Structural Change in Africa

Debates on African development continue to downplay the achievement of the continent: economic achievements are diminished and the perception of a conflict prone continent continues. Many of the policy prescriptions externally imposed on African countries have done little to transform the continent, largely because they have been conceived and applied without context.

Using literature from diverse origins, this book expands our knowledge about Africa and makes practical suggestions as to how successful development in a complex, yet dynamic continent can be achieved. Widening the policy dialogue and providing alternative thinking on the key elements and full extent of opportunities and challenges towards achieving the socio-economic transformation of Africa, the book moves the debate from the rhetoric to reality.

As a considered reflection on the "Africa's transformation" narrative, it outlines the practical pathways necessary for Africa's sustainable development, providing policy makers and researchers with tested solutions. It will be of interest to all scholars, students and policy professionals working in African development, public policy, international political economy, economic policy and politics.

Carlos Lopes is a Professor at Mandela School of Public Governance, University of Cape Town and Visiting Professor at Sciences Po in Paris as well as 8th Executive Secretary of the United Nations Economic Commission for Africa (2012–2016).

George Kararach is a Lead Economist, the African Development Bank Group, Abidjan, Côte d'Ivoire; a Non-Resident Fellow, Payne Institute, Colorado School of Mines, Illinois, USA and until recently Senior Economist at the United Nations Economic Commission for Africa (UNECA).

The International Political Economy of New Regionalisms Series

Series Editor: Timothy M. Shaw

The International Political Economy of New Regionalisms Series presents innovative analyses of a range of novel regional relations and institutions. Going beyond established, formal, interstate economic organizations, this essential series provides informed interdisciplinary and international research and debate about myriad heterogeneous intermediate-level interactions. Reflective of its cosmopolitan and creative orientation, this series is developed by an international editorial team of established and emerging scholars in both the South and North. It reinforces ongoing networks of analysts in both academia and think-tanks as well as international agencies concerned with micro-, meso- and macro-level regionalisms.

The International Political Economy of the BRICS
Edited by Li Xing

Multipolarization, South-South Cooperation, and the Rise of Post-Hegemonic Governance
Efe Can Gürcan

Inclusive Trade in Africa
The African Continental Free Trade Area in Comparative Perspective
Edited by David Luke and Jamie MacLeod

The Political Economy of New Regionalisms in the Pacific Rim
Edited by José Briceño Ruiz and Philippe De Lombaerde

Structural Change in Africa
Misperceptions, New Narratives and Development in the 21st Century
Carlos Lopes and George Kararach

For more information about this series, please visit: www.routledge.com/ASHSER-1146

"This is the book so many of us have waited for and will welcome as an informed and rigorously empirical contribution to the challenges of our times – loss of biodiversity, fragile and fading social cohesion and the emergence of new forms of authoritarianism. It's narrative of possibility, based on empirical evidence and informed by pluralist scholarship, constitutes a new departure in the economics of development. It is a work that is invaluable, not only to the continent of the young and the future that is Africa, but for all scholars and policy- makers concerned at the insufficiency of current economic models in delivering a sustainable global world. We are indebted to Lopes and Kararach."

— Michael D. Higgins, President of Ireland

"Capturing the diversity and richness of African narratives about development - past, present and future – remains a complex challenge. In their endeavour to bring context and perspective to Africa's contemporary discourse about the future, Lopes and Kararach offer an eclectic yet compelling review of 'narratives about Africa' to demonstrate that perceptions often are not reality when it comes to reporting, research or rhetoric about Africa. Geography, demography and economy take centre stage in their search for greater African agency in articulating choices and pathways that will shape Africa's future development and transformation. A rich and thought- provoking book that conveys opportunity and excitement about Africa's diverse and fast changing prospects."

— Achim Steiner, Administrator, United Nations Development Programme

"This timely book presents one of the critical issues of development economics in the twenty-first century, namely Africa's structural change. It combines both theoretical perspectives and empirical evidence to examine the challenges and misconceptions surrounding Africa's structural transformation, and the central importance of industrialization. It will undoubtedly generate optimism about Africa. A must read to policymakers, researchers, and students!"

— Arkebe Oqubay, Ethiopian Minister and author of Made in Africa *(2015)*

"Western based depictions of Africa massively underestimated its size and just about everything else about the continent. New tropes, such as 'Africa Rising' are equally misleading. The continent urgently needs a new narrative to support a transformative agenda underpinned by African agency. This is exactly what Lopes and Kararach provide in their superb new book which is essential reading for everyone with any interest in the future of Africa."

— Kevin Marsh, Professor of Tropical Medicine and Director of Oxford Africa Initiative, Oxford University

"This book is different! So, a must read. It presents a rich and refreshing perspective on Africa's need for structural transformation with analysis based on diverse intellectual and philosophical approaches. Ultimately, it is Africans who must act to change mindsets by building a continent whose reality awakens and inspires."

— *Ngozi Okonjo-Iweala, former Nigerian Senior Minister, former World Bank Managing Director and Chair of GAVI and Africa Risk Capacity*

"This will be the first book I place in the hands of the emerging African leaders who study at the Mandela School. Not ignoring political economy challenges, Lopes and Kararach have written an articulate and persuasive exhortation to African agency in development, also describing the immense imminent potential of African economic development. It is comprehensively researched and eloquently copy edited."

— *Alan Hirsch, Professor and Director of the Nelson Mandela School of Public Governance, University of Cape Town*

"A forward-looking assessment of Africa's prospects and the pathways for achieving structural transformation and inclusive growth. This is a must read for policymakers and students of African economies."

— *Fantu Cheru, Emeritus Professor, American University, Washington, DC*

"This book debunks the dominant analysis of Africa economic and social condition, examine methodically the politics, policy prescriptions and knowledge production that have reworked and accounted for the gains (often neglected) and regressions (always highlighted) of the continent's development trajectory. It paints a rich and multifaceted future of an awakening continent. An essential reading for everyone interested in the future of Africa."

—*Mamadou Diouf, Leitner Family Professor of African Studies and History, Columbia University*

"This is a thought proving and timely book on the prospects of and barriers to Africa's economic transformation. Its arguments challenge a number of liberal ideas about the best paths to economic prosperity making it all the more interesting."

— *Jonathan Rosenthal, Africa Editor,* The Economist

Structural Change in Africa

Misperceptions, New Narratives and Development in the 21st Century

Carlos Lopes and George Kararach

Routledge
Taylor & Francis Group
LONDON AND NEW YORK

First published 2020
by Routledge
2 Park Square, Milton Park, Abingdon, Oxon OX14 4RN

and by Routledge
52 Vanderbilt Avenue, New York, NY 10017

Routledge is an imprint of the Taylor & Francis Group, an informa business

First issued in paperback 2021

British Library Cataloguing-in-Publication Data
A catalogue record for this book is available from the British Library

Library of Congress Cataloging-in-Publication Data
Names: Lopes, Carlos, author. | Kararach, George, author.
Title: Structural change in Africa : misperceptions, new narratives and development in the 21st century / Carlos Lopes and George Kararach.
Other titles: International political economy of new regionalisms series.
Description: New York, NY : Routledge, 2019. |
Series: The international political economy of new regionalisms series | Includes bibliographical references and index.
Identifiers: LCCN 2018057139 | ISBN 9781138348448 (hardback)
Subjects: LCSH: Economic development—Africa. | Africa—Economic policy. | Africa—Economic conditions—21st century.
Classification: LCC HC800 .L6723 2019 | DDC 338.96—dc23
LC record available at https://lccn.loc.gov/2018057139

ISBN: 978-1-138-34844-8 (hbk)
ISBN: 978-1-03-209163-1 (pbk)
ISBN: 978-0-429-43667-3 (ebk)

Typeset in Times New Roman
by codeMantra

Contents

Contributors viii
Acknowledgements ix
Abbreviations x

Introduction 1

1 Defining structural transformation 13

2 Seeking transformation? Africa is not alone 44

3 Industrialisation: understanding the role of industrial and related policies for transformation 88

4 Understanding other key enablers of Africa's structural transformation 125

5 Innovative development financing 155

6 Selected experiences: drilling into the country dimcnsions of transformation 173

7 African circumstances and efforts into the future 192

Appendix 205
References 209
Index 241

Contributors

Carlos Lopes is a Professor at Mandela School of Public Governance, University of Cape Town and Visiting Professor at Sciences Po in Paris. He was a Visiting Fellow at Oxford Martin School, University of Oxford in 2017. Professor Lopes has occupied several senior positions at the United Nations including the leadership of the Economic Commission for Africa (2012–2016). Widely published and the recipient of many awards, he is an Associate Fellow of Chatham House and a member of the Global Commissions for the Future of Work, Economy and Climate and Geostrategy of Energy Transformation. He is also a member of the African Union current Reform Team led by Rwanda President Paul Kagame and doubles as the organisation's High Representative for Partnerships with Europe.

George Kararach is a Lead Economist, the African Development Bank Group, Abidjan, Côte d'Ivoire; a Non-Resident Fellow, Payne Institute, Colorado School of Mines, Illinois, USA and until recently Senior Economist at the United Nations Economic Commission for Africa (UNECA). He has an outstanding background in policy analysis, development economics, and strategic planning. Dr Kararach has deep understandings of donor fund raising and the UN system as well as the operational activities of other agencies such as the African Capacity Building Foundation and the African Development Bank. He also taught Economics at several UK universities. His most recent books include *Macroeconomic Policy and the Political Limits of Reform Programmes in Developing Countries* (African Research and Resource Forum, 2011), *Rethinking Development Challenges for Public Policy: Insights from Contemporary Africa* (Palgrave Macmillan, with Hanson, K. and Shaw, T.M. (eds), 2012), *Development Policy in Africa: Mastering the Future?* (Palgrave Macmillan, 2014), *Development in Africa: Refocusing the Lens after the Millennium Development Goals* (Policy Press, with Besada, H. and Shaw, T.M. (eds), 2015), *Economic Management under Hyperinflationary Environment: The Political Economy of Zimbabwe, 1980–2008* (Oxford University Press, with Raphael Otieno (ed.), 2016). George Kararach holds a PhD in Economics from the University of Leeds, UK.

Acknowledgements

This book is the result of multiple efforts to influence the debate about Africa's economic development from the narratives and perceptions angle. A continent constantly mistreated by those who consider themselves or are legitimised by others as specialists of its history, politics or development performance deserves a fairer treatment. This is an attempt to address such a deficit. It would not have been possible without the support of many colleagues while we both worked at the Economic Commission for Africa, in Addis Ababa. We would like to mention the contributions of Chichi Bodart, Mestawet Mistir, Stephen Karingi, Bartholomew Armah and Adam el-Hiraika, without associating them to any of the shortcomings readers may find. We would like to also acknowledge the zeal of our friends Fewstancia Munyaradzi and Garth Le Pere for reading and commenting on the entire manuscript, thus sharpening our insights. The editorial guidance provided by Richard Sanders has also been essential to finalise the manuscript on time. We are indebted to their time and patience.

Finally, our families had to put up with the many extra hours such an endeavour requires. Carlos wants to recognise the role his wife Mara played in creating the conditions that enabled this achievement. George wants to thank his family who were equally a constant inspiration in debating African development.

Cape Town and Johannesburg, May 2019

Abbreviations

ACFTA	Africa Continental Free Trade Area
ACP	African, Caribbean and Pacific
ACP–EU	African, Caribbean and Pacific–European Union
AERC	African Economic Research Consortium
AfDB	African Development Bank
AGA	African Governance Architecture
AI	Artificial Intelligence
AIDA	Accelerated Industrial Development of Africa
APSA	African Peace and Security Architecture
ASP	average selling price
ARVs	Anti-retroviral
AU	African Union
AUC	African Union Commission
AuM	assets under management
BCG	Boston Consulting Group
BRICS	Brazil Russia India China and South Africa
CEEAC	Communauté Économique des États de l'Afrique Centrale
CEGIS	Center for Environmental and Geographic Information Services
CNOOC	China National Offshore Oil Corporation
CNPC	China National Petroleum Corporation
COMESA	Common Market of Eastern and Southern Africa
CSIR	Council for Scientific and Industrial Research
DBSA	Development Bank of Southern Africa
DRC	Democratic Republic of Congo
DRM	Domestic Resource Mobilisation
DVD	Digital Versatile Disc
EAC	East African Community
ECA	Economic Commission for Africa
ECOWAS	Economic Community of West African States
EEZ	Exclusive Economic Zones
EIF	Enhanced Integrated Framework
EITI	Extractive Industries Transparency Initiative

EMU	European Monetary Union
EPRDF	Ethiopian Peoples' Revolutionary Democratic Front
EU	European Union
FAO	Food and Agricultural Organization
FDI	Foreign Direct Investment
FT	*Financial Times*
GDP	Gross Domestic Product
GERD	Grand Ethiopian Renaissance Dam
GHG	Green House Gases
GSMA	Global System for Mobile Communications/Groupe Spécial Mobile
GTZ	Gesellschaft für Technische Zusammenarbeit
GVCs	Global Value Chains
GW	Gigawatts
HABITAT	United Nations Human Settlements Programme
HIV	Human Immunodeficiency Virus
IADB	Inter-American Development Bank
ICT	Information Communication Technology
IEA	International Energy Agency
IHDP	International Human Dimension Programme on Global Environmental Change
IMF	International Monetary Fund
IPCC	Inter-governmental Panel on Climate Change
IRPs	International Reference Prices
IT	Information Technology
IWMI	International Water Management Institute
LDCs	Least Development Countries
LLDCs	Landlocked Developing Countries
LPGs	Lowest-priced Generics
MAU	Maghreb Africa Union
MDGs	Millennium Development Goals
MGI	McKinsey Global Institute
MICs	Middle-Income Countries
MoU	Memorandum of Understanding
MTN	Mobile Telephone Network
NDS	National Development Strategies
NEPAD	New Partnership for Africa's Development
NSDS	National Strategy for the Development of Statistics
OAU	Organization of African Unity
OB	Original Brand
ODA	Overseas Development Assistance
ODI	Overseas Development Institute
OECD	Organisation for Economic Cooperation and Development
PIDA	Programme for Infrastructure Development in Africa
PRSPs	Poverty Reduction Strategy Papers

PTA	Preferential Trade Area
R&D	Research and Development
RECs	Regional Economic Communities
SADC	Southern Africa Development Cooperation
SAPs	Structural Adjustment Programmes
SDGs	Sustainable Development Goals
SEZs	Special Economic Zones
SIDS	Small Island Developing States
SNA	System of National Account
SSA	Sub-Saharan Africa
STI	Science, Technology and Innovation
TB	Tuberculosis
TRIPS	Trade Related Aspects of Intellectual Property Rights
TWh	Terawatt hours
UAE	United Arabs Emirates
UN	United Nations
UNCLOS	UN Convention on the Law of the Sea
UNCTAD	United Nations Conference on Trade and Development
UNDESA	UN Department of Economic and Social Affairs
UNDP	United Nations Development Programme
UNEP	United Nations Environment Programme/UN Environment
UNESCO	United Nations Educational Scientific and Cultural Organization
UNFCCC	United Nations Framework Convention on Climate Change
UNICEF	United Nations Children Fund
UNIDO	United Nations Industrial Development Organization
US	United States
WHO	World Health Organization
WTO	World Trade Organization

Introduction

> Africa is too big to follow one script, so its countries are taking different routes to becoming better places.
>
> (*The Economist*, 2 March 2013)

Africa's place on the global scene has not been without controversy and this relates in particular to its recent growth performance (Jerven, 2013). In historical terms, Africa has been portrayed through an accepted view that betrays the true size and developmental achievements of the continent. With a land mass of over 30 million square kilometres, Mercator's map has projected Africa's size to be equal to that of Greenland whose size is 14 times smaller. Mercator's 1569 cartographic depiction of the world became one of the most influential and widely circulated world map projections throughout the nineteenth and twentieth centuries. Whilst some have argued that the initial intention was mostly to provide a navigation tool for sailors because of the ease in ensuring angle and shape accuracy, this depiction became the recognised global map, adorning backgrounds of daily television news, homes, walls and the cover of many atlases.

In fact, despite recognition of these distortions, Google Maps has continued to use it as a basis of web projection. Many have also argued that the Mercator projection served to reinforce Western colonial attitudes towards Africa and has been instrumental in shaping images of European dominance (Peters, 1983; Henderson and Waterstone, 2009). In 1967, Arno Peters provided an alternative method of looking at maps as a means of correcting what he perceived as the inaccuracy and racism that was projected by the Mercator map.

We now know that the landmass that is Africa is the size of India, China, the United States, and most of Europe combined. Africa's blue or maritime economy is even bigger than its land mass, which offers huge untapped potential for development. The maritime zones under Africa's jurisdiction alone total about 13 million square kilometres, including territorial seas and approximately 6.5 million square kilometres of the continental shelf

(ECA, 2016a). Still, when Thomas Frederick Saarinen conducted a study in 1992 that tested the way Westerners viewed the world, the results suggested a diminished view of the size and importance of Africa (Meffe, 2013). Nearly two decades later, Kai Kruse attempted to address what he called "rampant immappancy"[1] and the extent to which the Mercator projection distorts the relative sizes of countries. He demonstrated this with a simple graphic illustration to depict just how "immense" Africa is (*Economist*, 2010). His objective was simple: "to create a simple graphical depiction of the statement: Africa is just immense – much, much larger than you or I thought" (*Economist*, 2010). This simple graphical illustration became a global sensation but did not correct the distorted perceptions of Africa and the extent to which this undermined its quest for development.

Some reflection of the misperceptions

Why does the parody and misperceptions of Africa continue to this day? To answer this there is a need to deviate somewhat from cartography and examine some fundamental historical assumptions that have played a part.

The roots of contemporary pessimism and scepticism about Africa's development prospects are obviously not new. During the European Renaissance, many authors and thinkers contributed to shore up various papal bulls that legitimised colonisation by the explorer Kings; this was extended to the demeaning portrayal of black people in the works of famous painters such as Pigafetta, Rubens, Velázquez, and Rigaud; and included the philosophical construct that Egypt as a more literate society was detached from the rest of the continent. Hegel, the German philosopher, captured the essence of this portrayal by proclaiming that Africans had no history before the arrival of the Europeans. Much later, Joseph Conrad's *Heart of Darkness* was even more egregious in its imagery of Africans as being "uncivilised" (Camara, 2005). More recently, Fukuyama (1992) has continued that tradition by proclaiming the dominance of Western civilisation which represented the "end of history" and thereby suggesting that cultures and traditions that did not fall within the Western orbit were rather insignificant.

In a dystopian depiction and in his travelogue *The Last Train to Zona Verde*, Paul Theroux describes Africa as "the awful, poisoned, populous Africa: the Africa of cheated, despised, unaccommodated people: of seemingly unfixable blight" (Theroux, 2013). On his way from Cape Town to Luanda, he wrote, "I became conscious of entering a zone of irrationality. Going deeper into Luanda meant traveling into madness." Another revealing bit is what he says about African rap music: "Naturally you wonder what is in the heads of the young here who have adopted these songs as their anthems. Are they merely idle, their minds colonised by the alien lyrics?" Theroux thus adds to the canon of misperception but from a distorted vantage point that he is writing seriously about Africa.

These considerations suggest that misperceptions about Africa are premised on three elements, namely: that geography does not reflect the true spatial coverage of human activity; the economy does not capture the true resource endowments and demographics underestimates the number of Africans in the near future – especially the emergent youthful population. We will explore how these issues of geography,[2] economy, and demographics have and will continue to influence Africa's development. This is very important in order to understand structural transformation as the core focus of this book. This relates to the processes by which African agency – at the levels of both state and society – is capable of charting autonomous paths of growth and development which render negative depictions nugatory and baseless.

Consequently, modern day misperceptions about Africa not only concern the injustices of current cartography or erroneous views portrayed in contemporary literature or arts. They also pervade risk perceptions, levels of conflict, problems of political stability and other spheres of human existence. Indeed, the global perception of Africa continues to be of a continent beset by crisis and as a risky environment for making investments. This is due, in no small part, to the nature of African conflicts and their world exposure, which attracts a different perception of endemic malaise (Makinda, 2012).

These negative portrayals also persist because of the images that are embedded in the African mind-set which excludes the possibilities of African agency (Fanon, 1952). These portrayals suggest an accumulation of problems that undermine the diversity of a continent which has nevertheless made remarkable progress since the start of the twenty-first century. Such portrayals come together as narratives which serve to create a gap between perceptions and realities regarding the transformative potential of the continent beyond strictly economic categories.

It is therefore important that we contextualise these narratives. At a fundamental level, this must include understanding what the African reality is vis-à-vis what are externally driven perceptions so that Africa is not deprived of its role in human evolution and history. The time has come to change the narrative such that Africa's new narrative transcends the much trumpeted "Africa rising" storyline. This will only be accomplished by a strong focus on the transformative agenda and the challenges faced by a fast developing continent which is underpinned largely by localised agency.

A big continent and the importance of structural change

Africa has experienced unprecedented growth over the last decade and a half and has remained the second fastest growing region in the world since 2000. Despite economic downturns and uncertainties since the global financial crisis of 2008, many countries in the region continue to grow and are some of the fastest growing economies in the world. The macroeconomic indicators are the best since independence. At the turn of the Millennium, Africa's GDP was $600 billion; this increased dramatically to $2.2 trillion in 2013, representing one of the fastest growth trajectories in history (AfDB, 2014). By comparison, China took 12 years to double its GDP per capita, India 17 years, and the US and Germany between 30 and 60 years (Barth et al., 2009).

The idea of a "big" continental Africa is often linked to its natural resources endowment. Onuoha (2016) argues that the abundance of resources provides the continent with the self-confidence and hope for continuous growth. The "Africa rising" narrative seeks to capture the huge growth potential of the continent. There is ample evidence to suggest that one of Africa's growth drivers has been a commodity super cycle that powered the economies of especially resource-rich countries. Indeed, new resource discoveries have fuelled increases in foreign direct investment in Africa from emerging powers such as China, India, Brazil, and Russia as they seek the necessary commodities for their own growth and development (Kararach and Odiambo, 2017; ECA, 2018).

The economic optimism of the past two decades has, however, been moderated by a combination of factors including volatility in commodity prices; the slowdown and rebalancing of China's economy; widespread drought, especially in eastern and southern Africa; and rising insecurity and instability in the Horn of Africa (Hanson et al., 2017). Such headwinds signify the importance of structural transformation. Such transformation will only occur through diversifying African economies, boosting their competitiveness in world markets, increasing their shares of manufacturing in GDP, and using more sophisticated technology in production. Economies will then become much more prosperous, less dependent on foreign assistance, and much more resilient to shocks (Kararach, 2014) – thus reflecting the growth successes of several Asian and Latin American countries over the past decades.

Structural change is mainly important because the global division of labour has caused African economies to lag behind other country groups by remaining dependent on primary product exports (Lawrence and Graham, 2015). More often than not, the prices of these commodities have been declining, thereby leading to a considerable decrease in Africa's terms of trade and share of world exports. In contrast, inter-African trade has been rising as has its trade with Asia (rising to 27.9 per cent in 2017, from 26.3 per cent in 2016) (Afreximbank, 2018). However, within this dependence on primary product exports, minerals have played an increasingly important role, and in some countries has exacerbated their vulnerabilities (Kararach and Odhiambo, 2016). While there has been greater diversification in the exports of developed countries in recent years, many African countries still have exports that are concentrated in fewer products such as oil, diamonds and coffee as exhibited by the Herfindahl-Hirschmann Index.[3]

The liberalisation of global trade has not helped African agriculture since its exports have declined and Africa is now a net importer of food.

Notwithstanding the logic of liberalisation, it is ironic that developed countries' agriculture continues to be heavily subsidised.[4] The liberalisation of trade, forced on Africa through "structural adjustment" programmes, has had equally negative effects on the continent's attempts to industrialise. And despite the pressure from developed countries to liberalise, this had not stopped the "tariff bias" against countries such as those of Africa which still experience high barriers against exporting to developed countries compared with the much lower tariffs that exist between the latter. The limited and largely capital intensive manufacturing that does exist in African countries has not created as much employment as it originally did in the developed countries. The median share of employment in industry across African countries is 11 per cent, while the median share of industry in GDP is 21 per cent as compared to 26 per cent and 23 per cent for high income countries in 2017 respectively. Hence the service sector and investment to transform agriculture has become especially relevant as a catalyst of structural change and employment generation.

Consequently, the availability of a large urban and better educated labour force suggests that African economies are well placed for greater manufacturing development. A strategy based on the processing of domestic resources in agriculture and mining could assist with generating a capital goods sector. This could be complemented by an active science and technology and research and development policy to adapt imported technologies to local needs. The challenge in manufacturing is to find a convincing way forward in order to produce basic goods for mass consumption (ECA, 2013; Lawrence and Graham, 2015). However, simply reproducing or trying to imitate the path of industrialisation taken by the now industrialised (or post-industrialised?) economies may not be the best way forward nor is it bound to happen (Chang, 2002, 2007; Kararach, 2014).

As advanced capitalism itself changes with new forms of social organisation, identifying economic activities of the future must take account of the growth of non-market networking activities, recourse to self-employment, and the shrinkage of the traditional industrial wage labour force. The increase of low wage jobs in the service sector also reduces the potential for the growth of markets, given the limited "tradability" of such services, which may also subvert an industrialisation strategy relying on a mass consumption market.

A changing Africa: the economics and demography

By 2050 Sub-Saharan Africa (SSA) will have a larger and younger workforce than China or India.[5] Fused with the continent's abundant land and natural resources, this workforce could be a competitive advantage and a great asset in driving economic transformation (ACET, 2014). African countries underwent a period of resurgence recently following decades of generalised economic stagnation, political turmoil, and conflicts (Cheru, 2002). High economic growth has been driven mainly by improved development policy together with a new-found commercial vibrancy in flourishing telecommunications, banking, retailing, mineral and construction sectors (Kararach, 2014). Crucially, public sector reform has significantly enhanced state effectiveness. We also cannot ignore a new scramble for Africa's economic opportunities and resources by both Western countries and emerging economies (Carmody, 2011). This has placed the continent at the centre of international relations, economic negotiations and agreements, and geopolitical transactions (Cornelissen et al., 2012).

Urban dynamics are at the core of Africa's renewal and growth potential, as manifested in the growing size of the middle classes, the concentration of (urban) consumers and markets, the emergence of new welfare challenges, and need for creative solutions and innovation to rapid rates of urbanisation.[6] There is strategic need for urban transformation (Versi, 2014) driven by effective and sustainable solutions for associated development challenges (Grant, 2015). Areas that need such attention in the post-2015 era include provision of adequate housing, transportation, infrastructure, and other services, while also dealing with concerns over power shortages, food insecurity, and pollution (D'Alessandro and Zulu, 2017).

Industrialisation strategies, including the creation of industrial parks and hubs, special economic zones, and multi-modal transportation corridors also underline the importance of geography to transformation and development. Even job creation and private sector development – as key drivers of social and economic development – are connected to a number of direct and indirect rural–urban changes. The new emphasis on green economies and industries contributes to attracting attention to the environmental impacts of economic activities and to the overall quality of life of populations and communities. This consideration must be the core target of transformative development. If properly managed, Africa, particularly Sub-Saharan Africa (SSA), could increasingly be the new frontier for development in the twenty-first century (Grant, 2015).

Some progress has also been recorded in the critical area of food production and security. The United Nations Food and Agriculture Organization (FAO) noted: "African food security prospects are brighter than ever" (FAO, 2015). The 2015 State of Food Insecurity in the World (SOFI 2015 report) reported a 31 per cent decline in the prevalence of overall hunger in SSA between the base period (1990–1992) and 2015. This represented a huge step toward halving the share of Africa's population suffering from hunger. At least seven countries (Angola, Djibouti, Cameroon, Gabon, Ghana, Mali, and Sao Tome, and Principe) achieved both the MDG1 and World Food Summit (WFS) targets of halving the number of hungry people by 2015 (FAO, 2015).

Whilst there is wide regional variation in progress, major transformational forces have taken root over the past 25 years. This includes significant demographic, economic, and political changes that have contributed to sustained economic growth. Such growth, in turn, has driven the above gains in reducing hunger and substantially improving the livelihoods and welfare of millions of Africans. Yet, there is much work to be done. Nearly 218 million people (one in four) in SSA remained undernourished in 2014–2016 – a 24 per cent increase compared to 1990–1992 when 176 million people were undernourished. Important questions about appropriateness and effectiveness have been raised by the technology-heavy (including the use of hybrid seeds, fertilisers, and pesticides) and productionist approach fuelling Africa's "New Green Revolution", which is increasingly being promoted as the best strategy to enhance food production (D'Alessandro and Zulu, 2017). This approach tends to be built on public–private partnerships, donor-driven private sector promotion, and links between African farmers, input suppliers, agro-dealers, agro-processors, and retailers and with increased supermarket penetration into poorer neighbourhoods, and is even proffered as a solution to urban food insecurity (Moseley et al., 2015). In essence and despite the noted progress, challenges remain about how to achieve deeper and more equitable gains on food security in SSA (FAO, 2015).

Rapid urbanisation and technology diffusion have resulted in a surge in the services sector, which now accounts for over half of Africa's growth. Increased consumer spending and affluence means that, by 2020, Africa will have over 1.1 billion consumers which will be more than the populations of Europe and North America combined, with twice as many affluent consumers as the UK (BCG, 2016). Internet connectivity is improving, with some countries reaching 83 per cent connection rates. By 2020, virtually all Africans will own a mobile phone and half of them will have a smart phone. As the world grapples with issues of sustainable development, African countries have real opportunities to develop carbon resilient economies. The potential of its renewable resources are immense. Africa is well endowed with natural gas deposits, which remain largely unexploited; it has more than 350 GW of hydropower; over 100 GW of wind energy; 10,000 GW of solar energy; and 15GW of geothermal energy (IEA, 2014). There is now greater optimism that Africa will tap into the potential offered by the "internet of things" to transform its own production systems.

Nevertheless, Africa's impact on the global economy is yet to be really felt and there is a simple reason for this absence. The aggregate remarkable economic performance has not spurred the kind of transformation capable of creating enough productive employment, improving living conditions, and adequately tackling the challenges of inequality. More recently, the African growth success has proven to be vulnerable to volatility in commodity prices as well as demand and perception fragility. These shortfalls have been linked to the limited investment and growth in the domestic economies of many African countries.

African countries must, therefore, pursue a process of transformation in order to create jobs and increase incomes and wealth. Indeed, this agenda now dominates the continental discourse of African leaders. That translates into a clear realisation of what has not happened – as reflected in low agricultural productivity, a contraction of value-added in manufacturing, limited poverty reduction, and lack of jobs and inclusive policies. African countries are at a juncture where a number of odds are in their favour, especially megatrends such as demographic, technological, and environmental changes, and rapid urbanisation. Its natural resource abundance – about 12 per cent of the world's oil reserves, 40 per cent of its gold, and 80 to 90 per cent of chromium and platinum group metals – can be used to spur the kind of dynamic industrialisation that would lead to structural transformation.

Diversification and industrialisation, including green industrialisation, are critical not only for national economies, but also for the geographical spaces, stakeholders, social groups, and communities that will benefit from the changes brought on by industrialisation. The examples of Ethiopia and Tanzania – putting in place industrial clusters and encouraging coordination between urban transformation and industrial development – show that economic policies and activities can have a positive impact on the multiscalar economic geographies of Africa, including in local infrastructure such as ports (UN-Habitat, 2014; Léautier et al., 2015).

However, we have to confront and change the negative narrative first. And as observed, this cannot be achieved without changing the African collective mind-set. It goes without saying that, central to this is the role of the African agency in owning and leading the transformation process. A distorted perception complex makes the case for structural transformation inordinately difficult. We must therefore attempt to promote the rich, multiple narratives of the past and present African experience. Failure to do so will result in the continuation of negative and derogatory attitudes towards Africa, dictated and written mostly by others, but surprisingly including Africans as well sometimes.

Beyond structuralist approaches to Africa's development

It has been correctly noted when discussing development issues in Africa, that it is not sufficient to simply stress the ubiquitous nature of failure, malnutrition, disease, predatory states, and war (Rutten et al., 2008). We also have to recognise that important aspects of the lives of millions of ordinary people have been transformed over the last five decades. It is therefore critical for analysis to be rooted in empirical research, and this must include factors at local, regional and/or national levels in different African countries, as well as a broader pan-African view. We also need different analytical perspectives that take into account the heterogeneity of poverty and deficits in development processes in Sub-Saharan African in order to confront the ideas, concepts and assumptions that lie behind pro-poor policies. It is important to encourage policymakers to choose realistic policy prescriptions that are capable of moving people out of poverty.

In recent years, institutions such as the United Nations Economic Commission for Africa (ECA, 2013; 2014a; 2015a) and the African Development Bank (AfDB, 2014) have pushed the centrality of a "developmental state" and "developmental regionalism" with renewed vigour as a basis for transformation of the continent. Mkandawire (2001) has also argued that a developmental state was a real possibility in Africa. Part of the renewed interest in "developmentalism" reflects the reality that conventional explanations of poor African economic performance generally fail to pay adequate attention to the actual causal mechanisms of growth, decline, and stagnation. Several African economies have experienced investment booms after independence but, in contrast to East Asia's newly industrialising economies, these were not anchored in a virtuous growth circle involving complementary increases in savings, exports, and necessary job creation. While structural adjustment programmes dismantled state-mediated development without putting viable alternatives in place, it failed to tackle those structural constraints which especially impede productivity growth in agriculture and the wider economy (Akyüz and Gore, 2001).

The notion of the developmental state derives from the non-neoclassical view of the economy that gives explicit recognition to the possible failure of the market mechanism to optimise economic and broader development outcomes. State intervention may thus be necessary in at least three instances: a) whereby there are missing markets and hence, the need for market creation; b) when markets fail to produce optimal outcomes due to factors such as information asymmetry or anti-trust behaviour by profit-seeking firms; and c) role allocation whereby the social returns on investments are higher than those of private returns such that private firms avoid engagement in sectors that provide "public goods." In these three instances, the state has the capacity to make strategic decisions that unleash market dynamics by instituting regulatory and other incentive mechanisms (Kararach, 1997). The state therefore engages in productive development policies and programmes (IADB, 2014).

The developmental state is both ideological and structural in nature (Mkandawire, 2001). In terms of ideology, the raison d'être of the state is to focus on development and structural transformation as primary objectives, interpreted as virtuous growth, industrialisation, job creation, and so on. Structurally, the state must exhibit the ability to plan and execute these developmental and transformation objectives independent of social forces that may negate such efforts. The state therefore needs to have the capacity to mobilise the necessary financial and human resources and social and political coalitions for development. With respect to coalitions, this implies navigating the various political economy dynamics and maximising the planned development outcomes, for example, by investing in the requisite infrastructure and skills. Essentially, it is important to acknowledge that the opportunities as well as challenges of Africa's development are complex and in a state of flux (Rucipero, 2001; Kararach et al., 2012). Because of such complexity as well as problems of local agency, Hart (2001) argued that it is necessary to revisit the underlying assumptions and applications of development policy and practice.

Diawara (2000) analyses the critical nature of local knowledge in shaping the dynamics as well as local agency in development. While structural characteristics may circumscribe development, they only partially shape its trajectory. It is therefore helpful to adopt a "post-structuralist" view of development and understand the implication of not only integrated local knowledge but also African agency. As an example, the cultural and political dimensions that touch age and gender of concerned groups shape how "development" is carried out by both governments and development partners. While the post-structuralist criticism of development is justifiable, there is need to give it a political economy flavour. Such an additional lens allows development specialists not to become the only focus of analysis, but to also include actors such as small farmers. Any approach aimed at understanding Africa's development and related challenges that ignores the roles of local actors but privileges large actors such as the World Bank misses the reality of development as a homogeneous activity. To block out any sterile theoretical excess, we must take into consideration the roles of different actors in society and consider how each defines its own reality of development.

A post-structuralist view of African development is important because the current forms of depiction breed both misperception and uncalled for exuberance. The "Africa rising" narrative gives a distorted and narrow meaning to development defined in terms of growth in GDP and assets by corporations without paying attention to issues of social inclusion, primarily with regard to the expansion of a vertical economy (Fioramonti, 2016). Pillay (2016) notes three reasons why the current narrative is misleading. First, as suggested by Morten Jerven (2013), Africa's growth spurts are generally from a very low base if reliable measures are anything to go by. Second, most of such growth originates from the extractive and enclave sectors, and do not consider the net loss to Africa of its resources due to crude exploitation by foreign firms. Third, development defined narrowly by investors' interests often does not translate into beneficiation and the improved quality of lives for ordinary persons.

The reality on the ground therefore is far different and is underpinned by forces that seek to expand Africa's marginalisation in the modern division of labour. In that regard, the "Africa rising" narrative is more like a call for investors and MNCs to assert their profit-seeking motivations with little regard for Africa's development imperatives (Landsberg, 2018).

There is, therefore, a much greater need to foster African agency. Instead of being bogged down in the exuberance of the "Africa rising" narrative, Africa must seek to rise up through its own endeavours and initiatives. Africa needs to defeat the "Curse of Berlin" – the legacy of colonialism that has engendered not only a mentality that places greater value on non-local knowledge and institutions, but also places higher premium on the "nation" state and sovereignty while at the same time undermining the evolution of local ideologies and belief systems that are critical for solving local problems (Adebajo, 2010). It is important to understand the "circumstances" and "efforts" that define the evolution of inequality, poverty, and underdevelopment at the individual and country level in Africa in order to ensure that we move debates on transformation beyond static structural and sectoral changes.

The continent's branding challenge and the purpose of this book

Africa is currently a continent with some of the best opportunities for high investment returns and rapid yet sustainable socio-economic development. Africa is very big because Africa's narrative, potential, and in some cases reality, is deliberately underestimated, corrupted but becomes different when growth data is known. For instance, the recent rebasing of the GDP of Ghana, Nigeria, and Kenya has attracted much attention because their economies were considerably expanded overnight (World Economics, 2016). This raises the question whether there are other African economies with systematically underestimated GDPs. Just what is the exact size of this underestimation? A study conducted by World Economics (2016) on a sample of recent rebasing exercises for 15 African countries suggests that there is an average 3.24 per cent uplift in GDP for every year since the given country's last rebasing. The average number of years passed since the last rebasing in African countries is 9.2 years. Taking the 3.24 per cent annual uplift rate per year and multiplying it with the number of years passed since the last rebasing gives us an estimate of how much an African country's GDP could be underestimated. These calculations suggest that Africa's GDP is underestimated by approximately 21.5 per cent.

However, while Africa undoubtedly has great potential, so too is the size of the challenge that African leaders face as countries prepare to take their place in the future global economy. They must transform their economies in the context of a harsh global climate, where patterns of industrialisation have changed, characterised by unfriendly trade negotiations, complex intellectual property rights, shrinking policy space, and fractured internal structures. While the growth in new technologies such as the internet presents opportunities in e-governance and service delivery, it is also laced with threats such as terrorism, cyber insecurity, the manipulation of big data, and fake news. As a result, African agency is constantly under threat from fractious internal and global forces.

The 2017 election in Kenya has raised concerns about using electronic platforms in managing elections and how electoral authoritarianism is perpetuated (the tendency for elections to be manipulated to entrench incumbent regimes). Equally, the emergence of populist governments such as that of Donald Trump in the US suggests a relatively protectionist future that the continent will have to confront (Hanson et al., 2017). There are additional problems related to drugs, organised crime, and human trafficking as well as religious extremists such as Boko Haram. Some may argue that developmental regionalism offers Africa the best option. The continent must therefore define and implement the correct development priorities and implement them in a volatile and increasingly uncertain globalised world. If the issues of transformation are to be seriously addressed, the solutions cannot be dissociated from the very elements that seek to undermine the immense transformative potential of the continent.

In this volume we will be mainly concerned with how Africa could harness its manifold "development" assets including geography, economics, and demographics for effective structural transformation. Our arguments are based on the premise that much of the policy prescriptions that have been externally imposed on African countries, such as the Structural Adjustment Programs of the 1980s and 1990s and the successor Poverty Reduction Strategy Papers, have done little to transform the continent, largely because they have been conceived and applied without proper context. Too often, these conventional policy recommendations focus on one-size-fits-all and business-as-usual models that do not accommodate Africa's diverse and fast changing realities nor do they allow for local agency. This volume is therefore a considered reflection on both the promise and fallacy of the "Africa rising" narrative and outlines practical pathways necessary for Africa's sustainable development.

Notes

1 The insufficient geographical knowledge of the land area of locality and the rest of the world.
2 See Jared Diamond (1997) and Acemoglu et al. (2001) for contrasting views on the influence of geography on economic development.
3 The index measures export concentration of individual countries.
4 For example, U.S. government presently pays about $25 billion in cash annually to farmers and owners of farmland.
5 Population projections from the United Nations estimate a workforce of 1 billion Africans by 2050, an increase in the continent's share of the global workforce from 12 to 23 per cent as compared to 212 million for China and just under 1 billion for India respectively.
6 The share of Africans living in urban areas is projected to grow from *36 per cent* in 2010 to *56 per cent* by 2050.

1 Defining structural transformation

Introduction

In 2010 the McKinsey Global Institute (MGI) described African economies as "lions on the move" because of a resurgence in growth. Overall, the continent achieved average real annual GDP growth of 5.4 per cent between 2000 and 2010, adding $78 billion annually to GDP (at 2015 prices). But growth has slowed since 2010. The question therefore is whether the gloss has disappeared from Africa's growth story? Several studies conclude that the answer is no, but it is important to observe that the continent's growth story has become a more nuanced one (ECA, 2013, 2014a, 2015a, 2016a, 2016b).

The MGI Report probably achieved its objective of bringing the attention of investors to the opportunities offered by African economies, buttressed by positive associated fundamentals. Foreign direct investment reached $73 billion in 2014, up from $14 billion in 2004. As of mid-2016 Africa had become home to 700 large – and increasingly pan-African – companies earning revenues of greater than $500 million. These companies together boast $1.4 trillion in revenues, and many continue to grow at a very fast rate. Large companies in utilities, transportation, and healthcare have achieved double-digit revenue growth in local currency terms between 2008 and 2014 (Barton and Leke, 2016).

However, despite the positive outlook and potential of African economies, policymakers undoubtedly will need to grapple with significant challenges ahead in order to achieve inclusive growth and sustainable development. Historically, poverty reduction has been essentially associated with a profound structural transformation of the economy, a process which entails a reallocation of economic activities from the less productive sectors to those that are more productive. The pace at which this process takes place has been a key factor that differentiates development levels across countries. The issue of structural transformation has been at the core of economic development debates through initial empirical analyses by Fisher (1935, 1939) and Clark (1940) who dealt with sectoral shifts in the composition of the labour force. Lin and Monga (2012) highlighted the fact that there was not a country that ever evolved from a low- to a high-income status without simultaneously transforming itself from an agrarian or resource-based economy to one that was industry- or services-based. Moreover, recent growth patterns have been neither inclusive nor sustainable. This is because such patterns draw their inspiration from neo-classical growth models[1] that have been embraced by many developing countries (McMillan and Rodrik, 2011; McMillan and Headey, 2014; Martins, 2015). The absence of structural transformation implies growth without development. This is so because whereas economic growth represents a necessary condition, accelerating the pace of structural transformation provides the sufficient condition for economic development and social inclusion (Ezeala-Harrison, 1996; Martins, 2015).

This chapter frames the concept of structural transformation and what it means for Africa. It answers the question of why Africa needs a new narrative of change and outlines the importance of reviewing Africa's strategic capacities for successful transformation. Accordingly, Africa must pay special attention to the fact that its resources are finite, and growth that is unmanaged and is not sustained will lead to deteriorating conditions for all African countries and societies. It is therefore important to reflect on African agency and answer the question regarding whether Africans are ready for the future by making the right choices.

On conceptual issues

The concept of structural transformation has evolved over time. The extant literature on structural transformation can be traced to the 1950s and 1960s and is largely based on the experience of Western countries. It shifted from a simple reallocation of economic activity across three broad sectors, namely, agriculture, industry, and services that accompanied the process of modern economic growth but also encompassed challenges of sustainability and enhanced workers' productivity. In general, structural transformation encapsulated longitudinal and historical change in the sectoral composition of output (or GDP), together with the sectoral pattern of labour employment. The sector shift in labour raises workers' productivity, which contributes to accelerated economic growth. Development takes place in the form of capital accumulation in the high-productivity industrial sector supported by the migration of labour from low-productivity subsistence sectors (Rostow, 1960). Because of these structural changes, the share of agriculture in the national GDP will decline while the proportion of national income derived from manufacturing activities increases substantially. In the process, countries can engage in extensive industrial upgrading and diversification, generate jobs, and be able to raise incomes substantially (Gerschenkron, 1962; Kuznets, 1966).

Timmer (2007) significantly expands the definition of structural transformation as a process characterised by the following factors: a decline in the share of agriculture in GDP and employment; a rural-to-urban migration that stimulates the process of urbanisation; a rise of a modern industrial and service economy; and a demographic transition from high to low rates of births and deaths. In order to bring these factors into a virtuous circle, proactive policies are required and state institutions must be actively engaged, coupled with strategic capacity to ensure that policies and institutions are appropriate for the job at hand.

The empirical dimensions of structural transformation have been a subject of research over time. Modern analyses of sectoral transformation can essentially be traced to Fisher (1935, 1939) and Clark (1940) who dealt with sectoral shifts in the composition of the labour force. As in most economic debates, one can find precursors to their ideas in earlier writings of Sir William Petty and Friedrich List. However, Fisher and Clark were the first to deal with the process of labour reallocation during the era of modern economic growth, and pioneered the primary, secondary, and tertiary sectoral divisions that are still used today (Syrquin, 1988, p. 212).

Kuznets (1966) provided the historical empirical measures as well as the conceptual framework for the modern analysis of structural transformation, although he did not apply econometric techniques. Chenery (1960) undertook the first quantitative analyses of patterns in the transformation process and was supported by his collaborators (Chenery and Taylor, 1968; Chenery and Syrquin, 1975). The first systematic effort to study the evolution of the structural gap between labour productivity in agriculture and the rest of the economy was that of van der Meer and Yamada (1990), who examined the productivity differences in Dutch and Japanese agriculture.

Since then much effort has gone into finding "patterns of growth", especially for various typologies of countries (Timmer and Akkus, 2008). The earliest was the classification by Chenery and Taylor (1968) of their sample of countries into large, small-primary oriented, and small-industry oriented. The goal has been to translate growth patterns in different typologies into strategies for development. However, the uniqueness of country circumstances, especially in terms of political economy, has largely thwarted that effort. Timmer and Akkus (2008) sought to bring the pressures[2] on political economy which flowed from structural transformation process itself directly into the analysis.

Evidence suggests that in the early stages of structural transformation, there is a substantial gap between the share of the labour force employed in agriculture and the share of GDP generated by that work force. This gap narrows with higher incomes. This convergence reflects better integrated labour and financial markets and is an integral part of structural transformation (Timmer and Akkus, 2008).

However, in many countries this structural gap widens during periods of rapid growth, a tendency seen in even the earliest developers. When overall GDP is growing rapidly, the share of agriculture in GDP falls much faster than the share of agricultural labour in the overall labour force. The "turning point" in the gap is generated by these differential processes, after which labour productivity in the two sectors begins to converge. The lag presents political problems because farm incomes invariably fall behind incomes that are earned in the rest of the economy (Timmer and Akkus, 2008). The long-term policy response then is to accelerate the integration of farm labour into the non-farm economy (including the rural sector), but the historical record shows that such integration takes a long time. It was not fully achieved in the United States until the 1980s (Gardner, 2002), and evidence presented here shows that the gap in productivity tends to be increasingly difficult to bridge through economic growth alone.

This lag in real earnings from agriculture is the fundamental cause of deep political tensions generated by structural transformation. Historically, the basic uniform response to these political tensions has been to protect the agricultural sector from international competition by providing direct income subsidies to farmers (Lindert, 1991). However, neither policy response tends to help the poor, even those remaining in rural areas.

Thomas Theisohn and Carlos Lopes in their book titled *Ownership, Leadership and Transformation* (2003) assess the role of national agency in relation to structural transformation. They argued that, traditionally, the notion of capacity originated in the engineering world, and was understood to involve the use of processes to transfer knowledge, especially technical and scientific skills (Morgan, 2001). Little attention was paid to sector-specific realms that were deemed to be less important but yet were conveyor belts of knowledge, including policy formulation, social and economic research, systems analysis, and review and feedback mechanisms. Today it is generally accepted that knowledge cannot simply be transferred; it must be acquired, learned, and reinvented. In addition, it encompasses a deep pool of local understanding that is the very foundation of learning, as well as a wealth of global information that can be reconfigured to meet local needs (Kararach and Hanson, 2011; Kararach, 2014). This entails a review of strategic capacities so that gains are not undermined by internal and external threats, including a poor understanding of new threats. When adaptation fails to happen, there is no ownership and consequently, no lasting capacity development (Lopes, 2019a).

Structural transformation is further perceived as more of a process whereby the relative importance of different sectors and activities of an economy change over time. In the African context, this implies a relative decline of low-productivity agriculture and low value added extractive activities, and a relative increase in manufacturing and high-productivity services (ECA, 2013, 2014a, 2015a, 2015b, 2015c). Developmental macroeconomic policies are also critical for addressing the three building blocks of human resources, infrastructure, and institutions while fiscal, monetary, and financial policies are key elements of that framework. Despite a litany of bad news, Africa as a continent has grown the most; its debt to GDP ratio has not changed dramatically even in the less favourable 2014–2015 period. In fact, it is negative in relative terms if reserves are considered. Rather than commodity prices per se, Africa's macroeconomic profile is more affected by internal policy blunders that can be corrected.

Such policy correction could be greatly complemented by current megatrends of rapid urbanisation, the potential of demographic dividends, and the fast diffusion of information and computer technology, all of which favour Africa's transformation. In this complex of issues, the role of the African agency and the imperatives of transformation are vital (Kararach et al., 2012).

However, there is a strong historical pattern of worsening income distribution between rural and urban economies during the initial stages of the structural transformation – a critical aspect of the "Kuznets curve" (Kuznets, 1955). Consequently, if urban inequality (the urban Gini coefficient) is higher than rural inequality (the rural Gini coefficient), inequality will initially rise, especially with the movement of people from rural to urban areas or from agriculture to industry during the process of transformation. Kanbur (2017) sets out these dynamics in relative detail.[3] Even countries that are now classified as rich did not escape this pattern during their early development stages in the nineteenth and early twentieth centuries. The good news, however, is that absolute poverty does not necessarily get worse during such episodes. In East Asia, for instance, the evidence reveals that absolute poverty declined very rapidly, albeit associated with inequality as distribution of income got tilted to the top quantile of the population.

These observations are supported by Chenery (1979) and Abramowitz (1983) as well as many recent empirical studies that documented the positive relationship between structural transformation and changes in institutional structures and social beliefs (McMillan and Headey, 2014; Martins, 2015). Key aspects of social change include rapid urbanisation through rural-to-urban migration, the emergence of production hubs in rural areas, and a demographic transition characterised by low fertility and mortality (Timmer and Akkus, 2008; Timmer, 2014). Thus, structural change may take various forms and could entail a demographic transition, changes in labour participation (through changing social preferences), and a spatial reorganisation of the population (through rural-to-urban migration) (Lopes et al., 2017).

Gerschenkron (1962), in his study of the "catching-up" process of European countries in the mid-1800s, found that capital accumulation was never a precondition for the success of many of these countries who lagged far behind Britain. Instead, there were particular institutional factors such as government agencies and banks that were designed to increase the supply of capital to budding industries that actually helped European countries to catch up with Britain. Capital accumulation as a precondition can be substituted through deliberate state action aimed at increasing the supply of capital to domestic enterprises in order to underwrite what private investors are unwilling to provide due to presumed risk factors.

While the analytical perspectives provided by Kuznets, Gerschenkron, Lewis, and Rostow on structural change reflect the experiences of Western

Europe and North America, it was the "flying geese" model developed by Japanese economist Kaname Akamatsu that caught the attention of many development economists and political scientists in the 1960s (Lopes et al., 2017). Japan was the only non-Western country that was able to make successful transition from a low productivity agricultural economy to an industrialised one. Akamatsu, focusing primarily on the development experience of Japan, used the "wild geese flying pattern" as a metaphor for an inverted V formation (Akamatsu, 1962, pp. 3–25). The metaphor describes the sequential order of the "catching-up" process of industrialisation by latecomer economies by transforming themselves as production platforms for low cost and low skill manufacturing sectors. As the "lead-country" moves up the product ladder to more sophisticated industrial production, the latecomers can move into the low cost and low skill manufacturing sectors that are vacated by the "lead-country" and thereby are able to "kick-start" their own industrialisation process (Lopes et al., 2017). Crucially, developed countries at the time did not "kick away the ladder" for Japan to climb up (Chang, 1996, 2002). Others point to the role of productive industrial policies whereby the state played an instrumental guiding role in the process of economic transformation (Okimoto, 1989; Amsden, 1989, 2000).

A pattern thus emerges whereby growing trade in parts and sectors of East Asia started with the dramatic growth of Japanese incomes and wages in the 1970s and 1980s, a phenomenon that is repeating itself in the case of China today (Lopes et al., 2017). The growth of wages eroded Japan's competitive advantage in manufacturing and triggered the movement towards lower cost countries such as Hong Kong, Taiwan, Korea, and Singapore (Wade, 1990). When these countries also experienced wage inflation and rising living standards, they looked off-shore to offload the most labour intensive phases of their production process to other low wage East Asian countries which included Thailand, Malaysia, Indonesia, and Vietnam (Lall, 2002; Lopes et al., 2017).

Knowledge of environmental impacts has become more sensitive, thus raising the momentum towards a more sustainable and inclusive structural transformation objective, accompanied by a relative decoupling of resource usage and environmental impact from the economic growth process (ECA, 2016a). In terms of the "flying geese" metaphor, the rise of China and other emerging developing countries offer less developed countries, particularly those of Africa, opportunities to move out of subsistence agriculture into manufacturing as these emerging economies move up the technological ladder and abandon low-cost manufacturing production (Lin, 2010; Lin and Monga, 2010). Lin (2010) suggests that China could herald the birth of the next group of "newly industrialising" African countries as it moves up the technological ladder. He estimates that this shift could create some 85 million jobs in the manufacturing sector as China moves up the technological ladder and as rising labour costs begin to directly affect China's global competitiveness (Lin, 2010).

As latecomers to this process, effective structural transformation for Africa means making significant productivity gains in rural areas, stimulated by several factors and primary of which are vibrant hubs of agribusiness and linkages across industrial activity; the translation of Africa's youth bulge into a demographic dividend; access to social services that meet minimum standards of quality regardless of location; reduced spatial and gender inequality; and progression towards an inclusive green growth trajectory (ECA, 2013, 2016a).

The literature on economic development as a process of structural change has demonstrated that *all* countries can make the transition from agriculture to industry, but that the catching-up process can vary from country to country, depending on their endowment structure, historical conjunctures, timing, and geography (Acemoglu et al., 2001; Lopes et al., 2017). Structural transformation requires a reallocation of labour between different parts of the economy as large productivity gaps exist between sectors as reflected in the dual economy model. However, several studies have demonstrated that structural transformation might occur through aggregate labour productivity growth due to the reallocation of labour across sectors as well as within sectors, resulting in increased production and export of high value-added products.[4] As such, large productivity gaps can exist even within the same sector or among firms and plants within the same industry (McMillan and Rodrik, 2011). Such productivity gaps are inherently associated with allocative inefficiency, signalling market failures and the need for state policy to reallocate resources towards higher-productivity activities across and within sectors, especially with regard to manufacturing and modern services (ECA, 2014).

Martins (2015), using data from 169 countries aggregated for 13 subregions in Africa, Asia, and Latin America, finds that "within-sector productivity improvements were the key drivers of output per capita growth in most sub-regions." Structural transformation in developing economies has substantially triggered economic performance through services rather than manufacturing as was the case in developed economies. Further, Martin notes that lower dependency ratios can generate a sizeable demographic dividend, while social preferences can impact on employment rates – through economic inactivity – which in turn affect economic growth. His analysis provides strong support to Chenery's (1982) notion of structural transformation as structural changes required to sustain a continuing increase in income and social welfare. It can be concluded based on existing theoretical and empirical literature, that there is no single common measurement of structural transformation.

Where is Africa with respect to structural transformation?

It goes without saying that some structural changes have occurred in many African economies.[5] For example, the changes in the relative share of manufacturing in most countries clearly reflect shifts in government policies and investment flows to support diversification. State-led development strategies of the 1960s and 1970s resulted in huge public investments in infrastructure and manufacturing with a focus on import substitution. Notwithstanding notable variations across countries, both manufacturing output and employment increased significantly during that time (Elhiraika et al., 2014). Unfortunately, these changes have not transformed the underlying commodity-based nature of most of these countries (Kararach et al., 2011). Furthermore, African economic growth has been proven to be vulnerable to volatility in commodity prices and demand as well perception fragility.

Despite a stream of bad news and renewed pessimism (see for example, Luengo-Cabrera, 2016), Africa is the continent that has registered the most growth in relative terms (Lopes, 2019a). As with Africa's current aspirations, other regions went through extreme periods of difficulty when they were embarking on their industrialisation process (Chang, 2002). However, and paradoxically, rather than dampening their transformation ambitions, the difficulties encountered contributed to raising their levels.

Agriculture remains the largest employer, absorbing over 60 per cent of the continent's labour force. However, its share in total employment has consistently declined across sub-regions and for the continent as a whole, from 73 per cent in 1960 to 52 per cent in 2014. With agriculture accounting for less than 25 per cent of total output, this implies that the largest proportion of Africa's labour force work in a sector that is characterised by extremely low levels of productivity. Indeed, average productivity in African agriculture was 0.5 per cent from 1960 to 2010, which is about 3 percentage points lower than agricultural labour productivity in Asia (McMillan and Headey, 2014). The prevalence of subsistence agriculture in most poor countries has been attributed to barriers and policy distortions that lead to allocative inefficiency and high transportation and transaction costs. Despite the existing substantial differences in sectoral productivity across poor African countries, the gains from reallocation would be relatively modest when labour is moved from high to low productivity sectors (Lopes et al., 2017).

Several empirical studies have been undertaken to show the productivity effects of structural change in Africa. McMillan and Rodrik (2011) find that structural shifts in 11 African countries were associated with diminishing overall labour productivity owing to migration of labour from higher to lower productivity employment; this typically occurred in the urban services sector. Labour productivity in these countries grew at only 0.9 per cent per year between 1990 and 2005 compared with 3.9 per cent annual labour productivity in Asia over the same period. Average labour productivity growth in Africa was 2.1 per cent within sector and a negative 1.3 per cent from structural shift transformation, compared to 3.3 per cent and 0.6 per cent respectively for Asia. Using productivity growth as an indicator, McMillan and Rodrik (2011) conclude that Africa has witnessed structural transformation in reverse. de Vries, Timmer, and de Vries (2013) extended the data for the 11 countries studies by McMillan and Rodrik to 50 years (1960–2010) with more detailed sectoral coverage.

The analysis by de Vries et al. (2013) found three distinct phases of structural transformation in Africa. In phase 1, 1960–1975, the continent witnessed substantial increases in labour productivity and the share of manufacturing in total employment thanks to migration of workers from agriculture to manufacturing. Labour productivity in manufacturing was 2.5 times higher than average labour productivity and about five times higher than labour productivity in agriculture. Both productivity growth and structural transformation stagnated during the second phase covering 1975–1990.

Between 1990 and 2010, growth recovery in Africa was characterised by static gains and dynamic losses in labour productivity. Static gains arose as labour migrated from both agriculture and manufacturing to the services sector, where labour productivity was higher than in agriculture. Dynamic losses resulted from the fact that labour productivity in the shrinking manufacturing sector was higher than in the expanding services sector. The structural transformation that took place in Africa between 1990 and 2010 made no contribution to productivity growth through manufacturing. de Vries et al. (2013) conclude that structural transformation (defined in sectoral shifts) in Africa has been limited and has not contributed to growth.

What have other countries done to achieve structural change?

Structural transformation has occurred across regions such as in Europe and North America and historical periods of the eighteenth and nineteenth centuries. As a latecomer, Africa has a great opportunity to learn from others' experience and leapfrog certain phases of the transformation process. The most cited recent experience is that of the East Asian "tigers", whereby neoliberal policies have been extolled by some commentators as the source of transformation. A few authors have delved into the issue of structural transformation either through historical or epistemological approaches.

For example, Karl Polanyi (1944) wrote of the great transformation to explore how industrialisation occurred in Europe. In his book, *The Great Transformation* (1944), Polanyi examines the social and political changes that took place in England during the rise of the market economy. One of the primary conclusions Polanyi comes to (which differentiates him from authors such as Keynes and Hayek), is that the nation state and the newly formed market economy are not separate entities but are one object of human invention which he refers to as "the market society." For Polanyi, this meant that any approach which sided with either market or state as the solution to our economic problems – for example, neoliberalism on one hand or state socialism on the other – was likely to be simplistic. There is, for Polanyi, an ongoing political struggle between the "dis-embedding" force of the free market and the "re-embedding" effects of social protection. His work represents a very useful way of understanding the politics of modern capitalism.

More importantly, Polanyi reset the tone of the argument in the African context. It is not only about whether markets function more efficiently. Quite fundamentally, it is about the human and environmental costs of allowing people and nature to be included as integral parts of the production process within the market economy. Polanyi thus provided a set of philosophical issues that Africa is still wrestling with today with regard to the "environment-versus-development" debate. This raises very basic questions (Kararach, 2014): are we content with allowing people to become ever more incorporated into the market society if it is not necessarily good for them? Are we comfortable with allowing more of the environment to be incorporated into a market society if we can show that this has detrimental effects? And who should really bear the costs of environmental damage during development?

In 1989 Alice Amsden, using a historical approach, published *Asia's Next Giant: South Korea and Late Industrialization*. In order to formulate the theory of late industrialisation, it was necessary to understand how the current period differs from previous periods. In that regard, Amsden recognised that context mattered, and that structural change required movement to a knowledge intensive economy with high productivity and income. This in essence was a very different set of tools than those used by earlier industrialisers. Her methodology was a welcome antidote to armchair theorising that has inhibited the relevance of economics as a social science for so many years. Her primary methodological tool was fieldwork, during which she talked to people. It is from this research and 'conversations' that her theoretical approach is based. Her quantitative approach was largely an extensive use of descriptive data as a means of verifying her hypotheses and claims (Seguino, 2014). If Amsden's (1989) core message is anything to go by, there seemed no way for the Africas of the world to escape their low-wage, low-productivity trap without purposeful and tailor-made development and/or industrial policies. With market liberalisation, and footloose foreign firms, it was well-nigh impossible for these assembly factories to serve as catalysts for the kind of manufacturing experience and structural change that would lead to the rapid productivity growth so necessary for economic development. Indeed, a similar set of points were made by Clive Thomas in 1974 in his book, *Dependence and Transformation: The Economics of the Transition to Socialism.*

In another detailed study, Ocampo (2006) showed how, over the period of 1950–1980, and like many countries in Latin America, Brazil crafted an industrial policy that was aimed at creating new industrial sectors by changing the prevalent pattern of specialisation in primary commodities and promoting technology-intensive activities. As a result, Brazil successfully entered many new industries, such as petrochemical and renewable fuels, especially ethanol, as well as established the bases for the development of new technologies. In addition, over the last 30 years, Brazil has been among the most active of countries that have resorted to policies that were specifically designed to expand natural-resource-processing industries and food production. Today, the country is among the top three producers and exporters of orange juice, sugar, coffee, soybean, beef, pork, and chicken. It has also caught up with the traditional big five grain exporters (USA, Canada, Australia, Argentina, and the European Union).

Box 1.1 Country examples of recent transformation

China is another example of a country that has transformed its economic structure through agro-based industrialisation in order to accelerate growth and development. The period 1978–1983 emphasised agriculture. In its Five-Year Plan (1981–1985), China encouraged foreign trade and foreign direct investment to facilitate the importation of advanced technology. Strategic industries identified in the Five-Year Plan of development were given targeted support such as protection from foreign competition and subsidised loans from state-owned "policy banks." On the basis of a deliberate strategy, China has combined a variety of policies to develop both its agricultural and industrial as well as its service sectors. As a result and within a span of two decades, China became the largest exporter of manufactured goods.

Another example of successful transformation is that of the United Arab Emirates (ECA, 2016b). The UAE diversified its economy essentially based on the crude oil sector, which accounted for about two-thirds of the GDP. This country developed its industrial base by investing its oil wealth in industry-related infrastructures. Furthermore, in 1985, the first free zone in Dubai, Jebel-Ali, was created with appealing incentives to foreign investors, such as allowing 100 per cent foreign ownership, no customs duties, unlimited repatriation of funds, and exemptions from certain labour laws. The UAE government also promoted several manufacturing industries through industrial policy in the fertiliser, oil refining, and cement sectors. As of 2010, manufacturing in the UAE accounted for around 10 per cent of GDP, a significant increase from the 0.9 per cent share in 1975 (World Bank, 2013b).

Between 1957 and early 1990 Malaysia achieved substantive economic transformation with the share of manufacturing in GDP rising from 14 per cent in 1971 to 30 per cent in 1993 (Lall, 1995). Malaysia's export to GDP ratio increased from 46 per cent in 1970 to 95 per cent in 1995 (Athukorala and Menon, 1999) and the share of manufactures in total exports rose from 12 per cent to 71 per cent between 1970 and 1993 (Lall, 1995). This period had three distinct phases of industrial expansion: import substitution in 1957–1970; the New Economic Policy in 1970–1985; and the New Development Policy of 1986 that moved the country's industrial policy closer to those practised by the East Asian Newly Industrialised Economies.

How should the continent deal with the transformation challenges?

A country's capacity to design and implement a successful transformation agenda can be undermined by internal and external factors. Gains can be reversed if there is inconsistent policy implementation or poor understanding and management of new threats (Kararach, 2014; ECA, 2016b).

Internal factors include: poor economic management capacities typified by macro-economic instability; poor planning design and implementation capacities; weak institutional and individual capacities; limited investments in social and economic infrastructure; limited investment in technology and R&D; and political instability (Lopes, 2002).

On the other hand, external factors include: limited policy space; barriers to trade that undermine export revenues and constrain the export of manufactured goods; the disproportionate concentration on dealing with ODA focus areas rather than handling it in its real macro dimension; and the concentration of FDI in extractive mineral and gas sectors of the economy with limited investments in value addition. Furthermore, in recent years, climate change has emerged as a threat to development through its destructive environmental and human impacts.

To address these challenges and promote sustainable and inclusive structural transformation, the role of institutions and of the state is indispensable (ECA, 2013). The emerging consensus (see for examples Chang, 2003, 2007; Cheru, 2017) is that a developmental state is central to the process of accelerated economic growth and transformation of any country. The state's role in bailing out the economies in Western countries, following the 2008–2009 global economic crisis, reaffirms the important role that it can play in sustaining the transformation process and has taken the dust off Keynesian debates.

A developmental state is a state that prioritises economic development in government policy and is able to design effective instruments to promote such a goal (ECA, 2011). More specifically, a developmental state must deliver several desired outcomes (ECA, 2016b):

- Scaling up public investment and public goods provision. Africa at its stage of development requires a big thrust in public investment – in the real economy, and across regions and continent-wide – in the coming decades. Without committed public investment, sustained private investment will not be made, causing overall productive investment to fall below the level needed to keep the growth momentum going.
- Maintaining macro stability in order to attract and sustain private investment. In fact, macroeconomic stability is essential, as high uncertainty and risks deter private agents from making forward-looking productive investments. At the same time, harsh fiscal retrenchment and overly restrictive monetary policy aimed at only achieving the stabilisation objective cannot move the transformation agenda forward.

- Coordinating investment and other development policies. Public investment using scarce resources should be made selectively, sequenced and directed at achieving the highest development dividends in the long run. This requires that public and private investment be well coordinated across sectors such that strong aggregate demand spills over to facilitate "a move from a bad to a good equilibrium" (Murphy et al., 1989), especially given well-known market failure of coordination.
- Mobilising resources and reducing aid dependence over time. This requires a solid framework for developing banking and non-banking financial institutions and deepening financial markets.
- Securing fiscal sustainability by establishing fiscal legitimacy. This urgently calls for developing state capacity in prudent and efficient public finance management. However, this must be the bedrock of a relationship between the government and domestic actors because fiscal sustainability can only be secured in the medium to long run on the basis of such a foundation.
- Other development policies critical for structural transformation include trade, technology, financial development, oversight regulation and competition, education and health, and sector-specific policies such as those for industry and agriculture.

Africa needs structural transformation not structural adjustment

Africa's "Growth Miracle" since 2000 has not been job-rich, sustainable, and inclusive (Kararach et al., 2011), with most African workers still trapped in the vulnerable agriculture and informal sectors. Meanwhile, services are absorbing most African jobs, leaving employment in industry stagnant while progress in social development remains limited, especially in relation to poverty, inequality, and social protection. Fluctuations in commodities prices have made such growth even more precarious (Kararach, 2017). As a consequence, structural transformation is critical for accelerating and sustaining growth, creating decent jobs, and reducing poverty and inequality. It is therefore imperative for African countries to put in place effective strategies for their economies to transition through increased value addition in the primary commodity sector and diversification into higher-productivity employment-generating sectors, especially manufacturing and modern services (ECA, 2014a).

Lopes (2014a) and Elhiraika and Sloan (2014) highlighted both the opportunities and challenges for Africa's structural transformation. To repeat the essential point of this book, the continent is big because it is endowed with huge untapped natural resources including arable land, oil, and minerals. These resources provide strong comparative advantages for African countries to successfully embark on commodity-based industrialisation and

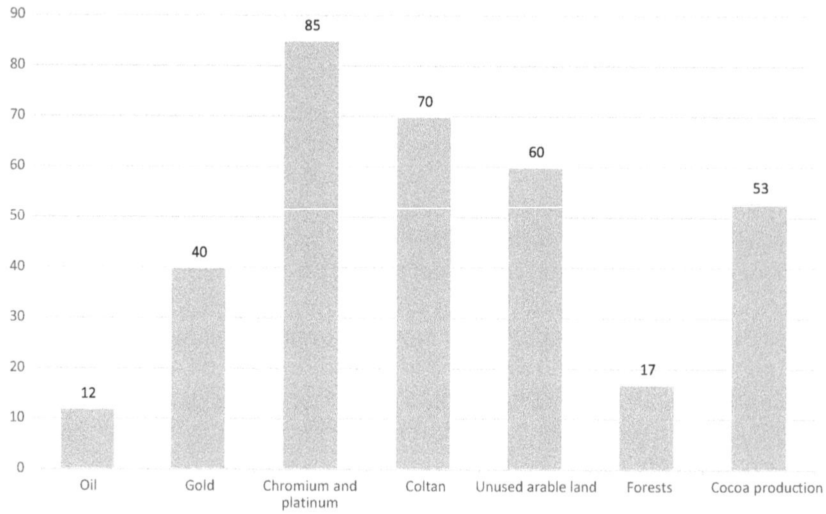

Figure 1.1 Some of Africa's untapped resource potentials (percentage of world resource)

Source: Lopes, 2014a.

Note: cocoa production accounts only those of Côte d'Ivoire and Ghana.

rapid structural transformation (Lopes et al., 2017). Adding value to minerals, oil, and agricultural endowments would allow African countries to exploit their comparative advantage and thus generate greater employment- and income-generating benefits from their commodities (ECA, 2013). Moreover, with proactive government policies, African countries can utilise any commodity windfall by allocating resources and rents from extractive industries in order to build capacities, especially infrastructure and human skills. Importantly, such policies can also promote new competitive industries in various sectors through diversification (Elhiraika and Sloan, 2014). Promoting competitive advantage is the most certain route for African countries to enhance their global competitiveness and to ensure sustainable, inclusive, and transformative development in the long-run. Successful experiences in both developed and emerging economies often followed a combination of these strategies (Auty, 2004; Lin, 2010).

The rationale for much of the current discourse of the "African Moment" and "Africa Rising" is clear, since some of the fastest growing economies in the world are indeed African. This performance has been due to several factors, including improved macroeconomic management, increased exports of natural resources, and a rising middle class (Lopes et al., 2017). For example, Lagos now has a larger consumer market than Mumbai, and spending in continental households exceeds those of India and Russia.

However, this growth experience is not sufficient. It falls short of 7 per cent, which is the minimum required to double average incomes in a decade (Atta-Mensah, 2017). This is partly because far too many of African economies are dependent on the production and export of primary commodities and far too many remain highly unequal societies, where large numbers of people are caught in the grip of unrelenting hunger and poverty. As the continent extols the fact that seven of its countries are in the top ten of global growth, we must also bear in mind that a similar number are in the top ten of global inequality.

It is useful to focus on the Asian experience for what it can teach us on the importance of bad press and regional branding. Although there is now greater awareness about specific conflicts in Asia, they are often viewed in isolation. Thus, the Mindanao conflict in the Philippines, the Sabah insurgency in Malaysia, or border clashes between Thailand and Cambodia do not receive much international public attention. Even rising India, with the Naxalite insurgency and issues of Kashmir, is not singled out, not to mention that South Korea sits on the border of a belligerent sister state. Despite the widespread nature of these conflicts in Asia, the region is not branded as unstable but is rather seen as a dynamic contributor to global growth. It is true that there are conflicts in Africa such those in Mali, the Great Lakes Region, South Sudan, and Somalia but these are the remnants of a declining trend of conflict in Africa. In other words, although there is a downward trend in African conflict and the numbers of casualties are smaller than Asia's, the global perception of Africa continues in many media outlets as that of a continent beset by crisis and as a risky environment for making investments (Araya, 2007; Oguh, 2015). If one exception is to be made, it would be about the rising number of casualties from Jihadist movements in Africa. But Asia faces the same increase in terrorist activity (Human Rights Watch, 2017).

In fact, two examples capture the essence of this point. There were about 29 piracy attacks in 2009 off the coast of Somalia, compared to 150 attacks in the shipping channel of the Strait of Malacca in 2005. Yet this did not lead to generalised negative perceptions about the economic prospects of Malaysia and Indonesia. It should be noted in a similar context that despite its unstable business environment, Pakistan is the second largest textile exporter in the world. If these perceptions were isolated from the narrative about Africa's performance, in general there would be no reason to accord them greater importance than those in Asia. However, the argument about why Africa is incapable of transformation is all too often linked to the enduring perception of its insufficient political and environmental fundamentals (Lopes, 2019a).

There are several ways in which structural transformation can be emphasised and defended (see Lewis, 1954; Kuznets, 1955; Anand and Kanbur, 1985; Kanbur, 2012, 2017). The sense in which it is used here is the large-scale transfer of resources from one sector to another due to changes in economic fundamentals and policies. In empirical terms, this requires a significant change in the sectoral composition of gross domestic product (GDP), with the share of the primary sector in employment and output shifting to industry and modern services. It also implies a greater use of technology and increased productivity across sectors. This is what some countries in Asia accomplished even though they had similar conditions to Africa at the beginning of their journey.

Simply put, Africa needs structural transformation and not structural adjustment or any realignment that simply fits the current configuration of the world economy which has tended to marginalise the continent (Lansberg, 2018; Zeleza, 2018). Industrialisation is indispensable for this objective since it will help to generate employment, increase incomes, and enable diversification, especially of exports, as occurred in Asia.

It must be remembered that Africa has attempted industrialisation before. In the 1960s and 1970s, newly independent Africa emulated other regions of the world in undertaking import-substituting industrialisation. It did result in some remarkable progress but was ultimately stymied by the limits of the model and abrupt changes in the global political economy. Import substitution strategies and the associated state-led development model proved unsustainable for a variety of factors, including externalities such as the oil price hike of the 1970s and subsequent turmoil and rising interest rates in global financial markets as well as the skyrocketing debt burden for poor countries. There were also internal factors such as macroeconomic mismanagement and undue political interference in the operations of state owned enterprises (ECA, 1990). Equally, market-led development models that were inspired by the Structural Adjustment Programmes of the 1980s and 1990s did not only fail to foster growth and poverty reduction in Africa but also compromised the capacity of the State to design appropriate policies for country-specific conditions (Cheru, 2017; Lopes et al., 2017). African countries therefore must be very mindful of the vagaries of the current global context and the associated political economy.

In this regard, one approach with prospects for success is commodity-based industrialisation (ECA, 2013). Rather than exerting our energies on trying to diversify away from commodities, we should focus more on using them as effective drivers of industrialisation. In addition to the broader benefits of industrialisation, as Chapter 3 will show, a commodity-based approach offers immediate scope for value addition and plenty of opportunities for exploiting forward and backward linkages. Given the dominance of global value chains and intense cost competition in the trade in manufactures, Africa can enter the industrial sector using its huge commodity and natural resources base. The fact that agro-processing is already one of the most developed manufacturing sectors in the continent is proof that this approach can work.

However, achieving success in this regard will not be easy (Kararach, 2014). It will require innovation and the determination to overcome infrastructural deficiencies. It will require a robust knowledge base of industry structures and global value chains. Indeed, African economies must continuously invest in knowledge, skills, technology, and innovation. The trading landscape, including barriers and preferences, must be well understood. Above all, boosting intra-Africa trade remains an overall imperative for creating the markets needed for successful industrialisation.

Africa must ponder the kind of society that it wishes to bequeath its children and grandchildren. Such clarity of vision must also be accompanied by a clear understanding of Africa's historical experience as well as its current economic and political context and policy environment, all of which become germane in achieving the continent's development objectives in a rapidly changing global environment (Lopes, 2019a). This process will benefit from the insights of several vital constituencies, including Africa's business and political leaders.

The starting point is for a political leadership that provides a clear vision and mobilises all sectors of society behind the development imperative (Leautier, 2014). African countries must change their approaches, attitudes, and priorities. They must nurture a highly educated, healthy and skilled population that can integrate technology and build the necessary infrastructure, both of which are indispensable for progress. African states must similarly strengthen their bureaucratic capacity to undertake dynamic long-term planning and the coordination of economic activity (Kararach, 2014).

For finance, Africa must begin to pay more attention to domestic resource mobilisation while it is accelerating the pace of regional integration to reap greater economies of scale (AfDB, 2018). The continent will increasingly require more robust data and better statistical systems to better measure and monitor progress.

Indeed, the quest for structural transformation will require a better use of Africa's economic strengths so as to enable all sectors of society, particularly women and youth, to fulfil their agency roles. The mantra going forward must be "Africa First" or putting the interests of the continent first. It means addressing emerging and other issues from the perspective of their impact on Africa. This means that the continent must drive the process of structural transformation based on its own vision and priorities. Africans must tell their own stories and for this to happen, they must generate their own data and statistics. This approach must define the continent's partnerships across the board as Africa seeks to promote coherence and deepen the impact of its nascent development trajectory.

On the enigma of Africa's growth story

The quality of economic growth in Africa has been persistently questioned. Sachs and Warner (1997) sought to provide econometric evidence on the sources of slow growth in Sub-Saharan Africa. The evidence suggests that the continent's slow growth can be explained through an international cross-country framework, without the need to invoke a special explanation that is unique to Sub-Saharan Africa. They find that poor economic policies have played an especially important role in the slow growth, most importantly about Africa's lack of openness to international markets. In addition, geographical factors, such as lack of access to the sea and a tropical climate have also contributed to Africa's slow growth. This evidence-based research is intended to empirically refute what many African specialists emphasise as explanatory patterns of the continent's growth, which include Africa's colonial history, and its ethnic divisions.

However, one could also argue over the last decade that Africa has been remarkably resilient to any form of global economic volatility. The continent has made significant strides in all dimensions of human development, comparable with other regions of the world which are in similar economic trajectories. As we shall show in subsequent chapters of this book, one thing always rings so true of the continent. As Pliny the Elder once said, "Ex Africa semper aliquid novi" (There is always something new out of Africa). The Hellenic and Roman worlds were amazed by the bountiful and exotic products they encountered from the continent including human beings who seemingly were not "human" compared to varieties of flora and fauna that had never been known to them.

Before the advent of Leopold of Belgium in the Congo and the subsequent "Scramble for Africa", the most contact Europeans had with Africa was limited to a string of coastal outposts from which trade in rubber and slaves was organised (Rodney, 1972). The limited engagement with the continent changed with colonialism, which required a physical presence in order to maximise the exploration and exploitation of natural resources. Europeans made enormous efforts at collating and establishing an impressive knowledge base of the continent, from which the world was able to learn about and indeed, use to redefine Africa. Despite these huge efforts, the rest of the world seems unable to fully comprehend all the complexities of the continent. As a sad consequence, many unnecessary and, very often, costly mistakes have been made in shaping Africa's transformation and development agenda.

Up to the late nineteenth century, the African interior was such a vast mystery that Western observers, many of whom had often not set foot on the continent or without benefit of concrete knowledge, wrote the most fantastical tales of Africa and its inhabitants. The "explorer" approach to knowledge and debates about Africa persist to this day. The "Africa Rising" debate typifies this mirage of information and knowledge. Jerven (2013) rejects outright the idea that Africa is rising because of data problems that characterise GDP estimates. Such data issues bedevil all economies and that is why national accounting is evolving all the time. It is possible that Africa's GDP could be underestimated as was the case of the recent rebasement of Nigeria's GDP.

Walter Rodney (1972) ably described the establishment of dependency relationships between Europe and Africa during colonialism, which would develop the former at the expense of the latter. Meanwhile, a combination of economic dependence, weak state authority, and divided societies encouraged the consolidation of "gatekeeper states" which have often been mired in recurrent economic and political crises (Ekeh, 1975; Cooper, 2002). To reproduce their economic and political power, both local and foreign elites sought to control the seat of the internationally recognised sovereign government which served as a gateway to resources that they could subsequently redistribute at their discretion so as to "remain" in power. Managing and sustaining a dense network of patron–client relationships has been essential for political survival. The endemic corruption that would result from these dynamics only served to further exacerbate economic underdevelopment (Beresford, 2015).

Against this background, a more optimistic than corrective narrative has emerged. It has been said that Africa as a continent is "rising" despite centuries of economic underdevelopment, limited transformation, and the supposedly ineluctable and neo-patrimonial fashion in which African politics "works" (Chabal and Daloz, 1999). The optimistic story is based on a range of factors to demonstrate Africa's rise, including the increasing attractiveness of African markets to foreign investors; positive and sustained rates of GDP growth, productivity growth, ambitious new infrastructure projects; and the emergence of a middle class.

Whether one accepts or rejects the "Africa Rising" narrative, there is a danger of conflating the symptoms of new dynamics in the continent's development with forms of a new and distinct historical trajectory (Beresford, 2016). It is therefore contestable whether African countries' recent economic performance constitute a definitive break with long-term relationships of dependency and recurrent crises afflicting many African states. Taylor (2016) argues that "the dynamics which are accompanying a notional 'rise' of Africa... are actually contributing to the continent being pushed further and further into underdevelopment and dependency" (p. 8). Taylor insists that Africa's "rise" has actually been underpinned by an intensification of African states' dependency on primary resource exports. Commodity dependency has contributed to processes of deindustrialisation, rather than bringing about a definitive change in the global balance of industrial power. The counter argument to both Taylor and Jerven is that China has played a major role in stimulating Africa's recent GDP growth through its sizeable investments in African infrastructure, as well as other private investments which have taken advantage of its untapped resource potential.

However, in most African policy circles there is now an acknowledgement of the potential fragility of economic growth due to resource dependence (Kararach, 2017; Cheru, 2017), with the consequent widespread call for structural transformation. Measuring economic progress by privileging "growth for growth's sake" tells us little about broad-based development. Africa must address the social problems that the new economic growth spawns, such as inequality – problems that are too often neglected by the Africa Rising narrative (Mkandawire, 2014).

Several studies have re-examined some of the older "resource-curse" debates regarding Africa's position in global relations of unequal exchange (Phillips et al., 2016; Kararach and Odhiambo, 2016; Kararach, 2017). They have highlighted the importance of a political economy perspective on development because power relationships shape and transform the nature of resource dependency; hence, African agency will remain a critical part of future continental development. In contrast, the neoliberal notion of good natural resource governance demands stringent adherence to acknowledging the "economic realities" of resource extraction and comparative advantage, creating and maintaining private property regimes, and stimulating foreign investment in ways that do not foster a radical break from the resource-based development trajectory of the continent. As Bush (2013, p. 15) argues: "Opportunities for sustainable growth and development lie not with greater integration with the world economy but with, among other things, local political and economic struggles in Africa for greater participation in local decision making and control of international capital." In Ghana's case, while the oil sector is likely to stimulate the kind of GDP growth revered by those claiming to witness Africa rising, there are serious doubts that this will augment more broad-based development that will benefit those not already enjoying economic and political power.

Africa needs critical self-reflection by identifying unique pathways for its future development. This requires a rejection of both the core assumptions of reinvigorated modernisation theory and the uncritical rehashing of the dependency theories of the middle twentieth century. While many of the old patterns of dependency remain, it is critical to understand the changing patterns of accumulation and the complex and constantly renegotiated political settlements that underpin them, including the forms of protest and resistance that they generate. Such dynamics of late capitalism not only reproduce social injustice but also generate massive contradictions for elements of civil society who might otherwise play a central role in shaping alternative pathways of development (Amaizo, 2012; Beresford, 2016).

Self-reflection is urgent because Africans themselves sometimes misread the reality of the continent's dynamics of change. Indeed, both citizens and institutions have at times taken positions that seem unanticipated. One major area of such misreading relates to the importance of constitutionalism and democratic rule. Leaders that tried to extend their rule have been confronted with situations that are precarious and unpredictable. In Burkina Faso, Blaise Compaore did not understand the mood of his people when he overstayed his welcome and tried to entrench his rule. And in Zimbabwe, Robert Mugabe imagined that his political writ was permanent until he was unceremoniously removed in a "soft" coup. Similar movements have occurred in Algeria and Sudan recently.

Growth in itself is not the issue that troubles policymakers or intrigues development scholars. What has confounded observers is the origins of growth (*Economist*, 2017) and its associated socio-political context. In 1954 Arthur Lewis argued that development occurs as labour shifts from an unproductive "traditional" sector – activities such as subsistence farming, or petty trade – into modern, capitalist activities. Based on his thesis, there are at least two traditions of thinking about growth. One focuses on raising labour productivity within sectors of the economy, by adding capital or improving skills and technology. The other stresses structural change, whereby workers move between sectors. The output of the average African manufacturing worker is five times that of the agricultural counterpart. It then follows that growth will occur if people move from farms to jobs in factories or high-value services. However, structural change is more than about factories but also refers to an enhanced quality of life which must include political voice, participation, and inclusion.

Defining the nature and character of the post-colonial state in Africa

While the developmental state is critical for Africa's transformation, it ignores the need for a better understanding of the post-colonial state in Africa. Through the work of Samir Amin (1990), John Saul (1974), and others, the analytical purchase on African economies has begun to progress, especially with respect to the contradictions inherent in the post-colonial state. There are three major variants of these analyses: one anchored on modernisation theory, the second on Marxist theory and an off-spring literature, and the third which adopts a structuralist stance. Modernisation theory is premised on the failure of development in Africa where "pre-modern" institutions undermined the emergence of a modern economy and prevented the continent's "take-off", as predicted by Rostow (1960). The Marxist interpretation suggests a different approach, as outlined by Saul (1974). Borrowing from Hamza Alavi, Saul avers that the political analysis of the post-colonial state in Africa has lagged far behind notions of political modernisation and one-party states, thereby falling short of any radical scientific understanding of the political dynamics. He notes that Hamza Alavi has provided an important starting point by using the historical specificity of post-colonial societies, a specificity that arises from structural changes brought about by the colonial experience.

The structuralist tradition, just like the Marxist one, urges us to get a better understanding of the structural constraints that have underpinned post-colonial Africa, including various resources such as human and financial resources. For example, Saul (1974) quoting Alavi (1972), argues that the state in post-colonial Africa is ill-suited to promote development. First, the colonial state is therefore equipped with a powerful bureaucratic-military apparatus and mechanisms of government that enable them through its routine operations to subordinate the native social classes. The post-colonial state instead inherits that overdeveloped apparatus of state and its institutionalised practices through which the operations of indigenous social classes are regulated and controlled in ways that undermine autonomous development

Second, the state in the post-colonial society directly appropriates a very large part of the economic surplus and deploys it in bureaucratically directed economic activity in the name of promoting economic development. Since these two features both characterise the East African situation, they also serve there. Alavi (1972) demands of us to "differentiate the post-colonial State fundamentally from the state as analysed in classical Marxist theory".

Third, Saul (1974) argues that in developed capitalist societies the state is the "dominant classes' political power centre" and, in this respect, comes to have an important ideological function. What is clear is the centrality of the state in the post-colonial social formation, including the importance of those who staff the state apparatus within such a formation, as the case of formerly colonial Ireland might suggest – especially the critical importance of an efficient and accountable bureaucracy.

Essentially, the post-colonial state stifles organic evolution and transformative development. Zeleza (2018) argues against a simplistic interpretation of the post-colonial experience. There is thus need to acknowledge the "twists and turns in virtually all sectors and dimensions." From a post-structuralist perspective, we are encumbered to acknowledge the painful history of slavery, imperialism, and colonialism alongside the tensions of contemporary African trajectories and agency fostered by external forces, agents, and institutions whose diagnosis, prescriptions and interventions are mediated by local realities and lived experiences. There is thus need for a broader agency anchored on a coalition of academia, professional groups, trade unions, and civil society. The agenda must present a new social contract between people and state with a focus on improvement of the conditions of lives on the continent for all.

The burden the state has to carry in structural transformation

There are many prejudices about Africa, including descriptions and analytical treatments of the state, religions, and ethnicity. For example, Handley (2008) makes a hasty and unjustifiable claim about how ethnic divisions have been instrumental in the capitalist development of South Africa and Mauritius. She argues that despite claims to the contrary, ethnic diversity creates healthy and vibrant capitalist economies by opening up avenues for engaging the state in economic policy issues. In South Africa, and to a lesser extent in Mauritius, ethnic ownership of the state and the economy took root in two separate kinship and cultural worlds, which meant that such ownership capacity was created purposefully. In both countries, economic success has been based on "the way that ethnicity had historically separated out their respective political and economic elites" (p. 243). This ethnic and racialist separation have allowed for "contestation" between the business class and the state, resulting in efficient and effective economic decision making and development.

It is clear from the authors such as Handley (2008) and Bates (1981) that characterisations are formed by hasty judgment or special interests. These subsequently circulate among intellectuals and laypeople, and lead to comparisons between what is to be seen from a Western standpoint and analyses of African societies based upon Western societal models and ideological orientations. Over the long term, such views have led to the branding and stigmatisation of African states having "colonial roots", or being "external", "quasi-state", and "artificial" or "pseudo-state." In an attempt to challenge this tendency, Jean François Bayart (1989) presents a historical view of the state in Africa as being built upon by the bases of pre-colonial state traditions and the colonial experience. He correctly argues that contemporary African states have been influenced both by colonialism and from pre-colonial kingdoms and empires, and reflect both rule of law and ancestral political traditions. These alternately are close to as well as keep a distance from religion. Such phenomena are complex, thus making understanding and management of the African state that more challenging (Saul, 1974).

Colonialism in Africa imposed itself upon structured societies and established specific relations of exploitation. However, in most cases, it did not take land ownership from the hands of the people, a primary condition for capitalist production according to Marx. Neither did it make wage labour a general rule. It left domestic society with its own social relations, which were conserved and/or adapted to serve colonial interests. Key in all these processes has been the effort to speed up the creation of a pool of labourers by either expunging communities of traditional property relations or instituting a wage-based economy. The result was a subsistence economy sitting side-by-side with one based on capitalist/colonial exploitation.

Meillassoux (1977) argues that colonial exploitation resulted from the reproduction of a cheap labour force and income transferred from domestic to capitalist society. Essentially, a dualism develops whereby subsistence food production remains almost entirely outside the capitalist sphere and maintains direct or indirect links with the market economy, either by providing workers to the domestic sector, or through the production of export goods produced by farmers from their own harvests. This food economy is partially capitalist because it provides a fed labour force while at the same time remaining outside the sphere of capitalist production, since no capital is invested and relations of production are of the domestic non-capitalist variety (Saul, 1974; Milazzo, 1977, pp. 155–156). In themselves, the relations between the capitalist and domestic sectors cannot be sufficiently binding to explain unequal exchange. The exploitative relationship is established through the reproduction of a cheap labour force for the benefit of capital. Access to a cheap labour force by colonial as well as post-colonial economy, through maintenance of domestic society, meant the maximum exploitation of workers while paying wages below their real value. This is because the labour force, when not employed "productively" by capital, assumes subsistence activity within domestic society and thus may not evolve as a major segment of a fully-fledged wage-based and industrial society (Leys, 1975).

As noted by Zeleza (2018), the African state has been characterised by contradictory tensions. This notion, and that of the different world-views of various players, is important for understanding the behaviour of populations in contemporary Africa. Africans are not simply passive agents; articulation is a play of forces, and the domestic community, even when subordinated, has ways of defending itself against changes that may not advance its broad interest. There is a relative independence of the domestic sector in relation to the capitalist sector, which becomes even more apparent in certain historical circumstances. Indeed, this articulation may preserve the domestic economy for purposes of exploiting it, and yet on the other hand, produce the elements for its destruction in the long term. These are the dynamics of economic underdevelopment requiring a redefinition by a developmental state.

Ironically, it was from among those that most benefited from the colonial capitalist project and yet felt marginalised that the nationalist leaders of most African countries emerged. In that regard, the modernisation of society may be compatible with the ideological perpetuation of pre-existing forms of social and political control over the oppressed. Thus, modernising and traditional values and practices may remain side-by-side and did indeed overlap, thus placing the burden of structural transformation squarely on the modern African state.

In essence, there is a need to conceptualise the state and review its diverse interpretations after decolonisation (Young, 2012). While the state in Africa has always been elusive, it has remained an authoritative actor in the last half-century in shaping continental development or the lack thereof. It is almost received wisdom that the premature evolution of the colonial state to the post-colonial state prevented African nations from gradually consolidating the necessary components of performing developmental state functions. The failure of these countries in their developmental functions forced many to regress into one-party states, military states (as a result of coups d'état), or hybrid states. The challenge is therefore for African states to manage the burdens of structural transformation placed upon them by both history and rising societal expectations.

African economic prospects

There is no doubt that the new Africa story about growth, investment, and expanding opportunities has been seriously shaken by recent developments in the world economy. After successful affirmations, the new narrative in many forums, including the EU–Africa Summit and President Obama's US–Africa Leaders' Summit, alarming predictions with regard to the economic impact of the Ebola epidemic on the continent's performance started a negative news cycle that spread very fast. The tone was set by recessive global demand, the commodities' price slump, high volatility in the oil and gas market, and bad news from a variety of conflicts. Gains of the past decade and a half were so fragile that many signalled that they were actually reversible.

Zeleza (2018) notes several factors that underpin Africa's growth prospects, including improvements in democratisation and governance, declines in conflicts, demographic shifts, and shifts in the globalisation process through better technology and social innovations. The emergence of new technologies present the continent with opportunities for innovation (Kararach, 2014).

Box 1.2 Cutting edge innovations in Africa

Recently, TerraPay and Instant Cash partnered to enable real-time cross border money transfers to mobile wallets. The partnership will make cross-border money transfer – to all major mobile wallets in Tanzania, Uganda, and all mobile numbers in Nigeria – faster and more convenient for the migrants. The platform, which uses TerraPay's global clearing and settlement service for mobile wallets, will allow Instant Cash's global agent network to expand their service offerings by offering cross-border transfers to mobile wallets, which is powering growth in many emerging markets. Such an innovation will enable customers to send remittances to mobile wallets in Nigeria, Tanzania, and Uganda. In Nigeria, migrants can send money to any mobile number as well as bank accounts. In Tanzania, migrants will be able to send remittances directly to Vodacom M-Pesa, Tigo Pesa, Airtel Money, and Zantel Ezy Pesa wallets. In Uganda, the friends and families of the migrants can receive money in their MTN and Airtel Money wallets. Other IT linked innovations are expected to enhance cultural exchanges including the streaming of music as well as sharing electronic contents.

Africa must remain strategic and exploit nascent opportunities. Economic stagnation in Europe and Japan has seen the introduction of stimulus packages that dwarf Africa's economic size. Yet the public deficits there continue to grow, and the malaise of deflation has become their number one concern. When some growth in the US contributed to the phasing out of its quantitative easing, there were enormous consequences for the currency markets, eroding most of the gains from largest exporting regions of Asia and Latin America. Russia's economy has also been contracting fast. China has started a cycle of reduced and slow growth and is recalibrating its economy to greater domestic consumption and away from exports.

The IMF has been lowering its global growth forecast despite, for example, the theoretical incentive that cheap oil and other commodities should provide to industrialised economies (IMF, 2009). The extent of the damage caused by the 2008–2009 crises is still being assessed. Many pundits believe that the world is not yet out of the doldrums, justifying strong calls by the US and the European Central Bank for new un-conventional monetary policies. Under this calamitous pressure, Africa seems to be doing better than other countries and regions of the world. Its forecasted growth has been revised downwards, but in a scale that puts the continent above any other at around 5 per cent for well over a decade (ECA, 2014a, 2015a). However, if the lessons of previous crisis cycles are taken into account, Africa will continue to be affected by global trends nevertheless.

There are seven major reasons influencing Africa's prospects. *First*, the unfavourable headwinds of falling *commodity prices* remind us that Africa cannot continue to remain at the lower end of the value chain. Geopolitics is at play in the decline of the global crude oil prices. The drop of 44.1 per cent between June and December 2014, or a monthly average decline of 7.4 per cent, happened on the back of the US shale gas boom, coupled with huge accumulated stocks; there was the need to exhaust the artificial price increases of the recent past and manage limited demand in emerging economies.

Second, most of Africa's recent growth is actually coming from *internal consumption*. The continent is less at the mercy of commodity markets since telecommunications, transportation, and finance are all expected to spur economic growth. Better fiscal policy is playing an important role. Financial markets have heeded the call from African countries to fund their huge requirements for investment in infrastructure and services through sovereign debt. Kenya, in the midst of its fight against terrorism, received $2 billion (Lopes, 2015a). Ethiopia, Nigeria, Senegal, Rwanda, Ghana, Zambia, and Côte d'Ivoire have all had demand outstripping their bond offers. Morocco and Djibouti accessed funds directly. However, it is important to note that this ease of access may be over. The lower rates some obtained will increase in light of heightened risk perception. This will make debt control calls more strident and buyers more cautious.

Third, Africa has managed to grow as an investment destination, albeit slowly. It only attracted 3.7 per cent of the $1.530 trillion global investments in 2014. About 20 per cent went to South America and 30 per cent to Asia. However, Africa's value proposition is equally attractive to China as it is to India. Total investment stocks held by China and India are very similar, even though Chinese investments tend to attract far more attention. India, like Malaysia, is the holder of the largest developing country investment stock in Africa, and has been quietly buying its way into various sectors of African economies. Africa's strategic direction will thus influence the nature of old and new partnerships.

Fourth, one cannot discount the impact of conflicts that divert major productive resources. Local conflicts are becoming affiliates or franchises of global terror networks. Economic transformation ought to make resources available to manage African diversity. Pastoralists who have missed economic transitions in marginalised Sahelian countries have found a haven in terrorism. Extremism, particularly religious extremism, as practised by Boko Haram in northern Nigeria, Seleka, Anti-Balaka, Al-Shabbab, and some of the Libya militia, or other AQIM and Mujao, are manifestations, in part, of African inability to leverage the productive forces of the continent. The situation in Somalia is a stark reminder that conflicts have regional and continental implications. Trafficking and organised crime must be tackled as they affect human security. Their impact in the continent's economic performance stretches from missed opportunities to contagious risk perceptions to loss of lives.

Fifth, while the rise of urban centres certainly offers a growth pathway, they also present a huge challenge. Africa's rapid urbanisation offers a potential springboard for economic diversification. However, building cities that work will require reforming land markets and urban regulations, and coordinating early infrastructure investments. For urbanisation to generate the benefits that it should, cities must become less costly for firms and hence, more appealing to investors. In addition, cities must become better living habitats for their residents by offering services, amenities, and housing for the poor and the middle class (World Bank, 2016b; ECA, 2017). However, if the Kuznets-Lewis effects persist in a developing economy, there would be a need to devise spatial and social protection programmes to protect lagging regions and rural areas from the backwash of structural transformation (Kanbur, 2017).

Sixth, the increasing role of trade will influence Africa's choices. Sub-Saharan Africa has seen a significant increase in the importance of trade over the years (SCB, 2012). In 1996, Sub-Saharan Africa was responsible for 1.2 per cent (Yeats et al., 1996) of global trade, compared with 3 per cent in 2012. Since 2004, Africa's trade and investment levels have been relatively steady. The level of trade and investment as a share of GDP now resembles that of regions such as East Asia. Trade is equivalent to 60 per cent of GDP, while foreign direct investment accounted for 3 per cent by 2012 (World Bank, 2012: World Development Indicators). These figures, however, hide important changes in the type of trade that Africa is engaged in. Figures from the IMF show that Sub-Saharan Africa is shifting away from its traditional trading base among the most developed economies at a faster rate than other emerging regions of the world such as Brazil, India, and China (see various IMF's Sub-Saharan Africa Regional Economic Outlook; also Ali (2007, p. 117)). These links are changing the nature of Africa's international economic relations, bringing both opportunity and risk. Regional trade within Africa has doubled since 1990 and constitutes 12–13 per cent of all African trade. The fact that this trade is growing shows that African economies are now differentiating from one another, and that trade barriers are starting to fall, proving great prospects for the success of the Africa continental free trade area.

Seventh, the demographic profile of the continent is changing fast. Sub-Saharan Africa has the youngest population in the world, with an average age below 20. The workforce is also expanding rapidly relative to the non-working population, thus lowering the dependency ratio. If young people are adequately educated, this factor, often referred to as the demographic dividend, will drive consumption and production in the future. Sub-Saharan Africa's workforce is forecasted to grow faster than the workforce in all other economies, meaning that the region will become increasingly competitive for labour-intensive activities compared to countries such as China where wage levels are rising. There are also opportunities for agricultural improvement to drive economic growth.

The demographics and the youth bulge raises the urgency of productive development policy and structural transformation (Kararach, 2014). African countries need to pay special attention to the potential problems that may be caused by mass migration if the youthful population are not absorbed into the wider economy (Adepoju, 2005).

So, what's next?

Africa as a continent must make radical reforms in order to deliver its transformational agenda and, especially, in making headway in exporting higher-value goods and services (Landsberg, 2018). It must move beyond the exporting of raw materials and importing of machinery and finished goods. The unfortunate state of affairs is that some of the finished imported goods are made with Africa's own exports, such as oil. One reason for this is "tariff escalation", which is a form of protectionism whereby raw material exports face lower export tariffs than higher value-added finished products. For example, the tariff for exporting coffee and cocoa beans is much lower than that on instant coffee and chocolate bars. Structural transformation will be a major tool to break this straightjacket on African development (Zeleza, 2018; Murphy et al., 2014).

Growth, cash, and jobs need markets to expand. Africa's trade performance has been relatively impressive with strong increases, especially since 2000. However, it failed to diversify its exports away from primary products and natural resources, and thereby limiting the potential for industrialisation. This can be explained by the highly ineffective design, implementation, and coherence of trade policy. Moreover, the asymmetric trade agreements which African countries continue to sign have led to insufficient incentives for industrialising through trade. African countries must therefore be bold and courageous when they negotiate. If Africa operationalises the common market of the Africa Continental Free Trade Area (ACFTA), it will have the size of China's population. If it cannot do it, who will believe in Agenda 2063?

As of early 2016, Africa's 3000 richest individuals had an accumulated wealth approaching $400 billion, while $400 billion is kept by Africa's central banks (Lopes, 2015b). If these figures are examined in terms of Africa's own capacities and resources, the way forward can be charted. The new Africa narrative is alive and well but it is also shaky and vulnerable without effective development policy and planning.

Traditionally, the responsibility for articulating appropriate development strategies and policies rested with the state through constant dialogue and contestation with key social and economic agents on the sides of production, supply, and consumption (Okimoto, 1989; Amsden, 1989, 2000; Chang, 2007; Mkandawire, 2001, 2017). However, economic transformation demands the use of appropriate policies, incentives, and sanctions to ensure that both public and private resources move in an optimal direction. Because policies result in gains and losses, the state therefore has a responsibility to negotiate the associated conflicts between social groups and, over time, to articulate development policies that promote economic growth and transformation without unduly sacrificing important equity and social considerations.

Another critical ingredient shaping the structural transformation and development pathway is the ability to implement blueprints and plans (Karach, 2014). The implementation of development plans and policies requires both state capacity and competence to carry out this critical task. Key planning institutions need to be established and given the power and autonomy to do their work effectively and efficiently. The design and implementation of plans and policies will involve monitoring and evaluation, as well as assessment and review of the relevant plans and policies under implementation, with broad stakeholder participation and involvement. However, there is need for a caveat here. As noted by Rodrik (2013) and Hausman (2012), developmental states have historically differed in their evolution, context, trajectory, and manifestations and, hence, there cannot be a "single model" in how the role of the state is engineered or fashioned. Rodrik (2013) further notes that the transition to high growth and transformation may require limited state intervention, if only to suggest that there may be many development recipes. In that regard, countries should consider context specificities when designing their transformational agendas.

Conclusion

Those who see the continent as a new source of investment opportunities, especially for corporate shareholders, have framed the narrative of "Africa rising." It is argued in this chapter that there is a need to reframe this narrative with a voice that champions structural transformation. Essentially, Africa's structural transformation is possible. Development requires making strategic choices in order to navigate the complex challenges alluded to and take advantage of opportunities. It is about how Africa preserves its policy space, while having a common set of goals and priorities. Under particular circumstances, countries often find their space for making domestic policy choices constrained. This tension arises from dilemmas of how countries can keep the manifold benefits of extensive international development engagement free of conditionalities. To do that, African countries must resolve a number of internal contradictions.

Improvement in governance must be deepened. Good governance will create the space to reduce conflict and improve human security. Such positive effects in governance will enhance Africa's position to utilise its huge natural resources for sustainable structural transformation. However, natural resource abundance in some African countries has often been associated with the distortion of incentives for economic diversification and transformation. This in part, has been a result of weak economic and corporate governance as well as inadequate rule of law that emphasises rights and responsibilities associated with the economic activities of all players. Africa's vast natural resources must be put to good use to raise the massive amounts of financing required for development. Through Agenda 2063, Africa has an ambitious plan for structural transformation and a redefinition of its position in the world.

Economic diversification is of paramount importance. Excessive dependence on exports to the United States and the EU has long been identified as a problem for developing countries. Product and market diversification should be part of any trade or development strategy. In an effort to lessen their dependence on traditional export markets, many companies have paid more attention to emerging markets during times of crisis. For large emerging economies, this has translated into a greater focus on domestic markets. For the poorest countries, the shift in demand has resulted in the arrival of new brands and new investors from emerging countries.

Trade and investment with non-traditional partners must be prioritised. Indeed, the crisis in advanced country markets has inspired different export strategies among developing countries. Africa has boosted South–South trade in the case of intermediate goods, where South–South trade increased to 50 per cent of the world's intermediate goods trade in 2009 compared to about 25 per cent in 2000. The shift in markets to the global South has two components: the growth of South–South trade, including a greater focus on domestic markets in large emerging economies; and the increased interest of exporters in the North in emerging markets in the South. Local producers in emerging economies, particularly in Brazil, China, India, and South Africa, have tried and have increasingly succeeded in competing with foreign producers at home.

Rapid urbanisation is another important driver and factor in shaping the evolution of African economies. There has been a rapid increase in the size and density of populations in urban areas with a corresponding increase in rural–urban nexus. Many explanations have been advanced for this rapid growth, including failure in the economy to stimulate productive activities in both the rural areas and urban centres. This has resulted in an incompatible increase in unemployment, poverty, and slums as well as a general struggle to maintain means of livelihood. Socio-economic and political institutions should be strengthened so as to ensure that political elites do not use state power to convert public investments into their personal wealth. Indeed, urbanisation can bring about the much-desired economic and political development of Africa if used as hubs of economic dynamism and growth.

Enhancing social inclusion and reducing inequality is equally important. Enhancing economic governance as part of the reform and structural transformation agenda is thus critical. The quality of socio-political institutions as means to enhance inclusion is a major determinant of growth performance, and it is therefore futile to recommend good macroeconomic or microeconomic policies if the institutional structure does not exist to support them. The African experience has shown how weak institutions lead to inequality, intermittent dictatorship, and that there is a lack of constraints capable of preventing elites and politicians from plundering a country. Reforms also need to tackle constraints related to structures of the economy, including over-dependence on primary commodities with consequent jobless forms of growth, the large informal sector, and poor corporate governance. Better quality services must be provided as means to enhance inclusion and citizens need to claim greater political participation to enhance their voice and to demand more accountability in the economy.

Africa must continue working towards a converged and harmonised approach to realise the gains of any transformation agenda. The continent can build on a number of enablers of development such as infrastructure, peace and security, human rights, and favourable demographics. These will require priorities that can be translated at national, regional, and continental levels whilst recognising the need to integrate policies at the international level. There are different and varied needs for African countries, given the opportunities and challenges that arise. The normative glue that binds all these countries together is the imperative of structural transformation and not a cul-de-sac of structural adjustment.

Notes

1 These models emphasise the importance of comparative advantage and perfect competition in factor markets as drivers of growth. The three factors that can be perfectly substituted are capital, labour, and technology depending on their returns at the margin. The rewards to these factors depend on the marginal contribution in the production process and, in that regard, every player in the system gets a "just" reward. Inequality is therefore an outcome perfect market functionality.

2 Such pressures include conflict over resources, issues of income distribution, support during sectoral adjustments, contestation of policies, and demands for voice and accountability.

3 See Appendix for a detailed formal exposition.

4 See for example McMillan and Rodrik, 2011; ECA, 2011, 2014a; AfDB, 2013; ACET, 2014; McMillan et al., 2014; McMillan and Headey, 2014; De Vries et al., 2015; Martins, 2015; Yilmaz, 2015.

5 One could look at commodity concentration or an export similarity index to detect such changes.

2 Seeking transformation? Africa is not alone

Introduction

The colonisation of Africa imposed a reorganisation of the economic and political arrangements of the continent which were to prove instrumental to its underdevelopment (Rodney, 1972). The unfortunate reality of decolonisation is that it largely failed to lead to the establishment of viable, democratic African governments capable of meeting the needs and aspirations of their peoples. There has been a growing recognition in Africa that democracy and good governance are both "goods" in their own right and are critical to the achievement of other development goals. Moreover, they are essential to the sustained promotion and protection of human rights and the achievement of development (Sen, 1999). However, there is a general misperception that international agencies can promote democracy and good governance in Africa. UN members voted to establish a democracy fund; and both the World Bank and the G-8 have launched new initiatives to address the problem of corruption as if this largely originates from within the continent. A recent study showed that 95 per cent of firms engaged in corruption in Africa are foreign (ECA, 2016d). The questions are whether these efforts are well-conceived or are they based on the negative narratives about the continent? In addition, are they being pursued in ways that are likely to be effective? In what ways have Africans been involved in or how have they responded to these efforts to determine their future? How will the legacies of history condition African responses to the challenges of the future?

Contextualising Africa's transformation within the changes that are taking place both locally and globally is critical. Over the past two decades, the international order has undergone a qualitative change. Indeed, a new discourse has gained prominence in international relations theory that emphasises a rapidly changing global environment, characterised by an ever-growing confluence of major systemic challenges. These range from widespread poverty and undernourishment, financial and economic crises, climate change impacts, human insecurity, organised crime, drug trafficking, and all of these are linked in inextricable ways.

We therefore need go beyond a simple interpretation of the Kuznets-Lewis framework in order to understand the various drivers of structural change, including policy stances, institutional factors, dynamics of savings and accumulation, access to resources and finance, and political economy: in essence, those factors that circumscribe inequality and poverty, however defined, and how these, in turn, relate to circumstances and efforts that shape and define the underdevelopment/development process. These issues will be referred to and explored further in the remaining part of the book.

We argued in Chapter 1 that for Africa to achieve its potential and truly to be big in a developmental sense, then its constituent countries must pursue the norms and modalities of structural transformation. Africa's transformation pursuit is taking place in a world that is attempting to reconfigure problems into a singular, dominant global governance regime, thus triangulating both the circumstances and efforts of African peoples. This has made the arguments for revisiting the governance regime for sustainable development and structural transformation more compelling. How the continent will redefine its global relations, including how the rest of the world perceives it, will shape the nature of its success in structural transformation. The rest of this chapter makes a deeper exploration of the implications of not being alone by considering problems of misperception and the negative global narrative. The international community faces no greater challenge than that of putting Africa on the path to balanced and sustained development. No region of the world is in greater need of the kinds of services and support that the system of international organisations was created to provide. Competent and effective international institutions are essential to helping Africans address and solve their pressing political, economic, and social problems.

This chapter thus explores what reforms are required within the system of multilateral institutions in order to enable them to redefine the circumstances and efforts to support African countries in their transformation agendas. We look beyond the myth that multilateralism can solve the problems thrown up by globalisation. More specifically, the chapter seeks to understand the reasons for the international community's collective failure to solve Africa's development problems, despite billions in dollars in development and humanitarian assistance. Why has Africa continued to lag behind despite its huge resources, and in many instances, to fall further behind even as other parts of the world were making great leaps forward? Why has the international community been so unsuccessful in bringing the lessons of decades of experience in development to bear on Africa's problems? Where and how should we begin to adapt our international institutions to address these challenges? We examine issues of international governance and the challenge of designing competent and effective international institutions. The focus on some of these global dynamics and constraints is not to suggest that they are delinked from some internal pressures and constraints in Africa. We do return to some of the internal challenges and opportunities in the subsequent chapters in this book.

Structural transformation as realignment of circumstances: beyond markets and political dogmatism

The environment in which African countries are seeking their transformation has always been rapidly changing. There is greater consensus among African scholars on what needs to be done to accelerate growth, reduce poverty, improve governance, and assume leadership and accountability for their own development (Landsberg, 2018). The continent's promising potential can only be fully unlocked by the proactive development of the rural sector, investment in human capital development, including training in science and technology, the development of the required infrastructure, the promotion of private initiatives and creativity, and improved governance (AU, 2014). Many African countries are seeking to halt the productivity decline in agriculture by instituting enabling policies and investing in vital infrastructure. A similar effort is being made to reverse the decline in education and access to health care (Cheru, 2017).

The continent remains vulnerable to external shocks and the recent slowdowns in China and other emerging countries have had an enormous impact on commodity-dependent African economies (Kararach, 2014). The challenge for Africa in the years ahead is, therefore, how to build on the recent gains and begin the process of transition from the heavy dependence on commodities and minerals to economic platforms with strong manufacturing, financial, and service sectors that can contribute a larger share of the economy and generate employment and wealth creation (ECA, 2004; ECA, 2010a, 2010b).

Disequilibrium defines the changing way economies operate, and one of the virtues of the market economy is its ability to adapt to such changes (Stiglitz, 2017). There are various sources of shocks from weather variability to new product lines due to innovation, and policy uncertainty. Producers as well as consumers have to constantly adapt to the changing competitive and business landscapes. However, alongside such changes are shifts in structural variables that tend to be infrequent and far between. But when these changes occur, there are significant strains as both markets and the political process that govern economies struggle to cope (Kararach, 2011; Stiglitz, 2017). In this regard, structural transformation needs to be managed to reduce the backwash effects. This requires an activist state to shape the evolution of industrial policy to be able to guide the transition from an agrarian to an industrial society.

Stiglitz (2017) argues that there is a simple reason behind the failure of markets and politics in managing structural transformations. It is largely because economic and political structures are designed for stability, including the maintenance of existing power relationships. Both markets and political processes are adept at handling small shocks, but do not cope well when managing large-scale changes. In the economic sphere, such changes lead to huge (and typically unanticipated) changes in asset values. Historically, during industrialisation, as farmers migrated from the rural sector, the assets owned by farmers, in particular their homes, decreased in value. Their human capital was even more affected: farmers were well-attuned to the nuances of weather, disease, etc. in their locales as these nuances related to the production of the crops in which they specialised, but those skills were largely unrelated to the skills required for manufacturing. Because, and for good reasons, manufacturing occurs largely in urban centres, there was a tendency for mass movement of labour from rural to urban areas. In addition, the move from agriculture to manufacturing thus required a massive change in the structure of housing.

In a decentralised market economy, the individuals must put in the effort for obtaining the human capital that they need in order to be productive beyond basic education. Individuals are responsible too for relocation costs and resettlement. Adjustments from the old sectors to the new sectors are difficult, sluggish, and require significant resources. Structural transformation presupposes up-front capital expenditures in factors such as housing, infrastructure, institutional reforms, etc., but no firm promise of good returns on such investments. Large numbers of individuals who should be making the transition do not have the resources to finance it; and given the imperfections of capital markets – which can be explained in terms of imperfections and asymmetries of information – they cannot obtain finance (Stiglitz and Wiess, 1981). Additionally, structural transformation itself makes it even more difficult to obtain the finance and this points to the need to rethink development finance. Banks that have invested or lent substantial amounts in the rural sector (or "old" sector) also experience significant losses or a credit crunch. The fact that the value of housing in the rural sector has diminished implies that some loans will be defaulted upon. So too for loans made to finance other investments in the rural sector. Thus, the net worth of banks will experience a negative shock, thereby reducing their ability and willingness to lend (Greenwald and Stiglitz, 2003).

Equally, large changes in technology and consumer preferences may not quickly translate into enabling changes in the overall economy that one would have expected, assuming that the cost of resource mobility is zero. There are, in addition, large social costs. Individuals have built up networks of relationships that are not only a direct source of "utility" but also provide strong systems of social support.

As the experience of Africa shows, what is required is political intervention not for its own shake but that has a developmental orientation and ideology. Stiglitz (2017) notes that political institutions also perform poorly in the face of structural transformation as they tend to reflect existing power structures. The greater difficulty is that the existing power structures depend on dominant economic arrangements and the structural transformation can undermine both those structures and arrangements. As a result, rather than facilitating the transition, too often governments prefer to preserve the status quo and the power structures associated with them. Historical evidence suggests that in the movement from agrarian to industrial economies, the political institutions created in agrarian contexts gave undue weight to the interests of rural agrarian communities, and the mind-set of those communities was often at odds with that of today's dominant urban communities that tend to be mercantilist, acquisitive, and individualistic.

The above discussion provoked some of the major criticism against the Kuznets-Lewis framework since 1955 (Kanbur, 2017). First, and primarily in the 1970s, 1980s, and 1990s but even today, we tend not to find an inverse-U relationship between national inequality and national per capita income in cross-country regression analysis. This is true even when in more recent years, longitudinal observations have been added to the mix for a few countries. The second and more recent and prominent criticism by Piketty (2006, 2014) is that Kuznets built a theory to explain the facts of the time, namely, the levels of declining inequality over the previous few decades.

There are a number of ways in which one can go "Beyond Kuznets", within the Kuznets-Lewis approach itself. Kuznets' (1955) exposition is far richer than the simplistic characterisations of it in the subsequent literature. Roemer's (1998) formulation of the normative concept of "equality of opportunity", takes the debates beyond the initial conceptualisations in Kuznets. Instructively, the basis of Roemer's arguments is the very same sectoral frame presented by Kuznets. Roemer distinguishes between two types of determinants of income (or any other outcome variable) – "circumstances" and "effort". Circumstances are the factors outside the control of the individual/unit of analysis, while effort denotes factors that an individual or agent controls. Gender, ethnicity, parental occupation, or wealth, for example, may be thought of as circumstances. The variation of income attributable to variations in these circumstances is then deemed to be (in)equality of opportunity. The specific method is to decompose an inequality index into between-group and within-group components and use the fraction of the former in total inequality as a measure of inequality of opportunity (see, for example, Paes De Barros et al., 2009). Locality of birth is a major factor in defining circumstances. This is legitimately thought to be outside the control of the individual. In the global context, for example, country of birth is considered to be morally arbitrary, and thus the fraction of global inequality attributable to per capita income differences across countries to be "global inequality of opportunity" (around 75 per cent, see Milanovic, 2016).

The remainder of this chapter as well as the book will discuss how Africa can change the "circumstances" necessary for its structural transformation through the achievements of the UN Sustainable Development Goals (SDGs), multilateral trade and related policies, migration and related issues of demographic shifts, climate adaptation and mitigation, and industrialisation.[1]

The Sustainable Development Goals: an impractical tool for global governance and Africa's transformation?

Across Europe, Asia, and the Americas common issues of financial and political stability, conflict management, job creation, raising productivity, and climate change mitigation permeate daily domestic policy discussions. The recent domino effect of five central banks (in Denmark, Switzerland, Japan, Sweden, and the European Central Bank) slashing interest rates to sub-zero levels has certainly given many the chills. The global and interconnected character of the twenty-first century challenges calls for solutions that transcend national borders and that are based on strategic partnerships. These vulnerabilities have provoked the need to re-examine the nature of global relationships for sustainable development. Even if the continent has great potential, African countries are not alone and their engagements with the rest of the world must be expressed and managed in the context of a comprehensive development strategy for economic transformation.

Such a strategy must be cognizant of five factors that have come to affect Africa's recent development "circumstances" (Kararach, 2014). First, the emergence of a multipolar economic world that now includes the Global South as a source of new investment opportunities and export destinations, development experience and knowhow, as well as a new aid architecture that is forcing a redefinition of multilateralism, including attempts to correct bilateral failures by enhancing triangular cooperation. Second, there are demographic changes brought about by a young and increasingly urbanised continent of a billion people – a number that is expected to double to two billion by 2050, with two-thirds living in cities. As noted in Chapter 1, this increased human capital has the potential to revolutionise the productive base of the continent. However, the energy of the young population, if untapped through better employment opportunities, has the potential to become a source of instability and political chaos as migration becomes one mechanism for relieving demographic pressures. Third, there are continuing discoveries of large amounts of natural resource wealth, and the associated challenges of illicit financial flows and corruption in the natural resource sectors, but there are also opportunities that arise from managing and sharing that wealth. Fourth, there is a real opportunity for skipping development steps with technology, including mobile technology. Finally, climate change has the potential to generate significant conflict over environmental assets such as land and water, and can weaken biodiversity and threaten livelihood systems. These new realities require Africa to revisit the tenets of international cooperation and multilateralism.

Since independence, international development cooperation has always been high on the political agenda of African leaders. At the continental level, African countries recognised that in view of the fragmentation and small size of their economies, regional integration and cooperation had to be important components of their development strategies. Several experiments in cooperation and integration have been conducted in various sub-regions of Africa. These include the East African Community (EAC), Common Market for Eastern and Southern Africa (COMESA), Preferential Trade Area (PTA), Southern African Development Community (SADC), Communauté Économique des États de l'Afrique Centrale (CEEAC), Economic Community of West African States (ECOWAS), Maghreb African Union (MAU), African, Caribbean and Pacific–European Union (ACP–EU); these arrangements were expected to play the role of primary building blocks for the eventual integration of the entire African continent. Okafor (2018) argues that multilateralism will only be beneficial if African countries develop the capacity to negotiate and implement rules that accommodates their development aspirations and needs.

Most regional cooperation bodies have had limited transformative achievements to date in terms of the human and financial resources deployed. Because of renewed efforts by Africa to redefine its development trajectory, regional cooperation and integration have not lost their attraction. The pace of regionalism has accelerated, including people-to-people exchanges (Kararach et al., 2012). The signing in 1991 of the Abuja Treaty establishing the Pan-African Economic community inspired the launching of numerous sub-regional initiatives of different types. These efforts gave impetus to the formation of the New Partnership for Africa's Development (NEPAD), which was seen as the way out of Africa's age-old integration problems. It is also a symbol of a more self-confident Africa.

It is accepted that the opportunities and challenges of today's Africa and economic globalisation are closely connected. Opportunities to improve living conditions and raise educational and health standards through participation in global supply chains certainly do exist. While African countries are all competing globally, there is an equal risk of joining a race to the bottom when it comes to the environment and social conditions (Kedir et al., 2016). Africa needs development, but it must be sustainable – based on the concept of decent work and with the objective of guaranteeing living conditions also for future generations (Hanson and Léautier, 2013). The continent actively supports the Sustainable Development Goals. It is striving for a combination of economic success, social justice and peace, ecological balance, and political stability (Hanson et al., 2017). Africa has for almost a decade sought to rewrite its development narrative and correct old misperceptions in the context of NEPAD.

Agenda 2063 reiterates the millennial renaissance theme, which demands that Africans work together with global partners towards a new beginning, proceeding from decolonisation towards self-determination, and calling for greater regional integration, socio-economic development, peace, security, and democratic development; and advocacy for self-reliance is shaping Africa's destiny and a redefinition of its place in the globalised world (Kararach et al., 2015). Agenda 2063 acknowledges that Africa needs new institutional and governance arrangements to effectively shape its agenda for transformation. However, the exact nature, structure, and composition of these institutional arrangements are not defined. Although Agenda 2063 moves beyond the SDG-framework, this cannot be achieved unless countries establish institutions that are capable of balancing and resolving competing political interests. Africa must also take into account three other broad issues: the interpretation of global targets; the reconfiguration of global priorities in the current context of evolving global governance and associated re-evaluation of the social contract due to issues such as climate change and communicable diseases; and the importance of political economy in a globalised world.

African leaders accept that several actions must be taken to shape globalisation so as to ensure fair economic distribution, adequate social conditions, and appropriate environmental management. Additional regulatory instruments and penalties are needed to relieve pressure on the market and to ensure that development policies succeed. A major innovative instrument for sustainable development and tangible improvement of social and environmental conditions all around the world arguably requires the establishment of enforceable compliance and environmental standards.

In neoliberal theory, short-term individual economic interests diverge from medium- and long-term social and environmental interests (Kararach, 2011). Yet the price for the destruction of natural resources and environmental assets is high. In recent years, there have been attempts at change in the international economy towards the formation of new modes of production and the incorporation of a variety of stakeholders into the global value chain in order to foster a greener growth path (ECA, 2016a). From the supply side, public and private sector awareness of sustainable production is growing. Instituting standards builds consumer confidence and improves the selling positions of those who conform to them, giving them a competitive advantage. On the demand side, consumer behaviour influences cultivation methods, working conditions, and the earning capacities of employees and producers. Certification of compliance with environmental standards is increasingly seen as a market incentive: a signal for higher quality, a better business culture, and a factor for a better corporate image.

New development paradigms became dominant in the early 1990s, particularly in the work of UN agencies such United Nations Development Programme (UNDP), United Nations Children Fund (UNICEF), and the World Health Organization (WHO), in which human development and human rights were regarded as more important than income-based notions of economic development (UNDP, 1990; Jolly et al., 2009). This new discourse prioritised not only the transfer of resources from developed to developing nations, but also the implementation of civil, political, economic, social, and cultural human rights, including a right to develop, particularly for women, children, and the poorest of society (Weiss and Daws, 2007; Jolly et al., 2009; Arndt et al., 2016).

Even though context specificities were overlooked, the United Nations embarked on an ambitious quest for global development. There was a concerted effort to combine the interests of both the Global South and North, which in turn guided the thinking of the Bretton Woods institutions, bilateral aid organisations, and countless NGOs, to pursue a common goal (Weiss and Daws, 2007; Jolly et al., 2009). The setting of goals such as the MDGs in itself was not unique for the UN, but the goals managed to mobilise the global community in an unprecedented fashion, often accredited to their clear, quantified, and time-bound nature (Weiss and Daws, 2007; Jolly et al., 2009). They were also the most communicated and promoted goals ever to be set, raising awareness across all spectrums of society and inviting the entire global community to participate in the endeavour (Jolly et al., 2009). To some commentators, the resulting consensus on this multilateral development strategy represented a major advance in international development (Weiss and Daws, 2007).

However, there is a misperception in reading Africa's poor development outcomes of the MDGs. Some old reasons are rehearsed for this relatively poor performance of Sub-Saharan Africa, including its harsh climate, political instability, and a large head-start for the rest of the developing world in 1990 (Sahn and Stifel, 2003; Ahmed and Cleeve, 2004; Maathai, 2011; World Bank, 2016b). Fukuda-Parr (2008) allegedly found in a study of 22 countries (primarily Sub-Saharan African) that few developing countries took ownership of the MDGs. These countries were blamed for not actively committing themselves to achieving the goals by following UNDP guidelines that were specifically created to assist the poorest nations. There is no doubt that Africa has been exposed to those global processes that undermine its ability to achieve the MDGs and, by extension, sustainable structural transformation. Bond (2006) describes these processes as looting Africa. A total of $192 billion is estimated to leave the continent annually from illicit financial flows, transfer pricing, brain drain, corruption, and other resource draining mechanisms.

The notion of sustainable development was arguably born out of a historical context and may have little to do with the African experience. It was notionally an attempt to resolve the tension between environmental concerns resulting from the global ecological consequences of human activities, on one hand; and economic, social, and political or structural transformational concerns associated with poverty and inequality on the other. The central tenet of sustainable development resides in the concept of equity and social justice for all. This is often associated with Rawlsian theory that suggests a bias in resource allocation to benefit the least advantaged societies (Rawls, 1971). The intergenerational solidarity principle is then translated into the will that resource management of today should not compromise the well-being of future generations.

More than two decades after sustainable development as a concept was given visibility by the Brundtland Report, how it is understood is still evolving. Indeed, subsequent international conferences such as the World Summit on Sustainable Development of 2002 reinforced the need for change in the way societies produce and consume as a precondition for achieving sustainable development (ECA, 2009). In fact, the ECA's "Sustainable Development Report" emphasises the importance of moving towards sustainable consumption and production to fulfil the dual aspirations of economic growth and poverty alleviation.

Sustainable development also implies a balance, namely, the ability to use the different forms of capital (social, natural, physical) in ways that do not jeopardise natural support systems (Kates et al., 2001). The amount and distribution of the various capitals matter (Dasgupta, 2001; Kates and Dasgupta, 2007). The Brundtland Report noted: "the 'environment' is where we live; and 'development' is what we all do in attempting to improve our lot within that abode. The two are inseparable."

Despite this evolution, sustainable development continues to suffer from definitional vagueness and programmatic follow-throughs. Most critics of sustainable development tend to see it as far too normative and ambiguous and therefore, incapable of providing practical solutions to complex development and environmental problems. To break away from this inherent fuzziness and ambiguity, the term "sustainability" is invariably used as a substitute for the absence of clarity in the path towards development. As Holling (1973) argues, sustainability is the capacity to "create, test and maintain adaptive capability." Development, on the other hand, can be a process of environmental management that is evolutionary in nature.

The new "engines" of global growth such as Brazil, Russia, India, and China have a collective GDP becoming closer to that of Japan, France, the United Kingdom, Italy, Germany, and the USA put together. Yet, in spite of their colossal economies and growth trajectories, the roles of the former as models or champions for sustainable development have been overlooked. What is their potential for achieving sustainable development? China is an example of a country that has achieved growth but it is not necessarily growth that is linked to the principles of environmental preservation.

Critics argue that sustainable development as a concept needs to be more flexible and dynamic and should be grounded on ecological and social realities. Sustainable development is a process of transformative change – across scales and governance regimes. It requires an enabling environment, robust institutions, and a set of rules to be adhered to. These are not processes that one can "stumble" into – it will require continuous direction and focus. Obligations to future generations thus present a central ethical problem, both in terms of how to approach the reality of an ageing population in most of the developing countries and especially with regard to significant parts of Asia and Latin America, and a booming younger population in Africa. Let us consider this conundrum. In the interest of intergenerational equity, how can we draw up a new social contract that will take into account changing demographic dynamics?

The answer to this "riddle" will lie in the ability to correct the youth asymmetry that the world is currently witnessing. Population growth is likely to increase in the world's poorest countries, with high fertility rates, which are mainly concentrated in Africa. It is estimated that half of population growth between 2013 and 2100 will be concentrated in just eight countries: the Democratic Republic of Congo, Ethiopia, Niger, Nigeria, India, Tanzania, Uganda, and the United States.

In Africa, youth unemployment tends to increase with higher education levels. Another constant is that government programmes aimed at promoting youth employment tend to be inefficient (Kararach et al., 2011; Hanson and Léautier, 2013). The young demographic has great potential to expand Africa's productive work force, promote job creation and entrepreneurship, and harness the enormous resource endowments of the continent. Poor investment in youth could constitute both a blessing and a curse for the continent (AfDB, 2013). Balancing the development sheet must be done in ways that do not leave most of Africa's population disenfranchised. Given the relative stagnation of employment in the 15–24 age bracket, how can Africa ensure that marginalised youth are not written off so that they become more fully absorbed in the economy?

The challenge of the twenty-first century will be the ability to address this demographic mega-trend in a manner that will preserve the interests of future generations. Today's elderly generation in Europe or Japan can enjoy a relatively prosperous old age mainly because their working lives are comparatively more prosperous than those of their parents. To what extent can Europe or Japan sustain its social welfare system without renegotiating a new contract with Africa's youthfulness?

Rewriting a new social contract implicitly means that there is a level of dissatisfaction with the way our world is configured. How do we create a redistributive system that is "solidaristic" and helps to enhance both intra-generational and inter-generational equity? How do we create new institutions that can lift people out of poverty based on a social contract that seeks to provide security and welfare to the poorest in the remotest outposts of the world?

Arguably, the Rio Summit's rationale is not radically dissimilar to the ideal of freedom and justice and the need for a participatory form of democracy. A new social contract that will take into account intergenerational equity and will ensure that institutions are aligned to societal needs will be difficult to develop. However, there are real risks for policy makers and humankind in general if we dismiss these ideals as utopian. The collective interest is strongly rooted in the ability to institute the behavioural response which will ensure that, whilst cognisant of a risk sharing approach, opportunities are provided to future generations. It is, in part, with this in mind that the world adopted the SDGs with a universal sense of purpose (Evans and Steven, 2012).

Grappling with goals for sustainable development is not only a demanding task but also a big challenge. The world's resources are finite and growth that is unmanaged and unsustained will lead to deteriorating conditions for all. For future generations, it is important to explore lifestyles and paths of development that effectively balance opportunities with possibilities. Therefore, goals creation is an equally important dimension to sustain development. However, a major misperception in the context of Africa is that these goals are likely to be silver bullets that will rid the continent of its development challenges and constraints.

As African countries move towards the domestication of these global goals, several considerations must be kept in the minds of their leaders.

First, there is a need to constantly interrogate the concept of sustainable development in order to account for changing times and ensure we remain alert. When it comes to the needs of countries in special situations, sustainable development means different things to different configurations of countries. For the Small Island Developing States (SIDS), the greatest threat to survival (and consequently sustainability) depends on climate change and adaptability, whether it is frequent cyclones, hurricanes, droughts, or storms, since much of their infrastructure and population reside along the coasts. For African countries and many of the Least Developed Countries (LDCs) and Landlocked Developing Countries (LLDCs), the road to sustainable development depends on their economic structural transformation, underpinned by the need to create increasing numbers of jobs and increase their share of the world's wealth. There is also growing concern that within the Middle-Income Countries (MICs), pervasive poverty is affecting a larger number of people than LDCs, not to mention growing inequality. Even countries with hard-won gains on poverty reduction remain vulnerable to economic volatility.

Therefore, the question is: how will SDGs address the different needs of these countries, while taking into consideration their hopes and aspirations, in the context of different political, economic and social realities or circumstances and efforts? A possible calculus is to identify commonalities that are clear enough to allow differentiation in terms of targets and priorities. After all, the principles of universality have always been based on this interpretation.

Second, there is need to examine the relationship between sustainable development and the need for a new social contract. When 250 years ago Jean-Jacques Rousseau wrote the *Social Contract*, his key contribution was to move the inter-generational level of solidarity from a family to a community and then to a national level. The establishment of modern regional integration projects – such as the European Union or the African Union – increased that level of ambition. The balance between human beings and nature, as defended by Rousseau, is not different from our discussion of SDGs. In order for us to defend a world global compact – as called for by the SDGs – we need to rethink the concept of inter-generational solidarity and reconstruct it in a more refined form. It would imply for instance, mimicking Rousseau, to recognise the need of youthfulness in certain parts of the world in contradistinction to the population that is ageing. This has tremendous implications for how we perceive mobility and migration, values chains for industrial production, or regulation of urban life. It will not be possible to attain sustainability at world level without understanding demographic trends as much as climate and environmental generation trends.

Third, there is need to scrutinise the vulnerability and challenges associated with the sustainable development concept. We know that sustainable development tends to be forgotten once new challenges threaten mainstream views. The recurrent economic and financial crises in both developing and advanced economies undermine all three pillars of sustainable development. The crises are intensifying the pressure for budget consolidation at national levels, and are increasing the likelihood of cuts in social services throughout much of the industrialised world. One government after another is bringing forward a budget consolidation programme that cuts social protection. Invariably, the financial crisis has led governments to introduce indicators and measures based on financial concerns rather than social welfare. The situation is leading to new forms of protectionism. This becomes especially obvious when not only conventional tariff and non-tariff restrictions to trade are considered, but also the more subtle, hidden protectionist measures, which have been described as "murky protectionism", such as rescuing firms to safeguard national interests or manipulating currencies.

The tendency of governments is to support production capacities in order to manage the economic downturn. Usually under this assumption, any sustainable development agenda goes out of the window. In fact, we have implicitly been living with a hierarchy of the three pillars of sustainable development: we accept economics as the pillar we have to get right, and then once that is done we deal with the social; and, only afterwards, we add environmental concerns. The SDGs must avoid this "cappuccino approach" of considering coffee as the basis to which we add milk and then sprinkle chocolate. The correct interpretation should be one that is based on the potential of a humanised and environmentally friendly economy. These sequencings in responses may well accommodate the emergence of the Kuznet's curve (see Appendix).

Fourth, there is need to reappraise an understanding of the principle of common but differentiated responsibilities. This principle is one of the milestones of the Rio Declaration from 1992. Its Article 7 states:

> In view of the different contributions to global environmental degradation, States have common but differentiated responsibilities. The developed countries acknowledge the responsibility that they bear in the international pursuit of sustainable development in view of the pressures their societies place on the global environment and of the technologies and financial resources they command.

For the first time in history, governments recognised their differential present and historical contribution to environmental degradation and, thus, their differential obligation to pay for the remediation and mitigation. Since then it has become a key element of the Kyoto Protocol, but its application reaches beyond climate negotiations.

Global negotiation processes tend to be bogged down and often collapse when the principles of common but differentiated responsibilities are contested. This has meant that difficult issues were taken off the table. For instance, despite a perceived break-through in Bali, after almost 18 years without a World Trade Organization (WTO) sponsored agreement, critics have been quick to state that many major issues had to be dropped for countries to settle on a very limited trade facilitation agenda. The same limited agreement scope was also reflected in the climate change negotiations. The lesson is that unless countries reappraise their views on common but differentiated responsibilities they will have difficulties agreeing on any universal set of goals.

Fifth, is the challenge of data. Measuring sustainability has to be at the core of any sustainable development agenda with metrics for measurements in environmental, economic, and social sustainability and how the three pillars work together. For instance, GDP is currently the conventional method for measuring the total monetary value of goods and services. Yet it is a measure of raw economic activity and considered a very poor instrument for measuring economic development, let alone social progress and environmental regeneration. Despite this fact, GDP has become the dominant economic measure and benchmark of progress, even though it obscures or excludes essential aspects of welfare and sustainability in our economies and societies. On the other hand, the laudable MDGs measurement promoted a focus on common targets rather than effort levels. It is the equivalent of having the same finishing line with different points of departure. Ultimately, local statistical capacity and local demand for statistics must be part of the implementation of the SDGs, which is why the call for a Data Revolution from the High-Level Panel Report is important! Previously, targets were first identified, but less thought was given to where the data would come from. Now all stakeholders realise that accurate statistics are a development investment (we return to this discussion in Chapter 3).

Sixth, Africa has been working towards a converged and harmonised approach to the implementation of the SDGs through its Agenda 2063 (ECA, 2016b). The African Common Position took into account the challenges of the MDGs, whilst calling for a structural transformation agenda based on a set of enablers of development such as infrastructure, peace and security, and human rights. While there are challenges to translate SDGs at the national levels whilst recognising the need to integrate policies at the international level, this effort may be moderated by the experience of African development. There is great coherence difficulty, on the one hand, when it comes to weaving country specific development goals into the diverse and often fragmented development initiatives of the African Union with those of the rest of the world on the other. Involvement of international players has tended to squeeze the policy space of African countries (Cheru, 2017).

Seventh, the SDGs offer little analysis of the drivers of global poverty. They say nothing about the unfair trade regime of the WTO, or many other bilateral trade and investment agreements that liberalise global markets at the expense of the poor. Goal 17.10 calls for more trade liberalisation and more power for the WTO. Instead of demanding an end to the financial speculation that has caused food prices to spike since 2007, pushing 150 million into hunger, the SDGs ask that countries "ensure the proper functioning of food commodity markets". Although it is unclear what this means, it can easily be interpreted as yet more liberalisation, which is what caused the food crisis in the first place (Hickel, 2015). Indeed, issues around food security and how this will be delivered remain a huge gap in the SDGs (Battersby, 2016).

Eighth, the SDGs evade the issue of debt and eradication of absolute global poverty. They refuse to call for debt cancellation, even though debt service drains developing countries of more than $700 billion per year – money that could be directed instead toward poverty reduction. On the contrary, clauses inserted by the EU in another backroom deal ensure that borrowers must shoulder full responsibility for over-indebtedness. The SDGs are also equally silent on the need for greater regulation of financial markets and big banks. Goal 17.13 notes the need to "enhance global macroeconomic stability" through "policy coordination", with no specific targets. Tax evasion and tax avoidance, which drain African countries of $30–60 billion each year, are not prioritised, despite the impact on Africa's ability to raise domestic resources. Equally, there is a need to point out that the $1.25 poverty baseline is actually not adequate for human subsistence in many African countries.

Ninth and finally, there are some failures of governance, which apply across developed, and developing countries. The current young African population – source of strong social capital – are reacting against these forces of inequality and unfairness. Faced with the burden of past and current global failures, they are seeking and supporting leadership that could be more transparent, sincere, committed, and able to achieve universally sustainable and inclusive development. Failure to pay special attention to the inclusion of marginalised groups means that development in Africa will be derailed (Kararach, 2014; Kararach et al., 2015).

While the SDGs are significant consensus-builders, and a natural progression of the MDGs for global sustainable development, several questions around planning and implementation remain, including to what extent can universal sustainable and inclusive development be achieved by the SDGs? How far can local and national governments go toward committing to any targets? What role and resources (technologies, finances, technical knowledge sharing, etc.) can and will international organisations be able to commit to? To what extent will it be possible to achieve consensus where required between national, intergovernmental, international governance, and nongovernmental (private, social, charitable, civil societies, etc.) organisations? Is the new multilateralism encapsulated in the ideals of the SDGs and the UN truly conducive to the transformational aspirations of Africa? Or is there a need for deep reform of the global governance architecture? Moghalu (2014) worries that international organisations such as the UN, if not utilised with care, may become the platforms that undermine Africa's development, as such organisations tend to be dominated by countries that have very different political and economic agendas.

Globalisation as a challenge to multilateralism

We have seen in Chapter 1 how, for many years, Africa was seen as a very risky yet exotic market. Since the turn of the millennium, however, those risks have declined. Africa now faces a new set of risks, including that of climate change and a lack of regulation in several markets, despite its increasing integration in the world economy though global value chains. There is therefore a need to address these new risks as a matter of urgency. The continent must pay attention to supporting African countries in funding their own development through sound financial management, better use of market resources, and greater reliance on domestic savings. Another priority is to create a single market out of the fragmented markets of each country and to increase the free movement of people between countries (Kararach, 2014) by, for example, implementing the ACFTA.

The argument for structural transformation draws on a stylised fact that developing economies are characterised by large productivity gaps between different parts of the economy (McMillan and Rodrik, 2011. Dual economy models have typically emphasised productivity differentials between broad sectors of the economy, such as the traditional (rural) and modern (urban) sectors (Lewis, 1954). More recent research has identified significant differentials within modern manufacturing activities as well. Large productivity gaps can exist even among firms and plants within the same industry. Whether between plants or across sectors, these gaps tend to be much larger in developing countries than in advanced economies. They are indicative of the allocative inefficiencies that reduce overall labour productivity.

McMillan and Rodrik (2011) note that allocative inefficiencies can potentially be an important engine of growth. When resources, including labour, move from less productive to more productive activities, the economy grows even if there is no productivity growth within sectors. This kind of growth-enhancing structural change can be an important contributor to overall economic growth. High-growth countries are typically those that have experienced substantial growth-enhancing structural change. They note that the bulk of the difference between Asia's recent growth, on the one hand, and Latin America's and Africa's, on the other, can be explained by the variation in the contribution of structural change to overall labour productivity. Indeed, in many Latin American and Sub-Saharan African countries, broad patterns of structural change have served to reduce rather than increase economic growth since 1990.

Developing countries, almost without exception, have become more integrated into the world economy since the early 1990s. Industrial tariffs are lower than they have ever been, while foreign direct investment flows have reached new heights. Clearly, globalisation has facilitated technology transfer and contributed to efficiencies in production. Yet the very diverse outcomes we observe among developing countries suggest that the consequences of globalisation depend on the way countries integrate into the global economy. In several cases – most notably China, India, and some other Asian economies – high productivity employment opportunities have expanded, and structural change has contributed to overall growth. But in many other cases – in Latin America and Sub-Saharan Africa – globalisation appears not to have fostered the desirable kind of structural change. Labour has moved in the wrong direction, from more productive to less productive activities, including informality most notably.

Deepened import competition has forced manufacturing industries in Latin America and elsewhere to become more efficient by rationalising their operations. Typically, the least productive firms have left the industry, while remaining firms have shed "excess labour". It is evident that the top tier of firms has closed the gap with the technology frontier – in Latin America and Africa, no less than in East Asia. However, the question left unanswered is what happens to the workers who are thereby displaced? In economies that do not exhibit large inter-sectoral productivity gaps or high and persistent unemployment, labour displacement would not have important implications for economy-wide productivity. In developing economies, on the other hand, the prospect that displaced workers would end up in even lower-productivity activities cannot be ruled out, especially in services and the informal sector. That is indeed what seems to have typically happened in Latin America and Africa. An important advantage of the broad, general equilibrium approach we take is that it can capture changes in inter-sectoral allocative efficiency as well as improvements in within-industry productivity.

Three factors explain whether (and the extent to which) structural change may be positive and contribute to overall productivity growth. First, economies with a revealed comparative advantage in primary products are at a disadvantage. The larger the share of natural resources in exports, the smaller the scope of productivity-enhancing structural change. The key here is that minerals and natural resources do not generate much employment, unlike manufacturing industries and related services. Even though these "enclave" sectors typically operate at very high rates of productivity, they cannot absorb the surplus labour from agriculture. This is the essence of Kaldor-Verdoorn's law (Kararach, 1997).

Second, countries that maintain competitive or undervalued currencies tend to experience more growth-enhancing structural change. This is in line with other work that documents the positive effects of undervaluation on modern, tradable industries (Rodrik, 2008). Undervaluation acts as a subsidy for those industries and facilitates their expansion.

Finally, countries with more flexible labour markets experience greater growth-enhancing structural change. This also stands to reason, as rapid structural change is facilitated when labour can flow easily across firms and sectors. By contrast, we do not find that other institutional indicators, such as measures of corruption or the rule of law play a significant role (McMillan and Rodrik, 2011).

It is clear from our discussion on structural transformation as realignment of circumstances earlier in this chapter that the emergence of a new discourse in international development is reflective of the rapidly changing global environment, characterised by an ever-growing confluence of world-scale challenges as well as opportunities due to globalisation. New technologies, including the transportation revolution, are further exerting a profound global influence by increasing a sense of interconnectedness within the human community to unprecedented levels. Interconnectedness runs counter to our traditional modes of thinking and organisation, which are highly compartmentalised. A holistic approach is needed for an effective response to many of the emerging global challenges if Africa is to reclaim the coming centuries (Hanson et al., 2012).

We can discern at least five broad areas where important megatrends have become visible in the current political, economic, and social landscape, all of which have significant implications for the continent. First, the world financial crises of 2008/2009 unleashed broader discussions about the need to improve global economic and financial governance systems. Globalisation, characterised by free market ideology and financial deregulation, has resulted in growing inequalities, financial speculation, and economic structures where the financial sector dominates the real economy instead of serving its needs. Financialisation has undermined the focus on production as a means of creating wealth (Sawyer, 2016).

In Africa, the social impact of the three-decade long economic liberalisation wave was largely negative (Cornia et al., 1987; Campbell et al., 1992; Cheru, 2017). The first decade of the twenty-first century was perceived as successful, given the growth rates in the developing world. At the time it seemed that the MDGs somewhat alleviated the impact of deregulated markets on social policies and helped to drive the development agenda and poverty reduction efforts.

However, the adoption of the SDGs shows that there are several MDGs where the world was still not on track despite the significant progress made by many countries (Wakiaga, 2015). The problems of growing inequality and rising unemployment have resurfaced on the global agenda, hence challenging the predominant economic model by calling for a stronger state presence in the economy, and more robust national and public policies.

Second, climate change, loss of biodiversity, and environmental degradation are closely interlinked with issues of economic and social development (Besada et al., 2013, 2015a). Indeed, the predominant economic model has been questioned, and the adoption of the Paris Agreement on Climate

Change reflects a growing realisation of a pressing need to include environmental and social dimensions in economic thinking and the measurement of economic performance. COP 21 in Paris was an unambiguous success of African agency. African nations seized the chance to shift the climate narrative from one of dependence to one of opportunity and transformation. Africa has made some advances in low-carbon energy while defending its right to exploit fossil fuels. With the cost of solar energy falling rapidly, huge opportunities exist (ECA, 2016a).

As the evidence from the US shows, with President Trump pulling out of the Accord, political commitment on behalf of governments is crucial to making progress in the implementation of the Paris Agreement. However, any political solutions must be complemented by specific and efficient measures aimed at promoting truly sustainable growth.

The exponential growth of consumerism is currently driven by ever-higher aspirations of the upper and middle layers in rich countries, as well as the expanding demand of emerging middle-classes in developing countries; all this at a time when inequalities continue to grow, and a significant proportion of the world population live in poverty (ECA, 2015c, 2016c). Africa's true ambition should be therefore to create incentives for the profound transformation of attitudes and consumption styles. In this context, education will play a major role in making the continent "carbon ready" (Nhamo, 2013).

Third, the UN's peacekeeping work became the focus of increased attention and significant criticisms in the 1990s, following the end of the Cold War and an eruption of a high number of conflicts not only in Africa, but also in Europe and other continents. However, the situation has changed again and requires a new vision. Compared to the previous decade, there is an emergence of new types of conflict. While they do not necessarily represent an immediate threat to the national sovereignty of a state, a variety of expressions of political instability and low intensity conflicts characterise the current landscape: they include political violence and coups d'état, natural resource conflicts, high levels of crime, terrorism, challenges to governance systems by various non-state actors, and separatism.

Most conflicts are intrastate, and highly politicised; and as a consequence, are often inextricably intertwined with various criminal activities such as drugs trafficking, human trafficking, money-laundering, financial criminal activities, and use of small arms. The actors themselves have changed, and their actions are no longer predictable because they tend to have a global narrative and discourse, complemented by attempts at spreading a global ideology based on radicalism and fundamentalist beliefs.

The concept of peacekeeping has evolved from imposing cease-fire on the two belligerent states, to covering a broad range of activities from civilian protection, support for government-led reconciliation efforts, to countering organised crime. Furthermore, there is an expectation that UN peace operations should adequately support national capacity development in areas of public administration, rule of law, and security. Indeed, UN peacekeeping has helped to restore some levels of development in Africa (Moghalu, 2014, p. 254). These evolutions, together with the evolving international normative framework, offer a window of opportunity for promoting peace, justice, and human rights. Conflict prevention must be prioritised as part of the development agenda and should include deeper structural measures aimed at addressing political, social, and economic fault lines.

Therefore, there is justifiable concern that the failure to extend rights of citizenship to the masses of the people has transformed post-colonial states in Africa into decentralised despotisms (Mamdani, 1996). "Subjects" are "citizens" who are not protected by the state, who do not have usufructuary right to land outside of their villages, who can work only in the district of their birth, and are treated as foreigners in the rest of the country. Because of mass abandonment, the African people are attracted to centrifugal ideologies that provide fertile ground for social movements that threaten national unity and progress. In many of Africa's conflicts it is therefore not difficult to identify local links that deal with the concerns and legitimate grievances of the people with those that are global, including primordial loyalties with roots that are external to the society, such as religion, diaspora politics, and irredentism. The local legitimate grievance is typically subsumed into the global concerns as external groups hijack the local cause as theirs (Zack-Williams, 2013).

Fourth, is the rapidly changing demographic configuration noted earlier and linked to such phenomena is increased mobility (further discussed in the next section). Migration has resulted in the transformation of the ethnic composition and the monolithic character of the host societies, as well as the emergence of trans-migrants with multi-layered identities. In this area, there is a pressing need to create a solid international migration governance framework to increase the development gains of migration and protect migrants' rights.

Fifth, the spread of ICTs has created unprecedented opportunities for connecting people and providing access to information. They make people in one part of the world ever more aware and concerned about things happening in other parts of the world. The spread of ICTs, the increased access of populations to information, and the means of communication has already resulted in a formidable expansion of social participation and civic mobilisation. ICTs are qualitatively transforming our perceptions, communication, governance, and negotiation systems. This highlights the need for reflection on how to make better use of opportunities generated by ICTs in order to promote a more inclusive governance and efficient negotiation methodology.

The global and interconnected character of the twenty-first century challenges calls for solutions that transcend national borders. There is a need for renewed multilateralism that would be based on an integrated approach as opposed to the traditional thematic clustering and isolated handling of problems such that the concept of global public goods is embraced, and the effective use of partnerships with multiple state and non-state stakeholders is promoted. The very notion of sovereignty is currently being affected by multiple systemic crises, and renewed multilateralism should, in the first instance, be conducive to shaping more effective and equitable global governance structures. This is not to suggest the death of the nation state (Trachtman, 1998) but to imply a greater rationale for development – one based on global compacts (Skidelsky, 2012).

Lin and Wang (2014) argued that multilateralism is critical because it can provide more learning opportunities for emerging partners, enhance triangular knowledge exchange, and hopefully, improve the effectiveness of both the established and emerging donors by better targeting development financing. They note, for example, that China Eximbank and the China Development Bank both signed memorandums of understanding (MoUs) with the World Bank in September 2013 to conduct tri-lateral collaboration. The outcome has been concrete "parallel projects" which are being prepared in Africa as part of the evolving development financing architecture. China has also contributed to the African Development Bank, Development Bank of Southern Africa (DBSA), and Inter-America Development Bank (IADB) as part of this evolution. In addition, China has co-operated with United Nation's Food and Agriculture Organization (FAO) on tri-lateral co-operation in agriculture. There are, however, obstacles on this path that have not been addressed, for instance, related to enhancing the voice of Southern partners in global economic governance such as in the WTO, the International Monetary Fund (IMF), and the World Bank.

Moreover, we are witnessing a global gridlock in multilateral negotiations and understanding about how to tackle different types of crises. The examples of multilateral negotiations that did not lead to a desired outcome in crucial areas are many, including for example the absence of progress in the WTO's Doha round negotiations. This negotiation deadlock results from a discrepancy between the current forms of the organisation of international life which is dominated by the state-based approach as well as critical trends shaping global society (Moghalu, 2014).

Three main areas where the challenges to multilateralism can be identified are in concepts, methods, and institutions. First, concepts are becoming volatile and eroded by problems of a global dimension such as climate change and communicable diseases that must be managed to cross national borders (Kararach, 2014). Other examples include national sovereignty versus human rights concerns or international criminal justice decisions, environmental and health problems. We have reached the critical level as far as international public law is concerned where the number of international conventions having multiplied over a few decades.

Second, the negotiation methods and techniques do not capture the complexity of modern society. On the one hand, analogies from IT such as open software modes in terms of organisation, contributions, negotiation, and decision taking might be better suited to the modern challenges.

The negotiation experience of the scientific and technical communities could provide helpful information in learning how to handle those challenges that are not purely political. On the other hand, the use of sectoral approaches in practice runs counter to intrinsically transversal concepts such as that of sustainable development.

Third, existing institutions do not reflect the increasing role of regionalism and the changing balance of power. UN Security Council reform is still being discussed after a few decades, and despite recent progress, there is a problem of inadequate voting rights for emerging and African economies in the IMF and World Bank. The rapid emergence of new global players such as Brazil, Russia, India, China, and South Africa (BRICS) has profound implications for negotiations and international governance. Emerging powers are building alliances and common positions in various international fora. African countries increasingly realise that they can better defend their interests when speaking with one voice.

The above considerations suggest that the international governance system is outdated, both in terms of the distribution of power among the states and its essentially state-based nature. As a result, inherent tensions lead to major gridlock in all the main negotiation areas. Multilateralism has become more complex today than ever before and creating a global consensus on what sustainable development should mean is even more complicated.

African migrants: payback time? Challenging the migration debate

As African countries prepare to realign their relationships with the world economy, mounting pressures on their economies have generated significant population movements. As argued in Chapter 1, structural transformation is also underpinned by population movements from poor to rich areas, rural to urban, or "declining" to "booming" sectors. Noticeably, out-migration from Africa continues to mistakenly dominate the international policy and news agendas and yet most of such movements are internal, across countries and regions of the continent (Adepoju, 2003; Kararach, 2014). There are, however, concerns that we do not know enough about migration in Africa due to a paucity of both qualitative and quantitative data (Ratha and Shaw, 2007; Uberti et al., 2015). Many African countries have begun to tackle the underlying forces driving this trend by fostering greater participation and development. At the same time, the global dialogue related to the movement of people from Africa to Europe must shift from being seen as a crisis to a potential win–win if managed more proactively (Kararach, 2014).

The fact of the matter is that increased mobility and migration are now a part of the consequences of globalisation. The recent relentless flow of images from the Italian island of Lampedusa, the city of Calais where the Eurotunnel starts, Bodrum in Turkey, the eastern islands of Greece, and the Spanish enclaves of Ceuta and Melilla in Morocco, are invading television screens and media outlets. They portray the massive scale of attempts to reach European countries, leading to a comparison of the worst migrant crisis since World War II. But is this really the case? Perhaps it is perceived as such in Western Europe but, understanding why is important because the wave is not over. Clearly, Africa is undergoing dramatic demographic changes due to factors such as migration, urbanisation, and population growth, all of which have significant implications for capacity building and skills development, and for the overall socio-economic transformation of the continent. So why discuss migration issues?

The discussion is important in the context of capacity building and skills development because it can change the lives of those individuals who move, the societies that receive them, and even those who remain behind (Sriskandarajah, 2005). Migration may be voluntary or forced, depending on factors ranging from economic determinants, conflict, trade, human trafficking, the rural-to-urban interchange, and the environment. Different types of migration flows are likely to occur in different parts of a country and may require a research approach that disaggregates the determinants at sub-regional level as well as between countries and individual localities (Cross and Omoluabi, 2006).

Migration is part of the human journey. The history of humanity is so rich and complex that one may have difficulty relating to a very remote common origin, except for historical assessments and philosophical reflections. It is easier for all to relate to a more recent past, especially one that shaped our identities through events and social interaction. Human beings have a selective reading of history. For most, compensation will be justified for a wrong done to some, but not to the other. Apologies will be fine with some, but not for others. Peace offers will be morally acceptable to some, but not to others. This is after all mimicking individual behaviour at a larger, societal level including the fabricated fear-mongering raised about the issues of migration in many parts of the world.

There have been several theories that explain migration dynamics (see also De Haas, 2008). Many of these originate from early models of competing or differential economic opportunities and constraints in rural and urban sectors and in different localities. The best example of this type of model is the Harris-Todaro model of rural–urban migration (Harris and Todaro, 1970).[2] While Todaro's (1976) work stressed job access as the driver of migration, Lipton (1995) argued that migration is dominated by differential and competitive labour absorption between different areas, and not just about jobs at the urban nexus.

To Bryceson (1999, 2000), migration in Africa is the outcome of an inescapable reality in which the rural economy is changing rapidly as land comes under pressure, yet terms of trade have moved against African small producers. These households can no longer rely on what is often an inadequate income and members may migrate as a means of diversifying their income base. It has to be noted that socio-economic improvements may actually increase migration, as this may widen people's aspirations for self-advancement. Indeed, migration takes place within socio-economic as well as the political contexts, where migration becomes part of a household survival strategy (Mafukidze, 2006).

Migration may also arise due to structural as well as political economy issues – whether at the level of the household, region, country, or globally, based on dependency pressures (see Wallerstein, 1974). For example, as women's role in economic activity expands, the need for greater income diversification and increased access to cash drives female migration. Research on the South African experience by Posel (2004) highlights a new trend where women migrants aspire to succeed and secure economic security. It is also important to know how people in different categories move in relation to the resources they can mobilise to remit and support one or more migrants (Kok et al., 2003). International migration often takes place over great distances and is both resource and finance intensive, while rural-to-urban and rural-to-rural migrations within the country of origin do not share these intensities. Information flows and asymmetries, and network connections have great influence on migration. In the Sub-Saharan African context, migration research needs to take account not only of socio-economic realities, but also other factors that may determine who can migrate and who has the "kind of resources and connections that facilitate migration" (Cross and Omoluabi, 2006).

Adams and Page (2003) pointed out that over time migration is both poverty-driven and poverty-limited: that is, it starts to happen as incomes begin to rise and people in disadvantaged communities learn about opportunities outside their own localities, often spurred on by the spread of communication technologies and information flows which become reinforcing factors. Without initial resources to support movement, poverty is an obstacle to migration. Migration tails off and stops when local incomes have risen past a point of relative adequacy. This point is reached as the area becomes relatively developed and offers its own competing opportunities. The conceptual model is one of a steep curve that rises sharply and then falls. The income-migration curve is thus bell-shaped.

De Haas (2008) argues that there is a persistent myth about the nature of migration from Africa. Essentially, African countries receive many more migrants than the continent exports abroad. In fact, the bulk of Africans looking for opportunities outside their countries go to another African country. Less than 2 million seek a destination abroad every year, which is a small number in relation to migrant stocks, particularly in Europe. In 2015, more than 1 million people crossed the Mediterranean to reach Europe, many through Italy. This is a much larger number than in previous years. Of that number, about 68 per cent were from Syria, Afghanistan, Iraq, and Pakistan. Of the top ten nationalities represented, only one in ten was African. The European agency dealing with the issue, Frontex, acknowledges that the number of irregular migrants from Africa pales in comparison with regular arrivals.[3]

Population movements are also driven by pull factors (Todaro, 1976). Europe's pull factor is to be understood by a variety of developments that define circumstances and efforts, from information access (6 billion cell phones in the world), human rights proclamations, as well as a call for universal moral values all the way to unfair distribution of income and inequality across the globe. Terrorism and religious extremism have played a card as well. Equally, it seems the strong European rights advocacy has worked to its detriment.

Pockets of war such as that of Libya and its surrounding deserts, the Great Lakes and its neighbourhood, and Somalia are generating political asylum seekers and a huge number of refugees as well. In turn, oppressive African regimes also contribute their lot. African leaders flinch when migration is a theme and it is equally disturbing for other fellow Africans. However, still this does not give us the full picture.

Africa has struggled more than most to find a way out of poverty and inequality. As already noted, the continent has performed better economically and socially in the last decade (Kararach, 2014). Yet the narrative about the continent seems to be fixated on migration and negative assessments about its performance. It is therefore important, first, to understand why Africa is perceived to be generating more migrants today than ever before.

Hatton and Williamson (2003) argued that the policies necessary to tackle challenges related to migration and those related to poverty are not necessarily the same. Indeed, the very poor usually do not have the resources, capacity, and skills to easily support migration, and international migrants do not tend to come from this group. Indeed:

> People who migrate are most often those who have begun to raise their expectations, have accumulated some resources and some information, and also have access to trans-local networks – they are the middle poor and upwards, not the destitute.
>
> (Adepoju, 2006, p. 6)

The distinction between internal and international migration within Sub-Saharan Africa may be spurious because of close cultural affinities between homogeneous peoples on opposite sides of national borders which may also enhance population and migrant absorption. As a result, migrants often regard intra-regional migration as an extension of internal movement given the connectedness due to lineage (Adepoju, 1998). Deepening poverty and socio-economic insecurities have transformed some of the migration patterns that would otherwise take place internally into replacement migration towards urban areas and emigration across borders to more prosperous countries (Adepoju, 2000). Due to climate change and environmental degradation, Africa's fragile ecosystems are also forcing rural populations to migrate from hinterlands to coastal regions; from the rural areas to the cities, and in some cases to neighbouring countries. The scarcity of local jobs in the face of worsening urban and youth unemployment reinforces the persistence of migration in the region (Léautier, 2009).

With the global economic downturn, fewer migrants can find stable and remunerative work in traditional regional destinations, and modes of circular and repeat migration have expanded to a wide variety of alternative destinations (Findley et al., 1995). It is likely that most Italians forgot they created entire nations such as Argentina and Uruguay because of migration. The British may not necessarily relate to Australia and New Zealand or the Spanish and Portuguese to most of South America as countries and a region that was spawned through migration. When referring to Indochina, the Chinese must have only a vague idea of why that region carries their name. Americans may find it in bad taste to mention that part of the present US was bought from Mexico. And on it goes.

Interestingly, Africa is the only continent in recent history that has never been associated with migration to colonise or profit from another region's richness! If anything, Africa is rather known for suffering from slavery, the plundering of its natural resources, and unfair international treatment which has been material in its underdevelopment (Rodney, 1972).

In every moment of history, growth has generated outward migrants from the same location. Growth reproduces chances for a new life but its distribution, particularly at the early stages of a country take-off, is uneven and unpredictable. Those who see their neighbour with the means and hope they do not have, invariably venture out. During sailing to South America, it would have been absurd to propose bombing those boats that were full of migrants escaping the misfortunes of the aftermath of two World Wars. These migrants were seeking better lives and yet their native countries were growing like never before, thanks amongst others to the Marshall Plan.

Arguably, those Africans dying in the desert or the sea in attempts to reach Europe are the determined lot. They do not accept their fate and are ready to risk their lives. The youngest population of the world sees the developed nations of Europe as the closest beacon of hope. For them it is the home of human rights that will, certainly, understand their plight and welcome them to work!

Africa's youthfulness will keep expanding while the rest of the world will be ageing. World demographics are changing so rapidly that it is not possible to maintain the current patterns of wealth distribution. It is difficult to demonstrate to the polity that austerity will not solve the twin problems of large debts and ageing populations. Most countries with high debt also have a structural challenge – their population ageing. The difficulty of admitting that the current state's welfare policies in all ageing countries is unsustainable has led to the most bizarre economic policy proposals. Accepting that there is a demographic challenge would imply a vast overhaul of social and political choices necessary to sustain the economy. As we all witness the limits associated with the transfer of value from production and labour to knowledge and financial control, we are also seeing the limits of the prevailing economic model. A demographic equilibrium is still essential despite technological progress and productivity gains. Robots or intellectual property cannot contribute to social security or pension funds; it indeed needs people, workers, and productive workers. As part of the payback, this is why Europe will have to come to grips with its need for migrants. Are these some of the signs that Africans are laying claims to their future?

Are Africans ready for their future?

Given the demographics, the imperative of industrialisation, attaining equitable outcomes for the majority, and – in the context of the 2030 Agenda for Sustainable Development – eliminating poverty remain the core national prerogatives for countries, both in terms of agenda setting and problem-solving. In the current context, globalisation, rapid urbanisation, free trade, and the ongoing fragmentation of production are the main factors that determine economic outcomes globally. In terms of these dynamics, the nation state is often heavily circumscribed (Breznitz, 2007; UN-Habitat, 2013) although not completely irrelevant (Moghalu, 2014). States continue to determine how economic gains can be captured and translated into social outcomes, in a manner that is sustainable at the national level vis-à-vis the global community and the environment at large (Sampath, 2016).

It must be repeated that the region's history is crucial to understanding some of its challenges of transformation as well as its potential. Views oscillate between those who espouse a commodities-based industrialisation pathway to development (Lin, 2011; Morris and Fessehaie, 2014) and those who vehemently criticise the overdependence on commodity rents, arguing that it leads to entrenching countries in product spaces that are not conducive to upgrading in general (Hausmann and Rodrik, 2005; Hausmann and Klinger, 2006; Hidalgo et al., 2007). Nevertheless, unprecedented changes have called for a reality check on Africa's readiness to embrace the future. In the coming decades an expected lowest dependency ratio in the world will be coupled with unparalleled urbanisation (ECA, 2017). Projections indicate that between 2010 and 2025, some African cities will account for up to 85 per cent of the continent's population. This will mean a transition from a rural to a predominantly urban society, with the largest cities on the continent such as Lagos and Kinshasa growing to 15 million people by 2025, while others such as Dar es Salaam reaching 7 million. Cities in Africa generate approximately 55 per cent of the continent's total GDP compared to developed country cities, which generate approximately 90 per cent of their GDP. Being cognisant of the related challenges, such as the need to ensure essential services to cater for this phenomenon, the opportunities and challenges for economic growth, poverty reduction, and human development are profound. Approximately 54 per cent of Africa's youth is currently unemployed and more than three-quarter live on less than $2 a day. A correlation and lessons to learn can be drawn from Asian emerging markets, where 40 per cent of their rapid economic growth between 1965 and 1990 was attributable to an increase in the working age population (ibid.).

However, a youthful population of such magnitude also indicates that the challenge of the twenty-first century is the ability to address this demographic imbalance in a manner that will preserve the interests of future generations (Kararach, 2014). As noted earlier, the benefits of a demographic dividend are sorely needed. This will require a new intergenerational social contract that is driven by the necessity to balance the needs of current and future generations; between a young Africa and an ageing population elsewhere in the world.

The continent must struggle to contain any bad news that might affect a new, robust narrative capable of reaffirming a new Africa. It is sometimes a thankless task when confronted with the sceptical eyes of many purveyors of mainstream public opinion. It is, nevertheless, a task that no Ebola epidemic, Boko Haram extremist group, bad electoral process, or commodity price downfall should discourage the continent from accomplishing. It has taken too long for Africans to regain a sense of urgency about constructing a common future (Moghalu, 2014; Kararach, 2014). Moreover, it requires renewed agency, as articulated well in the jubilee celebration of Africa's mother institution, the African Union. The celebration of 50 years of Pan-African institutional history is a time for reflection. Africans must look into their past to create their future; acknowledging their previous mistakes and learning from them but also celebrating their successes and building on these.

Many still do not see Africa as having the requisite capability to develop because of the misperceptions that abound. Africans can only move ahead or overtake their competitors if they make sure that others see and feel what they are up to and are aware of what they consider an imperative. Two very different perspectives have been used to examine and explain Africa's position in world politics and economics: the dependency and the decolonisation approaches. On one hand, the latter view emphasises change rather than continuity, choices rather than constraints, symbols instead of structures, and ideals not economics; it is based on the premise that formal independence generates real power to act in the international system (Shaw and Newbury, 1979). On the other hand, the dependency approach suggests that political and legal independence does not necessarily produce a new political economy of transformation; it indicates instead that internal underdevelopment and external dependence have been perpetuated despite any appearances to the contrary (Amin, 1973, 1990; Thomas, 1974; Zartman, 1976; Shaw and Newbury, 1979). From the decolonisation perspective, the foreign policies of African states are reflective of their national interests and are based on their ability to make their own independent decisions. There is therefore a natural evolution towards new patterns of relations between Africa and other world powers. In contrast, the dependency approach notes that, given Africa's subordinate place in the global economy, its foreign policies are largely determined by external forces and tend to advance such interests. Dependency suggests that any reduction inequality is unlikely because of this structural dynamic. These two distinct modes of analysis have major implications because African foreign policy choices are seen and for the assumptions that determine how Africa will face the world and shape its own future.

The seeming contradictions between the two approaches may be partly resolved by making distinctions between policy and practice and by recognising several different issue areas and levels of interaction (Shaw and Newbury, 1979). First, Africa's ideologies of nationalism and Pan-Africanism, non-alignment and self-reliance, are responses to its inheritance of dependence and underdevelopment (Thomas, 1974; Shaw and Newbury, 1979). If one examines only the rhetoric and declarations, then Africa would seem to enjoy the fruit of independence. However, after examining its external economic and strategic relations, a rather different and much less autonomous image emerges. African states may display all the trappings of independence in diplomacy – they establish overseas missions, participate in the UN, and bring pressure to bear through developing country coalitions in international organisations. Yet in the economic, strategic, and social spheres they are dependent and even penetrated; they are characteristically vulnerable to external economic fluctuations, strategic demands, and social changes (Shaw and Newbury, 1979; Kararach, 2014). Africa's political decolonisation may be contrasted with its economic dependence and political vulnerability, particularly where the great powers in the world economy are concerned.

African states interact at several levels: with their neighbours, in the African Union (AU) constellation, and in the wider world economy. Within Africa and in terms of AU sovereign membership, countries appear to have more equality and autonomy among themselves than they do in the global system. In the latter, inequalities and asymmetries are substantial, with African states being concentrated at the lower end of the hierarchy. There is international dependence rather than interdependence. In addition to its established geographic and racial identity, Africa has its own regional organisations and laws, but it continues to be dependent on economic and military exchanges with the world political economy. While Africa has recaptured its political independence, its autonomy is still limited by continued dependence on external trade and investment, skills and technology, and military and development assistance (Shaw and Newbury, 1979; Kararach, 2014). There is thus a basic discontinuity between continental diplomatic interdependence and global economic dependence. There is continental supra-nationality in politics and global supra-nationality in economics (Mazrui, 1972, 1973).

Although the primary Africa-related actor in the international system is still the state, the number of non-state actors has increased rapidly since independence. These agents can collectively create the potential for greater African autonomy, particularly if duplicative extra-African links are reduced (Shaw and Newbury, 1979). The most influential African organisations tend to be economic or political in their function and are mostly concentrated at the continental level. For example, there are some 30 continental organisations in the AU/Economic Commission for Africa (ECA) system, including the African Development Bank Group, the Association of African Central Banks, the Association of African Airways, Afrexim Bank, and the Inter-African Coffee Organisation. There are another 70 concerned with social issues, such as the All-African Conference of Churches, the Supreme Council for Sport in Africa, the Association of African Universities, and the All-Africa Trade Union Federation. A complex set of relations exists among this broad range of actors: that is, between the UN, its specialised agencies, the AU, regional organisations in Africa, and African States. They exchange support proposals and define their respective roles in order to enhance their mutual compatibility.

The construction of Africa's future will obviously benefit from Africans' own actions and agency (Moghalu, 2014). That by itself does not necessarily mean Africans would drive their own future and development trajectory. The nuanced difference between being "part of" and "being the driver of" the transformation of one's reality is indeed what matters. After so much suffering and so many missed opportunities, the time has come for Africa to claim its future. This was aptly captured in the theme for the AU's 2013 celebration, "Pan-Africanism and African Renaissance". A focus on African renaissance provides an opportunity to reflect on Africa's self-reliance trajectory and the need to demystify, appropriate, and popularise its history, its shared values, and its narrative about the state of Africa today as a means of inspiring current and future generations.

There is an accepted principle that ownership is central to the success of any enterprise (Mugobo et al., 2016). Ownership is essential to overcome the problems of agency in any strategy, programme, or project that requires implementation (Fama and Jensen, 1983; Shleifer and Vishny, 1986; Zhou, 2001). In the twenty-first century, Pan-Africanism reflects Africa's conscious need for not only political independence, regional integration, and improvements of its living standards, but also the throwing off the shackles of economic bondage and democratic stagnation that saw it reverse the short-lived prosperity of the independence era (Hanson et al., 2012). This has meant devising a new economic positioning and new forms of partnership in which Africa, as an equal partner, would negotiate with the rest of the world, while fiercely defending its own defined priorities. Without losing the key elements of unity, cultural heritage, and freedom, the reinterpretation of Pan-Africanism in the form of an African renaissance is very relevant. It is a new phase that requires popular participation and mobilisation of the African people behind the goals of structural transformation. Indeed, Africa's renaissance can only be complete when the African voice will be heard and seriously considered (AUC, 2013).

However, if Africa does not take ownership of its own development trajectory given the pressures of globalisation, then others will either do so or, worse still, the future of the continent will be left to the vagaries of chance. Africa must avoid the dangers and pitfalls inherent in the wholesale adopting of received paradigms (Moghalu, 2014) because isomorphic mimicry has its own fault lines (Pritchet, 2010; Kararach, 2014). The continent cannot continue to fall prey to different and the sometimes-ulterior motives of some actors on the international scene.

For Africa to determine its own future, the thinking underpinning its political, economic, and social development must emanate from the continent and its diaspora by exploiting the potential offered by historical and local knowledge. This is a contentious point in the sense that the generation or use of knowledge should not be constrained by geographical or indeed psychological barriers. After all, ownership of ideas is nonsensical. What matters is ownership in a different sense since all ideas, learning, and knowledge can be deployed for development, no matter what their origins might be (Hanson and Kararach, 2013).

In pursuing any bold transformation agenda, a few risks must be appreciated and tackled head on (Moghalu, 2014; Léautier, 2014). The current challenges facing most developing countries are very different from the past two decades. Addressing economic inequality, expanding opportunities for all, reducing illiteracy, and creating the enabling conditions for the growth, development, and protection of nascent local industries are just a few of the myriad tasks that, if not adequately solved, will certainly continue to drag Africa down the world scales of development indicators.

The most important component of Agenda 2063 is its clear commitment to the structural transformation of the continent. Put simply, Africa must industrialise as a catalyst for sustained growth, creating jobs, and extracting maximum value addition from its natural resources. This in turn, requires credible macroeconomic frameworks, infrastructural development, and adequate financing. We must remember that while articulating macroeconomic frameworks to underpin structural transformation, the benefits of austerity are at the best short term and are sometimes even damaging to the very foundations of structural transformation (Lopes et al., 2017).

How can African countries capitalise on geopolitical changes?

Naidu et al. (2009) argue that the contemporary shift in the geopolitical environment has seen Africa's traditional relationships with the Global North being offset by competing and increasingly influential interests from the Global South, most notably China and India. However, they assert that there are complexities that arise from the growing competition resulting from Africa's engagement with emerging powers of the South. Cornelissen (2009) notes that one of the legacies of the end of the Cold War has been a shift in the relative influence of economics over politics in determining trends in international relations. For Africa in particular, the contemporary global state of play has important implications for its development.

The prominence of emerging powers necessitates a better understanding of international hierarchy, hegemony, and power (Ellis, 2013).

Africa's attempts to capitalise on changing global dynamics have been in the offing for decades. The Organization of African Unity (OAU), established in 1963, laid the foundation for the unity of the African continent. It aimed to rid the continent of remnants of colonialism and restore Africa's dignity and pride after centuries of domination; promote the integration of the continent; and defend its interest in a Cold War arena. As the continent evolved, the OAU, heralded as the most notable result of Pan-Africanism, was replaced by the Africa Union in 2002. The African Union symbolised a new era for the continent. Its foundational philosophy aimed to accelerate the process of economic integration, resolve socio-political problems, intensify continental unity, and enable Africa to play a more meaningful role in the global economy (Hanson et al., 2012). How then, in terms of these aims, can Africa capitalise on recent global changes?

Africans can start by taking control of their natural resources (Besada et al., 2015a; Hanson, 2016). Africa's industrial potential had been stifled by the legacies of Africa's colonialism, which left behind weak institutions, and an infrastructure designed to enhance the extraction of its resources. The Structural Adjustment Programmes of the 1980s and 1990s had particularly negative effects on technological accumulation, human capital development, and export performance (Awoyomi, 1989; Igbedioh and Aderiye, 1994; Momoh, 1995; Owusu, 2012). However, it is worth recalling that Africa's resource wealth accounts for approximately three quarters of the world's platinum supply; half of its diamonds and chromium; one fifth of gold and uranium supplies; just over half of the world's uncultivated arable land, with the potential to become the breadbasket for the world; and it is home to gas and oil production in over 30 countries. The moral of this story is that, with the abundance of resources and the rising global demand for them, Africa must manage its resources carefully (Kararach and Odhiambo, 2016).

A major consequence if this moral injunction is not adhered to is that by being dependent on the production and export of primary commodities, many African economies are generating prosperity, jobs, and opportunities of development for other countries and regions of the world instead of those in Africa. The continent runs the risk of marginalising its own role in international trade if it does not add value to its commodities. Commodity-based industrialisation therefore offers the scope for value addition as well as forward and backward linkages (ECA, 2014a). Ethiopia's leather industry and Nigeria's oil supply industry provide good yet random examples of linkages that are not only developing, but also deepening into high value-added activities. Such initiatives to enhance value addition must become the continental norm (Moghalu, 2014; Kararach, 2014).

Africa's economic future will be determined by how it designs and implements effective policies to promote industrialisation in an ever complex and changing world (ECA, 2014a, 2015a, 2016c). There is an urgent need to address infrastructure constraints and bottlenecks; facilitate the development of the commodity sector and its associated linkages, boost the availability of unskilled and semiskilled jobs, provide job training in higher artisanal skills, and deploy data-driven evidence to inform planning (Kararach, 2014). These all present opportunities for Africa and its partners to better collaborate without depriving Africa of the benefits of its resource boom.

Africa can leverage new partnerships with emerging economies (Hanson et al., 2012). The influence of the Global North is diminishing in Africa and will have to change toward a new relationship with Africa. India, China, and other new players such as Turkey and Russia have increased their engagement in Africa in rather dramatic ways, by transforming Africa's traditional trade and investment relations. The largest increases in foreign direct investment to Africa in recent years have come from the BRICS (Cooper et al., 2007), targeting Africa's natural resources, from oil in Angola, Algeria, Nigeria, and Sudan to mining in Niger, Mauritania, Zambia, and Liberia. It is, however, a very partial view of what is going on. There is significant diversification of investments. For example, India is investing in social services, textiles, and medium-sized enterprises as well as technology and China is investing heavily in Africa's infrastructure and services sectors (Brautigum, 2009; Ellis, 2013). Ways of doing business have thus been revolutionised, and the template has been greatly enhanced by advances in technology.

This new paradigm of engagement reflects cooperation in which partners see themselves as peers in a set of mutually beneficial relationships (Hanson et al., 2012). The growing interest in Africa by a larger pool of partners favours the continent and is creating a different menu of choices. Africa in turn, is well positioned to be a more assertive player in the global arena and to capitalise from the different development models and comparative advantages offered by the array of partners. To benefit fully, Africa must strengthen its institutions, take the lead in negotiating, designing, and implementing strategies with partners to leverage their comparative advantages, as well as broker constructive and beneficial deals. Crucially, Africa must transform itself from being perceived as a price taker to becoming a price maker.

Traditional partnerships remain important, although their terms must be revisited (Moghalu, 2014; Kararach, 2014). Europe and Africa have been important to each other with ties stemming from their history and geography and the fact that their relationship connects two continents. Europe has been more of a trade, development, and investment partner while Africa has been a crucial source of hard and soft commodities for Europe, such as strategic metals and minerals as well as being a captive market. Having said this, perhaps the most successful thematic area in this long partnership has been in peace and security.

Over the last decade, the EU–Africa partnership has evolved under the auspices of the Joint Africa–EU Strategy. From one that was criticised as an unbalanced donor–recipient relationship, the strategic shift now promised a profound change in the EU approach to Africa. In 2007, the Joint Africa–EU Strategy was premised on principles of equal participation and representation, as well as treating Africa as a single entity. However, the promise of development and political cooperation between the two continents has not resulted in any fundamental transformation; instead, the gap has only become wider. This is attributable to factors such as dwindling development budgets that have been impacted by the Eurozone's sovereign debt crisis; in turn, the financial expectations under the Joint Strategy have not materialised into anything concrete. The emergence of new economies now rivals Europe's historic role and modalities of development aid cooperation in Africa (Hanson et al., 2012; Besada et al., 2013). Several partnership arrangements, such as the Cotonou Agreement and the Economic Partnership Agreement, reinforce the unbalanced nature of the EU–Africa relationship, thus fragmenting the Joint Strategy.

In the new landscape of multipolar partnerships, Africa needs a coherent strategy so that its development is not compromised by competition amongst potential partners (Moghalu, 2014). In doing so, mutual accountability, mechanisms of enforcement, and principles that foster compliance of multinational firms to international norms and standards should be indispensable features for the future partnerships. It is time for Africa to capitalise on the geopolitical changes, but it will only do so by driving and owning the process.

Small nations must unite for climate revolution

The issue of climate change and its potential impact on sustainable development is another major policy conundrum that requires global collective action. No nation is immune to the impact of climate change, but it is the world's poorest that will be hit the hardest. The Paris Agreement on Climate Change reminds us of the moral imperative to combat climate change. All countries, regardless of their level of development, must look to reduce their own CO_2 emissions and prevent further warming so as to reverse the trend. It is critical to mitigate the effects of climate change that are already being felt throughout the world (IPCC, 2007).

There is no doubt that climate change threatens to derail Africa's development and compromise the socio-economic gains made over the last decade and a half (Kararach, 2014). Africa's future relies heavily on climate-sensitive sectors including agriculture, fishing, and tourism. Agriculture alone accounts for 30 per cent of Africa's GDP and 50 per cent of the continent's total exports (ECA, 2015c).

The link between development and climate change is circular and cumulative. Most societies have always been subject to climatic factors, but the steep increase in greenhouse gases since the Industrial Revolution has transformed the relationship between society and the environment. Not only does the nature of climate affect development but development also affects the nature of climate. Left unmanaged, climate change reverses development progress and compromises the well-being of current and future generations. The impacts of climate change will be felt everywhere, but much of the damage will be in developing countries (Harrington and Walton, 2008; IWMI and CEGIS, 2007). Greater rainfall variability and more severe droughts in Africa will hinder efforts aimed at enhancing food security and combating malnourishment (Schmidhuber and Tubiello, 2007). The advancing disappearance of water catchment areas – which regulate river flow, generate hydropower, and supply clean water for over a billion of people on farms and in cities – will threaten rural livelihoods and major food markets (Bates et al., 2008).

Decisive and immediate action is needed. Even though the debate about the costs and benefits of climate change mitigation continues, the case is very compelling for immediate action in order to avoid unmanageable increases in temperature. The unacceptability of irreversible and potentially catastrophic impacts and the uncertainty about how, and how soon, they could occur require bold action.

Historically, the direct benefits of carbon-intensive development have been largely concentrated in today's high-income countries (Besada et al., 2015a). There is huge inequity in the global distribution of past and current emissions, and therefore in the spread of current and future damage. The window of opportunity to choose the right policies to deal with climate change and promote development is closing. Increasing people's opportunities and material well-being without undermining the sustainability of development is still the main challenge globally, as a severe financial and economic crisis wreaks great havoc across the globe. Stabilising the financial markets and protecting the real economy, labour markets, and vulnerable groups are the immediate priority. The world must exploit this moment of opportunity for international cooperation and domestic intervention to tackle the urgent problem of climate change.

Three conceptual issues are involved here: adaptation, mitigation, and greening growth or development. Climate change is directly linked to environmental degradation. Extreme weather events such as droughts and floods lead to desertification and erosion. In addition, reduced river flow leads to siltation and polluted water. "Adaptation" is a broad concept usually implying a process of adjustment to survive and, ideally, thrive in the face of change. In the context of climate change, adaptation takes place through adjustments that reduce vulnerability or enhance resilience to observed or expected changes in climate, and involves changes in processes, perceptions, practices, and functions (Parry et al., 2007). Adaptation may be initiated on a variety of scales, from institutionally driven policies and programmes at national or subnational levels to adjustments and risk management decisions within individual households (McLeman and Smit, 2006). For example, adaptation in agriculture refers to measures put in place to allow African farmers to live with the changing climate. Hisali et al. (2011, pp. 1245–46) view adaptation strategies as planned actions to moderate the effects of climate variability now and into the long term either to reduce the harm or expand emergent opportunities therefrom.

Mitigation is "any anthropogenic intervention that can either reduce sources of GHG emissions (abatement) or enhance their carbon sinks (sequestration)" (Rosegrant et al., 2008, p. 8). Appropriate mitigation measures could result in lower GHG emissions, which would result in less extreme weather events and other negative impacts associated with climate change.

The disruptions to socio-economic and natural systems caused by climate change are happening even now – that is, even sooner than previously thought possible (Smith et al., 2009). Changing temperatures and precipitation averages and a more variable, unpredictable, or extreme climate can alter today's yields, earnings, health, and physical safety and ultimately the levels of future development. Numerous sectors and productive environments, including agriculture, forestry, energy, and coastal zones in both developed and developing countries will be affected. However, developing economies will be more affected by climate change, in part because of their greater exposure to climate shocks and in part because of their low adaptive capacity.

Africa is highly vulnerable to climate change and of concern are water resources, agriculture, health, ecosystems and biodiversity, forestry, and coastal zones. The longer-term impacts will include changing rainfall patterns affecting agriculture and reducing food security. Water insecurity further exacerbates problems such as poor economic growth prospects and shifting vector diseases. According to a recent IPCC report, the cost of adaptation in Africa could be as high as 5 to 10 per cent of the continent's GDP (Field et al., 2014). There are several dimensions to sustainable livelihoods that arise from climate change.

First, over 95 per cent of Africa's agriculture is rain-fed. Agricultural production and food security in many African countries and sub-regions is projected to be severely compromised by climate variability and change. The area suitable for agriculture, the length of growing seasons, and yield potential, particularly along the margins of semi-arid and arid areas, are expected to decrease. In some countries, yields from rain-fed agriculture could be reduced by up to 50 per cent by 2020.

Second, Africa faces severe water stress (Oyama et al., 2012). Many African countries are in zones where a small reduction in rainfall could cause large declines in the river water. Climate models show that 600,000 square kilometres classified as moderately water constrained will experience severe water limitations. By 2020, between 75 and 250 million people are projected to be exposed to an increase in water stress due to climate change. Water scarcity is even more acute in North Africa due to very high population growth rates and already high rates of water resource use.

Third, communicable diseases are likely to increase. The health effects of climate change are likely to be overwhelmingly negative. Africa is already vulnerable to a number of climate-sensitive diseases such as Rift valley fever, which afflicts both people and livestock; cholera, associated with both floods and droughts; and malaria, where rising temperatures have resulted in malaria spreading to the highlands of Kenya, Rwanda, and Tanzania. These factors are superimposed on existing weak health systems and poor access.

Fourth, the risks to coastal areas could compel major population movements and social disintegration as well as human insecurity. The rise in sea levels resulting from global climate change threatens coasts, lagoons, and mangrove forests of both eastern and western Africa. More than a quarter of Africa's population live within 100 kilometres of the coast, and projections suggest that the number of people at risk from coastal flooding will increase from 1 million in 1990 to 70 million in 2080. Local food supplies are projected to be negatively affected by decreasing fisheries resources due to rising water temperatures, which may be exacerbated by continued over-fishing.

Fifth, the effects of climate change could further undermine peace and stability on the continent due to conflict over constrained resources such as water. Significant population migrations both internally and across borders may occur with severe humanitarian impacts further undermining peace and stability.

Sixth, there is a need to cost the impacts of climate change and to inform and sensitise domestic audiences. While the likely immediate impacts of climate change are known, greater effort must be made to assess and estimate their long-term socio-economic implications and cost the development characteristics of climate change by involving economists and development planners. Because most climate adaptation efforts take place at the local and sub-national levels, there is need to provide local audiences with more information.

That said, climate change must be seen as an opportunity to rethink industrial development. The climate debate should inform the decision making on financing, investment, technology, and institutional change. Leaders and the public at large must be prepared to integrate it into development decision making. This involves addressing the multiple yet, in some instances, competing goals involving equity, climate management, and social and economic development. Indeed, the very perception of trade-offs can prove a potent political barrier to integrating climate change and development. Experience has shown that differences in perceptions and conceptual frameworks across high-income and developing countries can and do get in the way of a meaningful discussion on how climate action can be integrated with development objectives.

To integrate the climate regime with development effectively, it is useful to identify and engage opposing perspectives with a view to transcending them. We identify four foci of tension between the climate and the development perspective: environment and equity; burden sharing and opportunistic early action; a predictable climate outcome and an unpredictable development process; and conditionality in financing and ownership.

First, burden sharing demands that countries set absolute reduction targets in order to avoid catastrophic climate change. Based on the recommendations of the IPCC, some countries have pressed for a global goal of restricting the rise in global temperature to not more than 2°C (which necessitates reducing global emissions by at least 50 per cent) by 2050 from their 1990 levels. In response, several high-income countries have submitted proposed national reduction targets for 2050 (EU, 2009).

Second, the climate challenge is quite different when viewed from a development perspective. Here, a recent strand of development thought focuses on institutions and problems of institutional inertia in development whereby formal "rules of the game" and informal norms, including those embedded in culture, are important determinants of economic incentives, institutional transformation, technological innovation, and social change. The political economy dynamic is central to this process, as different actors organise to change institutions and transform incentives but including what individual actors can bring to their engagement with the process. Three issues are relevant here: development is a process of change, largely driven from below; history and the past patterns of institutions matter a great deal, and hence common templates are only of limited use – one size does not fit all; and this characterisation of change applies equally to high-income countries, even though the challenge of imperfect and incomplete institutions appears less daunting, and top-down policy and price signals are considered to be the main drivers of change.

Third and finally is the issue of policy ownership and financing. Climate change related policies will not succeed if they compromise living standards – they should rather aggressively explore the co-benefits of development for promoting climate resilience. Nested within this longer-term objective, African countries could agree to short-term "best-practice" measures – notably for energy efficiency – that bring about both developmental and climate benefits. Agreeing to aggressively pursue these measures would provide some reassurance that predictable climate gains will be realised in the short term. Then, adequate financing would need to be sought.

Even if the present pledges to limit emissions by 2020 are fulfilled, global temperature is still predicted to increase by 3.5 to 4 degrees Celsius by 2100. Persistent drought and flooding are exacerbating food and water insecurity, threatening livelihoods and health. Severe droughts have affected the Horn of Africa and Sahel regions and are expected to continue with rising carbon emissions (Oxfam, 2015). In 2015, South Africa declared five of its nine provinces drought-disaster areas. Ethiopia also witnessed the decimation of crops, livestock, and water, which left 4.5 million people in need of food relief in 2015. The impact of the drought hurts African economies because 94 per cent of their agricultural output is rain fed, and the major source of energy generation is hydroelectricity (WWF, 2011).

The effectiveness with which Africa addresses the link between food production, water, and energy will determine how many millions are lifted out of poverty in the coming decades. A climate-smart agricultural revolution is needed to guarantee food security. Water management strategies must be developed to protect and rehabilitate groundwater sources and river basins. The energy sector should be geared towards the promotion and adoption of clean and renewable sources of power. In addition, African governments and business leaders must make significant investments in science and technology to support mitigation and adaptation efforts. While international assistance is vital, effective and sustainable solutions must be developed locally (Kararach, 2014). Developing countries have a great opportunity to "do it right". Partnerships must be created to share technology and best practice. We must end the spectre of national self-interest in a world where climate change knows no boundaries.

If emerging economies focus on growth at all costs, they risk handing future generations a terrible legacy. There is a wealth of evidence to show that the impact of climate change will be more expensive than the changes needed to halt its impacts.

However, what is clear is that Africa is no longer on the back foot. The continent is beginning to adopt a proactive approach to tackling climate change, empowering its people, and strengthening its institutions to enhance political and economic governance. Policymakers must develop ambitious plans to create clean and green economies across Africa. Partnerships must be forged between government, the private sector, and civil society so as to enable the swift implementation of national climate action plans (ECA, 2016a).

In the absence of global leadership from developed countries, which contribute most to climate change, small developing nations must do what they can to ensure that their interests continue to be represented before it is too late. Leadership is a critical factor in a globalised world if countries are to deal with complexity and risk (Léautier, 2014).

A new era for partnerships with the Global South

While the history of multilateralism has been largely punctuated by disappointment for Africa, there is no doubt that global partnerships can provide the impetus for tackling the key socio-economic development challenges facing the continent. This requires urgent reform in governance systems and making many of the institutions such as the IMF and World Bank fit for purpose (Woods, 2006). In the case of the IMF, Woods (2010) argued that attempts for reforms find only very limited shifts in the engagement of major emerging economies combined with efforts to preserve the status quo. Such difficulty in reforming global governance institutions may compromise Africa's ambitions (Moghalu, 2014). However, Africa can still tap into the huge knowledge depository of the likes of the IMF and the World Bank (Moghalu, 2014).

Africa needs to seek new partners, especially in the global South (Shaw, 2012), to give it the policy space necessary for reorienting its development agenda (Cheru, 2017) as well as searching for different ideas, knowledge, and forms of finance (Lin and Wang, 2017). The economic weight of southern actors at the global level over the last two decades has been unprecedented in speed and scale. Whilst growth levels of Western economies plummeted following the 2008–2009 financial crisis, developing economies continued to grow at high rates, largely driven by a variety of factors, including sound industrial policies and investments in human, physical, and technological capacities. Countries of the South have diversified their economies with large manufacturing and modern service sectors (Moghalu, 2014). India went from being one of the world's largest recipients of foreign aid in mid-1980s to become a net donor, with foreign aid constituting less than 0.3 per cent of its national GDP, and is now a member of the G20 and the BRICS. India's development performance is one of the most spectacular of the past 50 years. The country led an agricultural revolution which transformed it into a net exporter of food, thereby doubling its life expectancy and halving its poverty rate.

For the first time in 150 years, the combined output of the developing world's three leading economies – Brazil, China, and India – is about equal to the combined GDP of the longstanding industrial powers of the North – Canada, France, Germany, Italy, the United Kingdom, and the United States (UNDP, 2013a). This represents a dramatic rebalancing of global economic power and the possible restructuring of the global governance architecture (Lema et al., 2012; Moghalu, 2014).

The impact of this shift is also evident in demography and social development. The absolute number of people in the South means that its middle class will continue to grow in size, income, and expectations. Rapid economic growth and poverty reduction, especially in China, have led to a decline in the number of poor by 158 million between 2000 and 2011 (UNDP, 2013a). Investments in technology and innovation have led to southern economies sometimes outpacing their northern counterparts in technological entrepreneurialism and manufacturing capabilities, and so producing complex products for developing markets. Because of rising South–South trade, the share of developing countries' capital goods imports from other developing countries has increased steadily from 35 per cent in 1995 to 54 per cent in 2010, making developing countries the major source of capital goods for other developing countries.

Global partnerships can work for Africa if these are aligned with the strategic vision of the continent and buttressed by a unified continental voice (Moghalu, 2014). Efforts to increase the continent's share of global trade through Aid for Trade and preferential market access initiatives have yielded mixed results. Though Aid for Trade commitments have increased over the years, disbursements have fallen short of commitments. Furthermore, the proportion of developed country imports from Africa (admitted duty-free) has stagnated. These trends are unfortunate since trade represents an important mechanism for promoting enduring economic growth and employment in developing countries. However, Africa can capitalise on the rise in trade with the rest of the world outside of its traditional partners (Mandy, 2007).

Africa can learn from the successes and failures of these countries and use them as building blocks to design its own development. For example, the Brazilian *Bolsa Familia* Programme, which was implemented under President Lula da Silva, used cash transfers to alleviate poverty by linking social development, economic improvement, and education in a wide-reaching process that eventually took 50 million people out of poverty (Ceratti, 2014). While land productivity in China, Brazil, and India has grown over the past 50 years, Africa's has remained stagnant (Lopes, 2014a).[4] Africa's increasing ties with the South are particularly important also in view of volatility that still afflicts the world economy, compounded by the increasing signals for investors to reduce their exposure to hedging markets in light of reduced quantitative easing.

Although creating partnerships with other developing countries is not new, starting as far back as the 1955 Bandung Conference, these relationships were more political and did not provide much economic leverage for the continent. At the end of the cold war, Africa launched new partnerships arrangements with the Global South, driven primarily by economic rather than political considerations. Africa's trade increased from $34 billion in 1995 to $283 billion in 2008 (Agarwal, 2013). The fact that Africa's total merchandise trade with the South accounted for nearly 27 per cent of its total trade in 2013 further attests to this (ECA, 2015a).

Africa must be more aware of the challenges and disadvantages that may accrue because of opening its borders to its "partners". Many studies have shown the negative impact of cheap goods flooding African markets and undermining African fragile industries. For instance, a recent study by the African Economic Research Consortium on China's trade relations with Mauritius found that cheap imports have benefited consumers but that, more significantly, Chinese import competition has caused heavy losses to local industry, with small firms and those in sectors such as garments, footwear, and furniture experiencing a loss of market share (AERC, 2010). In this regard, Chinese engagement with Africa has to be constantly revisited to ensure that mutual benefits flow from Sino–Africa relations (Kararach, 2014; Shelton et al., 2015; Kararach et al., 2017).

Policies guiding trade must address the intrusion of cheap manufactured goods and dumping by emerging economies on African markets and out-competing domestic firms (Kararach, 2014). However, cheaper imported goods from emerging markets can benefit Africa's own industrialisation provided such goods are primarily industrial inputs as this will result in significant foreign currency savings.

African countries must avoid incentives to industries that lack focus, usher in opaque discretionary and arbitrary practices, insulate inefficiencies, and offer rewards without results. Unfocused policies also mean narrow windows of opportunity because of incoherence or slowness. For example, Africans fought hard to obtain preferential rules of origin for least-developed countries at the Ninth Ministerial Conference of the World Trade

Organization, held in Bali, Indonesia, in 2013. However, African countries have neither called for the implementation of those preferential criteria in their bilateral negotiations with the European Union under the Economic Partnership Agreements, nor considered them in the African Growth and Opportunity Act. It is clear that when engaging in bilateral negotiations with large trading partners, more vigour is necessary (Moghalu, 2014). Although the least developed countries obtained an extension of the transition period for the implementation of the Agreement on Trade-related Aspects of Intellectual Property Rights, the continent has not maximised this as an opportunity to innovate and promote new technologies.

To ensure a win–win situation, Africa needs to carefully devise new partnership arrangements with developing countries (Kararach et al., 2012; Shaw, 2015). Whether on a country-by-country basis, through the Regional Economic Communities (RECs) or at a continental level, it is imperative to design a workable plan for engagement with partners. Africa can take advantage in global geopolitics and related dynamics. For example, in 2006, China released an official China–Africa policy white paper, which covered a broad range of topics by which China will engage with Africa, from aid, debt relief, the promotion of Chinese culture and language, tourism, and alliance building. It was the first of its kind in China's diplomatic history with Africa, and it embodied the country's long-term plan for enhancing all-round and mutually beneficial cooperation with Africa. This is not to suggest that Chinese interest in Africa is benign but to implore the leaders to pay special attention to the protection of African interest(s) (Osei and Mubiru, 2010; Chatelard, 2012; Moghalu, 2014).

All said, Africa must assume greater ownership of its development agenda (Lopes, 2013a). This will require that countries undertake a critical assessment of their domestic resource potential and develop resource mobilisation strategies aimed at maximising that potential. Irrespective of some the constraints that come with state interests, African countries need to ensure that partnerships with developing countries work for Africa's transformation agenda. Regional bodies such as the African Union must work as fora to reach binding agreements amongst member states for a standard set of requirements for foreign involvement on the continent, whether with new or traditional partners. This collective action can also be leveraged, for example, to open up greater policy space for industrial investments that were utilised by the Asian newly industrialised countries during their economic transformation. The new framework must also take into consideration the initial conditions of each country. This is important since performance should be appreciated considering the road travelled, relative to the point of departure. We cannot repeat the methodological mistake of increasing every country's progress towards a universal goal as if they were all in the same line of departure. Africa must be prepared to apply history to suit its own ambitions such as regional integration (Ekpo, 2012).

Africa's engagements must be articulated and managed in the context of a comprehensive development strategy for economic transformation

(Moghalu, 2014, p. 277). A clear transformation agenda is required that enables Africa to shift from a largely agrarian society with acute dependence on primary resources towards an economic model based on industry and modern services, with significant employment generation and a more equitable distribution of income. Moreover, Africa must prioritise its interaction with traditional and emerging partners by clearly and unambiguously articulating its needs in infrastructural development, education and training, health, finance, and other critical areas.

There is a win–win situation that can be achieved. Africa has the natural resources, the land, the work force, and increasingly the markets that are and continue to be of strategic interest to the emerging economies of the South such as China, India, and Brazil (Lopes, 2014a). Such partners can provide the technical and expert assistance to address Africa's growth challenges. The story of the "Asian Tigers'" rise from low-income to high-income and developed country status (Amsden, 2000) is of course relevant to Africa. The economic history of these countries suggests a system of state planning, favourable interest rates for loans to specific exporting industries, major government investments in education, maintenance of export-led regimes, and low taxes, among others, which were all critical in their path to rapid industrialisation (Okimoto, 1989; Amsden, 1989, 2000; Chang, 2007).

The increasing trends in development cooperation between Africa and its partners present the right opportunities for such enhancing growth to fuel an economic transformation. Africa's key priorities should be identifying the means of cooperation with partners that have the greatest potential to foster its transformation, provide sufficient domestic investments to complement this cooperation, and engage external partners collectively in order to maximise the benefits of such cooperation (Moghalu, 2014, pp. 340, 341).

The South Africa–China Comprehensive Strategic Partnership presents a model framework whereby China will increase investment in South Africa's manufacturing industry and promote the creation of value-adding activities (Shelton et al., 2015). Such investments can focus on value-addition as a means to guide interest in Africa's natural resources to productive activities that yield a greater portion of global value chains for processing within Africa.

As the availability of loans and financing from external emerging markets increases, Africa must ensure that new borrowing does finance projects with significant employment-generating potential in order to absorb the increasing number of young people entering the labour force. The policy environment in Africa must ensure a stable and low-cost business environment conducive for investment, to attract jobs that are anticipated to relocate due to rising labour costs in Asia. Alongside this opportunity is the emergence of a new aid architecture which presents the continent for different development pathways (Kararach et al., 2012; Lopes, 2013b; Shaw, 2015).

Finally, future global partnership will have to include new sets of actors such as the private sector, parliamentarians, civil society, private foundations, women, and the youth. The engagement of these groups will be a major step in reforming the governance of development norms, structures, and processes and making them sustainable (Kararach, 2014).

Conclusion

There is no doubt that Africa's transformation is set to take place in a more complex environment. The linkages between developments in the world socio-economic system, Africa's quest for transformation, and factors that may seem remote from them are becoming increasingly apparent. For instance, the centrality of climate change to Africa's development is interlinked with Africa's fight against poverty and the impact of climate change. As demonstrated, climate change adaptation and mitigation are critical for Africa's development, and such strategies are interlinked with the fight against poverty. Conflicts in faraway places such as Afghanistan, Syria, and Iraq clearly show that there is a need for conflict prevention as a major priority of development.

The rise of the Global South as a major source of foreign investment in Africa has altered the direction of financial flows and the nature of development cooperation. Aid is no longer the only important source of development finance as remittances, driven by rising migration, increase. In addition, with increased globalisation, much is gained through enhanced trade and transfer of technology, but harmful economic forces also thrive which threaten "de-industrialisation", a prospect faced by many African countries.

Equally, global compacts such as the SDGs will always be important indicators of and frameworks for development based on attempts to revive multilateralism as mechanisms for exchanging ideas, knowledge, and resources. However, these can no longer be achieved by old architectures. Strategic partnerships, leadership, and vision all have their roles to play. Africans must seize the opportunities and redefine their relationships in the current but highly unstable and volatile multipolar world. The State in Africa has an important role to play in the continent's transformation. Nevertheless, it will not do so as long as it is weak and artificially propped up by external forces. In the next chapter, we address the challenge of industrialisation as a major vector of structural change and examine how prudent and functional industrial policy, aided by strategic government intervention, could assist the process of structural transformation.

Notes

1 These discussions build on our previous interventions on the topics and extend the arguments to illustrate the misperceptions that characterise the history of Africa's quest for sustainable development.
2 See Lewis (1954) as an earlier variant of this model.
3 See https://frontex.europa.eu/along-eu-borders/migratory-map/
4 China, Brazil, and India's grew from 1.21, 1.35 and 0.95 tons per hectare to 5.52, 4 and 2.53 respectively over the past 50 years. Africa's remained at 1.5 per hectare.

3 Industrialisation

Understanding the role of industrial and related policies for transformation

Introduction

The 2008–2009 financial crisis was a clear demonstration of the depth of global interconnectivity. At the peak of the financial crisis, in addition to its far-reaching impacts on the US, Europe, China, and Japan, innocent "bystanders" in countries as far flung as Indonesia and other developing countries found themselves feeling the effects of the investors' fears and trepidation. Yet, developments in the global economy such as commodity volatility and the rise of protectionism circumscribe the imperative for Africa to industrialise and trade in high value-added products and internally as much as possible. Industrialisation is thus critical if Africa is to achieve structural change that translates its recent high growth rates into significant social development through decent jobs. Promoting structural change requires sound industrial policies and strategic government interventions in the economy's production structure for purposes of shifting it towards more productive sectors. In this regard, manufacturing emerges as a key sector as it fosters forward and backward linkages, dynamic economies of scale, innovation and technology diffusion, and positive spill-over effects within and across sectors. It bears repeating that countries that diversify away from traditional sectors experience a decline in poverty rates and a sustained increase in technology accumulation and international competitiveness (McMillan and Rodrik, 2011; UNCTAD and UNIDO, 2011; Joachim and Poncet, 2012; Rodrik, 2013).

While the theoretical justification for industrial policy is persuasive, it faces numerous challenges in practice. Proponents of industrial policy point to the presence of market and coordination failures, knowledge spill-overs, and dynamic scale economies (Pack and Saggi, 2006; Rodrik, 2009; Stiglitz et al., 2013). While this view of industrial policy receives considerable support, at least in theory, critics also point to the inability of governments to precisely identify sectors or firms that any such policy should target. Obstacles such as corruption and rent-seeking, induced by government intervention as well as deficiencies in the transparency and accountability of state policies, may undermine economic performance. As a result, industrial policy may reduce allocative efficiency in an economy by interfering with the price mechanism (Altenburg, 2011).

Evidence suggests that earlier attempts by African countries to industrialise were mostly unsuccessful and economic production has remained largely agrarian and subsistence, and portrays limited value addition (Elhiraika and Mbate, 2014). The reasons for this failure include a weakly articulated policy notion of comparative advantage, domestic programmatic failure such as unsustainable subsidies of production inputs, inappropriate monetary and fiscal policies, political economy issues, and structural impediments such as infrastructural and human capital deficits (Chang, 2013; Stiglitz et al., 2013; Mkandawire, 2015). Consequently, manufacturing has either stagnated or declined over time. The share of manufacturing in Africa's GDP remained at around 13 per cent between 1980 and 2010, compared to 31 per cent in East Asia, where labour-intensive industrialisation has driven high growth and addressed challenges arising from job creation, poverty, and inequality (ECA and AUC, 2013).

Although the drivers of growth are diversifying, the continent continues to rely heavily on the production and export of raw commodities, and the share of manufacturing stagnated at around 11 per cent over the last decade. Many African economies are vulnerable to fluctuations in commodity prices, and the continent remains home to the world's highest proportion of poor people and to a growing population of youth (Kararach et al., 2017). Today, African countries feature in the ten most unequal societies. The growth experienced so far has been good but without quality and has not diversified production structures into higher employment-intensive activities.

We argued in Chapter 1 that industrialisation provides the theoretical underpinning for structural transformation by redefining the productivity base of the economy. For a number of decades African countries have mistakenly not prioritised industrialisation and value-addition as critical elements of their development strategies. Industrialisation is indispensable to structural transformation and must therefore be brought back in. The kind of industrialisation Africa needs should be inclusive and sustainable. Industrial and related policies become major tools in reshaping the circumstances that define development in Africa (Lopes et al., 2017).

African countries have a number of opportunities to industrialise by capitalising on the continent's abundant natural resources, adding value to them, while also supporting the development of infant industries. Being latecomers, they can avoid the pitfalls of others and leapfrog using innovation and advances in technology. It is very clear that the policy conditions for Africa's industrialisation are now more difficult, given greater levels of global competition and rising protectionism. Context will therefore be very important in addressing the conditionalities of "free market" policy orthodoxy (Chang, 2007). The state, thus, has a central role to play, especially as facilitators and enablers in the industrialisation process. The state, for example, is critical in shaping macroeconomic planning, ensuring some level of pragmatism, risk-taking, and constant adaptability to changing local, regional, and global conditions. Industrialisation is not a haphazard process; it occurs through strategic vision and deliberate actions of the state. Of course, the private sector is the ultimate agency of industrialisation but efficient state planning and implementation are essential.

Therefore, the importance of industrial policy for Africa and the rest of the developing world is shifting away from its theoretical justification to its practical implementation (Rodrik, 2013; ECA and AUC, 2014). While experts agree on the need for industrial upgrading and state interventions, there are divergent views on whether industrial policy should favour a country's comparative advantage or not (Lin and Chang, 2009). Practically, one wonders whether industrial policy should be based on commodities and natural resource endowment, which are abundant in most countries; or whether government interventions should help firms to venture into new growth sectors that are independent of natural resources as production inputs; or whether governments should implement industrial policies that are sector specific – vertical policies – or those which are broad and neutral – horizontal policies (Lin, 2012)?

For the African economic and political landscape to be ripe for change, it is incumbent on leaders and governments to drive industrial policies as part of structural reforms, characterised by Africa's increasingly assertive and vibrant citizenry, together with the private sector. The rest of this chapter further discusses Africa's industrialisation imperatives and opportunities.

Development planning in Africa: lessons and challenges in transformation

Development planning has a long and mixed history and as Africa sought to industrialise, the continent's development trajectory has been influenced by various approaches to development planning since the early stages of independence. Gumede (2014, p. 3) makes a strong case for development planning, arguing that:

> Very few, if any, developing countries have progressed in terms of economic development without a long-term development plan. Such an explicit development plan serves a country into its future. Successful long-term development plans integrate action for the short term (present), medium term and long term. A long-term development plan is crucial for the identification of the core priorities of a nation.

It is therefore an important mechanism for shaping the circumstances and efforts for development.

Since the 1950s, development economists formulated grand and visionary models of development strategy that aimed at effecting structural transformation with a central role assigned to the government in planning and programming development (Meier, 2001). However, given that both markets and politics may not deliver structural transformation (Stiglitz, 2017), there is need to qualify the basis for development planning.

While planning occurs within the context of many types of decision-making units, and is often defined as any attempt to select the best means to achieve desired ends, it should be understood to encapsulate those actions to purposefully bring about structural transformation and the associated future development of the economy. The policy content of development plans was anchored on the perception that:

> a less-developed economy was characterized by pervasive market failures. To correct or avoid market failure, they advocated central coordination and allocation of resources. The newly expanding subject of welfare economics also provided considerable rationale for government action to correct market failure.
>
> (Meier, 2001, p. 14)

Besides inherent market failures, state intervention was justified by the stylised facts that the supply of entrepreneurs was limited in these countries, and that major structural changes rather than marginal adjustments were needed to effect development. Thus:

> [T]he government of a developmental state was to promote capital accumulation, utilize reserves of surplus labour, undertake policies of deliberate industrialization, relax the foreign exchange constraint through import substitution, and coordinate the allocation of resources through programming and planning
>
> (Meier, 2001, pp. 14–15)

The economic case for development planning, while at times axiomatic (Bauer, 1971), has been broadly made in terms of the failings of an unregulated market economy (Lewis, 1951; Griffin and Enos, 1970; Gumede, 2017). Perhaps the major arguments view planning as a superior means of arriving at investment and other decisions affecting the future, with the market seen as supplying information that is a poor guide for such decisions, leading to avoidable uncertainties and myopia. Thus, Scitovsky (1954) and others drew attention to the interdependence of investment decisions and alleged that aggregate investment made up of atomistic decisions would be less than that which would result from "centralised investment planning" that could provide more realistic signals of present plans and future conditions. In other ways, too, planning is seen as a means for correcting discrepancies between private and social valuations, for example, the markets tendency to over-value unskilled labour. Under the influence of the "big push" approach, planning was also seen as the only way to mobilise resources on the scale necessary for a successful development effort, and as the only practical means of binding the various strands of economic policy into a consistent whole.

The first phase of development planning in Africa started much earlier, with colonialism. There were various levels of planning from national, local, and sectoral planning. It was a mixed bag of centralised and indicative planning with the objective of delivering the colonial project. For example, the history of the process of the production and reproduction of knowledge since the advent of colonialism is instructive. The object of education under colonialism was not as altruistic as it is often made out to be. The idea of a civilising mission, through which Africans were Christianised and taught to read and write, was first and foremost an attempt to produce Africans who would be serviceable for the project of colonialism; essentially, those Africans who would acquiesce to the strategy and tactics of the colonial project (Prah, 2011).

The second phase spanned the 1960s and was characterised by centralised planning with three to five-year planning phases. During this period, at least 32 African countries had a national development plan (Cheru, 2017). This first generation of development plans continued to the 1980s. These plans promoted state-engineered economies with resources allocated by governments. It was notably the period of state-owned enterprises operating in most of the productive sectors. However, Africa's development plans of the 1960s had limited success. This was due to a variety of reasons: certainly, deficiencies in the plan documents but also failure to implement them; ambitious formulation of targets; institutional and bureaucratic weaknesses; exogenous shocks; as well as political factors.

The third phase in the evolution of planning in Africa was marked by a wholesale abandonment of planning under neoliberal Structural Adjustment Programmes (SAPs), which emerged in the 1980s–1990s with the support of the Bretton Woods Institutions. SAPs aimed to reduce the role of the state in production and service delivery and placed emphasis on macroeconomic stability, downsizing of public sector institutions, privatisation, and reducing government spending and budget deficits (Elhiraika and Bodart, 2012).

The social cost of SAPs has been enormous. The downsizing of public sector institutions and massive privatisations led to net job losses; budget restrictions compromised social service delivery and human capital development; and most importantly, SAPs failed to yield the envisaged growth outcomes as the annual economic growth for Africa over the 1990s averaged only 2.1 per cent. Takahashi Motoki observed that by the "mid-1990s, the failure of orthodox SAPs to save Africa from rampant poverty and stagnation became unquestionable" (Motoki, 2001).

These past experiences in planning alerted policymakers and decision makers to the need to broaden the agenda of public sector reforms and to the importance of good institutions and greater ownership and legitimacy of the development process (Gumede, 2014), especially in the new context of globalisation.

In the early 2000s, SAPs were replaced by Poverty Reduction Strategies (PRSPs), which aimed at reversing the negative effects of a decade of Structural Adjustment on welfare and social conditions. PRSPs placed strong emphasis on poverty reduction as a condition for debt relief. Many African countries embarked on at least two generations of PRSPs, mostly to ensure eligibility for debt relief.

Notwithstanding the principle of ownership and consultations that underpinned PRSPs, they lacked credibility because of the externally driven nature of the process. Furthermore, PRSPs tended to place disproportionate emphasis on the social sector at the expense of the productive sector, thereby raising questions about the sustainability of the poverty reduction agenda (Amoako-Tuffour and Armah, 2007).

In the last decade, there has been increasing interest in, and a return to, more comprehensive development plans that go way beyond short-sighted PRSPs. Indeed, many African countries have adopted long-term development visions and planning frameworks with far more ambitious growth and social development objectives.

National Development Strategies (NDS) have now gone beyond the narrow objective of poverty reduction to encompass objectives such as accelerated growth, employment creation, structural transformation, and sustainable development. Unlike the 1960s, these plans employ a mix of state and market-based approaches and appreciate the critical role of both the public and the private sector in the development process.

Many African countries have developed long-term visions to guide their steps towards these ambitious objectives (ECA, 2016a, 2016c).[1] Stronger ownership from African actors and a consultative and participatory process involving a broad spectrum of stakeholders, including civil society, the private sector, decentralised constituencies, and development partners all characterise these long-term visions. Indeed, these broader national development plans often take into consideration various global and continental development goals and frameworks such as NEPAD.

Challenges, however, remain and it could be argued that the phases in planning are closely linked to that of industrial policy and strategies for industrialisation in Africa (whether through import substitution or export promotion). These challenges include: ensuring credible consultation processes, prioritising funding in line with development aspirations, coordinating donors, strengthening capacities to implement projects and programmes, and developing effective monitoring and evaluation systems that feed back into the policymaking process. In short, more work is required to improve the planning frameworks in Africa in order to translate development aspirations and priorities into concrete results. Another important aspect is coordination. Coordination between ministries of finance and the ministries or entities in charge of development planning, among others, is likely to better link the planning cycles to those of the budget, thereby ensuring an effective implementation of the national development plan.

Tony Killick noted a while ago (1976) some of the erroneous assumptions about the primacy of planning in delivering structural transformation. He noted the limited appreciation of political economy dynamics as a major weakness of planning in the developing world. He argued that development planning tends to be characterised by the virtual absence of systematic discussion of the implications of planning for political systems, or vice versa, even though authors often insist that a plan is essentially a political document. This is because "economists seem to find it more comfortable to get rid of this problem" (Killick, 1976, p. 166) by treating politics as creating "boundary conditions" that constrain the variation of targets and policy instruments (see also Tinbergen, 1967). The result is a largely unarticulated view of political processes, which appears to owe the greatest intellectual debt not to the study of government but to economists' own theories of the behaviour of individuals and firms (Simon, 1957).

The economist fails to note that politicians may not always have the social and national interest at heart and this thwarts their decision-making functions in ways that undermine development. Killick (1976) notes that economists expect a government to have a clearly defined set of policy objectives in the medium term and with a relatively high degree of internal unity, a shared objective, and operational discipline to implement stated development plans. However, in the real world, such expectations are violated.

The criticisms of planning being devoid of any savvy understanding of political economy is in large measure an explanation of the failure to deliver industrialisation as a tool for structural transformation in Africa. However, the continent's turbulent experience with development planning in the past is ceding ground to a more positive outlook for the future (Landsberg, 2018). Indeed, there are some good examples of success stories among African countries, which graduated from low income countries to middle income countries, including Cape Verde, Ghana, and Botswana. In addition, some African countries such as Ethiopia, Nigeria, and Uganda have adopted long-term development visions, policies, and planning frameworks with far more ambitious growth and social development objectives and strategies than those typically included in PRSPs. These countries have understood that planning is critical for turning challenges into opportunities and exploiting these effectively.

Building a developmental state and institutions is an important ingredient for renewing the growth narrative (Moghalu, 2014; Zeleza, 2018). If Africa is going to own its narrative, it has to be based on real changes. It is therefore opportune to focus on the practical and African-owned pathways necessary for transformation.

Statistics and planning for Africa's future

Over the past 20 years, Africa has moved from a position of Afro-pessimism, through to Afro-optimism, and now to a state of Afro-enthusiasm. Why has the narrative changed so drastically? Is the new narrative coming from Africa? Partly, yes. However, most of the narrative still represents an outside view, and for good reason. Those who control information flows and data control the narrative.

There have been lingering concerns about the quality of the data underpinning Africa's growth story (Jerven, 2013). The question is: can we verify the numbers behind telecoms, retail, banking, corruption, poverty, and the like? What is the statistical basis for generating these figures? Moreover, can they be corroborated by the facts on the ground? Rick Rowden (2013) questions the basis of Africa's supposed growth figures. He argued that due to unavailability and/or unreliability of data or what he refers to as "unhelpful indicators", it is difficult for economists and analysts to believe the sheer hype. Derek Blades, as far back as 1980, also suggested that estimates of African GDP levels had large errors and should rather be considered within plus–minus margins (Blades, 1980). In 2011, lead statisticians in 23 countries were asked the direct question: "do you think that GDP rates are fine?" Only Namibia and Lesotho answered in the affirmative. The other 18 country statisticians were convinced that their countries' GDP rates were underestimated. Figure 3.1 highlights the status of the GDP base year of African countries.

It might be helpful to recall how GDP is calculated. To work out real GDP, government statisticians use the prices of goods and services from a "base year" as a reference. It is recommended that base years should be changed every fifth year but only seven out of 54 African countries regularly do this. A study of 47 African countries by Morten Jerven found that only ten African countries used base years less than a decade old (Jerven, 2013). Up to seven countries still had base years in the 1980s and several others were unsure of their base years.

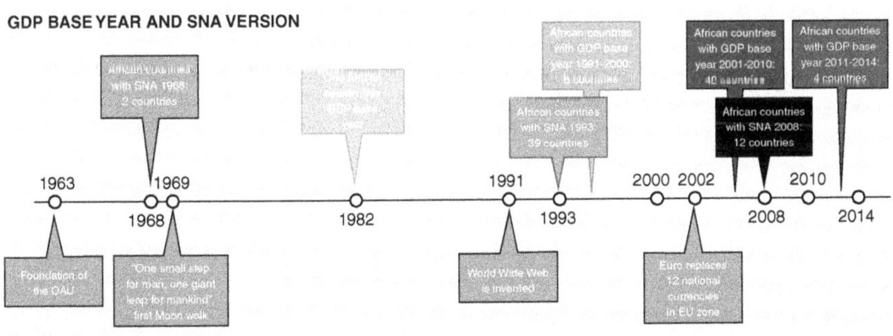

Figure 3.1 Rebasing of GDP of African economies could scale up the level of overall GDP

Source: ECA, 2016a.

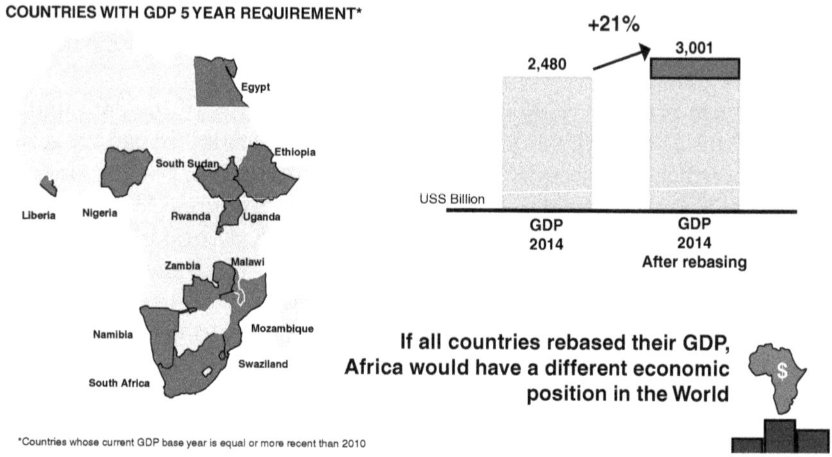

Figure 3.2 Underestimating Africa's GDP
Source: ECA, 2016a.

In 2010, Ghana revised its base year from 1996 to 2006, thereby dramatically increasing its GDP by 60 per cent. In 2018 it recently carried out a second rebasing, increasing GDP a further 26 per cent. This resulted in the World Bank re-classifying it overnight from a poor to a middle-income country. This meant in concrete terms that about $13 billion of economic activities had been systematically overlooked. In response, Todd Moss (2010) exclaimed: "Boy, we really don't know anything." Given this level of error margin in the GDP estimate on Ghana, arguably one of the most studied countries on the continent, what should we think about economic statistics that derive from many other African countries?

Nigeria's recent rebasing, from the rate of the 1990 base year to 2008, catapulted the country to becoming the largest economy in Africa, overtaking South Africa. Jerven's (2013) analysis on the impact of this rebasing within the economies of Sub-Saharan Africa leads to the conclusion that there are about the equivalent of 40 "Malawis" that are unaccounted for in the Nigerian economy to date. Figure 3.2 shows African countries whose GDP base year rate is equal or more recent than 2010.

But even with these drastic changes, can one be confident about these figures? Jerven (2013) further compares the World Bank's calculations of country specific GDP with GDP figures calculated by national statistics offices. He finds that only three country figures are totally consistent with this comparison and in a few other cases there are major discrepancies, such as 476 per cent for Ethiopia, or 10,432 per cent for Sudan.

In a second example, researchers from the London School of Economics argue that over the last 20 years, household consumption in Africa has actually been growing from 3.4 per cent to 3.7 per cent per annum, based not on the GDP calculations but on factors such as the number of households with TV sets, electricity access, or the percentage of people with mobile phones, compared to the 0.9 to 1.1 per cent suggested by income statistics (Young, 2012).

Another example is the estimation that there have been 316 million new mobile phone subscribers in Africa since 2000. How were these numbers calculated? The short answer is most likely with industry giving the figures of the sale of handsets!

According to the Food and Agriculture Organization (FAO), the quantity and quality of agricultural statistics from national statistical offices have been on a steady decline since the early 1980s, particularly in Africa. Consequently, official submissions from countries in Africa are at their lowest level since before 1961, with only one in four African countries reporting basic crop production data (FAO, 2010).

Take the MDGs for example. Only 17 African countries collected data to measure changes in poverty in the past decade and 47 per cent never carried out a household income or expenditure survey in more than five years.

Finally, there is need to acknowledge that census and demographic statistics may be wanting. Without good knowledge of how many people exist, where they are, and what their conditions are it is hard to give credibility to any statistics that finish with "per number of people". The issue is that the perception of Africa continues to be negative even when the basis of the evidence can be contested or is mixed.

The effectiveness of national planning systems largely hinges on the quality and availability of data. Data informs the setting of priorities and facilitates the tracking of performance. Governments in Africa are increasingly strengthening their statistical departments in line with the trend of developing longer term development plans. In 2012, PARIS21[2] supported several African countries to design or implement a National Strategy for the Development of Statistics (NSDS). Niger, Benin, Burundi, and Guinea benefited with other countries to follow but, sadly, most national statistical machinery is still quite deficient. Much more needs to be done. Such an innovation could take the approach of Henderson and colleagues (Henderson et al., 2012) who developed a statistical framework to use satellite data on night lights to augment official income growth measures. They show that for countries with poor national income accounts, the optimal estimate of growth is a composite with roughly equal weights on conventionally measured growth and growth predicted from lights. Our estimates differ from official data by up to three percentage points annually. Using lights, empirical analyses of growth need no longer use countries as the unit of analysis; we can measure growth for sub- and supranational regions. For example, coastal areas in Sub-Saharan Africa are growing slower than the hinterland.

As Schumpeter noted, "We need statistics not only for explaining things, but also in order to know precisely what there is to explain" (Schumpeter, 1954, p. 14). How can Africa catch up with the current momentum and enhance its statistical capacity without being able to plan? In addition, how can planning be meaningful without accurate and reliable statistics?

Undeniably, Africa needs to make use of technology in this new era of the "data revolution". The increase in the use and access to new forms of technology is not limited to the developed world. The spread of mobile phones and internet in Africa can and should be harnessed for improving and reducing the cost of collecting its statistics. It is estimated that while internet traffic will grow by more than 50 per cent in Africa and Latin America and the Middle East, it will only grow by 25–30 per cent in North America.

In addition, the collection of data with mobile devices can accelerate the rate of collection, analysis, interpretation, and use of real time data to solve the continent's problems. At the macro level, the use of technology in health, agriculture, surveys to collect and analyse proper data needs to be encouraged (Xie et al., 2016).

Another important development is "Big Data". The use of "Big Data" gives access to real time information and therefore makes it easy and quicker to analyse and respond to crises by projecting trends in areas as diverse as weather, agriculture, health, population, and so on. New technologies driving the "Big Data" revolution are creating huge opportunities for designing, monitoring, and evaluating policy decisions and for directing structural transformation and related actions (Abelson et al., 2014; Varshney et al., 2015). However, while rich countries are being flooded with data, developing countries are suffering from a data drought. A new data divide is emerging, with huge differences in the quantity and quality of data available. For example, some countries have not taken a census in decades, and in the past five years an estimated 230 million births have gone unrecorded (Independent Expert Advisory Group Secretariat, 2014). We will return to these issues when discussing the importance of algorithms and the evolution in block-chain technology.

There is, of course, a debate on the use of "Big Data" due to privacy and the possibility of revealing personal confidential information whilst doing analysis. Moreover, most of the data generated through these means are perceptions as opposed to facts. Notwithstanding this, however, there are some very good applications of "Big Data" which have turned out to be very useful in providing users with policy and development information that is timely and of good quality. African leaders and policymakers must make use of institutions, structures, and systems that can support the production of credible data as a means for effectively measuring our developmental growth in a credible manner.

Africa at a fork in the road?

The notion of an African renaissance has been a recurring theme in African social thought – the quest for a new beginning and changing the course of sustainable development (Zeleza, 2018). Pan-Africanists such as Edward Blyden (1872, 1887) and Leopold Senghor (1971); and nationalists including

Kwame Nkrumah (1965) and Pixley ka Isaka Seme (1905/6) all called for a "new Africa" anchored on five core pillars: spiritual balance, social regeneration, economic determination, mental emancipation, and national self-determination in order to change the circumstances of its development and agency (Zeleza, 2018). The question has always been: how should African intellectuals, political leaders, and policymakers understand and engage each other for renewal of the continent – especially at the grassroots in order to avoid an elite-driven transition (Bond, 2000)?

What is clear is that Africa is increasingly making its own choices, even though some of these may not be well strategised or well planned. Two dynamics will be critical when such choices are made: the building up of African agency and the fostering of a development state as the correct mechanism for creating the right "circumstances" and supporting "efforts" for structural transformation. At the African Union Summit of 2013, which celebrated the fiftieth anniversary of pan-African institutional history, the tone was about the need to avoid repeating mistakes; and to prepare for the next 50 years with a vision and agenda that will make sure Africans claim their share of global prosperity by 2063 (AUC, 2013).

The same boldness is evident in the elaboration of African-specific goals or in the negotiation of some key partnerships. A flurry of intra-African initiatives is keeping policymakers busier than ever before. The vast majority of peacekeepers in Africa are from the continent. Most of the economic debates centre on domestic resource mobilisation, arresting illicit financial flows, or better using investment streams (Cheru, 2017; Lopes et al., 2017).

Structural transformation now dominates the continental discourse of African leaders. This means that there is a clear realisation of what has not happened – as reflected in low agricultural productivity, a contraction of value added in manufacturing, limited poverty reduction, and a lack of jobs and inclusive policies. Today, then, the fork in the road for Africa points to one direction only and therefore, one choice: the need to use the favourable winds to achieve economic transformation, and to accomplish this through industrialisation. A number of commentators are therefore quite optimistic about the possibility of Africa building developmental states (Mkandawire, 2001; Gumede, 2017; Landsberg, 2018).

Learning from others

For Africa to grow and transform, there is need to have a clear understanding of the times and circumstances as well as efforts needed to realise these requisite changes. Africa is not new in the business of transformation. However, it must innovate in this business. Lessons from many parts of the world will help Africa to avoid mistakes, become more sophisticated and resilient (Lopes, 2015e).

The changing landscape of international trade and investment has completely overhauled our understanding of global value chains and the dynamics of inequality and poverty (Kaplinsky, 2000). Since the 1980s, there has been a growing trend for enterprises to be spread across several countries for different stages and activities of the production process. There is no longer any single firm that produces any product from A to Z and production is certainly no longer limited by physical borders (Kararach, 2014). The value of patents and intellectual property is more substantial than the value of physical goods. Complex and innovative financial systems, capital and venture arrangements, and global standards and dispute settlement mechanisms have all contributed to a world where crude protectionism does not work. However, there are many countries that practise smart protectionism, better defined as the ability to make the rules work for a particular country and outsmart the systems that typically attract investment, equity, and markets.

Previously, countries had to develop strong industrial bases before they could trade and compete globally (Lopes, 2015e). The difference is that now they can insert themselves into specific segments and sub-sectors of global production processes. The rise and expansion of global value chains is not primarily due to increasing trade in goods – rather it is focused on technology, finance, investment, and other modern services (ECA, 2014a). For example, this can be seen in the comparative advantage exercised by immigrant Chinese in Prato, a fading manufacturing hub of mills and workshops in Italy which made clothing and leather goods for major fashion houses. This was achieved not only because of cheap labour, but also because the Chinese have the ability to quickly produce and alter production patterns overnight. Thus, the strategic focus of industrialisation in the twenty-first century has to be innovation and flexibility.

This leads to a second lesson which is the acknowledgement that the requirements for industrial policy development are different today from those in the 1970s (ECA and AUC, 2013). Key changes include the fact that economic policy has become more open and comparable between regions and countries like never before (Lopes, 2015e). Interested groups want to be part of and contribute to the design of innovative multi-sector strategies and to give such strategies legitimacy (Gumede, 2014). Instruments of economic policy have also changed significantly, from an overwhelming reliance on administrative direction to placing greater emphasis on modifying market processes through taxation, subsidies, and public expenditure measures in order to correct market imbalances. In addition, industrial policy development has become more polycentric and eclectic, simultaneously pursuing a variety of objectives rather than simply promoting rapid growth.

The industrialisation models of import substitution used in Latin America or the Southeast Asian export-driven model are no longer an option for Africa. The latter was particularly based on the premise of mass production with cheap labour, great absorptive capacity, and significant resource savings. As a latecomer, Africa will find that this niche is occupied or mostly gone, even if its attractiveness could be taken into account.

The third lesson is that Africa must fight for a level playing field under very adverse weather conditions (ECA and AUC, 2013). The current trade and climate-change negotiations are not in its favour. Take the example of agriculture. Some of Africa's cotton farmers, like the Burkinabe for lint or the Egyptian for processed cotton, have achieved high productivity but cannot compete against the subsidies of developed countries' farming sectors. The subsidies are officially not permissible in terms of the categorisations of the WTO, but they have been replaced by equal or higher amounts through a battery of environmental and insurance premiums that blur the frame. If agriculture must play a fundamental role in Africa's structural transformation, given that 60 per cent of the labour force is employed in that sector, major internal effort is needed in order to increase productivity and take advantage of the continent's enormous reservoir of unused arable land.

Strategies to move forward toward industrialisation and structural transformation

External factors are equally pertinent and should form key pillars of any policy considerations. The generally opaque international trading system is not helping Africa to industrialise and this is not going to change easily. Africa needs to carefully understand and strategise so as to confront this reality head on (Lopes, 2015e). There are a number of arguments to support such as stance.

First, Africa must insist on value addition in those commodities in which it has a dominant position. For example, transforming its mineral export volumes by just 5 per cent before exporting them can create 5 million jobs a year. Recent estimates show that African countries spend some $30 billion a year to import processed food yet this could be negated by enhanced post-harvest management of agro-products. Specifically, this trend can be reversed through value added agro-processing, thereby creating countless jobs especially for the continent's growing population of youth. (This is further discussed in detail later in the chapter, in the section on greening industrialisation.)

Second, as a latecomer, Africa is not locked into any technology preferences; it can follow a green and clean energy pathway and leapfrog the old carbon-intensive industrial models (ECA, 2016a). (We also discuss this in later in the chapter in the section on African trade policies.) The growing awareness of environmental degradation and climate change is giving rise to new research and development priorities such as clean energy technologies which could be scaled up rapidly. The continent is well positioned to absorb, adapt, and build on the vast quantities of scientific and technical knowledge already available to speed up its transformation. Its vast hydropower, geothermal, biomass, wind, and solar power potential is an amazing asset. For example, only 5 per cent of Africa's hydropower potential has been exploited.

Third, Africa should focus on its domestic consumption to enhance the budding productive linkages. Africa's rising population growth, growing middle class, and rapid urbanisation trends will continue to raise demand for consumer goods. Agribusiness, particularly processed food, holds the key to meeting this demand. The shift from primary production towards modern, integrated agribusiness provides a lucrative opportunity for many smallholder farmers, the majority of whom are women, as well as for generating modern jobs for the continent's youth. Africa cannot continue to import products such as yoghurt or toothpaste, whose productions do not require extremely complex investments in requisite plants.

Fourth, industrialisation can and should be inclusive and cognisant of the rights of both workers and consumers. It should avoid having buildings collapsing with sweatshop workers trapped inside or migrants dying in the desert or sea. That means paying proper attention to the drivers of an integrated model – mostly the small and medium-scale enterprises.

Fifth, promoting greater regional integration across Africa is an imperative not only to give the continent greater global voice but also to create alternative market outlets for its good and services as well as pool resources for requisite development. The scope for regional integration is still largely untapped both due to tariff and non-tariff barriers to intra-African trade which currently stand at around 10–15 per cent. Africa's transformation will require renewed and bolder efforts to implement the Africa Continental Free Trade Area (ACFTA) as a mechanism to free the movements of critical inputs, goods, and services.

So, what are Africa's chances going forward?

Africa needs policy tools and economic enablers for industrialisation and structural transformation. The commonality between the investments in Prato, Guanajuato, and Itú-São Paulo is that they have attracted the attention of Africa's number one trading partner: China. The lesson for Africa is that industrialisation is a highly competitive business underpinned by constant innovation. The continent needs to develop its own recipe and pathways if it wishes to become one of the factory floors of the world. Africa's attractiveness will most likely not be found in producing a Prada outfit or a spare part for Ford, or in adjusting Apple's iPhone to the Brazilian market. Its attractiveness will be to challenge the prevailing dynamics and role play that its coffee has to be Starbucks, its cocoa Toblerone, or its coltan Samsung, without appropriating any slice of the industrial value chain that can also be called proudly African (Lopes, 2015e).

Late President Nelson Mandela captured the spirit of what Africa's attitude should be where the metaphor of a fork in the road is evoked:

> There is no passion to be found in playing small and settling for a life that is less than the one you are capable of living … I could not imagine that the future I was walking towards could compare in any way to the past that I was leaving behind.
>
> (cited in Lopes, 2015e, p. 51)

Busting the myths about industrialisation in Africa

While economic theory singles the manufacturing sector out as the premier engine of growth due to the existence of dynamic scale economies (Kararach, 1997), several myths are bandied about for why Africa's industrialisation prospects have been stunted. We therefore need to address a few myths that continue to plague Africa's drive to industrialisation and why there is no truth in these allegations.

Myth 1: Industrialisation is a fashionable developmental term that will soon be forgotten

There continues to be strategic and policy changes in the posture of African states regarding development strategies. One may remember buzzwords such as "structural adjustment", "trickle down-effects", and "poverty reduction strategies" that exercised an enduring influence on the direction of national policy. Although the concept of industrialisation has always existed in the development literature, it has now taken centre stage. The call for industrialisation is now linked to the structural transformation and a developmental state (ECA, 2013; Lopes et al., 2017). Africa's Plan of Action for the Accelerated Industrial Development of Africa (AIDA) is supported by the AU, ECA, AfDB, and NEPAD; it demonstrates the extent to which the link between industrialisation and structural transformation is being taken seriously. AIDA is based on four pillars: using Africa's own natural resource endowment as a basis for industrial transformation; developing an infrastructural system including energy and transportation; increasing research and development and the adaptation of technology; and promoting private sector development, especially the role of small and medium scale enterprises. It is hoped that these enablers will lead to the structural transformation of the continent's economies. In the 1970s, South Korea had neither the skill nor raw material for developing a world-class shipbuilding industry but decided to pursue this path based on a well-developed industrial policy (Chang, 2007; Aderemi, 2018). Today, South Korea is one of the three largest shipbuilding nations. These are examples we need to think about. Although we need African solutions and priorities, we can learn from such successes (Zeleza, 2018).

Myth 2: Industrialisation is all we need to develop

African countries must begin to view industrialisation as a tool for the social and economic transformation of their societies, with structural transformation being the key outcome. Deng Xiaoping's transformation of China's economy is an example of the need to address industrialisation as part of a wider integrated and intergenerational process of development (Lin and Wang, 2014). Structural transformation can be realised by paying attention to key developmental elements, one of which is industrialisation (Lin and Monga, 2011). For example, African countries have to still deal with a demographic challenge and transform it into a dividend, not to mention social cohesion that should result from less inequality, embracing diversity, and enhancing human security and inclusive governance.

Myth 3: African countries have tried industrialisation before and it failed, so why now?

In the 1960s, newly independent Africa emulated other regions of the world by undertaking import-substituting industrialisation. This led to some remarkable progress but was ultimately stymied by the limits of the model and the vagaries of the global political economy (Kararach, 1997). This is why today Africa should be mindful of a very different global context. Africa needs alternate models that play to its strengths and satisfy the need for transformation. Brazil's *Bolsa familia* programme, discussed in Chapter 2, is one such example of achieving economic growth with social equality. With up to 90 per cent of Africans still heavily reliant on the agricultural sector, commodity-based industrialisation (which is discussed later in the chapter) speaks to that African strength. Commodity-based industrialisation also offers immediate scope for value addition and plenty of opportunities for exploiting consequential linkages. Botswana's decision to add value to rough diamonds before exporting them (ECA, 2018) ensured an extra $6 billion of diamond sales which are now going through the country's financial centres. This created new jobs for its youth whilst boosting the infrastructure and tourism sectors.

Myth 4: Africa comes too late to industrialisation without polluting the environment

The world has changed since the times of the industrial revolution. Coming late to the club provides Africa with the opportunity to industrialise differently (Aderemi, 2018; Landsberg, 2018; Lopes, 2019a). It is not about privileging export-oriented or import substitution models. The new industrialisation model must be closer to the commodities' production centres, keeping in mind Africa's potential for market expansion and leapfrogging technology. Opportunities exist to take advantage of innovations, technologies, and business models on a pathway that uses our natural resources optimally and efficiently as inputs for an industrialisation process, powered by Africa's endowments of clean sources of energy.

Myth 5: Africa's current economic growth will lead to job creation

Current economic growth models do not create enough modern jobs. In fact, the highest growing African economies also have the highest levels of youth unemployment (Hanson and Léautier, 2013). Although growth is robust in many countries, it is propelled by internal consumption that does not benefit all (ECA, 2017; Lopes et al., 2017). To reverse this trend, proper planning should focus on modernising economies through more manufacturing production taken from other parts of the world where unit values are increasing fast. The starting point should be positioning Africa in relation to its natural resources and potential assets in renewable energy. This opportunity basket is unique when combined with a younger, more educated, urbanised, and connected work force. Africa must also enhance its trade competitiveness as a key element of its industrial strategy.

The reality is that, even with today's unfriendly global policy space, African countries have a number of avenues through which to pursue the process of industrialisation, whether it be value addition, agribusiness or low-cost manufacturing. None of these are out of their reach with deliberate and coherent policies that are entrenched into a coherent development strategy and enlightened by a transformational leadership. The next sections discuss some of the "how" of industrialisation or the varieties of industrial policies. We discuss value addition, green industrialisation, trade policies for industrialisation, and the value of global value chains.

How Africa's natural resources and other untapped opportunities can drive an industrial revolution

While not all African countries are commodity rich, the continent has 12 per cent of the world's oil reserves, 40 per cent of its gold, 80 to 90 per cent of its chromium and platinum, and the world's largest renewable energy potential. Africa is also home to 60 per cent of the world's unused arable land and has vast timber resources (Figure 3.3). Fifty-three per cent of the world's cocoa is alone produced by two countries – Côte d'Ivoire and Ghana (ECA and AUC, 2013).

The idea that these abundant natural resources could be the driver for an industrial revolution across the continent is gaining pace. The 2013 edition of the Economic Report on Africa (ECA and AUC, 2013) sets out how the continent's future will be determined by how policies that promote commodity-based industrialisation are designed and implemented.

We believe that such a transformation is both imperative and possible. Nevertheless, it requires courage, vision, and a new mind-set from the continent's political and business leaders to overcome the challenges, which continue to detract from building a successful and dynamic industrial base in Africa.

There is no one-size-fits-all solution to problems of development in developing economies (Kararach, 2011), and more importantly, to accelerating resource-based industrialisation. However, important lessons can be learnt from the success of countries such as Malaysia, Indonesia, Thailand, and Venezuela in promoting value addition, new services, and technological capabilities while keeping in mind the constraints of isomorphic mimicry (Pritchett, 2010; Kararach, 2014). Interestingly, almost all the countries of

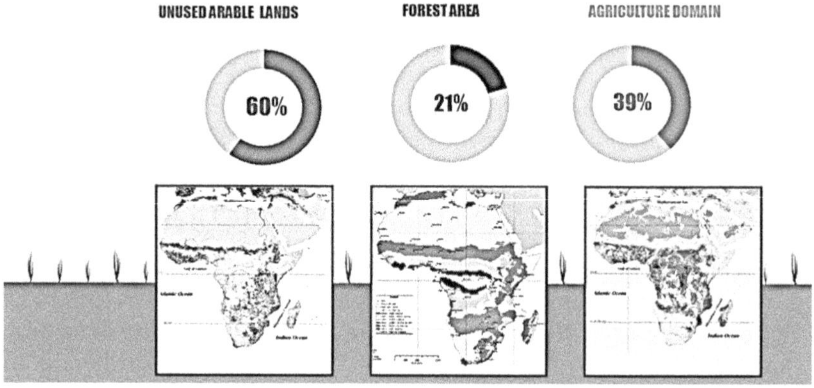

Figure 3.3 Africa's land status
Source: World Development Indicators, 2016.

East and Southeast Asia carried the baggage of colonialism just like Africa (Booth, 2007; Aderemi, 2018).

Malaysia, in particular, is an instructive example of how a commodity-based economy was transformed, through focused state interventions and an allocation of resources towards the industrial sector such that the country became a high-income and diverse manufacturer in only a few decades. Through a series of five-year development plans, centred on a vision to transform the structure of the economy and raise incomes in the medium- and long-term, investment was oriented towards industry. Today, Malaysia is a key manufacturer and exporter of a wide range of goods and services.

Governments, both individually and collectively, have an important role to play. A supportive policy and investment frameworks are essential to attract long-term investors. Policies to build local capacity and address inequality are also essential. Moreover, developing skills through training and incentives will ensure that local economies are able to grow and diversify (Kararach, 2014; Lopes et al., 2017).

However, a barrier to Africa's industrialisation that is not often talked about is the mind-set of private sector leaders – both in and outside Africa. Many are still indulging in the same historical rent-seeking attitudes that have resulted in the short-terms gains of crude, cocoa, and gold sales.

More business leaders need to change their thinking and understand that short-term revenue gains – as opposed to long-term value addition – offer little or no contribution to sustainable economic growth. Of course, there is a new cadre of African business leaders emerging who are building, investing, growing for Africa's future but they are rare. It is their efforts that will provide the jobs and income that will have the biggest impact on tackling poverty and driving wider social progress. Africa's private sector must take the lead in improving coordination between farmers, growers, processors, and exporters; in increasing competitiveness in the value chain; and ensuring the price, quality, and standards that markets demand are met.

There is a need to see national and regional champions created and supported, and to help foster effective collaboration between the public and private sector and the broader global development community. This is the essence of the emerging economic philosophy of "Africapitalism", a private sector led partnership mode focused on Africa's development.

There is already some real progress that has been made on the continent. Progress has been registered in forward and backward local linkages in the hard energy and soft commodity sectors in some African countries (ECA, 2018). Ethiopia's leather industry and Nigeria's oil supply industry provide good examples of linkages that are not only developing, but also deepening into high value-added activities. South Africa's input supplies industry and Egypt' textile/clothing industry are cases of well-developed linkages to and from the commodity sectors that are struggling to remain competitive. Ghana and Zambia are in the middle of the spectrum of linkage development. In both countries, the mining sector has been making a long and intrinsic contribution to socio-economic growth. Ghana has experienced an investment boom since the 1980s, and Zambia since the 2000s. In East Africa, the success of Kenya's fresh vegetable and cut flower producers in adding value to their exports has been remarkable (ECA and AUC, 2013).

The key challenge to African countries today is how to design and implement effective industrial policies needed to promote industrialisation and economic transformation (Aderemi, 2018). Important lessons can be learnt from the development success of China and other emerging economies in recent years (Lin and Wang, 2014).

However, when Africa only earns some 10 per cent of the income from its own coffee crop, there is much work that needs to be done. Africa today can create a new legacy. Sweeping political and economic changes over the last half century have reformed global power structures, reconfigured international relations, loosened old hegemonies and allowed new ones to emerge, and led to serious rethinking about alternate development paradigms (Hanson et al., 2012). These changes present a huge opportunity for Africa to emerge as a global economic power – and present a serious challenge too. Emergence will require leadership, vision, and strategies for long-term development (Kararach, 1997; Landsberg, 2018; Zeleza, 2018).

The lesson from resource-rich countries is that commodity-based industrialisation is possible – despite all the criticisms, which run along three lines: that it is as difficult as any other industrialisation path; that commodity sectors are unlikely to promote linkages and externalities; and that resource-based industries do not match Africa's factor endowments. The recent experiences of such countries as Venezuela, Argentina, Malaysia, and Thailand, Australia, Norway, and Scotland as well as the historical experience of Sweden, Finland, and the United States point to the contrary.

For African countries, success will require a good understanding of the critical factors that influence linkage development in particular and resource-based industrialisation in general – again an acknowledgment that one size does not fit all (AfDB, 2018). Upgrades in commodity processing require a supportive policy environment, domestic firm capabilities, and sector regulatory frameworks (Lin and Monga, 2011). Interventionist state policies will play a critical role and continental policy initiatives will present an opportunity for addressing some of the challenges.

Africa needs to frame specific, evidence-based policy for commodity-based industrialisation for each country in order to ground government initiatives that foster linkage development and accelerate the process within each country, sector, and dominant value chain. Value addition is still limited across Africa's nascent industrial sectors and the depth of linkages is more varied from country to country, mostly due to country-specific and/or industry-specific constraints that cannot be overcome by market forces. It is worth noting that up to 90 per cent of Africa's total income from coffee, calculated as the average retail price of a pound of roasted and ground coffee, goes to consuming countries. This clearly underscores the benefit to be realised and enjoyed by African countries if they were to increase value addition. Kenya's upgrading trajectory has been remarkable, as fresh vegetable firms have moved into high value-added exports. Effective collaboration between the public and private sector has played a critical role in designing and implementing strategies to support local upgrading processes. This sets an example for other countries.

Africa's economic future will be determined by how the continent designs and implements effective industrial policies needed to promote industrialisation and economic transformation (Mbate, 2016; Lopes et al., 2017; Okafor, 2018). Regional markets can facilitate local production linkages within and between African countries by providing learning opportunities and allowing domestic firms to build their production capabilities in a staged, systematic process (Oloruntoba, 2018; Konde, 2018).

With the abundance of its resources and the continued global demand for raw materials, African governments are currently forging new partnerships that are leading to increased infrastructure investments and the sharing of skills and technology. Nevertheless, Africa can do better. Instead of relying on exports of raw materials, African countries should add value to their own commodities to promote sustained growth, jobs, and economic transformation (Lopes et al., 2017).

Greening industrialisation

The green economy is based on the premise that social and economic progress must be achieved in ways that will not exhaust the earth's finite natural resources and that will cope with the concerns over lack of natural resources, environmental devastation, and climate change (ECA, 2016a).

Greening growth represents a new approach to industrial policy in Africa as leapfrogging is brought to the fore of the industrialisation process through smart technologies.

Since the 1930s, the most widely used measure of the strength of a nation's economic progress has been the GDP; a measurement of both the consumption and production within a country. This measure falls short of capturing the contributions to the economy of natural capital and ecosystems that are actually necessary for growth. Studies have shown that when GDP growth is adjusted to account for the actual loss of natural capital, in most instances growth actually becomes lower and in some cases is even negative. For example, if measured by GDP, the economies of China, the United States, Brazil, and South Africa grew by 42 per cent, 37 per cent, 31 per cent, and 24 per cent respectively, between 1990 and 2008. However, when assessed by the Inclusive Wealth Index[3] based on UNEP and UN University calculations, the Chinese and Brazilian economies only increased by 45 per cent and 18 per cent. The United States' grew by just 13 per cent, while South Africa's actually decreased by 1 per cent (UNU-IHDP and UNEP, 2012). Therefore, while the exploitation of natural resources may generate economic benefits in the short term, resource depletion will decrease the potential for economic growth and development in the long term.

We need a system of valuing resources that link economic concerns, natural resources, ecosystems, and human capital as part of development planning. Although quantifying costs of ecological and environmental damage can be challenging, a true measure of transformation must be the cost to countries if resources are lost.

The time has come for Africa to make the switch to a green economy. Natural resources are the backbone of the continent's recent economic growth, amongst the strongest in the world. In 2011, for instance, raw and semi-processed goods accounted for about 80 per cent of African export products, compared with 60 per cent in Brazil, 40 per cent in India, and 14 per cent in China. Agricultural commodities, timber, metals, and minerals, and hydrocarbons combined have accounted for approximately 35 per cent of Africa's growth since 2000 (AfDB, UNDP and OECD, 2013). They provide a basis for the livelihood of millions of people who depend on fertile soil, forests, fisheries, and other resources from nature for survival. Natural resources also sustain much of tourism and associated service industries.

Africa's structural transformation towards more value-added activities and modern jobs is closely linked to a strong natural-resource sector (ECA, 2018). This presents challenges. Since the start of the industrial revolution more than two centuries ago, industrialisation in Western countries has been a primary contributor to environmental degradation and global warming. Prosperity has been gained at the cost of the environment's regeneration, despite enormous socio-economic gains. Africa was a provider of the raw materials that contributed to progress in other parts of the world. The paradox of Africa as one of the regions causing the least harm to the planet is worrisome enough: its total CO_2 emissions per capita are less than one ton per annum and yet the entire continent has benefitted from this record. As a result, being at the end of the scale is no longer accepted. It accounts for just 2.4 per cent of world emissions yet climate damage as a percentage of GDP is higher in Africa than elsewhere in the world (Collier and Venables, 2012).

Africa can contribute to climate change solutions while industrialising (Kararach, 2014). For that, some key conditions must come into play, such as a global acceptance of the common but differentiated responsibilities principle. Those who have most responsibility for greenhouse gas emissions, and most capacity to act, must cut their emissions first. Africa needs recognition of climate justice so that it at least has some external help in its industrialisation path. Africa also has a variety of enabling opportunities of its own. As a latecomer at the early stage of industrialisation, Africa actually has the advantage of leapfrogging technology preferences to deploy those that are clean, efficient, and resource saving. This advantage would mitigate against wasteful consumption and resource depletion. While the technological and financial requirements of green industrialisation are considerable, reallocating investments towards the green economy will result in faster economic growth (ECA, 2016a).

The urban renewal potential

Urbanisation in Africa is growing at a rate more than twice the world's urban growth rate of 3.7 per cent a year (ECA and UN-HABITAT, 2016). This presents a rare historical opportunity for rapid industrialisation and socio-economic renewal. Africa stands to benefit from the rapid expansion of its cities much the same way Asia did. With the right public policies in place, marrying prosperity and density will result in economies of scale. Dense and compact cities can lower per capita emissions per square meter, while providing greater accessibility in terms of infrastructure and basic services. This in turn, can be a magnet for new talent and private capital investment (Glaeser, 2011).

However, the quality of the urbanisation process does matter, especially if it generates dynamic economies of scale and scope. Of all urban dwellers in Africa, 62 per cent live in slums, compared to 24 per cent in Asia or 43 per cent in Latin America. Between 2005 and 2010, the combined population of African cities increased by 17.3 million and projections indicate that between 2010 and 2050, Africa's urban populations will triple, reaching 1.2 billion people. In contrast to early-urbanised countries, Africa's urbanisation is occurring at low-income levels and with enormous infrastructure gaps, especially in energy and transport. Here lies an opportunity.

Climate change presents cities with an incentive for better urban planning and service delivery. Urbanisation is already jump-starting industrialisation; 40 per cent of Africa's population who now live in cities produce 80 per cent of its GDP. The continent is projected to be 50 per cent urban by 2030; so the potential for economic growth is formidable. UN-Habitat projects that by 2050, 20 African cities will be among the largest 100 cities in the world (ECA and UN-HABITAT, 2016). New cities are also likely to emerge as industrialisation and inter-regional trade generate increased activity. Cities are therefore central to realising the benefits of a green economy and gaining from employment opportunities, access to social services for human well-being, reduction of resource depletion and ecosystem degradation.

Energy is key

Sustaining the continent's energy demands and future growth will only be possible if fuelled by a much larger energy sector. At present, power generation is not reliable in most African countries. This impedes manufacturing from developing. Data suggests that industrial enterprises suffer an average of 56 days per year of power outages, losing 6 per cent of revenues (World Bank, 2018a: World Bank Group Enterprise Surveys). This slows investments.

Energy challenges are the norm in large parts of rural Africa as well. If current trends continue, almost 600 million people in rural areas will still lack access to electricity in 2030, and an even larger number will lack access to clean cooking facilities. It is estimated that by 2030, 1 billion people in Africa will depend on biomass as their main energy source (IEA, 2010). This is a critical concern, given that open fire stoves are widely used for cooking and will continue to have severe health impacts, particularly in the case of women and children under the age of five years, with indoor air pollution causing respiratory diseases such as pneumonia.

Africa's large agricultural sector and rural economy play an essential role in the continent's economic growth. Bringing power to isolated communities is essential to kick-start businesses and industries. For instance, Uganda used to have one of the lowest electrification rates in the world with only 2 per cent of its rural population having access to electricity. And now with just one investment, the Bujagali 250 MW hydropower plant will meet half of its energy needs while creating more than 3,000 jobs.

Africans currently consume only one quarter of global average energy per capita, using a mix of hydropower, fossil fuels, and biomass. Africa's renewable energy potential is substantially larger than the current and projected power consumption of the continent. Presently only 5 per cent of Africa's total hydropower potential is exploited. Africa, with an additional 900 TWh over 20 years, could provide full electricity access to all (AfDB, 2018). This amount corresponds to one year of current additional global power consumption. With gradually falling technology costs, Africa has the opportunity to capitalise on using its abundant renewable resources, for example, by using geothermal or solar thermal resources for heat or bio fuels and renewable energy-based electrification for urban public transport. At sea, the access to deep-sea resources, including shale gas hydraulic fracking or methane hydrates from deep sea floors, can benefit from more measured appetite in terms of Africa's great renewables potential.

"Greening" the blue economy

We note in Chapter 4 that Africa's oceanic mass is far greater than its land mass. The marine ecosystem and resources, as well the economy around the maritime industry, referred to as the "blue economy", are central to advancing Africa's socio-economic interests. The potential of its oceanic resources therefore offers a unique opportunity for Africa's transformation. In particular, it offers Africa's six Small Island Developing States (SIDS) and coastal countries opportunity to expand their resource base, which has traditionally been viewed as narrow. The consequences of climate change and rising sea levels exposed SIDS and coastal countries to both irreversible and life-threatening damage. SIDS are facing disproportionately greater vulnerabilities, given that, alongside marine fisheries, some of the more traditional economic sectors such as shipping, power generation, and manufacturing are concentrated around coastal areas.

By shifting to a green paradigm and using clean technologies such as greener refrigeration, improved waste management in fish handling, processing, and transportation, the ecological health and decline in economic productivity of marine and coastal eco-systems can be reversed. For example, the seabed currently provides 32 per cent of the global supply of hydrocarbons and is attracting further exploration. New frontiers of marine resource development are progressing, from bio-prospecting to the mining of seabed mineral resources, to tapping into the vast potential for renewable "blue energy" production from wind, wave, tidal, thermal, and biomass sources. In addition, aquaculture is also becoming a fast-growing food contributor, providing 47 per cent of global fish consumption.

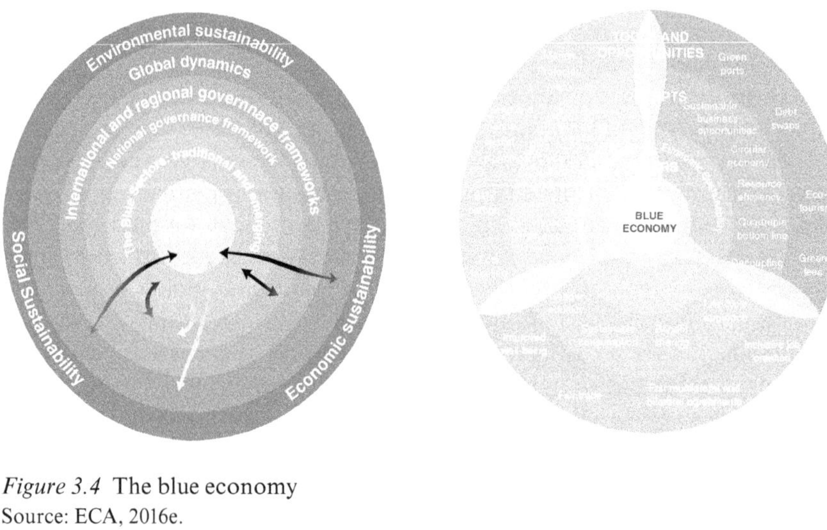

Figure 3.4 The blue economy
Source: ECA, 2016e.

In tourism, for example, the GDPs of Cape Verde, Comoros, Kenya, Madagascar, Mauritius, Mozambique, Seychelles, South Africa, and Tanzania are all largely dependent on "blue economy" strategies. A well-developed tourism industry in the Caribbean region is also attracting income of $1.9 billion from cruise operations; this could be an incipient offer in Africa.

Scaling-up green investments in marine and coastal resources and enhancing international co-operation in managing these trans-boundary ecosystems are essential if a transition to a low-carbon and resource-efficient green economy is to be realised. This involves for example, optimising the benefits to be reaped from fishery agreements or oil and mineral extraction and ensuring that Africa's interests are reflected in international ocean's governance mechanisms. Figure 3.4 shows a desirable blue economy framework for African SIDS.

Greening must be more than a slogan. It needs to be part of Africa's ambition for transformation that is premised on a different path from that which others walked before. The continent needs a careful reflection on how it utilises its resources and taps into opportunities to achieve the industrialisation imperative.

African trade policies have to match its industrialisation imperative

Trade continues to play a major role in Africa's economic growth performance and it has the potential to promote trade-induced industrialisation of the continent, provided that it is deliberately directed at industrialisation.

The key factors constraining trade and industrialisation in Africa are related to Africa's narrow production and export base, which is dominated by low-value products such as raw materials and primary commodities. Very high trade costs, tariffs, and non-tariff barriers to intra-African trade and Africa's access to international markets compound this constraint. The continent therefore has no other alternative but to increase its share of global exports. While in the 1970s, Africa accounted for 4.99 per cent of world trade and East Asia 2.25 per cent, by 2010, it had regressed to 3.33 per cent, while East Asia had soared to 17.8 per cent (ECA and AUC, 2013). Limited by poor infrastructure and inefficient logistics, lack of adequate skills and quality inputs, insufficient provision of credit and financial services, Africa's story has become one of lost opportunity. This helps to explain why Africa's current trade policy plays a major role in its inability to excel.

What we have learnt is that trade and industrial policies are now delinked from each other (ECA, 2015a). As a result, African countries exhibit high levels of protectionism with no tangible benefits in terms of productivity improvements. This is exacerbated by rent-seeking behaviour, which precludes the harnessing of dynamic comparative advantages. Accordingly, tariff structures often do not reflect industrial policy considerations but are the unsystematic result of successive rounds of reforms.

If one looks more closely at imported inputs, it is clear that tariffs weigh very heavily on the competitiveness of African countries. They stimulate neither the supply responses upstream nor the competitiveness of downstream industries. When properly applied, tariff structures are an instrument of a coordinated strategic approach and of consistency between trade and industrial policy frameworks. Such an approach could be called "smart protectionism" – better defined as making the rules work for you. All countries would like to practice it but African countries have not succeeded in making it happen.

Pursuing trade reforms in a strategic manner is a means of promoting and strengthening a country's competitiveness and creating favourable conditions for enhanced participation in value chains (ECA, 2016a). Where global value chains are concerned, there is a growing body of research that points to the relevance of the services sector in terms of its complex contribution to both value addition and employment creation (Low, 2013). Put differently, a dynamic services sector – for instance financial services or ICT – can exert wide-ranging spill-overs that lift productivity and enhance value along the chain. Within Africa, however, trade in services is still restricted by a number of mainly regulatory barriers.

It is vital that operationalisation of the Continental Free Trade Area also encompass intra-African trade in services. This would not only contribute to improving the scope for developing regional value chains but also ensure that the gains stemming from the creation of the Continental Free Trade Area are more fairly distributed among African countries, particularly those economies that are developing significant service hubs.

In addition, harnessing trade strategically means that African countries are able to ensure that the sequencing of trade liberalisation is consistent with their transformative agendas and commitment to regional integration. In other words, the sequencing of trade liberalisation should prioritise the reduction of tariffs and removal of non-tariff barriers within Africa. The fact remains that intra-African exports often face higher levels of protection vis-à-vis Africa's exports to the rest of the world, and the situation may worsen. The goal should be to have tariffs reduced between regional economic communities in order to avoid offering lower tariffs to Europe than those within Africa. This situation will have to be addressed in the context of the EU's Economic Partnership Agreements and its possible effects on the efficacy of the Continental Free Trade Area Agreement. Other limiting factors, such as non-tariff barriers, remain particularly pervasive and add to the burdens that weigh on the competitiveness of African producers since these barriers remain particularly high between regional economic communities.

Unilateral trade preferences alone can hardly enable the conditions required for the development of regional value chains. It must be realised that Africa can no longer afford to negotiate trade agreements as if industrialisation did not matter. We need to keep before us, as our lodestar, the message that trade can indeed support industrialisation but harnessing this opportunity requires a coherent policy framework, including a green industrial path.

Global value chains: greater diversification from agriculture and other commodities

Africa has missed the opportunity for more robust, diversified, and sustainable economic development. The Asian industrialisation experiences suggest there are good reasons for Africa to look at their models as a basis for its own industrial development. Specific industrial policies and programmes have worked in Asia and could be replicated in Africa. Among these are the sophisticated use of Global Value Chains (GVCs) and the Special Economic Zones (SEZs).

GVC operations concern the global division of labour in production processes and their concurrent effect on the distribution of income and profits between participating countries. Involvement in GVCs presents an opportunity for African economies to move beyond producing raw materials so as to enable them to build dynamic and competitive manufacturing sectors capable of processing the continent's abundant minerals and agricultural products. They also provide an opportunity to create sustainable jobs and stimulate inclusive growth while new markets for value-added products evolve both in the continent and among the industrialised and emerging economies.

SEZs are designated areas that have special regulations and economic incentives for organising production around processing and manufacturing activities (Lin and Monga, 2011). China's SEZs were key features of its early reforms, transforming coastal towns such as Shenzhen or Zuhai into industrial centres within a generation. In the context of its development cooperation with Africa, China has initiated and supported the operation of SEZs in several African countries (Lin and Wang, 2014) such as Algeria, Botswana, Egypt, Ethiopia, Nigeria, Mauritius, Tanzania, and Zambia.

African governments have granted favourable conditions to foreign investors in the SEZs, which they believe will create jobs and boost export earnings. With China graduating to higher-value industrial production, Africa stands to benefit from the outsourcing of lighter manufacturing businesses from China to African SEZs. With China about 85 million light manufacturing jobs to export, GVCs and SEZs could improve Africa's chances to win a fair share of this number and reverse its declining share on manufacturing (Lopes, 2013c).

The success of GVCs, SEZs, and other industrialisation initiatives requires the creation of an enabling environment that enhances requisite domestic capacity and capability, particularly in respect of physical and social infrastructure, human capital, technological innovation, financial systems, and governance (Chang and Andreoni, 2016). In addition, governments need to put regulatory frameworks in place for tackling market failures as part of a wider and all-inclusive industrial policy. The creation of such an enabling environment will help to realise the full potential of the African private sector.

Africa's vast unexploited resources and abundance of labour provide opportunities for development of the private sector and attracting private investments for economic diversification and value-addition. The phosphate industry in Morocco has positioned itself in all parts of the value chain from the production of fertiliser to that of phosphoric acid as well as derivative products. Its industrial strategy has led to continued growth and leadership, as it has been punctuated by the steady strengthening of the production tools and a policy of ambitious sustainable partnerships, supported by a prudent financial policy. The Office Chérifien des Phosphates has grown from several hundred people at its creation and revenues of $4.8 million (in 1920) to revenues of US $52.25 million (in 2010), and nearly 20,000 employees (Callaghan, 2013).

It should also be recognised that entrepreneurs in Africa continue to face greater regulatory and administrative obstacles and high transaction costs, which make doing business more difficult; hence, these obstacles and constraints must be addressed in any industrial policy. Finally, and importantly, deepening regional integration also offers the potential for Africa to tackle some of the challenges it faces in pursuing meaningful and beneficial industrial development.

The promotion of GVCs should be based on the complementarities between agriculture and industry, considering the potential of agricultural development to contribute to the creation of competitive advantage industries (Kaplinsky, 2000). In many African countries, given the dominance of agriculture in their economic structures, the sector will continue to be an important source of foreign exchange needed to import intermediate inputs for domestic industries. A major challenge in industrial policy, including its implementation through the establishment SEZs, is how to create mutually supportive linkages between the industrial and non-industrial sectors of the economy.

Some of Africa's natural resources that are exploited and exported represent irreplaceable, non-renewable assets; and their exploitation generally has weak economic linkages to the rest of the economy.

The upsurge in GVCs as a vehicle for economic diversification and the basis for resource-based industrial development is timely, given the increased demand for Africa's natural resources, together with increased urbanisation and consumer demand for processed goods within the continent. Domestic and sub-regional markets should therefore be a prime target. However, accelerating industrialisation through diversification of exports can also potentially contribute to the expansion of trade within Africa and between Africa and the rest of the world.

As part of the process of structural transformation, African countries should take targeted actions at national and regional levels to establish production and trade links and synergies between different actors along the entire agri-business value chain, through the provision of incentives for bolstering private sector investments and competitiveness (Konde, 2018). Together with SEZs, which have sprung up all over Africa recently, the shift from primary production towards modern integrated agri-business will undoubtedly be crucial for job creation and poverty reduction.

Preliminary evidence from some SEZs in Africa indicates that they are indeed creating new jobs and that workers in these zones are on average paid more than workers outside such zones. The macro-impact on jobs is still, nevertheless, limited to only a few countries. Ethiopia may be a good case for what needs to happen. The country is prioritising light manufacturing growth, particularly the leather industry, as part of its economic transformation programme. It recently landed a large investment by a Chinese firm producing designer shoes for the US and EU markets. Production is based at an industrial SEZ just outside Addis Ababa, Ethiopia, and it is estimated that over 25,000 jobs have been created through GVC and SEZ- FDI enterprises in the country.

Transformation beyond industry: examples of the creative and pharmaceutical economies

Africa's creative economy

A critical part of our argument is that Africa has grown in recent times but without transformation. Alongside the jobless growth, about 70 per cent of those employed in Africa are in vulnerable, low paying jobs, with many frequently falling in and out of poverty. To foster prosperity, African governments face the daunting challenge of tackling unemployment and creating millions of new jobs for a bulging population (Kararach et al., 2012). This is why there is a need to adopt a non-traditional approach to national development planning and strategies in order to boost not just individual efforts and circumstances for transformation. The creative and cultural industries are an increasingly important piece of the puzzle. These industries – design, fashion, film, television, radio, music, and much more – have all too often been overlooked as legitimate avenues for job creation and as contributors to the gross domestic product. African governments should embrace and support the creative industries in their efforts to drive sustainable development and create jobs. The creative industries should be an added layer in constructing more diverse and economically viable markets (Manzambi, 2017; Hruby in FT, 2018).

Africa's creative economy can trigger a value chain between artists, entrepreneurs, distributors, and support services across multiple sectors to provide modern jobs. Cape Verde is a good example of how a country can leverage such resources by placing the creative economy at the cornerstone of its development strategy (Lopes, 2015c). With few exportable resources,

Cape Verde is enabling its cultural assets to be a significant contributor to the country's economy. Its efforts have made it easier for artists and producers of creative goods to produce locally as well as for export. For instance, a micro-credit facility referred to as a Culture Bank was created in 2012 which facilitates access to "seed" money for small entrepreneurs and creative artists across the islands. To further encourage the creative drive, networks of crafts, art, museums, venues, and festivals have been set up across the islands so that everyday culture and arts help to stimulate the economy. The recent Atlantic Music Expo that took place earlier this year in the capital Praia was also a significant step that brought together a wide range of music industry professionals from across the world, connecting them to local musicians, entrepreneurs and distributors and helping to trigger the value chain.

It is estimated that the South African music economy will have an annual growth of 4.4 per cent between 2015 and 2020, fuelled by surging digital music streaming revenues. Similarly, in Kenya, the mobile music industry is starting to contribute to GDP in a measurable way: a $10m growth in industry revenue is projected between 2015 and 2020 (Hruby, 2018).

With respect to the fashion industry, building a network that increases opportunities for exposure, besides providing financial and knowledge support to individual producers, will enhance local markets in different African countries and boost the global presence of African fashion through trade. Euromonitor (2015) reported that Sub-Saharan Africa's apparel and footwear market is worth $31bn, and Africa together with the Middle East are expected to provide fashion's long-term growth. This is an expanding industry where efficient use of talents working in the informal sector can result in huge income generation.

More importantly, there is a growing class of new consumers associated with rapid urbanisation and sizeable incomes that have brought about a rise in domestic consumption and demand for products and services closely aligned with their lifestyles. This is propelling public spending and private investment in culture. Lagos has a larger consumer market than Mumbai and spending in the continent's households exceeds those of India and Russia.

Technology and the digital revolution have opened doors for the continent to be a trailblazer for frugal innovation. For instance, digital cinematography gave rise to Nollywood, allowing it to mushroom and to become the third-largest film industry by value in the world, after Hollywood and Bollywood. It generates an estimated $500 to $800 million annually and is one of the largest Nigerian employers by sector, second only to agriculture. On average, more than two thousand feature-length movies are made each year. A feature movie sells an average of 50,000 copies at about $2 a DVD, offering Africans an affordable entertainment option. Nollywood's model of rapid production and home consumption is now being exported across the continent, with countries such as Cameroon, Ghana, Kenya, and Mali adopting this model over traditional American or European features.

Africa's creative industry now needs to go "digital". Research suggests that the highest growth within the creative industry is in technology-centred industries such as software programming and video games; the lowest is in music and film. While animation and game development is gaining traction in some African countries, there is ample scope and opportunity to develop this further (Lopes, 2015c).

There is growing political recognition that creative industries can fuel growth. Numerous international summits and publications confirm this; for example, UNCTAD has been publishing Creative Economy Reports and two-thirds of African countries have signed the Convention on the Protection and Promotion of the Diversity of Cultural Expressions (FT, 2018). This convention calls for greater investment in the creative and cultural industries and for creative products from the Global South to have preferential access to Northern markets. At the continental level, there are several policy documents that support the development and growth of creative industries: these include the 2008 Nairobi Plan of Action on Cultural Industries; the 2010 Abuja Declaration and Charter for African Cultural Renaissance; and the more recent Praia Declaration focusing on the potential of young Africans in the creative economy.

The state has a key developmental role in designing, implementing, and monitoring robust institutional and regulatory policies that will commercialise and support creative forces. An enabling regulatory framework accompanied by legal protection is essential. Piracy, for instance, remains a major obstacle due to weak copyright and intellectual property rights regimes as well as poor enforcement capabilities. South Africa estimates that it loses 44 per cent of DVD revenues, 15 per cent of which is online (Lopes, 2015c). For the creative economy to grow, it is imperative to operate under a functioning system of intellectual property rights. This will not only regulate ownership and give creators or authors control over the use of their work but also facilitate trade as well as encourage serious investment in the sector.

Strengthened partnership with the private sector and civil society would go a long way in ensuring investments in all elements of the value chain, from building human capital to strengthening domestic supply capabilities. In the past, Africa has lost many artists trying to make a living and who are then obliged to accept the theft of their work. This is one of the reasons why many artists leave and live abroad. Africa can no longer afford a continued talent drain. Instead, the focus must be on strengthening and providing specialised education and training, including entrepreneurial and business service skills, support for artistic development, modernising production, strengthening distribution networks, and promoting consumption and branding. Given that the majority of the enterprises in the creative industries are small, partnering and facilitating access to finance, in the forms of credit, grants, and loans, are key.

Tapping into the pharmaceutical sector

Africa has 25 per cent of the world's disease burden but consumes less than 1 per cent of global health expenditure. It manufactures less than 2 per cent of the medicines it consumes. Over 70 per cent of the world's HIV/AIDS cases and 90 per cent of the deaths due to malaria currently occur in Africa (UNAIDS, 2012). In addition, the continent suffers from 50 per cent of global deaths of children under five, mainly due to neonatal causes as well as pneumonia, diarrhoea, measles, HIV, tuberculosis, and malaria. The tragedy is that these diseases are treatable: most related deaths could be prevented with timely access to appropriate and affordable medicines. Development in the pharmaceutical sector will go a long way in supporting the enhancement of the quality of human capital and broader delivery of the desired structural transformation in Africa.

Lakdawalla (2018) found that the pharmaceutical industry accounts for a substantial proportion of the US economy's research and development (R&D) investments, which have resulted in significant medical breakthroughs. These R&D investments are more driven by efforts to reduce product liabilities, thus enhancing firms' performance in horizontal and vertical industries. Unfortunately, Africa's capacity for R&D, which includes local drug production, is amongst the lowest in the world (Kararach, 2014). The problem of inadequate investments in this area continues. Overall, 37 African countries have some pharmaceutical production, although only South Africa produces some active pharmaceutical ingredients. Where there is local production in Africa, normally there is a reliance on imported active ingredients. As a result, the supply of African pharmaceuticals remains highly dependent on foreign funding and imports. The pharmaceutical market in Africa is now made up of 70 per cent imported content. Estimates further suggest that more than 80 per cent of antiretroviral drugs (ARVs) across the continent are imported (ECA, 2014a).

The reason African countries should prioritise investing efforts to change the circumstances in the sector is linked to the issues of intellectual property rights (IPR). Stiglitz (2006) notes that intellectual property rights grants "exclusive control of the use of a particular piece of knowledge, thereby creating monopoly power. Monopolies distort the economy. Restricting the use of medical knowledge not only affects economic efficiency, but also life itself" (p. 1279). He goes on to argue that the tolerance of IPR is based on a false belief that such restrictions might spur innovation, thus balancing costs against benefits. However, the costs of restrictions can outweigh the benefits. And:

> [it] is hard to see how the patent issued by the US government for the healing properties of turmeric, which had been known for hundreds of years, stimulated research. Had the patent been enforced in India, poor people who wanted to use this compound would have had to pay royalties to the United States.
>
> (ibid.)

The establishment of the WTO in 1995 saw the imposition of US style intellectual property rights on pharmaceutical products around the world. These rights resulted in the reduction of access to generic medicines. As generic medicines cost a fraction of their brand name counterparts, billions of people could no longer afford the drugs they needed. For example, a year's treatment of a generic cocktail of AIDS drugs might cost $130 compared to $10,000 for the brand name version. Billions of people living on $2–3 a day cannot afford $10,000, even though they might be able to scrape together enough for the generic drugs. And matters are getting worse.

It can cost much more for the new drug regimens recommended by the WHO as well as second line defences that need to be used as resistance to standard treatments develop. Developing countries paid a high price for this agreement. Drug companies have instead spent more on advertising and marketing; more on research on lifestyle drugs than on life saving drugs; and almost nothing on diseases that affect developing countries only. This is not surprising. Poor people cannot afford drugs, and drug companies make investments that yield the highest returns (ibid.).

The poor access and affordability of medicines are compounded by factors that include long lead times for international orders; infrastructure gaps such as poor logistics and storage capacity, as well as high transport and distribution costs. In addition, there have been scarce public finances and deficient public health procurement systems. It is estimated that there is a gross scarcity of essential medicines in both the public and private sector. People are also often being forced to buy medicines that may not be certified. A major consequence of this situation is that costs and other obstacles to accessing medicines have significant implications for the fight against poverty (Niëns et al., 2010).

Many African governments spend a disproportionate amount of their scarce resources on procuring medicines. For instance, in 2006, Mali and Burundi spent 2.3 per cent and 2.9 per cent, respectively, of their GDP on such imports. In a study of Swaziland, Mhlanga, and Suleman (2014) found that private sector original brand (OB) medicines were priced 32.4 times higher than international reference prices (IRPs), whilst lowest-priced generics (LPGs) were 7.32 times higher. OBs cost 473 per cent more than LPGs. The total cumulative mark-ups for individual medicines range from 190.99 per cent to 440.27 per cent. The largest contributor to add-on cost was the retail mark-up (31 per cent to 53 per cent). Standard treatment with originator brands cost more than a day's wage.

On the other hand, the public sector was procuring medicines at a slightly lower price than their IRPs. Half of the lowest-priced generic medicines were priced at 0.79 to 1.72 times their IRP. Trends now indicate that new health challenges facing the continent will generate demands for extra resources on the back of exorbitant costs. Non-communicable diseases, such as heart disease, lung disorders, diabetes and cancer, are increasing due to demographic and lifestyle changes. These conditions will account for half the deaths in Africa, surpassing those caused by infectious diseases.

An additional difficulty results from the excessive use of originator brands, with much higher prices than the lowest-priced generic equivalents. To add to this concoction, the poor quality of drugs and their regulation not only fuel illicit transactions but also contribute to health problems. It was not long ago that 64 per cent of antimalarial drugs in Nigeria were found to be counterfeit!

Scaling up pharmaceutical production is crucial for the effective health systems in Africa. It can enhance population access to vital medicines at a lower cost, including those in rural areas. Better health is central for people's opportunities and contributes to them being more productive. The economic costs of disease are well known for families and the national economies. The direct and indirect impact of malaria alone is estimated at $12 billion of annual African income (Global Fund, 2012). Local production of medicines is therefore possible and has become imperative.

In attempts to keep the costs of drugs and related products down, there have been experiments in advancing market creation or commitment – the idea that committing to purchase vaccines against diseases concentrated in low-income countries (if and when desirable vaccines are developed) as a way to spur research and development on vaccines for these diseases. Under such an "advance market commitment", one or more sponsors would commit to a minimum price to be paid per person immunised for an eligible product, up to a certain number of individuals immunised. For additional purchases, the price would eventually drop to close to marginal cost (Berndt et al., 2007). However, with economic growth projected to be buoyant and Africa pursuing an agenda for economic transformation, there is a huge market opportunity. Local manufacturing could create modern jobs, stimulate economic activities, and in many ways increase productivity.

The pharmaceutical industry involves legal, scientific, technical, fiscal, and financial aspects. In order to step up their production capability, countries need to tackle challenges on a variety of fronts. These range from R&D and exploring the full utilisation of the Trade Related Aspects of Intellectual Property Rights (TRIPS) flexibilities, tax, and tariff policies, drug regulatory and registration systems, and, of course, building infrastructure. Indeed, a few African countries such as South Africa and Uganda have benefited from the TRIPS exemption in the Doha Round with respect to certain medicines in the treatment of HIV, malaria, and TB.

In some pockets of the continent, predominantly in North Africa and in South Africa, the status of local manufacturing of pharmaceutical products has gained a sturdy foothold. For example, Egypt and Tunisia produce most of their national requirements for essential medicines. Morocco, the second largest African pharmaceutical producer after South Africa, has 40 pharmaceutical industrial units supplying 70 per cent of domestic demand and exporting 10 per cent of their production, particularly to neighbouring African countries. Significant production capacity is being developed and enriched in Tanzania, Kenya, Uganda, Ethiopia, Ghana, and Nigeria. Mozambique has just commissioned an ARV plant with the help of Brazil.

Indeed, Africa hosts some of the leading global innovators and generic manufacturers: Starwin in Ghana, Saidal in Algeria, Universal in Kenya, Aspen in South Africa, or Cipla in Nigeria and Uganda are home-grown manufacturers. This goes to demonstrate that Africa is producing medicines that meet international standards. However, to enhance the pharmaceutical industry generally, there is a need for fewer structures and better harmonisation of policies through regional integration. Intra-Africa trade offers the prospect for strengthening and better exploiting regional supply chains and expanding economies of scale. This would also make larger investments attractive. To be able to generate wealth and give its future generations a chance, Africa must take ownership of its health.

Conclusion

If the news about growth is good, then more is wanted and needed across the entire continent. It must deal with the challenge of industrialising and growing when its population and cities are increasing faster than in any previous historical period. It needs more growth which will have to be more rapid than any other region of the world. There is now a greater urgency to turn the "no hope" appraisal about Africa into a "rising" continent story predicated on meaningful change that will prove the sceptics wrong. This must be underpinned by embarking on a sustainable industrial pathway.

Five decades of development planning have not yielded the 7 per cent, which is the minimum required to double average incomes in a decade. Instead there are a range of highly unequal and vulnerable economies that remain entrenched in poverty. The evolution of industrial policy in Africa mirrors the evolution of development planning. These include the import substitution policies that took root after the independence era when planning was enthusiastically driven in the 1960s through to the 1970s; the structural adjustment programmes of the 1980s when planning waned and the state was rolled back; and then followed by poverty reduction strategy papers in the 1990s when liberalisation, deregulation, and privatisation were entrenched as methods of economic management. The weaknesses in understanding Africa as well as its misrepresentation during these periods has a lot to do with the deficits in industrial production and the incidences of de-industrialisation. This is ironic since most governments implemented various industrial policy strategies and interventions to promote industrial development (See Tekere, 2001; Mudenda, 2009; Grosen and Coflkun, 2010; Mohammed et al., 2011). Manufacturing as a share of output and employment decreased or remained low over most of these periods (ECA and AUC, 2013).

As African countries prepare to take their rightful places in the future global economy, they have a real opportunity to promote economic transformation through the industrialisation process by capitalising on the continent's abundant natural resources, adding value to them, while also supporting the development of infant industries. The manufacturing sector in particular has been the engine of economic development for the majority of developed countries, and very few countries have developed their economies without a strong manufacturing base, so much so that the terms "industrialised" and "developed" are often used interchangeably when referring to such countries.

As latecomers, it is clear that the conditions under which African countries could promote their own industrialisation processes are difficult. In order to forestall such difficulties, governments can and must develop industrial policies that build the necessary capabilities that respond to national and regional needs but within the confines of global rules. This would call for a systematic assessment of current trade and investment policies and agreements with a view to reviewing such policies and negotiating or renegotiating such agreements; and where possible, manoeuvring through the available flexibilities to ensure that reciprocal control mechanisms are in place. It would also entail examining the possibilities for "smart protectionism" measures – such as the use of tariffs, subsidies, foreign direct investment and other policies at the disposal of African countries – that are not directly trade-related and therefore not covered by the WTO or other trade and investment agreements.

Finally, establishing a solid political foundation requires that governments have embedded autonomy that invests in solutions that are rooted in the needs of their societies while having the conviction to execute "best fit" policies. The role of the state is therefore critical in shaping macroeconomic planning. Successful implementation also requires state pragmatism, risk-taking, and constant adaptability to changing local, regional and global conditions.

Having now made the strategic case for industrialisation and industrial policy as a key driver of the transformation agenda, the next chapter turns to understanding other dimensions that are relevant to our considerations. There is a particular emphasis on how agency can be a potent force of empowerment through better governance, bringing in the voices of women and youth, harnessing Africa's natural resource assets, developing the blue economy, promoting regional integration, peace and security and so on. Africa needs to seek all the key enablers of transformation.

Notes

1 Botswana, for example, has Vision 2030 to guide its diversification agenda. Other countries with such plans include Uganda, Ethiopia, South Africa, Kenya, Tanzania, and Nigeria, to name but a few.

2 The Partnership in Statistics for Development in the 21st Century (PARIS21) was established by the United Nations, the European Commission, the Organisation for Economic Co-operation and Development (OECD), the International Monetary Fund, and the World Bank to promote the better use and production of statistics throughout the developing world.

3 Aims at revealing the true state of a nation's wealth and the sustainability of its growth, beyond GDP.

4 Understanding other key enablers of Africa's structural transformation

Introduction

African countries have several other opportunities to change the circumstances and individual efforts that underpin current developments beyond those outlined in Chapter 3. This chapter builds on the discussion of the previous chapter and focuses on the other key enablers of structural transformation by outlining how they can be exploited positively for changing the "circumstances" and "efforts" of the continent. Here we extend the discussion on the importance of agency as a critical analytical tool for understanding how big the continent really is; and what can be tapped into as material for delivering the continental transformational agenda. Core to this perspective is that Africa has made significant progress with enhancing its political and economic governance frameworks and this has had positive effects on its development trajectory. For example, the continent has signed up to most international and regional instruments for advancing gender equality and women's empowerment. The recent increase of women in parliaments and other corridors of power has vastly contributed to giving them political and economic voice.

Furthermore, globalisation is in flux. The once dominant influence of the West is diminishing, and it will have to forge a new relationship with Africa. Meanwhile the new players, India and China, have increased their engagement with Africa in rather dramatic ways by transforming Africa's traditional trade and investment relations. In recent years, the largest increases in foreign direct investment to Africa have been from the BRICS. This new paradigm of engagement reflects cooperation in which partners see themselves as peers in mutually beneficial relationships. More importantly, the concept of pan-Africanism has continued to evolve, measured by the challenges and aspirations of the African continent. Pan-Africanism as an ideal enjoys renewed relevance which can be seen from its continuous attraction to intellectuals both on the continent and in the diaspora. Its effect, however, will be measured by the continent's collective ability to adjust to new demands and how new generations shape the evolution in African agency to change the "circumstances" of the continent's transformation.

The impact on African agency comes up against the reinforcement of negative perceptions about the continent. Reversing this dynamic takes place in the context of renewed activism by African states. This is both enabled by and contributes to the diffusion of power in multilateral forums and the subsequent evolution in the circumstances and efforts of transformation. At its most rudimentary, and in the absence of other means by which the bigger economies can dominate multilateral forums, "numbers count" and, with 54 states, Africa can play a crucial role in alliance formation and deal making (Lee, 2011; Zondi, 2011; Kararach, 2014). Such alliance formation strengthens the influence of developing country groupings such as the WTO-based Group of 20, and through the role of the "cotton club" in promoting a common objective.

Although the results have been patchy, these dynamics afford the continent the opportunity to re-examine the underlying factors and circumstances that influence decisions in multilateral forums. With UN reform, the Africa common position outlined in the Ezulwini Consensus[1] was arrived at through a consensus-forming process. Because of the need to accommodate disparate interests, it resulted in an implausible and inflexible negotiating position that left Africa marginalised in UN discussions (Zondi, 2011, pp. 9–11). This can be contrasted with the outcome of the Copenhagen negotiations on climate change in 2009, where there was a better common Africa position (Hoste, 2011). Yet the collective position could not withstand disparate national interests, with South Africa taking a key role in drafting the Copenhagen Accord without any AU oversight and following pre-summit bilateral deals and splits between Ethiopia and Sudan which undermined AU cohesion on climate change (Hoste 2011, pp. 6–7; Zondi, 2011, p. 15). These experiences cast a spotlight on the political limitations of pan-Africanism, continental solidarity, as well as the strictures of pooled sovereignty within the AU (Zondi, 2011, p. 5, 17).

That said, it would appear that "pan-Africanism" is being put in practice today through regional integration and trade. For many years, Africa has been a mere price-taker in global trade relations, having little or no influence on markets. It now has an opportunity to transform itself into a price-maker. The expanded avenues for South–South cooperation, notably intra-African trade through the continental free-trade area, break the monopoly of developed countries by providing a better environment for African policymaking and choice in trade partnerships. One of the key lessons for Africa from the EU's experience is that the institutional environment has to be conducive to the fostering of regional trade.

The continent essentially needs to put its various physical and soft resources to better use, including those that are not properly tapped. Noteworthy is the fact that Africa's informal sector has generated tens of thousands of individuals and multiple communities who essentially make a daily living through their own inventiveness. The contribution of this sector is largely unknown or estimated because of a lack of reliable data; but it is significant.

All this hidden talent is a key ingredient of the creative economy. Equally, Africa's natural resources wealth needs to be strategically tapped into.

However, for the continent to sustain its growth trajectory, there must be security of citizens and property. Greater peace and security is thus essential. Since the turn of the century, with the exceptions of the 2004 Gatumba massacre in Burundi, the Darfur conflict, extremist and irredentist activity across the Sahel region, and the perennial Somali war theatre, complex conflicts have not only been on the decline, but the very nature of warfare has also changed. Reduced conflicts have created both the material and institutional contexts for sustained growth. Understanding the other key development drivers will be essential in shaping the policy responses for structural transformation and the achievements of 2030 SDGs and Agenda 2063.

Emerging political and economic governance: beyond Pax Africana

There is growing evidence about how African agency has sought to shape the discourse and direction of African development (Hanson et al., 2012). Reforming governance is thus key for improving the impact of political, economic, and social decisions and functions. A number of actions are required in this area. Progress has been made. The need to address corruption in Africa is of primary importance, with a focus on easing the fiscal space and optimising resource mobilisation as ingredients for structural transformation.

Combating corruption

Delivering social equity as a means of combating corruption demands governance reforms that empower poor and marginalised groups by giving them a voice. This must include accountability which increases service providers' incentives to respond to the needs of the poor. Responsible and accountable service provision, in turn, enhances government revenue and expands fiscal space so that citizens are more willing to pay taxes (Kedir et al., 2016). Investing in the social capital of the most vulnerable is also paramount since it allows the populace to be active players in the setting and implementation of the transformation and poverty reduction agenda (UN, 2010; Bhengu and Wallis, 2018). Another core and complementary pillar of the inclusion effort is guaranteeing access to and protection of property rights. However, access to and protecting property rights is a complex issue since such rights derive from several sources such as legislation, government policy, customs, and religious practice. As such, the history of property rights is usually context-specific. Strategies for legal and other reforms need to consider these complexities when it comes to providing for marginalised groups, combating corruption, and expanding access to essential services.

The greatest challenge to Africa's structural transformation agenda is not corruption of the sort in corporate and public-sector scandals; fraud and bribes can be effectively tackled with improved supervision and more stringent enforcement of governance rules (Kaufmann, 2006). In general, fundamental economic governance problems are found on an entirely different level, namely, the inability of both the public and private sectors' managers to act effectively by enhancing programme delivery and optimising results (Kararach, 2014). Furthermore, effective regulatory frameworks should strike a balance between fostering private sector development and enhancing social transformation for better service delivery (Bhengu and Wallis, 2018). In this regard, a wider approach to the structural transformation agenda needs to be adopted by focusing on actions that not only tackle corruption but also enhance wider economic and corporate governance (ECA, 2016d).

Combating corruption must also include international and regional instruments that advance gender equality and women's empowerment, and that are non-discriminatory and socially responsive. A concerted effort and collaboration between legislators and other arms of government is essential since laws and policies alone do not necessarily introduce the changes needed. While they do provide a normative framework for protection and support by the state as well as a basis for engagement amongst stakeholders, they cannot be isolated from other socio-economic improvements.

Women's empowerment

Research is needed that correlates the gains in social equality and progress in equal representation in legislative bodies; however, the latter is a demonstration of strong public opinion that favours diversity recognition.[2] Changing the plight of African women thus needs laws that incentivise transformation. These must be able to regulate heritage, access to assets, and capital; provide equal opportunity to girls and boys; and protect the girl child from being married at an early age. The importance of women parliamentarians in such critical processes is obvious because as mothers and providers, they have faced situations which their male colleagues only hear about (Ocran, 2014).

Over the past 20 years, the representation of women in parliaments around the world has increased and Africa has been no exception (Bauer, 2013). By 2012, 11 African countries were among the world's top 36 houses of parliament that reached the 30 per cent threshold which is considered necessary for women to have an impact on decision making (ECA, 2014c). Amongst the countries in the world with the highest number of women elected to parliament, seven are African, with Rwanda occupying the top position. As of 2014, Rwandan women made up 64 per cent of the Chamber of Deputies and 38 percent of the Senate. With these figures, Rwanda has exceeded the gender parity targets set out in the Beijing Platform for Action as well as in the Protocol of the African Charter on the Rights of Women in Africa. This is by all means an historical achievement.

Indeed, the Inter Parliamentary Union shows an increase in percentages of women in parliaments across Africa; including 49 per cent in Namibia, 44 per cent in the Seychelles, 43 per cent in Senegal, 42 per cent in South

Africa, 40 per cent in Mozambique, 37 per cent in Angola, 31 per cent in Burundi, and others such as Algeria and Tunisia with over 30 per cent (ECA, 2014b). These figures make Africa a top performing continent in securing women's political agency. In seven African countries, at least 30 per cent of cabinet ministers are women, with Cape Verde recording the highest number at 50 per cent, ranking second globally after Finland's 63 per cent.

South Africa, Burundi, Tanzania, and Guinea-Bissau also rank among the top 20 countries globally with the highest numbers of women ministers. The adoption of gender responsive electoral models, the use of affirmative action as well as quotas have also helped ensure an overall representation of up to 20 per cent of women in parliaments across the continent. The speed with which gender quotas have been implemented depends on the parliamentary systems adopted: those with first-past-the-post electoral systems such as Ghana, Malawi, Nigeria, Botswana, and Zambia have been the slowest (Bauer, 2013; Ocran, 2014).

The ascendance of female cabinet ministers into "hard" portfolios, such as Defence, Foreign, and Home Affairs has defied the stereotypes of women being confined to "soft ministries" that address welfare issues (Ocran, 2014, pp. 69–70). Africa is starting to become used to prominent female leaders such as Presidents Ellen Johnson-Sirleaf of Liberia, Catherine Samba-Panza of the Central Africa Republic, or former President of Malawi Joyce Banda; and there have also been a few Vice-Presidents, including Inonge Wina, from Zambia. Indeed, one of the foremost African international figures is the former Chairperson of the African Union Commission, Dr Nkosazana Dlamini-Zuma. Women in such positions of authority are contributing to changing the mind-sets about the role of women in governance and multilateral cooperation (Kararach et al., 2013).

Indeed, increasing educational achievements by women and their rising participation in the labour market have not been matched by better conditions of employment or prospects for advancement and equal pay (WEF, 2017). At the current rate of progress, the ILO estimates that it would take more than 75 years to reach equal remuneration for work of equal value. Dynamic African countries will not be built if women and girls, who form most of the population, remain marginalised or excluded. The question therefore is what legislative action could remedy this situation?

For a start, labour market policies could bolster women's access to income by guaranteeing adequate minimum wages and equal pay for work of equal value. Additionally, carefully designed social protection policies could increase women's income security as well as strengthen their voices.

It is vital that parliamentarians focus strategically on leveraging the sectors that are poised to bring about the structural transformation needed in the continent. This entails the revitalisation of the industrial sector, including manufacturing, agri-business, and adding value to extractives with full women opportunities.

The Africa Regional Review Report on Beijing + 20 shows progress in the economic empowerment of women in agriculture, business development, and finance (ECA, 2014c). A number of countries since the 1990s have made tremendous strides in the successful institutionalisation of gender-responsive budgeting initiatives. This methodology has undoubtedly become an important tool for promoting gender equality. In 2012, more than 20 per cent of African countries had such initiatives. South Africa and Tanzania were among the pioneers of gender budgeting in Africa. In 1996, South African NGOs collaborated with Members of Parliament and jointly launched the South African Women's Budget Initiative. This has been cited as one of the most successful and institutionalised initiatives. Ethiopia, Rwanda, Tanzania, and Uganda have also considered women's concerns in their national budgets.

Despite these pockets of progress, gender inequality and women's empowerment still requires upstream policy formulation and re-energised efforts to close the gaps in sectors that are lagging behind (WEF, 2017). The first challenge is to effectively exercise an oversight role to ensure the formulation of inclusive gender and socially responsive legislation, particularly in transformative and productive sectors. For instance, a strong call must be made for policies, laws, and programmes to harness Africa's Green and Blue economies as well as women's economic participation in them as a response to climate change challenges.

Second, parliamentarians across all frontiers need to work together in advocating responsive policy frameworks for social equity. The range of opportunities and space offered by ICTs as well as a wide array of knowledge platforms facilitates swift communication and information sharing which could give the population more voice and stronger agency.

Finally, a woman farmer in rural Africa is quite removed from the daily news in Europe and the USA with regard to what women are doing to enhance their incomes. For instance, in 2015 *The New York Times* reported the growing number of women in the USA and Europe selling their breast milk, and hence, transforming it into a commodity. This example of market maximisation is just one more demonstration that the world needs a compass on ethics and development and women in parliaments are the most capable of providing it. However, widening socio-economic governance beyond parliamentary engagement has other positive side effects, including enhancing creativity and ensuring better natural resource management and associated strategic exploitation. Creating the conditions to allow "individual efforts" or human capabilities for structural transformation to thrive requires a governance framework that is people-centred, responsive, accountable, facilitative, and transparent (Bhengu and Wallis, 2018, p. 135).

Exploiting innovation and young talents

We noted in Chapter 2 that a core element of structural transformation is the notion of "individual efforts". Africa is endowed with "soft" resources that could be deployed to facilitate its structural transformation aspirations. One only needs to pick up a magazine or leading newspaper to read about innovations that are sweeping across Africa. This includes M-Pesa, a mobile money transfer service invented in Kenya that has revolutionised African banking practices; and South Africa hosting the Square Kilometre Array, the world's largest and most powerful radio telescope ever constructed. Africa has led science and innovation since ancient times (Diop, 1974; 1987). Its accomplishments, however, have seldom been attributed or publicised. They range from algebraic equations born some 35,000 years ago to the engineering genius of the pyramids; from the astronomical brilliance of the Dogon people, to architectural masterpieces of Timbuktu or Great Zimbabwe.

However, advancing Africa's science, technology, and innovation (STI) and its effective application to economic transformation is the new challenge for transformation. According to UNESCO's science report 2010, R&D in Africa still attracts less public funding than the military, health, or education sectors. A survey of 19 Africa countries by the AU-NEPAD in 2012 revealed that only Malawi, Uganda, and South Africa had invested more than 1 per cent of their GDP in R&D, while the rest spent between 0.2 and 0.5 per cent. UNESCO's science report of 2010 estimates that only 0.3 per cent of GDP is dedicated to R&D on average across the continent (UNESCO, 2010). This is seven times less than the investment made in industrialised countries.

The continent has also only registered 0.6 per cent of worldwide patent applications, compared to 51 per cent in Asia. Africa recorded 0.4 per cent of gross domestic R&D expenditure compared to 1.6 per cent for Asia. Although innovation is pervasive, the value of innovations made, their quality, relevance, and impact are overshadowed by limited investment in knowledge generation and commercialisation. The situation is further compounded by the shortage of highly trained scientists and engineers. In 2007, one could count only 164 researchers per million Africans against a world average of 1,081. Despite lagging behind globally, there is an air of excitement brought about by the rapid adoption of new technologies and the explosion of frugal innovation hubs, which are helping drive the continent's transformational agenda.

African countries such as Kenya, Rwanda, Morocco, Nigeria, and South Africa have the ingredients to take-off in the same way as technology leaders such as China, the Republic of Korea, or Brazil did during previous technological revolutions. China's rise, for example, took place over a period of just three decades under reforms introduced by Deng Xiaoping which lifted more than 400 million people out of poverty. Its most successful ingredient was the establishment of numerous Special Economic Zones (SEZ) and their industrial clusters (Lin and Wang, 2014), as discussed in Chapter 3. In just 15 years from their formation, the clusters accounted for half of China's high-tech gross industrial output and one-third of its high-tech exports. Today China is the second largest economy in the world. If other nations could make it, Africa should have the same.

Africa's often-criticised informal sector happens to also be one of the most inventive environments (Daka and Toivanen, 2014; Links et al., 2014). It is a breeding ground for frugal innovation and resilient entrepreneurs (Welter et al., 2015) who can literally make treasure out of trash, from tools to grass-cutting machines to water pumps, and anything one may need in that environment. Technologists of this informal economy represent a huge pool of indigenous talent that Africa must engage in its industrialisation process. The informal sector constitutes a very important size in the economy. Traditionally, it was associated with increasing poverty and weak employment conditions. It now includes investment by entrepreneurs seeking to reduce costs related to wages, retirement pensions, and other social benefits. Organising the informal sector and recognising its role as a profitable activity (Malyamkono and Bagachwa, 1990) will contribute to further harnessing Africa's STI potential as well as formally recognising and recording it.

The advent of the ICT democratisation is offering Africa's polity opportunities to leapfrog the industrialisation stage and bridge technological divides. Africa is already bypassing traditional means with technologies such as wireless, satellite bandwidth, and frugal mobile technologies that have relatively lower physical infrastructure requirements and investment costs. Ecobank has built a financial transactions platform that now covers 35 countries, while Airtel rates first worldwide in introducing common rates for voice and data use in 18 countries. The continent is well positioned to absorb, adapt, and build on the vast quantities of scientific and technical knowledge that is already available worldwide to solve its local socio-economic challenges from agriculture to health and environment. Regional economic integration could create more solutions. Without strong integration, the narrow market size of most countries will act as a liability. Africa needs to embrace the concept of locomotives where key hubs act as pullers for the rest.

Africa is the second biggest mobile market in the world. Mobile penetration rose from 1 per cent in 2000 to 73 per cent in 2015, surpassing the number of mobile users in the US, India, or Europe. Unique mobile subscription has been growing at an annual average rate of 11 per cent over the last five years, with 557 million subscribers in Africa by the end of 2015 (GSMA Intelligence, 2016). Estimates put the total value-added contribution of Africa's mobile ecosystem to GDP at around $50 billion in 2015 (GSMA Intelligence, 2016).

Africa has applied its own genius and adapted the use of mobile phones to new areas. Mobile and e-initiatives are revolutionising a range of sectors. For example, they help healthcare agents to target out-of-reach beneficiaries; allow farmers access to real time market information; and create virtual classrooms in education or monitoring elections. There are apps that have been developed and tailored by Africans. These continue to flourish with innovations such as Mafuta-go, Afritab to the VMK elika smartphone driven by the desire to balance price and quality so as to match limited purchasing power across the continent. Affordability has been the key restraining factor in developing markets, but this constraint is rapidly diminishing. GSMA Intelligence's 2016 report showed that smartphone average selling prices (ASPs) fell from $230 in 2012 to $160 in 2015 (GSMA Intelligence, 2016). Many providers have also produced smartphones that cost less than $50. For example, MTN Nigeria's Smart S720i sells for $50 and Orange has recently launched Orange Rise 31 for $40 (GSMA Intelligence, 2016).

Mobile financial services continue to deepen, thanks to advancements in mobile money. A 2015 study conducted by the European Investment Bank reported that Africa leads the world in mobile banking (EIB, 2015). Financial inclusion is also on the rise as a result. Africa accounts for over half of the 271 live mobile money services in 93 countries, and 64 per cent of all active mobile money accounts globally (GSMA Intelligence, 2016). Africans are finding it more convenient and efficient to use mobile money as a means of cross-border money transfer – 17 of the 29 expanded corridors on cross border remittances initiatives are in Africa (GSMA Intelligence, 2016).

To boost innovation, entrepreneurship, and R&D infrastructures, there are currently over 200 specially supported projects called Hubs. These include Innovation Hubs, Technology Labs, Fablabs, Science & Technology Parks, and incubators and accelerators in over 30 African countries. An additional incubator is mushrooming every fortnight. Examples include Kenya's iHub, Liberia's iLab, Nigeria's Co-Creation Hub, which concentrate on the use of social capital and technology, as well as Senegal's ICT incubators. Soon, Africa will also be host to technology cities such as in Konzo, Kenya, which is now called the Silicon Savannah. Major IT companies such as IBM, Samsung, Google, PwC, Nokia/Siemens, and Huawei, amongst others, have hosted labs or African Headquarters in Kenya. Recent data shows that, in 2015, $185 million was raised by 125 African tech start-ups (GSMA Intelligence, 2016).

The continent has been also testing sophisticated technologies. Examples include Joule, an electric car; the Ahrlac, the first defence orientated aircraft to be made and assembled in Africa; LifanX-60, a sports car designed for Africa and assembled in Ethiopia; as well as a growing aerospace industry in Morocco and Tunisia. Like Toyota at its foundation, some of these ambitions are not being noticed. Nevertheless, it is a beginning that can be essential for mastering the innovation curve.

Creating high-tech, scientific, and innovative industries attracts skilled human capital. There are indications that many of Africa's growing economies such as Nigeria, South Africa, and Ghana have significantly increased the retention of educated workers. The next step is to attract skilled diasporas back to African countries. Similarities can be drawn with the creation of science parks in several countries in Asia, including India, which triggered the return of former migrant engineers and researchers trained abroad because of remarkable market growth.

Why do Africans still have to go abroad for research and training when sophisticated innovations are emerging across the continent? A strong relationship exists between the strength of a country's higher education system and its overall ability to innovate. Secondary education in Africa has expanded considerably in recent years, according to UNESCO's Global Education Digest 2011, but still lags behind all other regions in the world (UNESCO-UIS, 2011). A large gap remains in the quality of the education provided. Few African universities offer advanced degrees and research programmes responsive to the knowledge needs of the economy while the overall cost of higher education is prohibitive. These challenges require a number of practical actions.

First, measures such as improving human resource training to offering technical skills as well as promoting linkages between businesses and educational institutes are valuable for inserting Africa into the higher end of global value chains. Lessons can be drawn from Brazil's success over the last four decades. Approximately 80 per cent of the top Brazilian universities have at least one incubator, and many are involved in the establishment of science and technology parks, thereby creating closer linkages with industry across the academic world.

Second, Africa's STI advances have to face a more regulated space than other regions when they made their jump. Intellectual property rights have evolved so much so that today they are anything but friendly to new entrants. Protecting indigenous knowledge systems, practices, innovations, and technologies is no longer enough. A much higher ambition is necessary to insert Africa into global value chains in order to propel the continent to acquire new technologies.

Third, several conditions will determine whether Africa can lead a technological revolution. These include adequate financing, strengthening linkages with research and academic institutions; access to qualified human resources; and access to reliable infrastructure such as communications, energy, and transport. Without adequate infrastructure, further technological and scientific developments are simply not possible (Kararach, 2014).

Fourth, Africa's problems are not unique. To compete, participate, and be recognised in the global economy, STI in Africa must be made a prominent focus of national development plans across the continent and progress must be made to improve R&D investment, efficiency, and policy coherence. Global financial institutions and bilateral development agencies must also devise more comprehensive strategies to integrate STI into their development efforts. The success of China can be attributed to the priority in its national development strategy to policies aimed at enhancing long-term growth prospects, including policies on technology, human capital, and institutional development.

Finally, to fully harness the opportunities before it and to build on its remarkable achievements so far, it is essential for Africa to go beyond the sum of individual capacities. It must build on existing capacities, assets, and the ability of its people and institutions; but above all it will only accomplish this ambition through integration. Essentially, there is need for self-confidence as Africa's creative talent continues to be showcased across the continent. It must optimise the use of its "soft" resources alongside those of other natural resources. Indeed, bolstering creativity will define how other resources, including minerals and agro-commodities, are utilised and their beneficiation enhanced.

New natural resource finds

We noted in Chapter 1 that natural resources are the other enablers of structural transformation. Natural resources such as hard minerals, oil, and gas are increasingly playing a greater role in the development of African economies (Kararach, 2017; ECA, 2018). However, Africa's political economy has a deeply ingrained history of exploitation and (mis)management of mineral and natural resources. More than 500 years after commercial exploitation of Africa's resources, Africa continues to host many of the large and unexploited deposits of minerals globally. Yet, with minor exceptions, Africa does not consume or add significant value to these and other mineral products which it has in abundance. Rather, African countries are net exporters of raw materials that fuel prosperity and development for other countries and regions of the world. Africa is largely seen as a price-taker rather than a price-maker, with a marginal role in international trade.

The question that arises therefore is why the continent continues to struggle with limited economic transformation, low or no resource rents, and scarce employment. In the last ten years commodity prices rode the wave of a super-cycle and yet Africa's share of windfall earnings have been miniscule, compared to what mining companies have realised. Average net profits for the top 40 mining companies grew by 156 per cent in 2010, whereas the proportion for governments grew by only 60 per cent. Most of this was accounted for by Australia and Canada, two countries that graciously want to share their experience with Africa. Indeed, most African countries got much less than this, due to generous tax holidays given to mining companies!

There is large but controversial literature on the natural resource curse on Africa (Kararach and Odhiambo, 2016; ECA, 2018). The range of concerns for African countries include but are not limited to declining terms of trade for commodities, exchange rate pressures, price volatility, poverty, and income inequality. The net effects of these factors upon growth and development outcomes remain inconclusive and at times dependent on the nature of governance and related institutions.

Economic institutions are a critical factor in economic growth and development (North, 1990). The focus of the policy debates is on the role of governance and institutions as determinants of economic growth and development in the presence of vast but depletable resource riches (Karl, 1997; Acemoglu et al., 2001; Rodrik et al., 2004; Brunnschweiler, 2008). In this context, any "curse" is associated with the impact of resource endowments on institutions and governance. In this scheme of things, resources induce distorted behaviours of rent-seeking, corruption, patronage, and other unethical ways of doing business. Deterioration in governance and associated institutions in the presence of natural resources therefore present developing African countries with real dangers to sustainable human development. Global Witness (2017) reported a deterioration in the quality of institutions in Uganda as more and more natural resources came on stream.

In equal measure and over the years, a wide range of solutions to enhance the positive development outcomes of natural resources has emerged. These include, amongst others: the pricing and taxing mechanisms of the natural resources (Dasgupta and Heal, 1979; Dixit and Newbery, 1985; Karp and Newbery, 1991); optimal extraction of natural resources (Hotelling, 1931); and enhancing intra- and intergenerational allocation of resource revenues (Takizawa et al., 2004). Most of the policy proposals are normative nature and suffer from limited practical implementation (van der Ploeg, 2010).

If the issue is looked at from another dimension, the profit made by the same set of mining companies in 2010 was $110 billion, which was equivalent to the merchandise exports of all African LDCs in the same year. It is fair to say therefore that the resource-to-development model puts raw materials suppliers at a significant disadvantage. The conclusion that can then be drawn from this situation is that the current resource-for-development model is not working to bring about equity or boost development.

Against this background, the African Mining Vision, jointly developed by the AU, ECA, AfDB, and other UN agencies, was adopted by the AU Summit in 2009. The Vision advocates the "transparent, equitable and optimal exploitation of mineral resources to underpin broad-based sustainable growth and socio-economic development" (AUC, 2009).

At the core of the African Mining Vision is the realisation that Africa's mineral resources can be better utilised on a number of fronts and to address: the continents social and economic needs; its focus on environmental and social sustainability; the advantages of regional and international integration with a focus on hard and soft infrastructure challenges; the emphasis on building backward, forward, and sideward linkages from the core mining sectors; and the promotion of equitable principles of fairness in benefit sharing and use of resource revenues.

To achieve the high aspirations of this vision, Africa needs to get back to the fundamentals and rectify some of the initial problems that have continued to plague the management of the continent's natural resources. Central to this endeavour is the capacity of governments to get the best deals for their countries during contract negotiations. Capacity deficits have also been identified in the critical areas of auditing, monitoring, regulation, and improving resource exploitation regimes. In the DRC, a government committee reviewed 61 mining deals over the decade up to 2006 and found none were acceptable. It recommended renegotiating 39 and cancelling 22 (IPIS, 2008).

In the wake of increased international copper prices and after years of subsidising large multi-national companies working in its copper belt,

Zambia successfully raised taxes for mining companies from 25 to 30 per cent, and introduced a windfall tax for exceptional profits. This earned it an extra $415 million in supplementary revenues. Other African countries have initiated similar cancellation or review of resource contracts, including Guinea, Zambia, Tanzania, Liberia, and Nigeria, in order to increase their resource revenue bases (ECA, 2018).

International processes such as the Kimberly Process for diamonds and the Extractive Industries Transparency Initiative (EITI) for other minerals, though with their own weaknesses, have contributed to improving transparency and accountability in contract negotiation processes from the production side. In addition, the Dodd-Frank Wall Street Reform and Consumer Protection Act in the USA and other similar acts have also created avenues for fair play within international circles (Shaw and Polonenko, 2015).

On the other hand, reducing the policy space available for Africa within international trade negotiation processes must also be checked. Unfair trade treaties and rules set out by international bodies that penalise Africa's value addition process to its primary commodities need to be reviewed. This is especially important considering increased demand and competition for Africa's minerals from the rising South, especially China and the Far East.

Second, and in geological terms, Africa is still the "unknown continent", with vastly unexplored quantities of extractive potential. Geological mapping and mineral inventory have not covered the entire continent, thus leaving its true geological potential unknown (ECA, 2018). African governments do not have the capacity to take stock of their mineral resources and have to rely on trans-national companies in order to assess the commercial capacities of newly found discoveries, especially oil and gas. This lack of verified data severely compromises negotiation capacity and the continent's bargaining power. New technologies abound that will make it easy for Africa to have a better appreciation of its natural resource base but this is held back by a lack of sustained and well-financed commitments, with exploration largely left in the hands of the private sector.

A third and important structural measure is a better integration of Africa's development policies. Africa needs to embed long-term development objectives firmly into the processes for extracting natural resources. For mining to benefit Africa's people, strong backward and forward linkages in the local economy should allow local entrepreneurs and industrialists to take advantage of service provision and technology transfer opportunities because of proximity to the mining industry. This means investment in infrastructure, research, and human capital development by insisting on conditionality for local content. This is what other regions have done and this is what Africa needs to do.

Within this paradigm of development-led mining, the potential of small-scale mining should also be harnessed in order to improve rural livelihoods and integration into both the rural and national economy. There are other necessary prerequisites such as the building of human and institutional capacities towards a knowledge economy that supports innovation, research, and development; the promotion of good governance of the mineral sector in which communities and citizens participate in decision making and in mineral assets; and in which there is equity in the distribution of benefits.

However, the importance of the mineral sector must be seen in perspective. Tumbling commodity prices have refocused attention on the sustainability of growth in Africa. For over a decade, high demand and rising prices for Africa's commodities have contributed significantly to growth on the continent. However, and since 2011, the continued fall in the price of oil and natural gas, and more recently other minerals, have threatened to turn tailwinds into headwinds. Declining demand in major emerging economies, coupled with continuous fragility in developed economies as well as volatility in the currency and shrinking confidence, all call for a reality check.

The global commodity price index declined from between 125 and 150 between August and December 2014 to below 90.5 in December 2015. Crude oil prices dropped from over $100/barrel in September 2014 to less than $37/ barrel by December 2015 (see www.bloomberg/energy). Average annual metal prices declined by 17 per cent in 2015 and continued falling in 2016. In fact, some stipulate that the prices of minerals and metals are now at their lowest since August 2002. Mining companies are trying to allay fears about profit losses by reducing production, with some estimates suggesting cuts in capital expenditures by up to $20 billion for 2015.

It is not only African countries that are subjected to bad weather. In emerging and developing economies, GDP growth has declined from 4.3 per cent in 2014 to 3.8 per cent in 2015. Brazil faces trade deficits estimated at $40 billion, from a trade surplus of $20 billion in 2010. Russia has similar challenges with growth of only 0.5 per cent in 2014, compounded by geopolitical tensions and associated sanctions. Colombia, Turkey, Mexico, and Chile have all seen their currencies fall between 20 per cent and 50 per cent against the dollar during 2016–2018. Stock markets have responded to declining prices with continued drops in prices, some often quite steep. However, the slowing down of growth in China is by far the most impactful and the lowest in a quarter century (*Economist*, 2018).

However, African countries remain resilient: the impact of recent decline in oil prices on Africa's growth has been less than expected (Kararach and Odhiambo, 2016) and indeed, has only had a marginal impact. In fact, Africa's growth is more attributable to internal demand as well as improved macroeconomic management. Progress in economic growth and rising wealth are contributing to the estimated $1 trillion projected rise in Africa's assets by 2020. This is a nearly a threefold increase from a total of $293 billion in 2008, according to research by PricewaterhouseCoopers across 12 African markets (PwC, 2015). Indeed, Africa's traditional assets under management (AuM) is expanding aggressively, supported by megatrends such as its demographic surge, fast growing middle class, increased use of technology, and rapid urbanisation.

Food security remains a critical challenge for Africa. Despite remarkable macro growth figures, food security has eluded much of Africa over many decades. The continent is faced with two broad tendencies: a rapidly rising population implying a rising demand for food. The other feature is one where farmers in African countries are subject to a variety of risks resulting from, *inter alia*, droughts, floods, and other natural calamities that undermine agricultural productivity and sustainable food production. The role of technology and research in African agriculture in a bid to transform the sector, raise its productivity, and secure food availability is generally accepted (Kararach and Kedir, 2019). Science and technology strategies are essential to improve agricultural productivity and food security in Africa (InterAcademy Council, 2004). Minten and Barret's (2008) research clearly indicated the need to support technological investments for improved agricultural production as one viable source of economic diversification and as an important part of any strategy to reduce the high rates of poverty and food insecurity that have stubbornly plagued the continent for many decades.

Many years of growth research shows the high returns associated with R&D investments in terms of growth and poverty reduction. Robert Solow won the Nobel Prize in economics in 1987 for his discovery that technical change is the engine of growth. Apart from the fundamental inputs to production such as land and labour, investment in science, technology, and agricultural research is what brings about technological change as well as the structural transformation of agriculture with interlinkages to other sectors of the economy. To achieve agricultural productivity, food security, poverty reduction, and their role in the transformation of Africa, there is an increasing recognition of the need to invest in technology and research. Strong political commitment is also needed, given the predominant rural nature of poverty in Africa and the persistently low levels of R&D investment, particularly in agriculture.

Another area requiring urgent investments in R&D is the energy sector. Energy is equally of utmost importance, from driving domestic consumption, health and education services provision to its industrial use. Africa is well endowed with renewable and non-renewable energy resources that far exceed its energy demand requirements for the next century. Paradoxically, most African countries are characterised by energy poverty and poor energy access, even for energy-producing countries such as Nigeria and Cameroon. This is partly a reflection of their low-income status and general state of economic underdevelopment. Energy security and development are thus more interlinked in Africa than in other energy producer regions of the world. Reducing "energy poverty" should be an essential component of African development policy. Many producer states are authoritarian, and their populations exist in conditions of deep internal poverty. Natural resource governance initiatives such as the Extractive Industries Transparency Initiative and the African Mining Vision as well as principles of prior and informed consent are yet to be seriously adopted (ACBF, 2012;

Kararach and Odhiambo, 2016). This exists in a few African countries such as Angola, Sudan, Chad, and Uganda. The link between development and energy security should be applied in all contexts. Several African economies have experienced rapid expansion in recent years. Improving terms of trade due to the solid global demand for commodities, and greater inflows of capital and debt relief schemes are some of the drivers contributing to these high growth rates. However, the great challenge facing African economies is how to meet all the Sustainable Development Goals (SDGs).

These goals call for progress on a number of fronts, as well as GDP growth rates that are even higher than those that currently exist. This calls for higher levels of domestic investment in a few areas and increased productivity of the economy in order to attain sustainable and inclusive development for the continent. Real GDP growth rates need to be 7 per cent or more per annum. Yet the productivity and overall performance of African economies are hampered by the state of the energy sector, among other factors. Lack of energy services, or poor access to them, militate against African economies' ability to realise their great potential. Measures to overcome energy insecurity are continually attracting the attention of governments, international lending agencies, non-governmental organisations, and other stakeholders.

Historical and empirical research has revealed a close correlation between the use of energy and broader economic growth and quality of life (e.g. Kraft and Kraft, 1978; Akarca and Long, 1980; Yu and Hwang, 1984; Yu and Choi, 1985; Erol and Yu, 1987; Ammah-Tagoe, 1990; Abosedra and Baghestani, 1991). Surveys undertaken in the 1990s established that developing countries' achievement of sustainable socio-economic growth could be measured by energy consumption. For example, for annual electricity consumption below 1,000 kWh per capita (where 60 per cent of the world population falls), indicators such as literacy rates and access to potable water remain under 40 to 50 per cent, respectively. However, when per capita consumption reaches 2,000 kWh, the same indicators rise to 85 to 90 per cent. This correlation has also been established for human development indicators such as infant mortality or life expectancy (Gaillard, 2010).

It is projected that worldwide demand for energy will increase significantly over the coming decades, particularly among developing countries (Gaillard, 2010). Three-quarters of the projected increase in carbon dioxide and other green gases emissions will come from fossil fuel consumption in developing countries and commercial energy supply will be concentrated in a small number of them. These patterns of global energy production and consumption are set to give rise to multiple challenges: global warming and other environmental concerns, geopolitical conflicts, significant rises in fuel price, and the depletion of fossil fuel reserves (Kararach, 2014). Consequently, the social dimensions (the fight against poverty), the economic dimensions (competitively priced energy and security of supply), and the environmental dimensions of these energy demand and supply patterns constitute a huge challenge to the achievement of sustainable development objectives (Monga, 2010).

High and highly volatile energy prices make Africa vulnerable to energy-based shocks and have pushed energy security to the top of the political agenda. Energy security is a core pillar of the Programme for Infrastructure Development in Africa (PIDA) (AfDB, 2009/10). Unavailability of energy services is an obvious cause of energy insecurity. Compared with other parts of the world, energy deprivation or the lack of access to energy is most prevalent in Africa (Monga, 2010). Over the last four decades, the gap between energy supply and demand in Africa has grown and is expected to continue to do so (UN-Energy, 2007) due to the recent economic expansion and steady population growth. Challenges for the energy sector include the use of renewable energy; improving energy efficiency;[3] the diversification of energy supply; the development of energy infrastructure; and the promotion of new energy technologies by exploiting innovative models of technology transfer (Kararach, 2014).

Other challenges are energy trade and regional integration; reform of the continent's electricity industries; and the economic vulnerability of African countries to oil price fluctuations. Within Africa, the situation differs dramatically between rural and urban regions as well as between Northern, Sub-Saharan, and Southern Africa. North Africa is heavily reliant on hydrocarbons; Southern Africa depends to a very high degree on coal; and in Sub-Saharan Africa (except South Africa) traditional biomass is by far the dominant fuel source (Monga, 2010). This high degree of intra-African variability requires differentiated approaches to tackle the issues related to the continent's energy security (Kararach, 2014).

Water is another important constraint on the structural transformation of African economies. Issues around water have led to debates about the possibility of "water wars" (Wolf, 1998; Chikozho, 2012). Countries need to build resilient systems to ensure access to water for all people, and to improve water-delivery and sanitation provisions for Africa's rapidly growing populations, especially in urban areas (Kararach and Yepes, 2017). The continent must expand the capacity to harness wastewater. With investment and proper management, wastewater can become a sustainable source of wealth for many Africans, with added benefits for human health, agricultural productivity, and environmental sustainability.

Only a few African cities collect and treat any more than 20 per cent of the wastewater generated through centralised wastewater-management systems. The remaining 80 per cent constitutes a huge untapped source of potentially valuable liquid and solid waste. With the right investment, foresight, and commitment, this underappreciated resource can create jobs and deliver sustainable growth.

Wastewater management is thus a central feature for the improvements of Africans' quality of life. It is capable of boosting public health, achieving gender equality, creating jobs, and increasing communities' resilience to the effects of climate change. Water will also play a key role in industrialisation and sustainable-farming objectives.

The continent must invest to reduce the frequency of flood incidents. In February 2017, flooding and strong winds from Tropical Storm Dineo devastated the coast of Mozambique and had a severe impact on the local population. Such incidents point to the need for Africa to develop business innovations for affordable and sustainable sanitation services.

Improving the quality of life for all Africans will require political commitment, public–private partnerships, and robust public involvement. All stakeholders – across Africa and internationally – must redouble their efforts to ensure clean and affordable water for all as part of the broader structural transformation agenda.

The fact remains that many of Africa's fortunes are still driven by the commodity sector (Cheru, 2017). Over 80 per cent of total African exports are still linked to commodities, with extractive industries taking the lion' share. The amount of value addition is estimated at just over 10 per cent. The formal employment generated by mining is only 1 per cent on the continent. These two elements are obviously related: Africa is simultaneously exporting its commodities and jobs. While African countries have done little to reverse such an appalling situation. Africa needs to catch up with its expanding labour force and do so fast. Equally, the continent needs to view its resource base beyond what exists above and under the ground to include sea and oceanic resources. The blue economy may be considered the real next frontier that could spur Africa's development.

Exploiting the blue economy

Recently, oceans governance and the term blue economy has been motivated by three factors. First, is the sheer extent and significance of oceans for development: oceans cover 70 per cent of the earth's surface; fish provide a critical source of protein for international markets and coastal communities; and, new sectors such as deep-sea mining and aquaculture are developing rapidly (Campbell et al., 2016). Second, most oceans are beyond national jurisdictions with many resources held in common and where UN-led multilateral governance is fragmented. Third, state and private interests in ocean conservation and development are high, as reflected for example, by the launch of the World Bank Global Partnership for Oceans (Campbell et al., 2013; Abbott et al., 2014). Arguably, a range of actors employed the term "blue economy" at Rio +20 in order to bring ocean conservation and development to the attention of the broader global environmental governance community, to raise priority problems as well as preferred solutions.

The term "green economy" is part and parcel of global environmental governance (Brand, 2012; Onesti, 2012). Green economy proponents espouse a conservation and development vision based on the notion of "new environmentally friendly technologies" and "a global policy network of private and public actors" (Haas, 2012, p. 95). The prominence of this term and the associated governance practices and mechanisms, can be read as part of a longer process. This is where the scientific and social justice underpinnings of global ecology give way to a managerial ontology of natural capital (McAfee, 1999; 2012).

The desire to conceptualise nature in economic terms has underpinned environmental policy, funding and programme implementation in the past 10 to 15 years (Suarez and Corson, 2013, p. 65), and although valuation methodologies are debated (Dempsey and Robertson, 2012), nature is now embraced as a solution to socio-economic crises as well as aspirations. Protected areas, payments for ecosystem services, biodiversity derivatives, and so on are seen as remedies for environmental problems and flagship opportunities for accumulation (McAfee, 2012; MacDonald and Corson, 2012). Rather than needing to pay their way amidst competing political–economic priorities (as in McAfee, 1999), species, resources, and ecosystems are recast as "the driver for the global economic recovery" (Corson et al., 2013, p. 3). As Silver et al. (2015, p. 138) put it: "A core difference between green economy and sustainable development is the former's grounding in the logics of capitalist growth rather than in recognition of its contradictions and inequalities."

The UN Convention on the Law of the Sea (UNCLOS, est., 1982) has formalised the right of coastal states to claim, access, and manage resources within 200-mile exclusive economic zones (EEZs). Through this framework nation states have claimed and utilised coastal seas and in-EEZ marine resources over the last 50 to 60 years (Mansfield, 2001; Steinberg, 2008). However, EEZs represent only 42 per cent of the oceans (Suarez-de Vivero, 2013).

The ECA (2016b, p. 16) has argued that:

> Africa would be better served by a sustainability approach for the development of the Blue Economy, which goes beyond a narrow focus on increasing national wealth and focuses more directly on the achievement of inclusive growth, social inclusion, environmental conservation, and protection of ecosystem services.

There are several African countries with coastlines. More importantly, of the world's 52 Small Island Developing States (SIDS), six are in Africa. They include Cape Verde, Comoros, Guinea Bissau, Mauritius, São Tomé and Príncipe, and the Seychelles. These countries range in size from the smallest, the Seychelles, which is composed of 115 small islands representing the largest number among African SIDS; to the largest, Guinea Bissau, which comprises over 80 islands. For most, these countries provide romanticised images of tourist heavens characterised by tranquil beaches, palm trees, clear turquoise waters, or colourful coral reefs (Lopes, 2014b).[4]

Economist E.F. Schumacher's seminal work in 1973, *Small is Beautiful*, sought to counter arguments to well-rehearsed economic maxims such as "growth is good" and "big is better", and succeeded somehow, in casting some doubt on widely held views on growth and expansion (Schumacher, 1973).

While most African SIDS would meet Schumacher's categorisation of smallness and classify them as beautiful, such images tend to hide the many vulnerabilities such small island states face (Haskins, 2012). Some of the challenges include geographical isolation, food insecurity due to limited agricultural base, labour shortages, climatic pressures, commodity and broader trade dependence; and precarious geopolitical existence.

Among the many threats facing African SIDS, climate change is probably the one issue demanding urgent continental attention. The distinct coastal zone concentration of their populations, infrastructure, and socio-economic activities make these countries vulnerable to any sea level rise due to climate change. For example, about 80 per cent of the infrastructure and population of the Seychelles is concentrated along the coast of just a few islands. In addition, SIDS have a limited physical size and are susceptible to frequent and intense cyclones, hurricanes, droughts, and storms.

The criteria that define SIDS are ambiguous and ignore the huge potential afforded by the associate oceans or blue economy. For instance, not all SIDS are technically "islands", although they lie along the coasts, for example Guinea-Bissau; nor are all SIDS "developing states". On the contrary, Cape Verde, Mauritius, and the Seychelles are middle income countries. By coming together, SIDS have been able to form a unified group for addressing their general vulnerabilities. For example, they have been recognised as a "special case" in multilateral environmental agreements such as the United Nations Framework Convention on Climate Change (UNFCCC).

Despite this, the distribution, scale, and severity of idiosyncratic shocks tend to vary across the SIDS, yet all SIDS tend to be lumped together in one category. The lumping is a "natural" outcome of the commonalities that define SIDS such as smallness in size and domestic market, geographic remoteness, proneness to natural disasters, environmental fragility, limited ethnic fractionalisation, better governance, dependence on foreign sources of finance, openness to trade shocks, and small populations and skill shortages (Briguglio, 1995; Tisdell, 2009; Read, 2010). Both the homogeneity and heterogeneity of SIDS must be appreciated. In absence of this, the current international architecture has a reverse effect on actually widening the solution space at national and local levels. International processes should instead be used to emphasise the need for customised and home-grown solutions for SIDS that reflect and are aligned to their own climate resilient development trajectories (Lopes, 2014b). For example, according to the Human Development Report of 2013, about half of the population in Guinea Bissau live below the poverty line of $1.25 per person per day. This is a stark contrast with the Seychelles with less than 1 per cent of the population living below the poverty line, which places this country among the healthiest countries in the world.

The consequences of climate change and rising sea levels for SIDS is damaging. The signs are evident from environmental degradation of diverse marine ecosystems and resources which are utilised for livelihoods and food security (Read, 2010). Coastal erosion also disrupts human settlements, infrastructure, social services, and tourism facilities as well as agricultural subsistence. Water management-related challenges are also limiting freshwater resources while the risks of saline intrusion increase. Already vulnerable populations are threatened further by health risks stemming from vector borne diseases such as malaria or dengue.

In their entirety, such consequences only cause additional social, cultural, and economic stress on SIDS, posing a threat to their very survival through reinforced vulnerabilities (Briguglio, 1995; Tisdell, 2009; Read, 2010; Haskins, 2012). In contrast, larger economies are predisposed to spreading the risks and burdens of shocks, both over time and space, thus absorbing the overall impacts of climate change. The choices for SIDS are reduced due to their geographic dispersion, remoteness, and isolation from global markets. Coping strategies tend to be fewer, with heavy reliance on external assistance for post-disaster recovery programmes. The paradox is that SIDS are paying far more than their fair share due to their smallness and are "subsidizing" the cost of managing climate challenges that they are least responsible for (Lopes, 2014b). The combined annual carbon dioxide (CO_2) output of all SIDS accounts for less than 1 per cent of global emissions and yet SIDS face disproportionately greater vulnerabilities.

What then are the opportunities for SIDS to address their vulnerabilities and better prepare for the impact of climate change? First, social capital is of fundamental importance in the recovery and coping strategies of vulnerable communities. Investing in kinship and other forms of social capital improves the chances of being able to bounce back after disasters. Even with the loss of biodiversity, biophysical losses can be compared with the kind of cultural losses that no amount of adaptation can fix. For instance, what would constitute a cultural fix for women rice growers in West Africa, faced with problems of salinisation and "predatory" mangroves? How could they find a substitute to this tradition that has formed an essential part of their economic culture?

Second, strong institutions are fundamental enablers to an effective response strategy, either through adaptation or through mitigation. They can provide the basis for formulating and supporting green economy policies that will allow Africa to stay on course. Institutions can act as stewards and regulators for the management, distribution, measurement, and ownership of natural resource goods and services. To graduate out of a special category, SIDS will need to think through innovative choices and solutions that will further insulate them from climate extremes and shocks. The good news thus far is that most African SIDS have limited fractionalisation and perform highly in terms of governance.

Third, the economic and structural transformation of SIDS requires the engagement of a multiplicity of actors – the state, private sector, civil society, and public–private partnerships. For example, the quality of institutions needed to usher in a new form of deliberative democracy based on the principle of "common but differentiated responsibilities", is one that can leverage opportunities in the energy and agricultural sectors to prepare for climate risks. The current primary product-driven and export-led growth model needs to build in value-adding export diversification to reduce both commodity and market dependence. This is partly needed to broaden the revenue base and spread the rewards of growth across a larger section of the population. SIDS also need to invest in infrastructure to maximise trading opportunities, enhance regional integration and boost the inflow of investment to their economies.

Fourth, "small is beautiful" in terms of the abundance of natural resource endowments offered by the blue economy. SIDS need to better exploit their natural resource endowments. Inclusive green growth is a frontier that could focus on affordable renewable energy services, the promotion of green jobs, and the reduction of poverty. Already, there is growing interest in these areas and the role of low-carbon development to reduce dependence on fossil fuels. For example, Cape Verde's renewable energy targets and objectives for 2020 to 2030 include increasing electricity network coverage to 100 per cent of renewable sources and increasing energy efficiency by 30 per cent through the promotion of new technology. Mauritius plans to increase the share of renewable energy such as solar power, wind energy, hydropower, biogas, and landfill gas, to around 35 per cent by 2025. SIDS are ideal locations and have the size for pilot projects in renewable energy and other areas and such innovations can then be rolled out in other countries on a larger scale.[5] After all, the smallness of SIDS could actually be a blessing as "localised" impacts of interventions can be demonstrated quickly on a national scale.

In addition, SIDS have the potential to incubate good technological options that enable them to sprint towards greening their economies. Hard engineering solutions can insulate them from vulnerabilities such as oil price volatility, while pursuing integrated development will increase the resilience of ecosystems and improve human security.

Among key growth sectors, tourism is a major source of revenue. Tourism is currently the economic bloodline of most African SIDS, and holds huge potential for growth and development. Ecotourism can provide employment, generate income, and help conserve natural resources, while promoting implementation of a biodiversity action plan.

Climate services and observational infrastructure that are used to predict weather patterns and identify climate related extremes tend to be weak in places where they are most needed. Investment in climate science and climate services would facilitate the production of high quality data and the development of early warning systems. In addition, it would initiate much needed research in the fields of climate change impact, vulnerability, and adaptation. All this activity would better inform policy decisions.

Finally, while SIDS have made major efforts to carry out climate change adaptation measures, progress so far has tended to focus on public awareness, research, and policy development rather than on implementation; this is largely due to financial constraints. This might have to do with only a limited number of financing options dedicated to adaptation such as the GEF specialised adaptation facilities, the Adaptation Fund, and the World Bank Catastrophe Risk Insurance Facility. Neither option is capable of providing the scale or magnitude of resources needed to address the climate change problem. If SIDS are to have a chance, new financing players and partners are urgently needed to support adaptation responses to climate change. Regional integration and its strength in numbers presents a practical way to deal with such challenges of developing a critical mass.

Regional integration and trade

Betrayed by a Mercator map projection, the common view of the size of Africa has been diminished in pretty much the same way as other characteristics of the continent. The reality is that the Democratic Republic of Congo (DRC) alone is about half the size of the European Union and with huge potential for trade and provisions of other resources if properly integrated within the continent. However, even in a single country, such as the DRC, national integration remains a major a challenge: in 2002, it had a public budget smaller than the city of Brussels. The point is Africa has a long way to go!

Integration in every region and corner of the planet has been a tale of many challenges as the experience of the EU and BREXIT show and Africa is no different. The EU, long considered the most mature integration achievement, has itself started to experience serious difficulties and major shortcomings, particularly relating to the Eurozone.

Africa has a longer history of monetary unions than Europe but the large size of the European Monetary Union (EMU) and the challenges it has faced since the 2008–2009 financial crisis, provide important lessons for both existing and proposed monetary unions in Africa. Europe worked hard to consolidate its single market and achieve a high degree of trade integration before the use of the euro. Over time, the Eurozone countries built an impressive architecture of processes, institutions, and regulations.

One of the key lessons for Africa from the EU's experience is that the institutional environment has to be conducive to fostering of regional trade. Another lesson for Africa is the importance of stable macroeconomic policies. When there are wide differences in the degree of fiscal discipline across member countries, these can create challenges for the survival and stability of any union. The Eurozone experience also underscores the need for countries that are about to participate in a monetary union to have a credible and feasible mechanism for fiscal transfers. This will enable them to respond and adjust to asymmetric shocks. In the absence of such a mechanism, any monetary union will be susceptible to enormous pressure when its members are hit by asymmetric shocks. There are, however, concerns that the adoption of stringent convergence criteria will limit policy space to address current and emerging development challenges.

In the context of economic integration, the importance of monetary, fiscal, and financial policy harmonisation cannot be overemphasised. Monetary unions are normally defined as involving two components: exchange rate union, that is, an area within which exchange rates bear a permanently fixed relationship to each other and convertibility, or the permanent absence of all exchange controls, whether for current or capital transactions within the jurisdiction. The work of Jacob Viner and subsequent followers document the evolution of thought on regional integration and associated complexities (Viner, 1950; Bloomfield, 1992; Bhagwati et al., 1998; Midelfart-Knarvik et al., 2003; Markwell, 2008).

Africa's realities make the regional integration effort more daunting and yet worthy to pursue. Administering 54 sovereign states with an array of national policies and inefficient government apparatuses constitutes a massive resource-draining overhead cost on Africa's fragile and undiversified primary production-based economies. An assessment of progress towards macroeconomic convergence in Africa's eight officially recognised Regional Economic Communities in Africa shows that, while some progress is being made, it is generally below the targets set in their monetary integration programmes.

If Africa were a business, the management costs of this type of structure would be uncompetitive. The cost of governing such a fragmented production structure is simply too high for Africa to afford or sustain. Thus, the contribution of regional integration to the promotion of intra-group trade, growth, development, and social and political cohesion is unquestionable. The stark conclusion that can be drawn from these facts is that Africa must integrate (or in business parlance, "rationalise and merge") in order to reduce its overhead costs.

The debate about integration, however, has mostly been centred on the political dimensions and the paramount pan-African ideal that has historically been shackled by narrow nationalism (Mbeki, 2009). Seemingly, Africa has broken the cycle of hopelessness and has hewn a much more optimistic future for itself through rapid and strong economic growth since the start of the century. The time has now come to move to a more technical debate and focus, partly in order to give credence to such noble political ideals but also because the speed of global transformation will not wait, especially for latecomers. Accelerating the pace of and achieving structural transformation remains the greater challenge for the future. In fact, the majority of African countries continue to struggle to diversify their narrow-based economies.

Addressing these challenges will require due attention to an appropriate macroeconomic policy framework underpinned by a long-term development strategy that facilitates transformation of economic and social structures and ensures a positive feedback loop in the investment-growth nexus beyond mere mercantilism. Such a macroeconomic policy framework for structural transformation should encompass five main components (Lopes, 2019a):

- scaling up public investment and public goods provision;
- maintaining macro stability to attract and sustain private investment;
- coordinating investment and other development policies;

- mobilising resources and reducing aid dependence over time; and
- securing fiscal sustainability by establishing fiscal legitimacy.

These key elements of transformation are not optional when discussing monetary unions in the African context. Regional Economic Communities (RECs) had better pay attention; otherwise, they risk not being taken seriously about such ambitious goals. The rhetorical question is, therefore, what role is there for trade?

Traditional approaches to regional integration have tended to focus on trade. It goes without saying that trade has significant potential to help achieve sustainable development and has increasingly played an important role in the strong economic performance of African economies during the past decade. Indeed, trade performance has shown great resilience even in the face of the ongoing economic crisis.

Intra-regional formal trade in Africa has historically hovered around 10 per cent to 12 per cent, although this could be much higher (ECA, 2014a). These figures do not consider statistical deficiencies and informal trade. Still, trade within regional economic communities is growing faster than African exports to the rest of Africa, and to the rest of the world (trade within the RECs have been growing at 30 per cent plus annually). The Common Market for Eastern and Southern Africa alone has increased its intra-African trade almost fivefold since it launched its free-trade agreement in 2000. Southern African Development Community trade grew more than threefold and East African Community trade grew more than twofold.

Regional value chains, if properly exploited, can help Africa gain the critical capacity needed to compete as the continent moves up the global value chain. This can be achieved by promoting cross-border opportunities that allow countries to contribute with different inputs to the production of intermediate and finalised products. This could lead to a multitude of positive outcomes such as employment creation, productivity gains, income generation, and the creation of backward linkages into the economy, all of which could lift millions of people out of poverty. Trade has yet to serve a transformational purpose for the benefit of human development in Africa as it has done in many other developing economies, and it is through its positive linkage to development that trade can play a pivotal role.

It is commendable that the AU is making African countries rethink the regional integration agenda beyond the issue of trade. One such area that has gathered momentum within the context of a regional approach has been peace, security, and the strengthening of democratic governance because preserving human security is a key ingredient in sustainable development.

Greater peace and security

A rise in African agency has ushered in a new wave of democratic dispensations as citizens demand more accountability from their leaders and development partners (Kararach et al., 2012; Shaw and Polonenko, 2015). Since the early 1990s, most African countries have witnessed the emergence of varied democratic transitions. Almost all democratic transitions have had to navigate the complexities and challenges of managing diversity in its various forms: the distribution of power and characteristics of political structures; issues of ethnicity and religion; definitions of citizenship; or the rights and concerns of marginalised groups.

Even where governments have reformed their institutions or put in place policies and legislation to better manage diversity, unresolved conflicts continue to linger. There are several elements that are central to consolidating democratic transitions and that not only require analysis but must be addressed. These include the quality of elections, promoting diversity in constitutions, understanding how deeply embedded diversity should be in the public space and institutions, as well as ensuring state capacity to mediate and rise above sectarian interests.

Conflict-ridden elections in many countries illustrate the distance that some African countries still must go in managing diversity and the importance of improving electoral processes to uphold fair, inclusive, and democratic elections. However, the biggest mistake of all is to believe elections are a silver bullet for resolving the challenges of national cohesion. It is naïve to think that a vote is all that is needed to solve all problems that have contributed to exacerbating entrenched positions or that have provoked polarising political tensions. The lack of accompanying elements fomenting social cohesion can have a vicious effect on any stated objective of inclusiveness.

In many African countries, human insecurity can certainly be linked to bad governance and lack of democratic practice (Kararach et al., 2012). When democracy provides the means for conflict resolution it plays a stabilising role by ensuring that points of view get a fair hearing. The way this is done, though, is important. Like in any social construct, the simplification of a blueprint may not provide the appropriate answer. Groups should feel that their rights are protected and that their economic interests can be fulfilled so they do not resort to conflict to break or assert a claim to self-determination.

Evidence also suggests that Africa is losing significant resources through illicit financial flows. Annual estimates have ranged from $20 billion before 2000 to $50 billion in the last decade (Ndikumana and Boyce, 2018; ECA, 2018). Obviously, the hidden nature of these flows has a devastating impact on tax revenues and public spending capacity. The continent is being deprived of huge financial resources needed to boost investment on infrastructure and services delivery, undermining the state's hopes for a distributive economic and social development agenda. Regulating such staggering sums of illicit outflows has become one of the main challenges for structural transformation (ECA, 2013; 2018).

Because illicit financial flows are intentionally hidden from the plain view of countries' financial authorities, their records, impact, and consequences are underestimated in many counts, particularly regarding peace and security. In fact, there is a strong nexus between illicit financial flows and conflict. Illicit financial flows of all types are associated with either ineffective state functioning or illegitimate use of state authority (Ndikumana and Boyce, 2012). They present a threat to governance by undermining both political institutions and confidence in them; and further weaken policy and institutional safeguards when tensions arise. Equally, conflict undermines institutional resilience and governance systems designed to address inequalities; and fuels corruption which hinders incentives for long-term investments as opposed to short-term rent-seeking activities.

Despite the ongoing responses by continental and international organisations, Africa's growing political space and influence have not always been leveraged to quell its conflicts. Most internal conflicts in Africa can be traced to contestation over political legitimacy, national identity, state building, and distributive justice; all these factors are often interconnected.

The involvement of the external interests has had serious consequences for domestic and regional security. A plethora of initiatives (see Wachira, 2017) including the African Governance Architecture (AGA) and the African Peace and Security Architecture (APSA) have not yet necessarily provided adequate solutions to the quest for peace and security. Some intractable conflicts are difficult to resolve because their underlying causes are often deeply entrenched and complex. Conflict resolution strategies that fail to account for that complexity are likely to be ineffective and quick wins have proven deceptive. Together with the Bosnia conflict, the Rwanda and Somali wars are credited to have contributed to the overhaul of a faltering peace keeping doctrine to a more interventionist approach (Werner, 2015. It is fair to say these changes played a part in the drastic reduction of wars, but it is less clear whether they reduced other forms of conflict that persist to demonstrate that we are facing a new but decisive moment.

Africa has begun to reap the effects of a peace dividend. Fewer conflicts have generated growth and opportunities for greater social change and human security (Kararach et al., 2012). For some countries such as Liberia and Angola, the end of conflict has become synonymous with the availability of fresh resources that were previously devoted to military expenditure and thus contributed to the stimulation of economic activity.

The challenges of maintaining peace and security are shifting to the nexus of human security, an increase of intra-states conflict, and emerging transnational threats. The multiplication of domestic insecurities highlights new trends such as radicalism, terrorism, drugs and human trafficking, all with trans-border dimensions. This can be seen in the case of Boko Haram networks with Al Qaeda in the Maghreb and Al-Shabab. Drugs trafficking explains the vitality of Sahara-based rebel groups (Shaw, 2018); indeed, the Libyan military and political crises have created a space for the proliferation of trans-border arms and human trafficking.

In addition, natural resources have been at the forefront of provoking conflict for resources control (Collier and Hoeffler, 2004; Collier, 2004).

Natural resources have traditionally been one of the main driving forces behind the continent's economic fortunes but also a contributor to some of the most violent conflicts. The highest illicit financial flows were recorded in African countries that are resource and mineral rich mainly in oil, precious metals and minerals (ECA, 2016d). The policy and legal frameworks for the mining sector have traditionally been designed to attract investment and raise resources for rent-seeking or un-strategic spending rather than to encourage transformation. Moreover, the share of resource rents retained by African countries has often been limited on the account of overgenerous concessions that are always made in the race to the bottom for mining investment as well as to the information asymmetries, which typically characterise the mining sector. It is estimated that between 1970 and 2008, illicit financial flows linked to trade mispricing alone cost the continent $854 billion (ECA, 2018).

The lost resources on the African continent are a clear indication that governments need to enforce and implement principles and standard operating procedures which could reduce the amount of leakages that are incurred through illicit financial flows (ECA, 2018). They also need to negotiate better! To begin with, the setting up of financial intelligence units to curtail, track, and repatriate illicit financial flows will be crucial in ensuring that resources lost can be tracked and eventually returned. The implementation of the Extractive Industries Transparency International guidelines will help to ensure transparency in negotiations between companies in the extractive industry and governments. Frameworks such as the Kimberley process will see to it that diamonds are not illegally traded, while initiatives such as "publish what you pay" will enforce more transparency in the industry. The blood diamonds syndrome still exists and what actually happens with Coltan or logging is no different.

Improved institutions, governance and leadership are vital in addressing the important concerns of turning natural resources into a boon for development (Kararach, 2017). African countries must re-evaluate their approach to governance to discern whether they are adequately equipped to provide stability, while being flexible enough to address the variety of issues relating to illicit financial flows. Interestingly, promoting a developmental state provides both opportunities and limitations in pursuing these goals (ECA, 2018). A developmental state facilitates coherence, drive, and better allocation of resources. However, it also has the potential to limit dissent if proper organic forms of inclusion are not considered, given the experience from Asia. For a developmental state, addressing illicit financial flows and strengthening regulatory and governance institutions is important. A more effective approach is needed in order to address the root causes of illicit financial flows. Long-term development visions and strategies can promote better resources management and less corruption. Given the trans-national ingredients of both illicit flows and conflict, it is necessary to comprehensively address the problems of peace and security in the African neighbourhood.

Conclusion

Africa should not underestimate its potential and must seek to understand all possible drivers or otherwise of its transformation. This exercise requires a mental shift and redefinition of its development narrative. For instance, Africa's natural resources are a blessing and not a curse and therefore, can be used as a precursor for the continent's continuous rise in the face of an insatiable global appetite for natural resources. To make this possible, frameworks such as the AMV must be implemented and used as a template at country and regional level. There is need to enhance beneficiation as well as ensuring better management of natural windfalls.

Most of Africa's economies are over-dependent on commodity production and the export of agricultural and mining products which explains why the continent remains the least industrialised region of the world. If GVCs and SEZs in Africa are to be sustainable and successful as showcases of industrial progress and structural transformation – as they have been in Asia – there is a need for forceful and workable policies. More specifically, industrial strategies have to be introduced as a matter of urgency in order to remove existing constraints on value-addition and economic transformation. These constraints are weak infrastructure, unreliable energy supply, an underdeveloped and inefficient private sector, and the shortage of skilled labour.

The continent also needs a rethink on how it utilises its oceanic resources so as to avoid the tendency whereby African SIDS are overlooked in the policy discourse about climate change. Their differing vulnerabilities are drowned in a debate that focuses on biophysical impacts with only superficial reference to the issue of social vulnerability. It must be stressed that local communities are in the frontline of the impacts of climate change and, as a result, they are already adapting to climate variability and change. After all, they have a history of surviving social and environmental changes with a wealth of indigenous knowledge that includes intricate systems of weather forecasting as well as mitigation and adaptation practices.

However, effective and modern pathways for future adaptation will not happen in a vacuum. They will need to be facilitated, structured, and organised within an institutional setting, including the regional economic communities. The solution space must therefore be widened for facilitating the means for cost-effective, participatory, and sustainable implementation and, crucially, regional integration does provide that space.

Schumacher may not have been wrong after all and perhaps small is beautiful. The beauty of SIDS resides in the ingenuity of its people, their entrepreneurial spirit, and ability to meet the many challenges of climate change. In the face of adversity, they have managed to reinvent themselves by finding renewed resilience in their institutions, social ties, networks, and alliances of reciprocity. However, the creativity of Africa's people cannot be optimised without ensuring peace and security. Tapping into the other key drivers of Africa's development must therefore exercise the minds of its leaders as they advance the structural transformation agenda.

The analytical and discursive reflections of this chapter are very relevant for understanding how and in what ways development financing could be a strategic catalyst of Africa's structural transformation. In the next chapter, therefore, we turn our attention to innovative forms of development finance and the articulation of their modalities in Africa and globally. Our purpose is to highlight the nature of the debate, including the role of foreign investment and to examine how innovative policy and institutional mechanisms could enhance and support financing for development.

Notes

1 The Ezulwini Consensus is a position on international relations and reform of the United Nations, agreed by the African Union in 2005. It calls for a more representative and democratic Security Council, in which Africa, like all other world regions, is represented.
2 This recognition has prompted the Beijing Declaration and Platform for Action (1995); and later the usage of quotas bring about social/gender equity (Dahlerup, 2002; 2006).
3 This is defined as changes in the energy/GDP ratio that are not related to changes in the relative price of energy.
4 Most of the discussions on the SIDS draw on an earlier blog by the co-author Carlos Lopes.
5 Mr. H.E. Danny Faure suggested this during his intervention at the 67th General Assembly General Debate, New York, 25–29 September and 1 October 2012: www.unohrlls.org/UserFiles/A%20Synopsis%20of%20the%2067th%20United%20Nations%20General%20Assembly%20General%20Debate.pdf.

5 Innovative development financing

Introduction

The linkage between development financing and structural transformation in Africa is critical. The outcomes of financing for development are important to Africa for two reasons. First, they inform the means of implementation of the structural transformation agenda and second, they determine the extent to which the aspirations of the SDGs and Agenda 2063 can be realised.

While financing requirements for sustainable development are demanding, the solutions lie in exploring innovative sources of financing. The working premise is that Africa has immense opportunities to generate the resources required for its transformation agenda.

New partnerships, innovative instruments for domestic resource mobilisation, the contribution of the private sector, and sources of climate finance are all avenues that could meet Africa's financing needs. Measures to unlock money at the national level include devising financing instruments that enable the integration of Africa into international financial markets and that facilitate intra-African trade. In this mix are harnessing sources of private equity; strengthening the role of bond markets, pension funds, and sovereign wealth funds to boost investments; improving the policy base and regulatory environment, from tax administration to legal reforms. There must be domestic recourse to governing the investment of public funds and international reserves of central and reserve banks; and building the requisite human, technological, and institutional capacities.

At the global level, financial and economic governance must also be reformed to improve the conditions of access to capital markets. This will assist with intensifying international cooperation for transparency in Africa's extractive industries; tackling the problem of illicit capital flight which deprives the continent of at least $50 billion a year; and to expanding Africa's fiscal space. However, it is useful that we first understand the nature of the debate.

Debating Africa's financing potential

Africa's development financing framework is closely linked to the global financial architecture and governance mechanisms anchored on domestic resource mobilisation, the use of ODA and financial markets and codes such as the Paris Declaration, BASEL III, and IMF debt sustainability framework. These frameworks and codes circumscribe the way finances are mobilised and deployed.

The ECA estimated what additional financial resources will be required to reduce poverty and inequality in Africa by half. Its estimates assume that savings, foreign direct investment, and official development assistance stay at their 2014 levels using different scenarios (ECA, 2015e). The ECA found that the additional financial resources required range from between $48 billion and $246 billion per year between 2015 and 2030. The higher figure of $246 billion applies when the target is to halve poverty and inequality simultaneously; while the lower figure of $48 billion applies when the resources required are only to halve poverty by 2030, with inequality remaining constant.

Remittances should reduce the additional financing resources required by between $6.5 billion and $204.6 billion per year (ECA and AU, 2015). More importantly, it must be noted that Africa has diverse financing potential that could be utilised more creatively (see Figure 5.1).

Africa has undertaken a number of policy initiatives aimed at addressing the financing gap by relying more on public and private domestic resources to ensure the delivery of structural transformation based on inclusive growth and sustainable development. The efforts of several African entities have been key in this regard and include the Planning and Coordination Agency of the New Partnership for Africa's Development (NEPAD), the Ninth African Development Forum, the High-Level Panel on Alternative

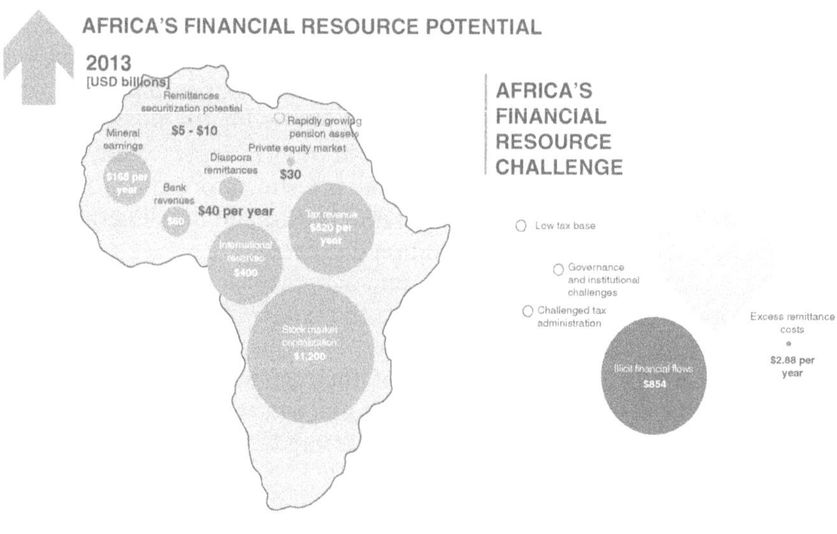

Figure 5.1 Comparative size and diversity of Africa's financial potential
Source: ECA, 2015e.

Sources of Financing, the African Union, and the High-Level Panel on Illicit Financial Flows, and the recently adopted Agenda 2063.

Africa has been seeking to move the debate on financing the continent's development away from the narrow focus of the Monterrey Consensus on the supply of funding by linking development financing to the broader issues of structural transformation, underpinned by capable, inclusive, and accountable institutions at national, regional, and global levels. The focus is therefore on the reform of the global financial architecture in order to create space for the mobilisation of local resources, for example, by lifting conditionalities imposed by agencies such as the IMF and the World Bank during economic reforms.

Stepping up domestic resource mobilisation (DRM) is critical because of the following reasons:

- reliance on domestic resources reinforces a country's ownership of public policy and strengthens accountability;
- domestic resources can spur the more effective use of development financing;
- external resources are not only unpredictable and erratic, but would not be sufficient to meet Africa's development financing needs; and
- most donor countries have failed to live up to their long-standing commitments.

As part of the DRM agenda, many countries have undertaken tax reforms with positive outcomes. Tax-based financing of Africa's development ranks second only to export earnings. The continent's total tax revenue has thus increased from \$331 billion in 2009 to \$527.3 billion in 2012 (ECA, 2015e). The tax-to-GDP ratio has also increased in the period 2000–2013 and is projected to keep rising until 2020 in middle-income African countries such as Mauritius and South Africa. However, the trend is expected to remain below the 15 per cent threshold in low-income countries, although that level is considered by many to be a reasonable target for their level of development (Kararach et al., 2015). Official development assistance must be a complementary tool to support low-income countries in their domestic resource mobilisation efforts. Development partners must step up financial and technical support to poorer African countries and improve their tax administration in the priority areas identified by governments.

It is generally accepted that fiscal policy can be used creatively to enhance the structural transformation agenda. Africa has great potential to mobilise domestic resources through taxation and this could be realised by broadening countries' tax base and improving tax administration. It will entail critical measures such as tapping into relatively underutilised sources of taxation, taxing financial transactions, improving the corporate governance of extractive industries in resource-rich countries, and combatting corruption and illicit financial flows (ECA, 2015d; Kararach et al., 2015). The establishment of independent tax agencies to address issues of capacity in tax administration has also been successful in a number of African countries such as Uganda, Rwanda, and Ghana. Addressing harmful tax competition among African countries in the hopes of attracting foreign direct investment will also help to raise needed domestic resources. For example, double taxation treaties need to be reviewed in light of the required reforms.

African countries must also review the regulatory and tax reform frameworks with a view to raising more domestic resources while enhancing equity objectives. The reliance in many African countries on indirect taxes such value-added taxes and customs duties, which tend to be disproportionally borne by the poor, needs to be revisited. One low-hanging fruit is fostering better tax compliance by providing affordable state pensions and other welfare packages. This relates to improved public service delivery at national, sub-national, and local levels because citizens are more likely to pay taxes if they feel that their lives would be improved in return (Kedir et al., 2016). This will be particularly helpful when bringing in the large informal sector into the tax realm, as its employees will see tangible benefits in this new form of citizen-based social contracts (Kararach et al., 2015).

There is also a consensus that more resources could be generated through public sector efficiency gains and the reduction of tax loopholes. Strengthening public expenditure and investment management through integrated public financial management frameworks does limit waste and graft as this enhances selection, design, and management of public investment projects, thereby improving the enabling environment for investment. Reforming regressive and harmful subsidy and corrupt procurement regimes could increase public expenditure efficiency and allow for more spending in support of poverty alleviation efforts and long-term transformation (ECA, 2016d).

The Panama Papers of April 2016 provided increasing evidence of the difficulties of delinking national solutions from global efforts in the fight against illicit financial flows. These flows have drained over $50 billion a year from Africa over the last decade. The Report of the High-Level Panel on Illicit Financial Flows from Africa noted that most African countries lack the means to verify the quantities of natural resources which are exported, relying instead on exporter declarations (ECA, 2015d). Self-regulation is the norm and African countries often use a variety of incentives such as tax breaks and promise of concession/contract renewals to encourage accurate reporting. The continuation of the problem of illicit financial flows speaks to the need for concerted, diverse yet harmonised actions by all players.

In spite of the various governance initiatives at the global level, the gaps in global governance relating to illicit financial flows remain acute. Such initiatives have been taken by the OECD, the Group of 8, and the Group of 20, and include the automatic exchange of tax information, base erosion, and profit shifting measures. However, current global measures do not consider the needs of African countries or those of other developing countries as enforcement mechanisms continue to be weak or non-existent. Efforts must therefore be made to ensure that Africa benefits from such initiatives without having to suffer the undue burden of compliance costs. One inclusive global solution would be to implement the recommendation of the Doha Declaration on Financing for Development to strengthen global institutional arrangements, including the United Nations Committee of Experts on International Cooperation in Tax Matters.

Eliminating the financing gap in Africa will essentially require effective collaboration between governments and the private sector at the national, regional, and global levels. The private sector has so far played only a limited role in the implementation of Africa's development projects, especially those relating to infrastructure and sustainable development, and it clearly can and must do more. Given recent improvements in the business environment – governance reforms, improved policy and regulatory frameworks, emergence of functional and effective public institutions – the private sector should step up its participation in infrastructure development on the continent. To this end, public–private partnerships need strengthening and new models of such partnerships and high-level platforms for public–private sector consultations such as the Programme for Infrastructure Development in Africa (PIDA) must be encouraged.

More efforts are therefore needed to enhance private domestic resource mobilisation. While reforms have been undertaken since the 1980s and 1990s to liberalise financial sectors across Africa, it remains unclear whether they have resulted in more savings or more efficient investment (Kararach, 2011). Basic financial sector information infrastructure, such as credit bureau and land registries, tends to be highly underdeveloped in most African countries. Building this financial infrastructure is essential for the development of housing and other long-term credit markets (North–South Institute, 2010). Mobile-phone and electronic banking are options that could be considered, along with programmes for strengthening financial literacy among the general population and building capacity for banking regulation.

Savings is also an important ingredient if Africa wants to exploit its great potential since mobilising domestic savings enhances the development of financial systems. Household savings provide a stable, reliable, low-cost, and low-risk source of financing compared to, for example, international private capital flows (ECA, 2015b). It is good news to note that domestic savings in Africa are projected to continue rising, except in low-income countries. This can be explained by the strong correlation between savings levels and per capita and national income as more and more Africans join the middle class (AfDB, 2013). This means that even where financial access is expanded, as it has in many African countries since 2002, savings rates remain dependent on economic growth (Beck et al., 2011).

Another important element of domestic resources is the levels of available credit. Since 2002, all African countries have seen an increase in domestic credit relative to GDP (World Bank, 2015). Domestic credit tends to grow in line with per capita income, reflecting financial strengthening as economies grow. However, how such domestic credit is used must be a matter of policy priority. In some African countries, growth in credit to the private sector has meant more credit for consumer finance and short-term businesses as opposed to long-term investments in sectors that are important for structural transformation such as agriculture, manufacturing, and infrastructure.

There is also now a growing call to revisit the roles of monetary policy and those of central banks (Chavula et al., 2017). Traditionally African central bank governors focused on price and financial stability to contain inflation and bolster the financial sector; yet this approach has not helped to bring down unemployment or spur inclusive growth. There is now a demand by their African principals for central banks to work together in order to solve social problems resulting from the failure of the traditional focus, suggesting that these banks must revisit their roles in the continent's development. Programmes aimed at improving access to finance, promoting financial inclusion, and fostering targeted interventions in the economy are increasingly being prioritised.

Financial and stock markets are other key sources of finance for development. Stock market capitalisation in Africa increased from $300 billion in 1996 to $1.2 trillion in 2007 but secondary financial markets on the continent remain largely underdeveloped (ECA, 2014a). The region's stock markets remain thin and illiquid because human, technological, and institutional capacity are persistent constraints on growth; and improvements in risk management and regulations have had limited impact on portfolio inflows. Irrespective, these markets still continue to have attractive investment opportunities (Allen et al., 2011).

The continent also has a very huge and yet underutilised resource in the form of central bank reserves. African central banks foreign reserves increased from $55.2 billion in 1995 to $573.8 billion in 2012, and then declined to $506.7 billion in 2013. Oil exporting economies accounted for more than 70 per cent of the total reserves of the region during 2011–2013. The accumulation of reserves has been accompanied by an appreciation of national currencies, with negative impacts on the export sector performance, domestic investment, and employment creation. African countries should therefore use their reserves to boost productivity, enhance public investment in industrial activities, diversify their economies, and promote value addition. Diversifying reserves holdings could also help to minimise losses from currency appreciation.

Harnessing foreign direct investment as financing mechanism

Unlike other private international resources, foreign direct investment (FDI) can be instrumental in developing productive capacities by contributing in particular to the easing of infrastructure bottlenecks, especially in energy and transport. Foreign direct investment flows to Africa have been generally increasing in recent years, reaching an estimated US $65 billion in 2017/2018, driven by market demand and infrastructure investment needs. Intra-African FDI, which tends to benefit structural transformation priority sectors such as manufacturing, has also increased, for example, from $2.5 billion in 2015 to $6 billion in 2016 (UNCTAD, 2017). However, the overall positive outlook masks steep declines in FDI inflows into some African sub-regions because of regulatory uncertainties, political turmoil, or lack of capacity by local partners. Sub-regions that receive such inflows see an improvement in their domestic environment for doing business, including relatively more diversified sectors. This has been supported by innovation, the availability of human capital, favourable demographics, and discoveries in the gas and minerals sectors. There is increasing evidence of FDI being diversified away from the extractive sector to other sectors, which bodes well for Africa's structural transformation (UNCTAD, 2017).

Dubbed the new investment frontier, Africa's attractiveness is becoming more visible to large corporations, institutions, and investors. Reflecting this, FDI flows have grown exponentially since the turn of the millennium. Countries such as South Africa, Nigeria, Kenya, Egypt, and Morocco are leading the way. This is highlighted in Figure 5.2.

High growth economies such as Zambia, Ghana, Tanzania, and Mozambique are also becoming important investment destinations. There is also a rapid growth in intra-Africa investments (UNCTAD, 2018). Financial services alone accounted for about 50 per cent of intra-Africa greenfield investment projects between 2003 and 2014 (ECA, 2015e). Table 5.1 shows the levels of mergers and acquisition in Africa. Cross-border M&A was higher in Africa than in the United States in both 2015 and 2016 – speaking to the buoyed mood on the continent.

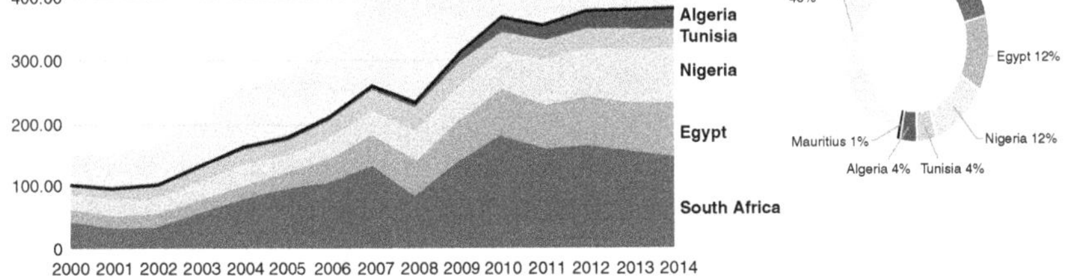

Figure 5.2 Trends in FDI in Africa 2000–2014
Source: ECA, 2015c.

Table 5.1 Cross-border M&As by region/economy, 2015–2016 (millions of dollars)

Region/economy	*Sales*		*Purchases*	
	2015	*2016*	*2015*	*2016*
World	21 259	9 689	3 533	6 061
Developed economies	22 357	−2 199	−165	5 792
European Union	18 605	847	490	3 131
France	612	236	−180	–
United Kingdom	201	596	161	965
United States	2 194	−3 085	−396	2 445
Developing countries	1 194	12 911	2 497	162
Africa	174	390	174	390
Morocco	81	–	–	375
South Africa	43	284	−9	–
United Arab Emirates	−616	9 187	1 543	–
China	53	2 932	279	–
Transition economies	–	−1 135	1 200	106

Source: UNCTAD, 2017, World Investment Report p. 45.

This trend is set to continue as more countries demonstrate sound economic policies and improved business environments. Major investors now include emerging economies such as China, India, Turkey, and the Gulf States. Manufacturing, a crucial trigger for industrialisation, was among the top business functions by capital investment in the region in 2014. Policymakers will no doubt be buoyed by this news. Capital investment in manufacturing accounted for 33 per cent of announced FDI in 2013, confirming that manufacturing output is finally expanding as quickly as the rest of the economy (ECA, 2015e).

For a while, the commodity boom remained a key driver of the region's growth. The extractive sector still receives the bulk of FDI getting \$14.5 billion in 2015. Current trends call for a sober assessment of the sustainability of this path. Moves towards diversification and increased value addition to the continent's abundant natural resources must be priorities. Africa's future will largely be determined by how well resource-rich countries harness natural wealth towards structural transformation.

It is encouraging to see that growth in the services sector is surging, bringing with it jobs and wealth creation. The sector is now Africa's largest sector in terms of FDI stock with \$70.98 billion in announced greenfield investments in 2016. FDI projects in real estate, hospitality, and construction have also increased. Rising urbanisation and a growing middle class continue to create opportunities and reorient investors towards a burgeoning African consumer market.

Nonetheless, the various trends in FDI flows into the continent represent mixed fortunes for Africa's heterogeneous economies. Some of the top performers in terms of value addition, as measured by manufacturing value added, are also amongst its smallest economies such as Seychelles and Swaziland. Because of their small size, these successes are not widely known.

In light of Africa's pursuit for structural transformation, it is imperative that FDI contributes to the region's integration and sustainable development agenda. As already noted, Africa's growth so far has not been accompanied by sufficient increases in productivity or job creation, nor has it significantly reduced poverty and inequality.

Getting a firm grip on the issue of industrialisation for inclusive growth will require answers to difficult questions such as: who is benefitting? How will the capacity and empowerment of the local private sector be impacted? Is competitiveness enhanced?

While the risk of over-dependence on FDI, given global uncertainties, demands cautions by African countries, it is clear that it is a significant source of financing for development. However, Africa's untapped savings as well as the quality of its regulatory environment and macroeconomic policies may attract bigger amounts in future (Lopes, 2015d).

Africa's transformation requires a new, ambitious vision with the right policies and incentives to back it up. Together with efficient institutions, this is as important as new infrastructure and access to capital. Some reformist governments as those in Rwanda and Ghana are showing the way (Zeleza, 2018).

Smallholder producers, who are most directly dependent on ecosystem services, are critical agents for the future of agriculture in Africa. They contribute to poverty reduction and food security, especially in the rural areas. Disappointingly, they are often excluded from debates on agricultural investments. This exclusion has become more pronounced in the debate on Large Scale Land Based Investments at the risk of land grabs and food insecurity.

Africa currently contributes 45 per cent of all the Large-Scale Land Based Investments globally, followed by Asia at 37 per cent. The top ten countries in Africa targeted by local and international investors account for 70 per cent of concluded land contracts and 54 per cent of Large-Scale Land Based Investments deals on the continent. Foreign-based investors representing 73 per cent of the deals drive the majority of cases in Africa. The high interest in these investments is principally driven by global challenges in food security, although industry, forestry, conservation, and tourism play an important role. The combined investment in agriculture and livestock totals 87 per cent of all cases (UNCTAD, 2017).

Despite the high Large-Scale Land Based Investments in agriculture, not much land is utilised to grow food crops. Large-scale agricultural investments in biofuels and other industry related crops take up a substantial portion of fertile land. Yet, if Africa is to be food secure, most of the agricultural land ought to be dedicated to food crops.

Large-scale crop production, agro-industry, and agri-business provide an opportunity to address Africa's yield gap and enhance job creation among the youth. These sectors are also likely to increase intra-Africa trade and improve infrastructure, mechanisation, productivity, and access to markets. However, the investments are also replete with risks because the acquisitions occur within governance and policy frameworks that substantially facilitate foreign investment and only minimally promote local community interests (Lopes, 2014c).

There must be sustained multi-stakeholder involvement in decision making, respect for human and property rights, monitoring of the investments, as well as accountability and transparency in the land deals. Without this there is the risk of water sources being jeopardised, family farming and smallholder food production being subverted; so, the land rights of local land African countries must also review the regulatory and tax reform frameworks with a view to raising more domestic resources while enhancing equity objectives. It is crucial that a balance is maintained between market needs and developmental, environmental and social interests. Smallholder producers are key to this process.

African countries have to entrench agriculture in the national agenda. The commitment under the 2003 Maputo Declaration to increase public spending on agriculture to a modest 10 per cent of their national budgets and raise agricultural productivity by at least 6 per cent is yet to be met. On average, public expenditure allocated to agriculture accounts for slightly over 5 per cent (Kararach, 2014; Lopes, 2014b). This under-investment in agriculture by African governments has created an environment for uncoordinated investment in land.

The success of large-scale agricultural investments on the continent will largely depend on the extent to which key land governance and policy reforms are undertaken by African countries. At the core of these reforms is an inclusive land tenure system. It would not only buttress the land rights of local communities, women, and youth but also increase economic development, promote gender equality, and inspire younger women and men to take up agricultural activities. An inclusive land tenure system would also improve efficiency of land use and climate change mitigation, and so help to contribute to Africa's economic transformation (Lopes, 2014b).

Fortunately, several countries such as Uganda, Zimbabwe, Namibia, and South Africa have set up processes for the formulation and implementation of land policies that would make land tenure systems more inclusive and secure. The African Union Commission, Economic Commission for Africa, and African Development Bank's Land Policy Initiative has been mandated by African Heads of State and Governments to galvanise support for land policy formation, implementation, and monitoring. To ensure systematic discharge of its mandate, the Land Policy Initiative is guided by the *African Union Declaration on Land Issues and Challenges in Africa* which calls for the application of the *Framework and Guidelines on Land Policy in Africa* in land policy processes.

When African states invest in effective land management and use, in accordance with the recently adopted *Guiding Principles on Large-Scale Land Based Investments*, they increase the opportunities for meeting the food needs of their populations, reduce poverty, and accelerate structural transformation of rural economies. In addition, by refocusing their energies on improving lives in rural areas through secure tenure, increased access to land, comprehensive land use planning and zoning, and innovative agricultural practices, a crucial step will be made towards sustainable development.

Finance for Africa's transformation

As the race to achieve the post-2015 development agenda is on, including global goals for people and the planet adopted by world leaders in September 2015 at the Headquarters of the United Nations, how ready is Africa to embrace this ground-breaking universal development agenda?

The past 15 years have been a journey of change for the continent. Despite starting at the lowest point on the MDG targets, African countries have done exceptionally well thanks to political determination and tremendous efforts. While not all the goals have been met, Africa can celebrate achieving some significant targets, such as halving the prevalence of underweight children under the age of five and considerably reducing the number of AIDS and malaria-related deaths. The last 15 years have seen life expectancy surge to between 20 and 42 per cent, with 30 out of the 37 countries that registered increase in life expectancy coming from Africa (Johnson, 2016). Africa has also experienced strong economic growth averaging 5 per cent per annum, consistently outperforming global economic trends (ECA, 2015a).

Notwithstanding these gains, many hurdles remain to be overcome if the continent is to move ahead and stay ahead. One of the most pressing is harnessing the energy and talent of its people, particularly its youth and women, as well as closing the growing inequality gap and reducing income poverty and unemployment. Challenges such as these undermine the continent's productive potential.

The continent's priorities in the African common position on the post-2015 development agenda and in Agenda 2063 have found congruence with the proposed sustainable development goals. These instruments will remain mere rhetoric, however, if the continent does not engender the necessary means to turn this vision into reality. The real change required is to rise to the challenge with adequate, predictable, and sustainable financing to drive this opportunity for powerful transformation.

The financing requirements for sustainable development in Africa are high but a creative policy paradigm will allow us to shift and unlock resources to finance this transformation. With declining development aid and the changing ecology of global development finance, there is consensus that aid must complement rather than be a substitute for Africa's development aspirations, as was the case in the past. The solution lies in exploring innovative sources of financing. These can be leveraged from new partnerships, innovative instruments for domestic resource mobilisation, the private sector, and sources of climate finance.

Innovative financing a must for Africa

After debating structural transformation and its imperatives, such as regional integration, the demographic dividend and urbanisation opportunities or climate change challenges, time has come to address more squarely the key question of how to finance Africa's transformation. Must Africa go the old way, begging for aid? Is there a new way? Is this a discussion which is more crucial for Africa than any other region?

Overall, many African countries such as Ethiopia, Uganda, and Rwanda are complementing the traditional sources of domestic financing identified above with alternative sources such as sovereign wealth funds, pension funds, remittances, and diaspora bonds (see Figures 5.3 and 5.4). However, their main challenge is to align these instruments with their broader development priorities.

A few African governments such as Nigeria and Botswana have established sovereign wealth funds to manage their large excess reserves and

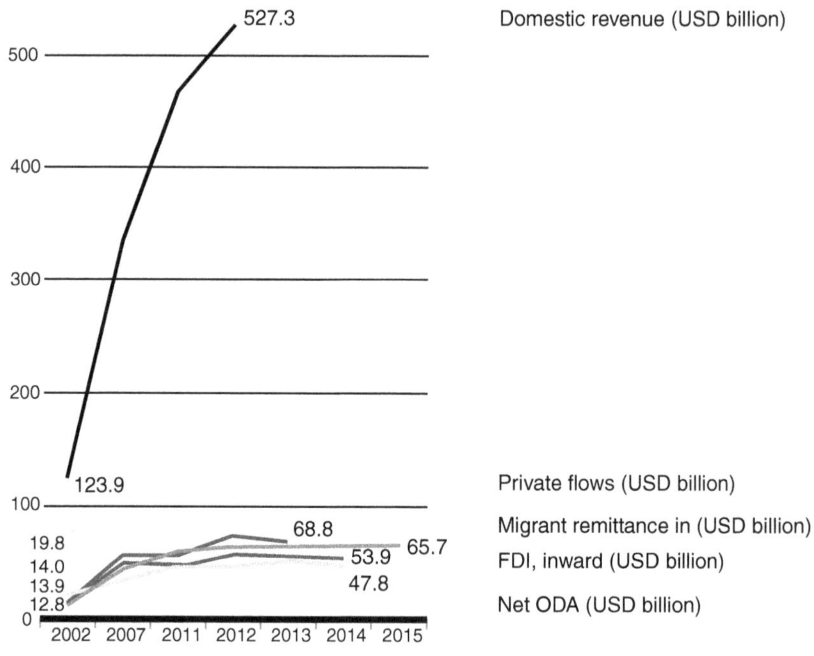

Figure 5.3 Trends in domestic resource mobilisation in Africa
Source: ECA, 2015e.

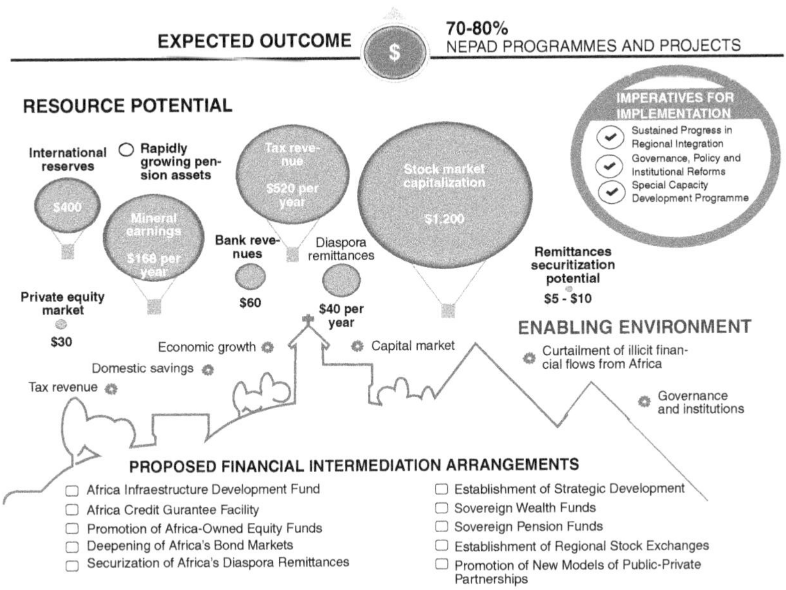

Figure 5.4 Variety of the innovative sources of finance for Africa's development
Source: ECA, 2015e.

resource windfalls. As of early 2016, 15 such funds had been set up. Although these funds can help to steer investment towards structural transformation, they suffer from poor governance, with a lack of transparency and accountability and weak institutions creating the risk of expropriation, abuse, and corruption.

Pension funds are another important source of domestic financial resources. African pension funds currently represent a growing domestic source of capital for private equity estimated at over $29 billion (Ashiagbor et al., 2014). If properly utilised, they can fuel investment in local businesses, infrastructure projects, and services that are desperately needed for Africa's continued transformation and growth.

The insurance sector also has similar innovative potential in the financing of Africa's development. For now, the sector is small and is still dominated by obligatory, state-owned schemes administered by national social security corporations. Most African countries have restrictions on how and where funds can be invested, which ultimately limits investment returns (ECA, 2014a).

With the reduction in conflict and better economic management across the continent, stable and predictable economic and political environments have lessened the risks for business investors, thus giving companies more confidence to exploit profitable investment opportunities in Africa. The continent learned the importance of building on strong foundations from the financial crash of 2008. This requires a paradigm shift in the minds of the fund managers as well as capital market perception and thinking about Africa.

We have to constantly remind ourselves about the caveats to Africa's promise. First, although Africa is a dynamic and growing region, considerable challenges and risks remain with most driven by activities of external players. Second, the continent's growth is often couched in figures such as gross domestic product but what really matters is how such growth is shared and distributed. If growth is not inclusive and broad-based, people will not feel that they are part of Africa's promise. Africa's population is young and growing but there are still large segments of the population that do not have enough money to cover their basic daily needs. Third, Africa's story is also about the continent's position vis-à-vis the rest of the world. Even though it is big, the continent needs transformation, and with that comes competitiveness from rivals for the same spot. Fourth, one has to be cautious about treating Africa as a single geo-political entity: countries vary from one to the other and differences regarding education, the health system, and rule of law matter. Lastly, Africa needs a strong political agenda in order to address challenges such as its infrastructure deficit and relatively underdeveloped financial system necessary for mobilising the requisite resources.

Under a decade ago, for example, the concept of private equity was not well known in Africa but is indicative of Africa's growing attractiveness to investors. These days, more and more capital is coming to Africa, and private equity is being discussed in many forums, which shows that the industry is gaining traction. In 2015 African private equity firms cashed in on investments at the highest rates in almost a decade, with investments being sold in 44 companies, in comparison to 39 companies in 2014 and 2013 (Ernst & Young and AVCA, 2016). Data from leading firm Preqin, which tracks private equity trends, revealed that the second quarter of 2013 was one of the strongest private equity fundraising quarters of recent years, with 164 funds securing an impressive $124 billion in aggregate capital (see www.preqin.com/products/preqin-pro/private-equity/22075). Indeed, statistics from the past three years indicate that there are some significant investments being made in the private equity industry. According to the African Development Bank, investment deals in Africa are reported to have increased from $890 million in 2010 to $3 billion by 2011, an increase of some 30 per cent. Meanwhile, according to estimates by AVCA, 823 PE deals were reported in Africa between 2010 and 2015, totalling $21.6bn (AVCA, 2016).

Private equity in Africa demonstrated that benefits do not only accrue to limited partners, general partners, and portfolio companies but also to Africans through local and regional markets. Africa, might have finally found a way to whet the appetite of private equity investors because it is an alternative source of capital that spans infrastructure, health services, and agriculture and with a high return on investment. Each success breeds new opportunities and could resound as an integral part of the transformation of Africa.

The ability to strengthen, build, and preserve capital in Africa is in line with Africa's search for innovative financing mechanisms. In the recent years, African governments have taken an active role in changing the investment landscape. Aid is no longer the panacea. This shift is associated with evidence-based policies. Economic activity thrives at the confluence of multiple sources of capital. As Africa builds its reputation in global capital markets, each success story establishes it as a destination for global capital flows. Steering them towards transformational projects is what is expected from governments that are strategic and focused.

The backbone of the transformation agenda is infrastructure. Here Africa offers opportunities in road, rail transport, aviation, energy, water, mineral resources exploitation, agro-business, and industrial development. The opportunity to diversify an investors' portfolio is not negligible. However, it remains a challenge, given the stark lack of liquidity and the scarce access to capital markets. African regulatory bodies need to engage meaningfully with private equity funds to understand the legal and regulatory requirements for a radiant African ecosystem.

African governments have responsibilities to fulfil in order to create an enabling environment. National, regional, and continental ecosystems must be upgraded to better support large-scale investments. Africa has come a long way, especially since it now has an increasingly stable and predictable economic and political environment. Reducing political and economic risk provides greater confidence for investors.

The real test is the confidence that capital will afford to Africa by committing to long-term engagement as opposed to short-terms gains. The reality is that Africa cannot rely on development aid for the transformation agenda; hence its appetite is moving towards private investment and domestic resource mobilisation. Indeed, the share of aid, including country-programmable aid, to least developed countries (particularly in Africa), has been falling in recent years and a reversal in this trend is not expected soon (OECD/DAC, 2018).

A similar trend is discernible in the case of small island developing states and countries affected by conflict. Beyond declining aid levels, OECD studies also highlight a shift in aid allocations away from the poorest countries to middle-income countries in the name of "efficiency" and reduction of risk exposure to such "investments". In contrast, current evidence suggests that development aid from countries that are not members of the Development Assistance Committee is growing rapidly, especially those that form part of the axis of South–South cooperation. Assessments and forecasts of aid flows from Africa's other major donors is, however, hampered by a lack of data and systematic reporting.

In a changing world, governments can no longer ignore the blurred lines between private and social sectors. Impact investing, with its focus on better outcomes, has the potential to transform social desires into successful outcomes. To better support Africa's developmental efforts, it is imperative that the post-2015 global partnership be consistent with the ongoing rebalancing of geopolitical and economic interests in favour of developing countries. In this sense, a fair reform of the multilateral trade and financial architecture calls for greater attention to the development dimension and a stronger voice for the developing world in key international forums (including the Bretton Woods institutions).

For instance, it is true that a key challenge facing Africans today continues to be food security, along with the development of a sustainable agricultural sector (Lopes, 2015d). In particular, the African agricultural sector is deficient in capital needed to improve farm productivity, enhance crop yields, and produce more food for local consumption. Studies show that growth in the agricultural sector has a greater impact on poverty reduction than growth in other sectors.

Climate finance offers unique windows of opportunity to deal with both climate change and repositioning Africa as a cleaner producer by leapfrogging technological platforms and tapping into the exceptional renewable energy potential of the continent. However, the climate finance architecture is too complex. Insufficient resources to meet African and global climate challenges are spread thinly across many small funds such as the Green Climate Fund and Global Environment Facility, with overlapping remits.

In addition to national capacity-related constraints, African countries also currently face a number of difficulties in accessing climate funds, some of which have cumbersome and complex access procedures. More financial resources need to be mobilised for the climate finance architecture to support climate mitigation and adaptation activities and the policy, regulatory, and enabling environments so as to encourage large-scale investments (Nakhooda and Norman (2014).

Africa could organise a forum where investments are speedily transacted along the lines of the World Economic Forum (Le Pere, 2018). The potential of domestic resource mobilisation is also immense. From better contract negotiations of extractive and other natural resources, to improved tax systems, or better use of sovereign funds and reserves, Africa has been short-changed by lack of appropriate policies. Illicit financial flows must be aggressively addressed. If the continent finds itself at the bottom of the Transparency Index, this has a lot to do with the current that serves the interests of those who are the local beneficiaries of corruption. Denouncing illicit financial flows is not just a moral imperative; it is also a good element of transformative policies.

Africa's migrants are remitting more than $50 billion per annum, besides paying the world's highest transfer fees on top of their human sacrifices (ECA, 2015c). The use of this asset class is far from productive right now. With a few exceptions, recipient countries have a long way to go in establishing attractive vehicles for these funds. Reducing the cost of sending remittances (both within Africa and into Africa from abroad) and developing financial instruments to channel such flows into development programmes and projects would optimise their developmental impact. Remittances routed through informal channels remain unquantifiable yet could be significant. Introducing new and alternative avenues for money transfer could also enhance financial inclusion and encourage the use of formal channels, which would in turn improve the measurement and reach of remittances and the assessment of their developmental impact.

Global impact investments accounted for about $8 billion in 2012, a third of it going to Africa. Impact investments are clearly an emerging and innovative source of finance that has the potential to become an important complement to traditional investments (UNDP, 2013b). Impact investments can have both direct and indirect positive effects on human development in areas such as education, health, and the environment.

The need for effective public policies to leverage FDI for the development of strategic sectors, including manufacturing, will continue to be of primary importance for Africa's structural transformation. African governments go to great lengths to court foreign direct investment, most prominently through fiscal incentives. Avoiding competitive and premature liberalisation in sensitive sectors while also retaining policy space for the pursuit of transformational goals will be paramount. Existing preferences under the rules of the WTO, for instance, will need to be safeguarded and not inadvertently relinquished in the quest for FDI and other private flows.

The continental dream is that when African children enter a history class and read Ibn Battuta's descriptions, they will feel like any other children from a modern, inclusive, and developed part of the world. African children should be amazed about how much Ibn has travelled but also, how much their own societies have travelled because they will know that their continent, Africa, is the new development frontier.

Conclusion

Africa has an opportunity to transform itself by seeking out various ways of financing its development. The expanded avenues for South–South cooperation, notably exploiting intra-African trade through the recently established continental free-trade area, will help to break the monopoly held by developed countries by providing a better environment for African policymaking and choice in terms of trade partnerships.

The fundamentals of policymaking, infrastructure, capital financing, and ensuring linkages between trade and other parts of the economy must be worked upon to make this a sustainable reality. Given its resource abundance, the continent could experiment with "finance-for-resources" funding mechanisms.

The reality of climate change adaptation measures requires focus on public awareness, research, and policy development rather than on implementation, especially the importance of financing mechanisms. Africa needs to exploit existing funding frameworks but also accommodate emerging ones such as the GEF specialised adaptation facilities, the Adaptation Fund, and the World Bank Catastrophe Risk Insurance Facility. Further innovation is required as the magnitude of resources currently needed to address the climate change problem is grossly inadequate.

Agenda 2063 is evidence of the commitment to structural transformation by the continent. Transformation requires credible macroeconomic frameworks, infrastructural development, and adequate financing. The plethora of initiatives that have been launched to attract and ensure financing for infrastructure projects, especially power, rail, road, and aviation projects must therefore be welcomed. The continent must move a step further to ensure a harmonised policy and regulatory environment for the requisite investments to take place.

Thus far, we have mapped the parameters of structural transformation and the various theoretical, conceptual, policy, and empirical logics that underpin the process in all its complexity and demands. We were also mindful of the tense interface between domestic challenges and external pressures which accompany the transformation agenda and what the appropriate response mechanisms could be.

In the next chapter, we cast the spotlight on five country cases of Tunisia, Cameroon, Cape Verde, Rwanda, and Ethiopia. These countries are not only representative of the diversity of Africa's size but are also very instructive samples of the types of development choices a country can make and the range of challenges that come with these choices.

6 Selected experiences

Drilling into the country dimensions of transformation

Introduction

In Chapters 3 and 4, we discussed the imperatives for industrialisation as key to structural transformation, setting out the primacy and avenues for industrialisation, as well as the enabling potential for transformation. As a latecomer to the industrialisation business, it was also recognised that Africa should not expect a friendly global policy environment in order to pursue its transformation agenda. However, in Chapter 5 we argued that Africa can finance its own transformation and showed the strategic areas of resource mobilisation capacities of the continent. Of course, it will not do this in a vacuum and the practicality of implementation will be a litmus test for how such capacities are used.

If great opportunities abound for Africa and the mega trends (highlighted in Chapter 1) are all in its favour, why did the process of transformation get off to a very slow start? Why do many countries still depend on the export of raw commodities – essentially exporting their jobs abroad? The answers to this question, as this chapter will show, are related to the contextual opportunities and challenges in designing successful transformation agendas. It draws lessons on "how" to effect transformation, given country specificities. In their heterogeneity, the context and characteristics of African countries play a major role in the kind of industrialisation policy choices their governments pursue. As such, context specific capacity developments will be crucial.

This chapter discusses five country examples to show how different countries can choose different development pathways with different outcomes. Indeed, even small countries can make significant progress if the "right" vision, strategies, policies, and political commitments mix are in place. The cases discussed are:

- Tunisia demonstrates how the context of excellent development indicators can be married with issues of governance.
- Cameroon is a country with enormous industrialisation potential which has been undermined by the absence of robust diversification policies.
- Cape Verde is a model and exemplary African country but is at risk of regressing due to inward looking perspectives on development.

- Rwanda highlights the importance of staying the course, where the role of leadership and governance has been paramount.
- Ethiopia presents an emerging archetype of a modern African developmental state.

The country experiences not only point to "how to transform" but underscore "how big the start-up challenges" are. While such challenges are not insurmountable, they nevertheless require carefully targeted intervention policies that are rooted in the needs of societies and grounded in the conviction to execute best-fit policies that change the circumstances and efforts of structural transformation.

Tunisia's economic future is in Africa

Tunisia, already at a political crossroads, must now also change its economic strategy and turn more towards Africa as opposed to Europe. Following a number of terrorist attacks since the 2011 Arab spring, Tunisia's central bank revised its growth estimates in 2015 as not likely to exceed 1 per cent for that year. Growth did not reach 1 per cent and recorded growth stood at 0.9 per cent (ECA, 2016a). This slowdown is partly due to the security situation. However, at a structural level there is also a slump in external demand for goods from Tunisia, which conducts 64 per cent of its trade with the European Union. Table 6.1 presents the outlook for the Tunisian economy 2014–2019.

Table 6.1 Tunisian Macro outlook indicators 2014–2019

	2014	*2015*	*2016 e*	*2017 f*	*2018 f*	*2019 f*
Real GDP growth, at constant market prices	2.3	1.1	1.0	2.3	2.8	3.2
Private consumption	1.8	2.3	0.8	1.9	2.8	2.7
Government consumption	4.2	8.8	8.9	−3.3	3.5	3.4
Gross Fixed Capital Investment	1.2	−4.5	2.2	4.1	6.5	6.6
Exports, goods and services	3.9	−3.2	3.2	1.7	4.2	4.3
Imports, goods and services	2.2	2.7	3.9	3.4	3.3	3.3
Real GDP growth, at constant factor prices	2.3	0.5	1.2	2.1	2.5	2.8
Agriculture	2.8	8.5	2.6	2.7	3.0	3.0
Industry	−1.1	−1.0	−6.6	−3.5	−1.2	−1.1
Services	3.8	0.0	4.3	4.2	3.7	4.1
Inflation (Consumer Price Index)	4.9	4.9	3.7	4.9	4.0	3.3
Current account balance (% of GDP)	−9.1	−8.9	−9.0	−8.4	−7.6	−7.1
Fiscal balance (% of GDP)	−5.0	−5.6	−6.0	−5.9	−5.5	−5.0
Debt (% of GDP)	50.8	55.4	61.8	66.1	68.5	67.5
Primary balance (% of GDP)	−3.2	−3.7	−3.8	−3.6	−2.8	−2.5

Source: Computed from AfDB database. Note: Annual percent change unless indicated otherwise.

Since the 1950s, Tunisia has sought integration in the European market and value chains, with a view to attracting textile, mechanical, automotive, aeronautical, and plastic manufacturing industries based imported technology (Moussa, 1998). This strategy was underpinned by the sustained growth in Europe and by Tunisia's competitiveness, based on its proximity to the Old World, the low cost of its labour, and tax incentives. This orientation towards Europe rather than Africa was justifiable at that time when the African continent was not seen as a market with great potential. This decision to turn towards Europe has been doubly disadvantageous for Tunisia, since the country now not only suffers from the economic downturn of its main economic partner but remains cut off from the African market.

One of the most significant changes over the last two decades regarding how global production and trade are organised is the growing importance of global value chains in the management and coordination of manufacturing and trade links between countries (Kaplinsky, 2000).[1] This has caused production to be more fragmented and for trade between countries to increase alongside inequality and poverty. Developing countries have started to change how they govern production to avoid tendencies such as the continuing decline in their terms of trade (Prebisch, 1950; Singer, 1950) by diversifying from primary commodity exports. In the case of Tunisia, expanding from a commodity such as oil and gas, citrus and vegetables to contract manufacturing of apparel and textiles as well as electronic products.

One way to cope with these changes is to develop regional value chains in a cooperative manner, both in North Africa and in the rest of the continent, thereby creating new and dynamic comparative advantages (Donna et al., 2017); and speeding up the strategic diversification primary commodities such as hydrocarbons and increased sophistication of the concerned economies (Behar and Freund, 2011; Rouis and Tabor, 2013).

As noted already, African growth is strong. It relies on both private consumption and investment supported by a growing middle class (Ncube and Shimeless, 2012). By 2020, more than 30 million Africans will have joined the middle class and will spend more than half of their income on outlays other than housing and food. This growth in consumption represents a powerful tool for the structural transformation of economies in the region, as demand grows for manufactured goods and a wide range of services. The Tunisian case shows that the levers of structural transformation can be developed for Africa.

Opening up to intra-African trade

Unfortunately, Tunisia is not particularly well integrated with the rest of the continent. In terms of its share of African exports in relation to GDP, it ranks twenty-ninth. While it has one of the best regulatory environments in Africa (fourth in terms of starting and operating a local business), Tunisia ranks only twenty-eighth in terms of attractiveness for foreign investment.

Accordingly, when we look at regional value chains, Tunisia ranks twenty-first in share of the total exports of intermediate goods within Africa.

A study that ECA has just conducted with UNIDO assesses the impact of various strategic trade agreements on exports for Tunisia and North Africa.

Thus, the Continental Free Trade Agreement has the potential to promote the export of Tunisian manufactured goods. These products, which in November 2015 accounted for nearly half of its exports (48 per cent), are expected to increase to $2.3 billion (an increase of 6.8 per cent) by 2020. This figure could be doubled (to $4.4 billion) if trade facilitation measures were enacted, boosting the effectiveness of trade-related administrative procedures by 25 per cent (ECA, AU, and AfDB, 2012). With these reforms, the share of manufactured goods in Tunisia's exports to the rest of the continent would further increase and would constitute the bulk of its exports.

A similar agreement with the other countries of the Arab League would encourage exports of mining products, while the strengthening of its Association Agreement with the European Union would more likely stimulate the export of agricultural products.

These findings clearly indicate that Tunisia, like other countries in the region, must ensure that its trade agreements are implemented in a sequence. Such action would be strategically advantageous to those companies exporting increasingly sophisticated manufactured industrial products, thereby creating modern jobs in urban centres. This will also entail trade facilitation reforms and investment in hard and soft infrastructure, primarily oriented towards intra-African trade but also as part of a wider export-oriented development strategy (World Bank, 2007[2]).

Tourism remains an asset

Tourism has been critical to the development of Tunisia (Smaoui, 1979; Poirier, 1995; Bleasdale and Tapsell, 1999). It contributed 14.2 per cent and 12.2 per cent of total GDP and employment respectively in 2017 (World Travel and Tourism Council, 2018). However, Tunisia will not be able to take full advantage of the WTO Bali agreement (focusing on trade facilitation) unless it first implements the recommended reforms, primary of which is strengthening its regional integration in the Maghreb and the rest of the continent.

Where tourist services are concerned, Tunisia has an important part to play at the continental level. In terms of volumes, the terrorist attacks have had different impacts on regional tourist arrivals (Jeffrey and Bleasdale, 2017). Between 2010 and 2015, visits by Europeans declined by 45.2 per cent, while over the same period those from Algeria went up by 35.6 per cent. This differential impact illustrates the need for Tunisia to reorient its strategy towards the African tourist market, whose numbers and purchasing power have experienced unprecedented growth. For purposes of comparison, 72.5 per cent of tourist arrivals in South Africa, which is one of the main African destinations, originate from other African countries (ibid.).

Tourism development is based primarily on an efficient air transport sector and marketing strategy and requires a presence in key emerging markets. Tunisair, the Tunisian national airline, has barely more than a dozen destinations in Africa, only five of which are in sub-Saharan Africa. By contrast, Royal Air Maroc serves more than 30 locations, including 27 countries outside North Africa.

Tunisia also has assets in many service sectors with high added value, such as medical tourism, higher education, engineering and consulting, which would enable it to capture a significant share of these rapidly growing markets. The examples are legion, but the message remains the same: the economic future of Tunisia is unquestionably in Africa.

Cameroon must roar: at a 7 per cent minimum!

Cameroon has vast resources for driving its industrialisation and agricultural transformation but it has been suggested that the country suffers from the resource curse and related rent-seeking activities (Yates, 1996; Wunder, 2005). Unfortunately, the economy's recent average annual growth of 4.6 per cent does not reflect the full potential that lies in the transformation of its country riches. The economy is relatively diversified through the exploitation of vast agricultural resources, forestry, mining, and energy. Oil, cocoa, wood, rubber, and cotton have dominated exports. This diversification and beneficiation of these resources could easily lend itself to economic transformation through industrialisation.

Table 6.2 presents the structure of the Cameroon economy as of 2018. The primary sector constitutes 17 per cent of the GDP and employs 62 per cent of the population. Before the development of the oil trade in the late 1970s, agriculture was the country's main economic pillar. Cameroon is one of the world's leading producers of cocoa, coffee, bananas, palm products, tobacco, rubber, and cotton. Fishing and forestry are two of the country's additional significant activities. Cameroon's mineral resources include bauxite ore and iron. The secondary sector accounts for 26 per cent of GDP and employs 9 per cent of the workforce. The tertiary sector accounts for more than half of the GDP (57 per cent) and employs 30 per cent of the active population.

Table 6.2 Sectoral composition of the economy

Breakdown of economic activity by sector	*Agriculture*	*Industry*	*Services*
Employment by sector *(in % of total employment)*	62.0	9.3	28.7
Value added *(in % of GDP)*	16.7	26.6	56.7
Value added *(Annual % change)*	6.8	3.2	4.5

Source: World Bank, Latest Available Data. Because of rounding, the sum of the percentages may be smaller/greater than 100 per cent.

In terms of its potential, the young and dynamic youth of Cameroon have a role to play in converting this cheetah's raw assets into the industrial products that will make the country proud. It is possible to transform agricultural products, wood, rubber, and cotton for the local, regional, and international markets. Indeed, Wunder and Sunderlin (2004) forcefully note that Cameroon's oil wealth has not been substantial enough to reverse forest loss or cause forest area to expand. But after 1989, the wood exports began to increase and reached a peak in 1994, the year of currency devaluation. The regional potential for speeding up transformation is particularly relevant. Given its geographical position and its ample access to the sea, the country can easily locate itself as a provider of goods and services between Central and West Africa.

Cameroon needs to work on value chains to maximise its economic base and general performance (Chenery et al., 1986; Devarajan, 1999). If cotton potential is considered as a demonstration it is possible to price the risk exposures (Douya, 2001). This can be done by developing strong linkages between the farmers and the nascent fashion industry based on factoring the quality demanded by consumers into the development of a textile industry. The opportunity to gain market share is very compelling, especially since local Cameroonians only control 1 per cent of the clothing industry. With entrepreneurs demanding locally sourced quality inputs, the proceeds from the clothing industry can be distributed to reduce the share of imports of new and second-hand clothes. The clothing industry is one area where the 64 per cent of the under 25s could redirect their energy, boosting economic growth. To achieve it, Cameroon has to devise and implement policy measures that support local enterprises in their endeavour to reap the benefits of their creativity in local and regional value chains. Their competitiveness will be enhanced when barriers to innovation and doing business are fully removed. Cameroon needs to implement reforms that reduce the significant structural and institutional rigidities that constrain the growth process (Kobou, 1993) and which will result in the requisite adjustments in the economy by agents (Herbel et al., 2002).

Fortunately, for Cameroon, there are other sectors with equal growth potential (Amin, 2002; Kobou et al., 2003). Young entrepreneurs are making inroads into the lucrative market of applications for smartphones and tablets. They have understood the space for frugal innovation. AppsTech, a company founded by Rebecca Enonchong and which is Oracle certified, specialises in the management of software for enterprises. Rebecca has entered the lucrative software solutions market at a time when the demand for these services is rising all over Africa. Another example is Tony Smith, who founded Limitless which specialises in tablet, smartphone, and flat screen conceptions. Such entrepreneurship can accelerate the changes required in a stagnant workforce by demonstrating that once jobs are not available we should strive to create them ourselves. ECA (2017) argues that governance reforms will remain a key ingredient in the transformation of resource rich African countries.

It is crucial that Cameroon's socio-economic policies reflect the needs of the 75 per cent young jobless population. The government will obviously not be able to absorb the unemployed through civil service jobs alone and thus needs a policy framework through which major human capital challenges in the formal and informal sector labour market can be addressed (Asek, 2017). Given Cameroon's resource endowments, its government has a real opportunity to address the mismatch between job seekers' skills and employers' needs. Solving this problem will prepare youth for those jobs that will come with economic transformation.

Jobs opportunities exist in the oil and gas sector. Its diversification could contribute to increasing the local content. The need for technical skills is real but companies should be made responsible for re-sourcing them locally. If they are not available, the companies will then have to contribute to training and fostering new skills. Hydrocarbons represent 8 per cent of GDP in 2011 (World Bank, 2014) and are set to expand, given Cameroon's natural gas reserves of 135 billion cubic meters, against the country needs of about 30 billion. The production and export of minerals, energy, and petrochemicals will diversify the skills that Cameroon attracts as well as the training that will be offered to the youth. Since 2012, production increases have required investment, technological upgrades, and trained human resources.

The construction of a deep-sea port with an extensive industrial zone for heavy, medium, and light industry is a positive step in increasing employment. Electricity supply will expand, thanks to the Kribi Power Project as well as hydroelectric dams in Lom Pagar and Memve'ele. In about five years, Cameroon should have completed the expansion and modernisation of its entire infrastructure which its industrial transformation depends on.

Cameroon needs also to improve entrepreneurs' access to financing by developing innovative banking credit products. Currently, a vast industrialisation drive has not been linked to the way in which export revenues are used. The role of small and medium scale entrepreneurs is crucial for shifting to a more labour-intensive model, especially since mining only employs less than 10 per cent of the workforce.

When it comes to trade patterns of the country, the three first import categories are oil, rice, and frozen fish. These are all categories in which Cameroon can produce itself and even export. Apart from mining, the country is blessed with amazingly fertile land, and vast sea and marine resources but, of course, one should not underestimate the amount of effort and energy needed for beneficiation in the three areas. However, the gain will be significant if Cameroon manages to steer itself along a more aggressive development path.

There is no doubt that Cameroon can do much better economically. Its strengths, as described, are solid. Nevertheless, it requires robust policies and leadership that is capable of overcoming its ethnic, regional, and linguistic factionalism, all which have dire consequences for transformation (Gören, 2013). Attaining 7 per cent should be its main goal since such a growth rate would allow the country to double its economy within a decade and create the conditions for drastic poverty reduction. Failing this, the country's development aspirations will be seriously compromised.

Cape Verde development trajectory: a lesson for Africa

Cape Verde is a real African success story (AfDB, 2012). It has a history of good governance and strong institutions, enhanced human capital, and reduction of vulnerability to shocks. In the space of 30 years, from 1982 to 2012, per capita income in Cape Verde has increased by a factor of 3.5 in real terms. This progress represents the formidable achievements of this small nation as has been documented (Halter, 1993; Marques et al., 2001; Bourdet and Falck, 2006; Batalha and Carling, 2008; Rocha et al., 2008; Challinor, 2008; Cardoso, 2004; Carling and Akensson, 2009).

There are a number of important lessons that support the Cape Verdean development trajectory (AfDB, 2012a, 2012b). First, there is the importance of development enablers. A key element of Cape Verde's success has been its ability to maintain fundamental preconditions for economic development. This has included securing peace and stability, building and improving sound institutions, realising the benefits of good governance, and maintaining macroeconomic stability. We learn that growth accelerations are a relatively frequent phenomenon, including in Africa; but the key difference between a boom-and-bust cycle and a sustainable development trajectory is preventing a subsequent growth collapse from offsetting the growth acceleration (Rodrik, 2003; Hausman et al., 2005), and ensuring that the latter is long-lived (Xu, 2011). Developing countries – especially those of Africa – should keep in mind that paying attention to development enablers is precisely a way of avoiding fatal mistakes, and through which continuous efforts could be made to realise the preconditions for sustainable growth.

A second lesson is the fundamental importance of forging a clear and consistent development strategy (AfDB, 2012b; 2014) which is shared amongst the various stakeholders and coherently spelt out in the various policy documents (Poverty Reduction Strategy Papers, Diagnostic Trade Integrated Study, Vision 2030, and the like). Forging a similar vision and building consensus around it is one of the primary roles of a developmental state (ECA, 2016c).

In addition, one can underscore insightful elements of Cape Verde's developmental vision:

- The attention it has paid to all the three dimensions of sustainability, namely, the economic with an emphasis on its efforts to maintain macroeconomic stability and spur new engines of growth; the social with an emphasis on the inclusiveness of growth; and the environmental epitomised by the commendable objective of achieving 100 per cent renewable energy use.

- The country has pursued economic integration not as an end. It embarked on a deliberate strategy to harness its geographical advantage of becoming a hub located within easy reach of some of the world's biggest markets. These include the EU, USA, and South America as well as an expanding market in Africa to mitigate the risks stemming from its heightened vulnerability.
- It has considered a sound and forward-looking assessment of the country's advantages and disadvantages. This audit has helped it anticipate risk factors such as the challenges arising from graduating out of the LDC category which has entailed taking appropriate mitigating measures to ensure a "smooth transition" while innovating. A good example is the role given to Cape Verde's creative economy.
- There have been sizeable long-term investments in economic infrastructure and continuous efforts to improve the business environment. These are key measures through which economic integration can become operational and bring about economic gains.

In this context, the Enhanced Integrated Framework (EIF) has been instrumental in providing a platform for development partners, recipient countries, and agencies to work together towards a more cohesive in-country trade integration strategy. The EIF has supported the mainstreaming of trade and regional integration strategies, in the conviction that Cape Verdean ownership of trade policy had to be a key principle.

A third important element of reflection from Cape Verde's development trajectory is the importance of strategically engaging a broad array of development partners and catalysing their support. Over time, Cape Verde has established close partnerships not only with traditional donors but also with emerging actors, most notably Brazil whose development cooperation is particularly active among Lusophone countries. With respect to traditional donors and in the context of the Fourth Global review of Aid for Trade, Cape Verde is one of the world's largest recipients of Aid for Trade: between 2009 and 2011, it received an average yearly disbursement of over $222 per capita. Of this disbursement, investment in Cape Verde's infrastructure attracted as much as 83 per cent of these funds; that is over $184 per capita annually.

Moreover, the country has retained close ties with its Diaspora community which continues playing a significant role in the country's development through remittances, investments, and knowledge networks (Resende-Santos, 2015). These ties validate much of the debate about the impacts of migration on development (Durand et al., 1996; Ratha, 2003; Bourdet and Falck, 2006; Skeldon, 2008; Faist, 2009; Ratha et al., 2011; de Haas, 2012; Schiller, 2012).

Some of the challenges that lie ahead for Cape Verde (AfDB, 2012b) include the unreliability of external development financing, climate change, trade dependency, and poor resilience to shocks.

The first challenge is to redress some of the imbalances emerging in Cape Verde's structure of production and in the composition of exports. The boom in tourism and transport services are but a confirmation of the potential role high-value-added services can play as engines of growth. However, it is hard to imagine whether poverty eradication could be achieved in a country of half a million inhabitants without boosting the productivity of the primary sector, especially agriculture and fisheries. Even in the context of a small island economy, this issue echoes the challenges confronting a number of bigger African economies where the agricultural sector still employs the majority of the labour force, and hence plays a fundamental role in poverty reduction and food security.

A related second point, which has to some extent been addressed in Cape Verde's Agenda for Transformation or Vision 2030, is the need to promote the emergence of industrial clusters. Given the small size of the domestic market, in this respect Cape Verde has no other alternative than to look to the world market. Spurring the emergence of firms capable of connecting to global value chains is all the more important to diversify the economy and generate more jobs. Similarly, it is important to promote stronger linkages between tourism and other activities by transforming the former into a more transversal industry. Once again, despite different context-specific conditions, the challenge of promoting industrialisation and connecting domestic firms to regional and global supply chains is common to all African countries, not just to Cape Verde.

A third challenge for Cape Verde's economy is the structural deficit in its current account, which on average exceeded 12 per cent of GDP in the 2002–2011 period. Far from being a problem of Cape Verde alone, this development challenge is fairly common across resource-poor African states, and even more so across the SIDS. Indeed, this represents a major dimension of SIDS structural vulnerability. African SIDS tend to be overlooked in the predominant literature on climate change. Their differing vulnerabilities are drowned in a narrative that focuses on biophysical impacts with only superficial reference to the issue of social vulnerability. Local communities are in the frontline of climate change impacts. They are already adapting to climate variability and change. After all, they have a history of surviving social and environmental changes through a wealth of indigenous knowledge that includes intricate systems of weather forecasting as well as mitigation and adaptation practices. Table 6.3 provides a summary of the current climate trends and projected future climate scenarios for the country. It shows projected increases in temperature, uncertain rainfall forecast, and a trend to increasing extreme weather events. The IPCC projects the sea level in this region to be between 0.13m and 0.56m higher by 2090 under all scenarios (AfDB, 2014).

However, effective and modern pathways for future adaptation will not occur in a vacuum. They will need to be facilitated, structured, and organised within an institutional setting. The solution dynamics must therefore

Table 6.3 Summary of climatic trends and future scenarios in Cape Verde

Period	*Temperature*	*Rainfall*	*Extreme events*
Historical (1960–2006)	Temperature increased by 0.6°C between 1960 and 2006, an average rate of 0.14°C per decade. The increase in the wet season (August, September, October – ASO) is higher, at 0.23°C per decade.	The average rainfall has not changed, although there could be large difference in precipitation year by year and island by island.	Some unusually extreme rainfall events happened in the latest decade.
2060s	Increase of 0.7°C–2.5°C. 16%–32% increase in hot days 23%–49% increase in hot nights	Models are not consensual, except for a further reduction in the rainfall in the dry season	Not enough data available
2090s	Increase of +1.2–3.7°C. 23–51% increase in hot days 31%–79% increase in hot nights. Cold nights decrease to zero in all scenarios.	Models are not consensual, except for a further reduction in the rainfall in the dry season	Not enough data available

Source: AfDB, 2014.

be widened and the means for cost-effective, participatory, and sustainable implementation facilitated.

Finally, Cape Verde remains vulnerable to a wide range of economic shocks such as instability of production, terms of trade fluctuations, and adverse weather events despite their relatively high income per capita. In this respect, Cape Verde confirms SIDS' specific needs for special support measures aiming at mitigating economic vulnerability. In so far as economic diversification is accompanied by the expansion of export revenues (or the relative decline in imports), it can contribute to mitigating external imbalances. Yet it seems unlikely that the structural external deficit will reverse completely, regardless of any smooth transition from Cape Verde's LDC status.

Rwanda National Dialogue and how to emulate the best in the class[3]

Compared to the other countries discussed in this chapter, Rwanda presents a unique case in championing structural transformation such that the last two decades have seen significant change with growth averaging 6 per cent per annum. Rwanda has thus attracted plaudits from diverse groups, ranging from international financial institutions (Tumwebaze, 2014; Lagarde, 2015) to mainstream (Collier, 2015) and heterodox scholars (Kelsall, 2013; Booth and Golooba-Mutebi, 2014). However, Rwanda's growth success has been accompanied by anxiety about limitations on freedom of speech and human rights (Reyntjens, 2011). Debates also persist with regard to whether or not inequality has been reduced in recent years (Ansoms and Rostagno, 2012; Booth and Golooba-Mutebi, 2014).

Notwithstanding some of the disquiet noted above, Rwanda's National Dialogue is a unique form of participatory democracy (Aldean, 2017) and provides momentum for sustaining the country's over two decades of development. Inclusiveness, togetherness, and unity, the topic of December 2014's national dialogue, Umushyikirano, resonated well with transformation. Rwanda's developmental state seeks to ground itself on addressing and narrowing cultural cleavages on the basis of the Imihigo which is aimed at ensuring that development outcomes are accelerated, and are equally shared and spread (Ndahiro, 2015). Rwanda also has several attributes of a classic developmental state: a transformative leadership with a developmental vision, closely intertwined business and political sectors to build an entrepreneurial society, and a highly effective public bureaucracy. What makes Rwanda different from states with similar developmental ambitions is its unique post-genocidal setting and special home-grown solutions (Booth and Golooba-Mutebi, 2012; Biedermann, 2016; Harrison, 2016).

Countries that show resilience in transforming their economies cannot wait for "favourable winds" or alternative political motivations (Mann and Berry, 2016). Often, they generate their own political developmental agenda to change the course of their economic and social history. Without making the historical mistake to compare 1965 to 1994, there are similarities between Singapore and Rwanda. Just like Rwanda (Crisafulli and Redmond, 2012; Johnson, 2013), good governance and leadership was a foundation to Singapore's economic transformation. Lee Kuan Yew led Singaporeans through rough waters by embarking on a route less travelled to deliver economic and social transformation. The government had to transform Singapore from a re-exporting economy under the colonial regime to an export-driven economy.

Unlike Hong Kong and Taiwan, there was no exodus of entrepreneurs from China to Singapore, there were no domestic savings, and regional markets were more likely to impose trade barriers to help their own industries. Singapore addressed these challenges by building its manufacturing base through FDI. In addition, domestic savings were mobilised through the compulsory Central Provident Fund very much like Rwanda's Agaciro is trying to do. Who could have imagined that Singapore would become the largest Asia port, have the most profitable airline in the world, and out-perform Switzerland as an attractive financial market? Can Rwanda emulate this remarkable example? In many aspects, the discipline and determination that made Singapore are legendary: it had its own governance models and standards, and never allowed anyone to teach them lessons about what would work. They were severely criticised, paid a price from the very beginning, but at the end they had the last laugh.

Much of the success achieved in Rwanda hinges on the power of its ideas, and notions of self-reliance and resilience as well as on the forging of home-grown and innovative solutions (Biedermann, 2016; Harrison, 2016) that are now globally known, such as Gacaca, Imihigo, Abunzi, Ubudehe, and Girinka, under the stewardship of able leadership (Crisafulli and Redmond, 2012; Johnson, 2013). As Rwandans deservedly celebrate their current achievements, the new challenge is how to shift into a higher development gear which is needed to reach the 11.5 per cent GDP per year growth target as stipulated in its plan.

The National Dialogue process offers a unique opportunity to fully explore possibilities for a dynamic change in Rwanda's fortunes. The magnitude of the shifts into higher growth sectors such as industry and services needs to accelerate (Tafirenyika, 2011; Karinganire, 2012). Policies such as those implemented in Finland could see Rwandan minerals follow a transformation path as the forestry sector did in Finland. Finland exemplifies the learning organisational model in which institutional environments mould the functioning of the economy, the manner in which economic agents go about running their businesses, and the nature of their interaction. Singapore shows adversity is the beginning of a journey, not its end. Uruguay also shows that small can indeed be beautiful in many unsuspected ways in that the country worked hard to become an egalitarian society and with high per capita income, low level of inequality and the almost complete absence of extreme poverty. In relative terms, its middle class is the largest in America, and represents 60 per cent of its population (World Bank, 2018b).

A national dialogue contributes to the development of institutional arrangements and social compacts between the governor and the governed (Aldean, 2017). To be successful and endure the test of time, these societal changes must be rooted in Rwanda's cultural, political, and economic history (Behuria and Goodfellow, 2016; Biedermann, 2016; Aldean, 2017). In this respect, it is for Rwandans to define the economic transformation that will make it an industrialised nation. This has already been very well articulated in Vision 2020 and its supporting planning and strategic frameworks. In defining this transformation, Rwanda, like Finland, Singapore, or Uruguay, ought to identify which key choices should shape a prosperous future for all in the pursuit of structural transformation.

The scale of Rwanda's trade imbalance is still large. To reverse the trend, Rwanda needs to master smart protectionism and take advantage of trade opportunities in regional markets, with full cognisance of the pitfalls ahead. The Northern Corridor is a good bet. The same could be said of Rwanda's overall strong regional integration agenda. For example, Rwanda has introduced visa on arrival for all African citizens and flexible work permits.

But beyond the regional market, Rwanda ought to look at emerging markets by investing in knowledge generation of value chains that it seeks to enter.

Being a developmental state must be strategic (Biedermann, 2016). This means that the government has transparent and adequate control over the geographical territory and demonstrates strategic visionary capacities. This also implies regular consultations with the people, who need their voices to be heard in policymaking and budgetary resource allocation to promote meaningful political participation and settlements (Khan, 2010; Whitfield et al., 2015; Aldean, 2017).

Strategic leadership, strategic management, and enterprise performance are pillars of Rwanda's transformation (Crisafulli and Redmond, 2012; Johnson, 2013; Behuria and Goodfellow, 2016). In addition, the application of principles of good governance rooted in *Abunzi*, *Ubudehe*, *Imihigo*, and *Umuganda* provide a unique Rwandan touch to the relationship between governed and governor (Ndahiro, 2015). The governed, in their contribution to Rwanda, have to use their judgement to make the process rest on a creative exchange for improvement. Diligence, motivation, and commitment from leaders will create and maintain environments that boost these qualities.

Leaders thus have a responsibility to increase their level of competency to contribute to the learning environment that made other nations succeed and prosper (Behuria and Goodfellow, 2016). In this respect, national dialogues as an accountability framework represent an honest assessment of the principles that guide the relationship between governor and governed (Aldean, 2017). It can take generations to achieve structural transformation. To withstand the test of time and to stay the course requires a solid social compact between the governed and the governor. Experiences from Finland, Singapore, and Uruguay show that success is an individual and collective responsibility.

Ethiopia: an experiment in developmentalism and structural transformation

Economic growth and the general transformation in Ethiopia in recent years has been impressive (Cheru et al., 2019). Between 2000 and 2013, Ethiopia ranked second only to Angola in Sub-Saharan Africa (and equal with Equatorial Guinea) with a GDP growth rate of 9.5 per cent a year against Angola's 11.1 per cent and a Sub-Saharan mean of 5.2 per cent. For 2015, Ethiopia's GDP growth rate of 9.6 per cent was the highest in Africa and the second highest in the world (World Bank, 2015). The drivers of growth are multipronged but are not natural resource-based as is the case in countries such as Angola and Botswana.

Table 6.4 shows the value added by sector as a percentage of GDP in Ethiopia and in African low-income countries over 40 years, along with the forecast out to 2030. In both Ethiopia and across low-income African countries, the agricultural share of GDP has been steadily declining while the service

Table 6.4 Ethiopia value added by sector (percent of GDP) in Ethiopia, 1990–2030

	Ethiopia			*Low income Africa*		
	Agriculture	*Manufactures*	*Services*	*Agriculture*	*Manufactures*	*Services*
1990	52	5	38	36	12	44
2000	48	6	40	32	11	46
2010	45	4	45	33	9	47
2015	41	4	43	31	8	47
2020	36	10	49	25	16	50
2030	22	11	62	17	17	56

Source: Computed from Global Trade and Analysis Project database using International Futures model. Note that the figures may not add to 100 per cent due to computational and data errors.

sector's share of GDP has been growing. Meanwhile, the share from manufacturing value added has slowly been declining. In low-income Africa, services have been the largest source of value addition for the past few decades, whereas the shift toward a service has dominated economic activity more recently. In 2016, the Ethiopian service sector accounted for about 43 per cent of GDP while agriculture and manufacturing accounted for 41 per cent and 4 per cent, respectively. The services sector is expected to expand significantly by 2030.

As a case study in developmental thought and practice, Ethiopia is both interesting and important. It provides an example of operationalising the idea of a "developmental state" in Sub-Saharan Africa, and a critical case of the applicability of this form of governance beyond East Asia. Clapham (2018) argues that the first rule in forming a development state is the existence of a state itself. Ethiopia has had centuries of statehood, identifiable as a political unit, characterised by entrenched habits of "authoritarianism" or central rule on the one hand, and civic obedience, on the other. Ethiopian statehood has had challenges, notably its historical origins in the northern highlands, and the often-brutal imposition of central control over other areas of the present national territory.

The culture of statehood in Ethiopia has long been – and remains – hierarchical and intolerant of dissent, resulting in much of the conflict from which the country has suffered which has also been a significant barrier to the development enterprise itself.[4] It has nonetheless created an idea of the state, spread much more widely through the society, allowing Ethiopian governments to conceive and implement projects of transformation to an extent that is difficult to imagine in much of post-colonial Africa.

Although Ethiopia has a similar difficulty of managing sparsely populated territories with other African states (Herbst, 2000), it does have a dense core around the capital Addis Ababa. Ethiopia also has a long history of entrenched experiences of statehood (Vu, 2010). Clapham (2018) argues that, more importantly, the country has had a tradition of developmental ideology since the reign of emperor Tewodros (1855–1868), although its implementation was limited by factors such as physical and cultural obstacles, the weakness of the state machinery, and the demands of other more pressing priorities including control of territories. Unlike in many African experiences of state creation based on external colonialism, state capacity in Ethiopia has been an indigenous process, initially war and subsequently revolutions such as those of the Derg and the Ethiopian Peoples' Revolutionary Democratic Front (EPRDF).

Ethiopia's recent developmentalism and structural transformation agenda seem to be heavily inspired by countries such as South Korea, Japan, and China (Clapham, 2018; Lopes, 2019b). While the government continue to pay attention to transforming peasant agriculture with a view to guarantee food security (Kararach and Kedir, 2019; Lopes, 2019b), infrastructure is now seen as necessary for industrial development (Oqubay, 2015). A three-pronged approach is at play. First is the drive to improve communications networks, which for a long time was a big hindrance to development in a largely mountainous country (Clapham, 2018). The road network, for example, has reportedly been expanded from 36,496 km in 2004 to 85,966 km in 2013 (UNDP, 2013b). The rail system to the port at Djibouti has also been reconstructed.

Second is human capital development as part of broader industrial strategy, through investments in higher education and requisite skills for the new economy; as well as expansion of health services to improve the health status of both the labour force and the wider population. The third is ramping up investments in renewable energy, the centre-piece of which is the Grand Ethiopian Renaissance Dam (GERD). After completion, the dam is expected to generate 6000 MW of electricity, to be used for domestic consumption as well as export to neighbouring countries. Ethiopia demonstrated a remarkable capacity to attract the capital required to build this infrastructure, in advance of any revenues that could be used to defray its cost, by ensuring every citizen paid a levy towards the effort. In addition, cheap energy, enhanced connectivity, and skills development have underpinned the development of agribusiness, industrial parks, and the policy for accelerated industrialisation (Lopes, 2019b).

Development financing came from three broad sources. First, retained resources or rents were used to promote the development agenda. The appropriation of rents prevents surplus funds from being wasted on excessive private consumption or the appeasement of social and political interests. In Africa and elsewhere, windfalls, especially from natural resources extraction, have entirely failed to provide long-term public welfare or development goals (Clapham, 2018; Ovadia and Wolf, 2018). Kelsall (2013) has argued that one of the four prerequisites for long-horizon rent centralisation that must form the basis for a developmental state is a somewhat authoritarian yet inclusive system. With exclusion and any greater democratisation, there may be proliferations of interests that could divert rents towards greater political patronage.

A second source of funds has been development aid and concessional loans. Ethiopia has a history of hostility towards neoliberal policy stances favoured by major Western donors. It has also consistently failed to meet "good governance" criteria, in terms of practicing multiparty democracy and respect of human rights that many donors typically insist on in exchange for any support.

However, Ethiopia has managed to reposition itself diplomatically in several areas. First as a force for "stability" in an unstable Horn of Africa region. Second, Ethiopia has made common cause with Western donors over poverty reduction, and its unique ability to deliver requisite development outcomes such as gender equality. Third, by taking advantage of alternative sources of finance to the "traditional" Western agencies, and especially using China. Unlike many African countries engaged with the Chinese, Ethiopia does not have significant mineral deposits of a kind that China loves to look for. China's role in Ethiopia can arguably be explained in terms of the country's overall importance in Africa's diplomatic landscape and ideological affinity (Clapham, 2018).

The final source of capital has been FDI from a wide range of sources, including Asian companies and countries such as Turkey, China, and Japan (Clapham, 2018). FDI to Ethiopia rose from $135 million in 2000 to $953 million in 2013 (UNCTAD, 2016), and to $3.6 billion in 2017 (UNCTAD, 2018).

The development state core concern is the need to prioritise the development agenda and create the ecosystem for any such transformative development to thrive (Mkandawire, 2001; Shumuye, 2015). The critical challenge facing Ethiopia has not been the ability of the state to meet its own "developmental" obligations, but rather the ability of the private sector to provide the requisite supportive productive capacity. Government has recognised the difficulties in providing requisite services (Donnenfeld et al., 2017) and has explicitly encouraged both FDI and private sector engagement for its developmental policies to succeed. Government has aggressively sought to attract private money, including remittances to fund developmental projects in the country. For example, remittances rose by 27.7 per cent a year between 2004/05 and 2012/13, from $400 million to $2500 million (Clapham, 2018). Reforms have also been focused on easing regulation, enhancing economic governance, strengthening planning, enhancing democracy and civic participation; and strengthening diplomatic relations with countries such as Somaliland, South Sudan, Sudan, Egypt, and Eritrea (Clapham, 2018; Lopes, 2019b).

The efficiency by which the Ethiopian state has pushed its developmental agenda has been equally impressive and purposeful (UNDP, 2015; World Bank, 2015; Donnefeld et al., 2017; Lopes, 2019b). This partly explains the startling absence of any negative reaction, especially from Western donors, to Ethiopia's historically weak democratic and human rights record until recently. While the presence of China as financier is one factor, Ethiopia's success in positioning itself as a beacon of stability in a highly unstable region is also a critical element. The centrality of the state in delivering the developmental agenda based on proximity to the people and development results should not be underestimated as a lesson to the rest of the African continent (Lopes, 2019b).

Conclusion

The case studies demonstrate how and how not to engender development in the context of the pursuit of developmentalism and the requisite associated state and institutional frameworks. The cases of Tunisia and Cameroon are symptomatic of underutilised potential. With respect to Tunisia, rising domestic security concerns have thrown the tourism sector into crisis. Equally, a slow recovery in Europe has hampered growth, despite a successful political transition, a record olive oil harvest, and the substantial fall in oil prices. The country needs to review its growth strategy for purposes of exploiting the huge potential offered by the African continent. Cameroon on the other hand, has not effectively exploited the energy of its youthful population. It also has to develop the necessary value chains as well as infrastructure critical for sustained transformation and development. The finance sector has remained underdeveloped and the entrepreneurial capabilities of its citizen's remains trapped.

On the other hand, Cape Verde and Rwanda have demonstrated that change can happen. Cape Verde has gained international credibility for its sound macroeconomic policies, good governance with low corruption rates, a simplified tax system, and a reformed banking sector. Since independence, successive Cape Verdean governments have fostered pluralism and a sense of citizenship, a participatory political process, and trust between the government and citizenry, respects for human rights and civil liberties, including a free press. Successive governments have, over the years, also adapted their policies and institutions to changes in the global economy by maintaining strong strategic partnerships with a variety of countries and institutions.

Equally, Rwanda has demonstrated that it knows where it is going. The country has undertaken wide-ranging reforms to improve the environment of peace and security. Strong institutions have been established and weaker ones strengthened to foster increased citizen participation in governance with a view to enhancing social inclusion. The successful implementation of the *Gacaca* or community-level adjudications and tribunals signal progress towards national peace, security, and reconciliation. Because of the various innovations in governance and economic management, Rwanda has registered marked improvements in its business environment and has been commended by the World Bank in its Ease of Doing Business Report as one of the top five growth performers in Sub-Saharan Africa (World Bank, 2018b).

The political and business leadership openly acknowledge that Rwanda's economic potential is fundamentally linked to the conditions prevailing in the neighbouring countries. As a result, Rwanda has consequently embraced regional integration to address these impediments.

It is clear from the above case studies that every country must discover its path to development by identifying its most valuable assets in each moment of its transformation, but very importantly, what use such assets will serve. Predictability can be more valuable at a point, inclusivity on another, safety yet on another, and so on. Many ingredients make up a successful development experiment but should not be a zero-sum game since each is shaped by a complex set of historical conditions and a unique mix structural circumstances.

The next and final chapter will provide a synthesis of the major themes of previous chapters and is devoted to drawing out their institutional qualities, governing principles, and policy measures with a view to defining a future orientation for the continent's growth and development. These qualities, principles, and measures are critical not only for averting economic crises but more as vectors of structural transformation on the road that Africa must travel to reach its true potential.

The next chapter will focus on the challenges that arise from Africa's size but will also highlight development opportunities and dividends that could irrevocably change the circumstances of African states and societies for the better. However, these come up against a difficult juncture of Africa's international relations and we therefore also consider the impacts of growing protectionism and populism for Africa's transformation agenda.

Notes

1 http://siteresources.worldbank.org/INTAFRSUMESSD/Resources/1729402-1150389437293/Kaplinsky_Value_Chain.pdf.
2 http://siteresources.worldbank.org/INTEXPCOMNET/Resources/Export_Diversification_in_Egypt,_Lebanon,_Jordan,_Morocco,_and_Tunisia.pdf
3 Taken from Carlos Lopes' speech at the 12th National Dialogue – Umushyikirano – Kigali, December 18, 2014, at the invitation of President Paul Kagame.
4 These dynamics have not abated even with the attempts at reforms by the new Abiy Ahmed's government. Indeed sections of EPRDF are reportedly complaining about the liberal reforms being introduced as a betrayal of Meles Zenawi's legacy.

7 African circumstances and efforts into the future

Introduction

The previous chapters sought to show how big Africa is and how many forces have shaped its economies circumstances and individual efforts as these define the scope of the challenges of structural transformation as well as the imperative for Africans to take control of its development narrative. For a while Africans' enthusiasm about the good economic performance of the continent had a contagious complacency effect in many minds. It was as if the road to a new continental status was a given, even while many frameworks and strategies that dealt with real structural transformation were in the process of being developed and approved. Unfortunately, the time for a wake-up call has now passed and a variety of worrisome symptoms of decline yet again dominate the African story line: a combination of renewed conflict; the drop in commodities' demand and prices, including oil; high currency volatility and rising interest rates; the choking of key economic locomotives; and the devastating effects of climate change.

Paradoxically, however, the fundamentals for Africa's economic prospects are present and intact. Africa continues to register the highest growth against a global slump; and while international reserves were negatively affected, debt levels remain low, public deficits are still under control, and there has been a steady increase in investment sources. Recent Summits with India and China demonstrated trust and confidence in Africa's future growth and development. Infrastructure projects have mostly not been affected by the global downturn, from a new Suez Canal to the largest ever dam in Ethiopia or world-size solar farms in three countries: Burkina Faso, South Africa, and Morocco. So, where then, we ask, are the key factors to be found that shift the mainstream narrative back to Africa's past of underdevelopment? Fundamentally, it is a combination of two factors: the pervasive fragility perception and lack of deeper structural transformation.

Globalisation has the potential to alter the growth trajectories of countries, with implications for poor people that directly or indirectly affect their access to assets and markets. Many African countries, however, are yet to translate any of the opportunities offered by globalisation into increased poverty reduction (von Braun and Mengistu, 2009). Moreover, for those that have, integration into global markets has some risks because these countries are more susceptible to global trends. Many global economic pressures – such as the recent global cycles of growth and downturn; levels and terms of trade; inflation, interest rates, and exchange rates; export subsidies in developed countries; and food and other commodity prices – affect country growth rates (Díaz-Bonilla, 2009). In addition, other emerging global challenges such as climate change and international migration now affect the status of Africa's poor.[1]

The ability of governments to implement the correct combination of short- and long-term policy measures is thus critical for sustaining social-economic progress and building greater resilience to shocks. However, determining the appropriate policy measures is complex. On the one hand, it requires specific technical capacities and capabilities in the organisations and institutions at the front line of the "crisis" response. On the other hand, it depends on the overall functioning of country systems and institutional qualities, including decision-making processes and consensus building among key stakeholders, the broader political economy dynamics, and governance structures that largely set "the rules of the game".

The previous chapters have demonstrated that despite the frequent allusion to a new "Scramble for Africa", the continent is planning, managing, and starting to finance its own destiny, in the wake of an African revival and renewal narrative. To address these challenges associated with this narrative and in order to promote sustainable and inclusive structural transformation, the role of institutions and that of the state is a sine qua non since without them the entire enterprise is bound to fail. Hence, the emerging consensus is that a developmental state is central to the process of accelerated growth and transformation of any country (Chang, 2007; Lopes et al., 2017).

In the long term, none of the challenges is insurmountable but solutions will require policy cohesion and resilience, creative leadership, careful choice of priorities and planning, and equally importantly, prudent management of scarce resources and transparency in both public and private sector operations.

Understanding the challenges: crises in changing times

More often than not, every society experiences its own crises moments. There are crises of values, pandemics, population growth, economic chaos, energy shortage, financial speculation, gaps in education, cultural pasteurisation, and poverty prevalent in a world of plenty, hunger, and lack of access to such prosaic matters as clean water. The issue is not to choose which crisis is more threatening. The real threat comes from a profound convergence of critical tendencies that ultimately are destroying our fragile planet as the home of humanity. There is thus a need to appreciate the links between ethics and development policy as well as the wider economy (Sen, 1987; Hausman and McPherson, 2006; Wilkinson and Pickett, 2010; Dutt and Wilber, 2010; Tirole, 2017).

In recent decades, the statistical horizon of the planet has been narrowed with the emergence of big data as a major variable in economic policymaking. Despite never-ending interpretations of the detail, we now have a better overall picture of what is happening. However, the abiding image that emerges is simply tragic. Initially it was seen in fragments through the prism of myriads of UN Conferences. In Rio de Janeiro, the world realised what was happening with the environment; in Vienna, with human rights; in Cairo, with population growth; in Beijing, with families; in Istanbul, with urbanisation; in Copenhagen, the social situation of the planet, and again in Copenhagen, the challenges of global warming. Even without this global summitry, we now know more about other areas, from extinction of species to acidification of the oceans and the disappearance of rare metals. The challenges are more systemic, where simple arrangements in how societies are organised and managed are not up to the task.

The sum of macro-tendencies during the historic period from 1750 until the present shows the convergence of areas traditionally studied separately such as demography, climate, automobile production, paper consumption, water contamination, extinction of ocean life and others. The interlinked nature of these tendencies become obvious, as does the magnitude of the environmental challenges. The *New Scientist* comment regarding macro-tendencies focuses directly on our own concept of economic growth and how such conceptualisation fails to appreciate the environmental limits of growth and the need for renewable resources and sustainability (Jackson et al., 2008).

The convergence of tensions for the planet has serious consequences. Africa can no longer be self-satisfied with increased "fishing" catches when life in the oceans is being extinguished or when the increase in crop production is eliminating aquifers or contaminating the planet's freshwater resources. The solutions therefore have to be systemic in order for Africans to take a broader view and thereby raise the overall level of awareness about the nature and depth of the challenges which cannot be minimised.

The dilemma is clear: what type of development do we want for the global community? Related to this, what kind of state and regulatory mechanisms will be necessary? With 7 billion inhabitants – and 75 million added per year – together with expanding levels of consumption and greater access to more powerful technology, the planet exposes all its vulnerability. The present mode of production places energy resources at the centre of productive activities and makes them a crucial element in the dominant models of exponential growth.

Box 7.1 Natural resources and the new scramble for Africa

We noted in Chapter 4 that Africa is rich in natural resources. Oil industries are at the heart of the "scramble" attracting foreign companies from the United States, the EU, and increasingly from China and other emerging economies. The fast growing Chinese presence on the continent has therefore provoked concerns by many. China operating through its state-owned or publicly listed corporations such as China National Offshore Oil Corporation (CNOOC), China National Petroleum Corporation (CNPC), and Sinopec in Sudan, Angola, Nigeria, Algeria, and Gabon (with growing interest in Central African Republic, Chad, and Libya) is now importing one-third of its crude oil from Africa. It became the second trading partner of the continent. China accounts for 50–60 per cent of oil exports from Sudan and 25 per cent from Angola (Southall and Melber, 2009, p. 14). The story with minerals extraction follows a similar pattern. A dramatic increase in minerals prices over the period between 2002 and 2006 was accompanied with a fourfold increase in minerals investments exploration, with China making significant investments in copper mining in Zambia, and copper and cobalt in DRC (Prichard, 2009, p. 250). Forests are another type of African natural resource that has come under stress. The growth of industrial fishing by foreign companies, sometimes illegal or under-regulated, creates further threats to local communities (Southall, 2009, p. 17). While large-scale industrial agribusiness expansion has constantly been brought to the public attention as threatening the interests of local farmers in terms of access to land, probably a less known aspect of the story is the danger to genetic resources stemming from bio-piracy. FAO noted that perhaps the main danger to genetic diversity was represented by "the marginalization of traditional production systems and the associated local breeds, driven mainly by the rapid spread of intensive livestock production, often large-scale and utilizing a narrow range of breeds" (Thompson, 2009, p. 308).

Africa needs inclusive and sustained structural transformation

Africa's growth is real: it is a significant historical achievement to almost triple GDP in one and half decades. The business of attribution is always a risky undertaking: to say that the Millennium Development Goals (MDGs) drove this achievement is very partial (Kararach et al., 2015 while to say that growth occurred despite the MDGs would be nonsense. Africa's growth was made possible by a combination of internal and external factors. Megatrends such as demographic, technological, and environmental changes have been crucial for the transformation of the continent's future. The policy space allowed by the transition from a prescriptive structural adjustment era to a goal targeting "do-it-your-way" mode has helped immensely as well (Cheru, 2017). Africa's agency benefitted from the confidence of new partnerships with rising developing countries' economies, which greatly contributed to attitudinal change in the African inter-state system.

However, the cold reality thus far is that Africa has achieved growth without quality (Hanson and Léautier, 2013). Africans are celebrating its potential more rather than the evidence-based results. The latter would require a focus on employment creation, inclusiveness, and poverty reduction (Kararach, 2014). Even though the MDGs remain unfinished business for Africa, there is no denying that the continent has accelerated progress on a number of goals and targets despite unfavourable initial conditions (Kararach et al., 2015). Significant achievements include increasing women's representation in national parliaments, enrolling more children in primary schools, bridging the gender gap in primary enrolment, reducing child and maternal deaths, as well as the declining prevalence of HIV/AIDS or malaria related deaths. In addition, notable progress in technology indicators have been witnessed with mobile telephone subscriptions that surpass the global average as well as the fastest annual average growth of internet users.

Focus on growing inequalities is, however, necessary since they are in part attributable to the lack of attention to economic and social inequalities in development interventions (Zeleza, 2018). And income inequalities may be the most pronounced form of inequalities where Africa is no exception, with a number of countries showing sharper increases in income inequalities. With an average Gini coefficient of 43.9 per cent over the period 2000–2009, income inequality in Africa is second only to Latin America, which averaged 52.2 per cent over the same period (ECA, 2014a). In 2010, six out of the ten most unequal countries worldwide were in Africa, and more specifically in Southern Africa, which appears as the most unequal sub-region of the continent (AfDB, 2014).

Notwithstanding the high levels of inequality in Africa, there has been a decline over time even though substantial country variations are observed. Out of a total of 35 African countries with data, 13 (37.1 per cent) experienced an increase in income inequality while 19 (54.3 per cent) experienced a decline over the period 1990–2012. In contrast, 58 per cent of countries in Asia experienced rising inequality versus 32.3 per cent that experienced falling inequality. Latin American countries also experienced net reductions in inequality during this period; inequality rose in 20 per cent (4 out of 20) of the countries in this region and fell in 70 per cent (14 out of 20) of the same.

For Africa to reverse its record there is a need to change its approach. More of the same policies and practices is not an option because Africa needs to rethink its ideological attachments and material conditions if it is to claim its rightful place in the world (Mkandawire, 1997). The need for the continent to pursue aggressive industrial policies is now widely recognised.

Such policies provide the virtuous circle for increasing agricultural productivity, benefiting from the urban and demographic dividends, and modernising economic sectors that depend too much on the survival of the informal sector (Lopes et al., 2017). The essential message is that the continent needs to bring back strategic planning in order to deal with the challenges of development.

Brexit, nationalist populism, and the return of protectionism

Africa must be concerned by the rise of populist nationalism in several parts of the world, more so with the election of Trump in the USA and the departure of Britain from the EU – commonly known as Brexit. Brexit in particular requires Africa's immediate attention. As Britain focuses on what its relationship with the European Union might be once it has left the bloc sometime in 2019, the rest of the world is already wrestling with the ambiguities of the post-Brexit era. For African countries, preparing for Brexit is not only prudent but may be a matter of economic necessity.

The EU is Africa's largest trading partner as a bloc, accounting for 36 per cent of its exports. The role which the UK plays in this trading relationship implies that Brexit will have unpredictable consequences for the continent although the UK accounts for only 4.3 per cent of Africa's total exports (Office for National Statistics, 2016).

At the end of 2014, British foreign direct investment in Africa was £42.5 billion ($54.1 billion), more than double the £20.8 billion that UK interests invested in 2005. British FDI has flowed largely to the telecommunications and financial services sectors but development aid and infrastructure projects have also been a focus.

This upward trend is likely to reverse if Brexit were to lead to an erosion of confidence in the British market. As Britain seeks to bolster its own economy, looking for opportunities abroad might seem less justifiable or even down right unattractive. In the short to medium term, those countries that rely on trade with the UK will feel the effects of Brexit, while other countries – for instance, those from the CFA zone such as Côte d'Ivoire, Guinea, or Cameroon – will be less affected. South Africa, Nigeria, and Egypt are the UK's most important trading partners on the African continent, with imports to the UK from these countries totalling £7.4 billion in 2014 alone. Other African countries accounted for £10.5 billion of UK imports in 2014. Another major area of economic relations is foreign direct investment (outward FDI): in 2014, the value of the UK's stock of FDI in Africa was £42.5 billion (Office for National Statistics, 2016).

Other damages may include: diplomatic where the historical, political, and economic ties strengthened over decades could fray as UK–EU negotiations move ahead, albeit in a very uncertain direction; peace and security as the EU has been a major supporter of the African Peace and Security Architecture (APSA) (Haastrup, 2013). Between 2004 and 2014, the EU contributed €740 million to the African Peace Facility and made available the same amount for the period 2014–2016 (Ansorg and Haastrup, 2016). This funding architecture has enabled the UK to contribute continentally rather than bilaterally to African peace and security under a Brexit scenario; negation of regional efforts being undertaken through the ACFTA, largely informed by the European model. Brexit fundamentally casts doubts on Africa's progress in promoting regional integration.

The challenges of artificial intelligence (AI) and disruptive technologies

We have noted that technology and innovation will be another important factor in shaping structural transformation in Africa. It has long been acknowledged that technological innovation drives firm level productivity gains and economic growth of countries (see Solow, 1956; Romer, 1990; Aghion and Howitt, 1992). It is agreed that more productive firms will displace less productive ones in a Schumpeterian fashion. The exponential rise in economic growth since the second industrial revolution and the massive increase in living standards serve as historical testament to the importance of technological innovation, notably in the case of the high-growth East Asian economies (Leipziger and Thomas, 1993). This was largely accomplished through leapfrogging, characterised by learning about and then absorbing technologies from abroad, along with successful resource mobilisation and building of human and physical capital (Yusuf, 2012).

Disruptive innovation, including technologies associated with artificial intelligence (AI), while dislocating existing firms, can also affect the labour market, the incomes of workers, and ultimately the distribution of income. Box 7.2 provides examples of how AI is being used in Africa.

Box 7.2 Cases of AI usage in Africa

1 Health

Kenya: Sophie Bot (a free chatbot that works on several popular messaging apps) relies on AI to process and reply to questions on sexual and reproductive health. According to an interviewee, people can access the application more easily and freely than going to a doctor.

South Africa: Citizens in regions without primary healthcare facilities are often reliant on the services of mobile clinics. Numberboost is a company working to develop a system to allow citizens to locate nearby mobile healthcare clinics – a service that could help improve citizen access to healthcare.

2 Agriculture

Kenya: Vital Signs analyses pixels' value and colour from satellite imagery data to estimate rainfall and drought patterns. Arifu provides curated access to information via SMS to help farmers determine, for example, what fertiliser matches their specific needs. FarmDrive offers credit for farmers in need of supplies (e.g. fertilisers) by relying on data such as the size of land, location, and crops to determine the risk and corresponding interest rates.

Nigeria: Zenvus seeks to improve decision making for farmers by providing insights based on data collected from sensors and other means.

South Africa: Aerobotics is assisting the agricultural industry by using drone aerial imagery to identify problems in crop yields, which is important considering the challenges faced by the industry including sustained periods of drought.

3 Fintech

Kenya: Tala uses a mobile app to assess and disburse loans to customers that do not have a credit history. Through the app, the company can assess these traditionally excluded customers by analysing Facebook and SMS data to determine a customer's risk of default.

Nigeria: Kudi.ai has developed a system that allows users to improve money transfers. Using natural language processing and artificial intelligence, Kudi.ai attempts to make peer-to-peer payment easier for Nigerians using a chatbot that works on popular messaging apps, such as Facebook Messenger.

4 Public transportation

Nigeria: RoadPreppers have developed a solution that allows users to navigate traffic congestion with driving directions and public transport options. In addition, the app lara.ng uses a chatbot to provide public transportation directions and fares for commuters in Lagos. Both are viewed as better than existing options, such as Google Maps; as an interviewee noted, they provide the commuter with more transparent information on fares from different public transport providers.

5 Natural language processing

South Africa: Council for Scientific and Industrial Research (CSIR) works on the use of automatic speech recognition to support language learning and translation. This is an important and complex task, given that there are 11 official languages in the country, with most existing language technology options limited to English and Afrikaans.

Conceptually, if disruptive technologies displace labour and median incomes continue to decouple from output, the associated economic growth and distribution of income become more unequal. Some such as Aghion et al. (2019) have made the analogy to the lines forming for airplane flights that are bifurcated into economy and other classes of travel. With lower demand for low-skilled and low-to-median wage labour due to work becoming increasingly automated, the owners of capital and unique skills are accruing a larger share of benefits. Should this process proceed without any offsets, such as transfer payments to compensate the income losers, one can imagine opportunities for others in related sectors to maintain their incomes also declining as innovation proceeds to lower consumption demand for a large part of the labour force. As such, inequality increases as a result of two forces: 1) the growing gap between labour income and capital income; and 2) the growing gap between high earners and low earners. To be clear, however, this is not a prediction, but rather an explanation of how the impacts of disruptive technologies may be felt.

A post-structuralist argument could be that it is largely up to individuals to alter their approach to education and work. Of course, this can be aided by access to better and more accurate information, even if this simply entails a recognition that there is less certainly in the labour force, and that skill fungibility is at a premium. That said, it is often the public sector that has a complementary role to play in sheltering individuals from sudden shifts in economic fortune that are outside their ken, and also in levelling the playing field for future workers by working to create an environment of better skill acquisition. If indeed technologies going forward will be more disruptive to economic livelihoods, this will inevitably place governments in the forefront of policy solutions. Unfortunately, many African governments are currently ill-equipped for this challenge let alone opportunity presented by growth in disruptive technologies.

Lines of action to exploit opportunities and tackle challenges

Our core argument is that the state and strategic planning must to be brought back into the development debate to redefine the parameters (i.e. circumstances and individual efforts) for structural transformation. Simplified versions of decision-making processes and linear input–output policy dynamics will no longer suffice in a world characterised by great volatility, uncertainty, and complexity. These factors of uncertainty and complexity affect the circumstances and individual efforts that shape structural transformation as defined in Chapter 1 (also see Appendix for formal representation).

In view of the above premise, the proposals or lines of action below therefore have a common theoretical and practical denominator: they have all been tested and are being applied in various regions of the world such as Latin America (Uruguay and Cuba) and South Asia (China, South Korea, Malaysia, and Vietnam), sectors, as well as different levels of socio-economic activities (see Figure 7.1). These proposals focus on five major action

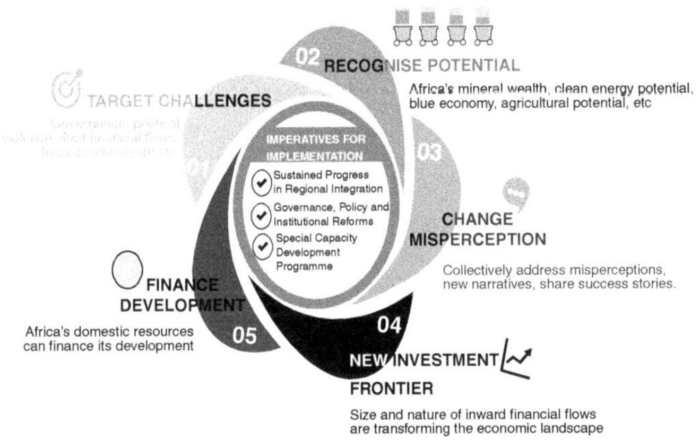

Figure 7.1 The five action levers to changes circumstances and individual efforts for sustainable transformation

Source: Authors' analysis.

levers: they target challenges, appreciate potential, correct misperceptions, identify new investment, and finance appropriately. The needs to identify development constraints and resolve them require a post-structuralist approach. Countries that managed to deliver on structural transformation also had to enhance integration of localities and markets, strengthen governance, resolve political economy problems, constantly renew policy and institutional frameworks, and develop capacity for programme implementation (see Acemoglu and Johnson (2005) on the importance of institutional and policy reforms in development).

Figure 7.1 presents a matrix of policy messages from the interactive dynamics of the five points that provide the strategic leverage for sustainable transformation:

Target challenges

As noted in the previous chapters, the challenges to structural transformation Africa faces are wide ranging. However, these challenges do present the continent with opportunities for reforms and innovations as well as a redefinition of the theory and context of change. As an example, governance reforms provide governments and communities a renewed chance to resolve conflict and reduce political violence, combat illicit financial flows, and expand the fiscal space (Lopes et al., 2017). Innovation is more than investing in new technology but also revamping business models beyond business-as-usual (Kararach, 2014). It is important for Africa to develop leadership capabilities in a complex world (Léautier, 2014). Africa needs a careful reflection on the nature and size of the challenges that have and will continue to define its position in world history by rising up (Landsberg, 2018).

Recognise potential

A core argument of this book is that inadequate attention has been paid to the true size of Africa: be it productive or market potential. The continent needs to work out strategies that optimise and ensure sustainable usage of the vast mineral wealth, huge renewal and clean energy potential, blue economy and agricultural assets. Exploiting this potential require actions in a number of fronts to change the trajectories around the circumstances and individual efforts for structural transformation. Such actions include better infrastructure, incentives, investing in innovation and new technologies, enhancing inclusion and institutions, better integration locally and regionally, and improved programme planning and implementation (Kararach, 2014; Kararach et al., 2015). Africa must develop a culture that nurtures leadership and learning to promote ambitions such as the delivery of Agenda 2063 and the ACFTA.

Change misperception

As correctly noted by authors such as Frantz Fanon (1952; 1963), Cheikh Anta Diop (1974), and Walter Rodney (1972), Africa must recognise the damage done by colonial experience as well as the opportunities this provides. Ngugi Wa Thiongo (1986) argues that Africa must decolonise its mind and world outlook. This demands that the continent should not only rewrite its own story but also engage in a rebranding exercise. There is need to correct misperceptions, create new narratives, and amplify success stories from the continent. The rebranding is particularly important to provide a proper sense of "how" big Africa is to both Africans and foreign investors and turn the continent's potential into a boon for transformation.

Develop new investment frontier

Africa also needs a new development compact that taps into the energy of the its people and brings the private and public sectors and the wider community in shaping and operationalising the structural transformation agenda. The continent can therefore proactively invest in new growth areas and sectors through better R&D (Lin and Monga, 2011). There is need to leverage and scale up investments in areas of new technologies including robotics and artificial intelligence to enhance the productivity frontiers of African economies. Countries need to devise appropriate regulatory regimes that reduce the capacity of the corporations to dictate the rules of the regulatory game.

Financing development

There is need to revisit the way development is financed by prioritising both policy sequencing and appropriate tool selection (Kararach, 2014). Finance is a critical ingredient in the structural transformation process (Kanbur, 2017). As an example, financing policies must be in harmony with industrial policies. Empirical evidence from Teixeira et al. (2014) suggest that Sub-Saharan Africa fails to ignite industrialisation due to the support for production processes that are beyond its human and financial capacities. They argue that most countries fail because they promote capital-intensive sectors rather than capitalising on their comparative advantage in labour and natural resources. Chang (2013) argues that what African countries need the most is a deeper understanding of how to get industrial policy right by implementing sound and timely government interventions. Therefore, these arguments should shape the design and the form of industrial policy but not negate its importance in accelerating a country's structural transformation process.

Conclusion

Historically, global financial institutions enforced neoliberal policies in the form of structural adjustment on African economies, despite the potential dangers of opening up to globalised markets. Unregulated capital markets have caused enormous social and economic damage in Latin America, Southeast Asia, and Africa.

However, recently the tables have turned: the Global North has emerged as the heart of resistance to globalisation. It has seen how free markets widen social inequality and learnt that effective regulation ensures that markets work better for people. The resistance to globalisation has given birth to neo-populist governments and protectionist tendencies. Economic uncertainty and the declining standards for the middle classes have engendered Brexit, isolationism, and the worrying spread of protectionism.

Notwithstanding this changing global context, Africa is at an exciting juncture in its development journey and is poised to become a new pole of global growth. To achieve this, however, Africa must continue to plan its development trajectory by enhancing its own policy space and making prudent decisions about appropriate strategies needed to achieve economic growth and structural transformation. A much more strategic approach is required in order to meet the various challenges discussed in this chapter. Indeed, it is commonly said that failing to plan means planning to fail.

The continent must protect a trajectory of peace and growth. It must generate enough jobs and business opportunities for the 17 million Africans who join the labour market every year, of which nearly 70 per cent are under the age of 25. To redefine and push its own growth and development agenda, Africa must chart a course of structural transformation. Africa is bigger than many have realised but without structural transformation, it is smaller than it can be. This paradox presents Africa's leaders with an arduous task of charting careful and strategic development pathways in what is inherently a deleterious and unstable global economy.

Note

1 The World Bank estimates some 414 million Africans will still be in extreme poverty by 2030.

Appendix

The Kanbur formalisation of structural transformation on Kuznets-Lewis lines

Based on Kanbur (2017), let the national economy be divided into two sectors indexed 1 and 2. If the frequency density of the national distribution of income y is $f(y)$, then the sectoral densities are presented as $f1(y)$ and $f2(y)$. Let the population share of sector 1 be denoted x, our key indicator of structural transformation. The national frequency density is then:

$$f(y) = xf1(y) + (1-x)f2(y) \tag{1}$$

Denote the mean log deviation (MLD) measure by L and the mean by m, with subscripts 1 and 2 to indicate each sector. Let $k = m1/m2$ denote the ratio of the two means. It is well known that the (MLD) measure can be decomposed into sectoral components as follows:

$$L = xL1 + (1-x)L2 + \log\left[xk + (1-x0\right] - \left[xlog(k)\right] \tag{2}$$

The first two terms on the right-hand side together constitute a weighted sum of the sectoral inequalities, and the sum is known as the within-group component of national inequality:

$$Lw = xL1 + (1-x)L2 \tag{3}$$

The last term on the right-hand side of (2) has an interesting and important interpretation. If the income distribution in each sector is equalised around its mean, the only inequality left would be that due to difference in the means of the two sectors. This is known as the between-group component of inequality and is given exactly by the last term on the right-hand side of (2):

$$Lb = \log\left[xk + (1-x)\right] - \left[xlog(k)\right] \tag{4}$$

Kuznets's (1955) interpretations of his numerical simulations, in effect, follow the paths of (3) and (4), and of their aggregate, as different variables evolve, under empirically plausible assumptions that the more advanced sector has higher mean income and higher inequality. Let the more advanced sector be Sector 1 and consider what happens when the population share of this sector increases from a low value to a high value where the vast majority of the population derives its income from the advanced sector. In this case it is seen that:

$$\frac{\partial Lw}{\partial x} = (L1 - L2) \quad (5)$$

$$\frac{\partial Lb}{\partial x} = \left[\frac{k-1}{x(k-1)+1}\right] - \log(k) \quad (6)$$

Thus, this Kuznetsian framework of structural transformation always increases the within-group component of inequality, as also argued by Robinson (1976) and Anand and Kanbur (1993), since it consists of moving population from the low inequality to the high inequality sector. Where then does the inverse-U shape come from? The answer is from the between-group term, the evolution of which is given in (6). The intuition is straightforward. Recall that the between-group inequality is what is left when everybody has the mean income of their sector. The income distribution in this case is a two-point distribution, with a fraction x of the population at the high income, and the rest at the low income. At the two extremes, when everybody is at one income level or the other, between-group inequality is zero. In between, inequality is zero. Thus, we must have an inverse-U shape as population moves from the low income to the high income sector.

While between-group inequality always follows an inverse-U shape, it is counteracted in its downward sloping portion by the increasing inequality of the within-group component. Thus, to get an inverse-U shape in overall inequality in the process of structural transformation, we need further conditions that (5) does not dominate (6), which will happen when the two sectoral inequalities are not too disparate. The specific condition is developed in Anand and Kanbur (1993a) and Kanbur and Zhuang (2013) and shown to be:

$$L1 - L2 < \frac{1}{k} - 1 + \log(k) \quad (7)$$

The role of factors other than structural transformation, as measured by the population share x, raises the question of how these other factors affect inequality and indeed move with structural transformation. Kanbur and Zhuang (2013) address this question by looking at the total differential of (2) and relating it to a series of elasticities.

$$\partial L/L = Ex(\partial x/x) + Ek(\partial k/k) + EL1(\partial L1/L1) + EL2(\partial L2/L2) \quad (8)$$

Where Ex, Ek, EL1, EL2 are elasticities of L with respect to x, k, L1 and L2, respectively, and are given by

$$\begin{aligned} Ex &= (x/L)\,[(L1 - L2) + [(k-1)/(x\,(k-1)+1)] - \log(k)] \\ Ek &= (k/L)\,[x/(1-x+xk) - x/k] \\ EL1 &= (L1/L)\,x \\ EL2 &= (L2/L)\,(1-x) \end{aligned} \quad (9)$$

Expressions (8) and (9) quantify the consequences of changes in the key Kuznetsian parameters. We have already, in effect, discussed Ex in the examination of the inverse-U shape of the relationship with the structural transformation variable, x. What about the other parameters? The expression for Ek shows that a widening of the gap between sectoral means will increase inequality, and that, similarly, a narrowing of the gap will reduce national inequality. Thus, to generate an inverse-U in national inequality, the sectoral mean gap will also have to follow an inverse-U shape. The advanced sector will have to race away from the lagging sector in the early stages of development and then be caught by the lagging sector in the later stages. It is this type of structural transformation that would re-enforce the inverse-U pattern induced by the pure effect of the population shift. Similarly, the expressions for EL1 and EL2 show that a widening gap between the inequalities of the two sectors will increase national inequality. Thus, if inequality in the advanced sector races ahead and is then caught up by inequality in the lagging sector, the result will be an alignment with the inverse-U path induced by other forces.

The above discussions lead us to a broader conceptualisation of sectoral transformation, rather than a simple shift of population from the low-productivity to the high-productivity sector. Arthur Lewis famously argued that inequality within the leading sectors would tend to increase:

> Development must be inegalitarian because it does not start in every part of an economy at the same time. Somebody develops a mine and employs a thousand people. Or farmers in one province start planting cocoa, which will grow only in 10% of the country. Or the Green Revolution arrives, to benefit those farmers who have plenty of rain or access to irrigation, while offering nothing to the other 50% in drier regions.
>
> (Lewis, 1976, p. 26)

Thus, certainly in the initial stages of development, inequalities within the advanced sector could augment, the mean income in this sector could increase rapidly, and these together with the population shift from the low-productivity to the high-productivity sector could increase inequality

What the expressions also make clear is that the impact of a change in x on national inequality depends on other sectoral variables as well. Thus, the bigger the average sectoral gap k, the more pronounced the impact of a shift in population on inequality will be. The same holds true for the gap in sectoral inequalities. Clearly, the links between structural transformation and national inequality are further complicated beyond the simple but powerful basic Kuznetsian forces identified in his classic paper.

References

Abelson, B., Varshney, K. R., and Sun, J. (2014). "Targeting Direct Cash Transfers to the Extremely Poor", pp. 1563–1572, in *Proceedings of the 20th ACM SIGKDD International Conference on Knowledge Discovery and Data Mining*. New York: Association for Computing Machinery.

Abbott, J., Anderson, J. L., Campling, L., Hannesson, R., Havice, E., Lozier, S., and Wilberg, M. J. (2014). "Steering the Global Partnership for Oceans". *Marine Resource Economics, 29*(1): 1–16.

Abosedra, S. and Baghestani, H. (1991). "New Evidence on the Causal Relationship between United States Energy Consumption and Gross National Product". *Journal of Energy and Development, 14*: 285–292.

Abramowitz, M. (1983). "Notes on International Differences in Productivity Growth Rates", in D. C. Mueller (ed.). *The Political Economy of Growth*. New Haven, CT: Yale University Press.

Acemoglu, D. and Johnson, S. (2005). "Unbundling Institutions". *Journal of Political Economy, 113*(5): 949–995.

Acemoglu, D., Johnson, S. and Robinson, J. A. (2001). "The Colonial Origins of Comparative Development: An Empirical Investigation". *American Economic Review, 91*(5): 1369–1401.

ACET (African Center for Economic Transformation) (2014). *African Transformation Report: Growth with Depth*. Accra: ACET.

Adams, R. and Page, J. (2003). "International Migration, Remittances and Poverty in Developing Countries", Poverty Reduction Group Working Paper 3179. World Bank Poverty Reduction and Economic Migration Program. Washington, DC: The World Bank.

Adebajo, A. (2010). *The Curse of Berlin: Africa after the Cold War*. London: Hurst & Co.

Adepoju, A. (1998). "The Role of Diverse Regional Economic Communities in the Politics of Migration in African Countries", in *Migration at the Threshold of the Third Millennium*. Rome: The Vatican.

Adepoju, A. (2000). "Issues and Recent Trends in International Migration in Sub-Saharan Africa". *International Social Sciences Journal, 165*: 383–394.

Adepoju, A. (2003). "Migration in West Africa". *Development, 16*(3): 37–41.

Adepoju, A. (2005). "Migration in West Africa". A paper prepared for the Policy Analysis and Research Programme of the Global Commission on International Migration, Geneva, Switzerland.

Adepoju, A. (2006). "Leading Issues in International Migration in Sub-Saharan Africa", in C. Cross, D. Gelderblom, N. Roux, and J. Mafukidze (eds). *Views on Migration in Sub-Saharan Africa*. South Africa: HSRC Press.

Aderemi, A. (2018). "Chalk and Cheese: Asia's Economic Miracle and Africa's Development Logjam", in C. Landsberg (ed.). *Africa Rise Up: Perspectives on African Renewal*. Johannesburg: Real Africa Publishers.

Afreximbank (2018). *The Africa Trade Report 2018: Boosting Intra-African Trade: Implications of the African Continental Free Trade Area Agreement*. Cairo: Afreximbank.

African Economic Research Consortium (AERC). (2010). *The Impact of China–Africa Trade Relations: The Case of Mauritius*. Nairobi, Kenya: AERC.

African Development Bank (AfDB) (2012a). *Cape Verde – A Success Story*. Tunis: AfDB.

African Development Bank (AfDB) (2012b). *Cape Verde – The Road Ahead*. Tunis: AfD

African Development Bank (AfDB) (2013). *Recognizing Africa's Informal Sector*. Abidjan, Côte d'Ivoire: African Development Bank Group.

African Development Bank (AfDB) (2014). *Tracking Africa's Progress in Figures*. Abidjan, Côte d'Ivoire: African Development Bank Group.

African Development Bank (AfDB) (2018). *Africa Economic Outlook*. Abidjan, Côte d'Ivoire: African Development Bank Group.

African Development Bank (AfDB) with African Union Commission (AUC) (2009/10). Programme for Infrastructure Development in Africa (PIDA). Tunis: African Development Bank Group.

African Development Bank (AfDB), United Nations Development Programme (UNDP), and Organisation for Economic Co-Operation and Development (OECD) (2013). *African Economic Outlook: Structural Transformation and Natural Resources*. Abidjan, Côte d'Ivoire: African Development Bank Group.

African Capacity Building Foundation (ACBF) (2012). *African Capacity Indicators Report 2012*. Harare: ACBF.

African Private Equity and Venture Capital Association (AVCA). (2016). *Annual African Private Equity Data Tracker*. London: AVCA.

African Union (AU) (2014). *AGA Framework Document, June*. Addis Ababa: AU.

African Union Commission (AUC) (2009). *African Mining Vision*. Addis Ababa: AUC.

African Union Commission (AUC) (2013). "Pan-Africanism and African Renaissance", Anniversary Celebration Theme, 23 May, 2013.

Agarwal, M. (2013). "*South–South Economic Cooperation: Emerging Trends and Future Challenges*". Background Research Paper Submitted to the High-Level Panel on the Post-2015 Development Agenda.

Aghion, P. and Howitt, P. (1992). "A Model of Growth through Creative Destruction". *Econometrica*, *60*(2): 323–351.

Aghion, P., Akcigit, U., Bergeaud, A., Blundell, R., and Hemous, D. (2019). "Innovation and Top Income Inequality". *Review of Economic Studies*, *86*(1): 1–45.

Ahmed, A. and Cleeve, E. (2004). "Tracking the Millennium Development Goals in sub-Saharan Africa". *International Journal of Social Economics*, *31*(1–2): 12–29.

Akamatsu, K. (1962). "A Historical Pattern of Economic Growth in Developing Countries". The Developing Economies (Tokyo), *1*, Supplement Issue No. (1): 3–25.

Akarca, A. and Long, T. (1980). "On the Relationship between Energy and GNP: A Reexamination". *Journal of Energy and Development*, *5*: 326–331.

Akyüz, Y. and Gore, C. (2001). "African Economic Development in a Comparative Perspective". *Cambridge Journal of Economics, 25*(3): 265–288.

Alavi, H. (1972). "The State in Post-Colonial Societies: Pakistan and Bangladesh". *New Left Review, 74* (July–August): 59–81.

Aldean, J. C. (2017). "Opportunities Just Beneath the Surface: Participatory and Deliberative Processes in Rwanda", MA Thesis, Naval Postgraduate School, June. Available at: https://pdfs.semanticscholar.org/f5df/728fe53fd74ce5e431a74ed5d2f527bbdec8.pdf

Ali, Z. (2007). "The Growing Relationship between China and Sub-Saharan Africa: Macroeconomic, Trade, Investment, and Aid Links". *The World Bank Research Observer, 22*(1) (Spring 2007).

Allen, F., Otchere, I., and Senbet, L. W. (2011). "African Financial Systems: A Review". *Review of Development Finance, 1*: 79–113.

Altenburg, T. (2011). "Industrial Policy in Developing Countries, Overview and Lessons from Seven Country Cases". Discussion Paper 4/2011. German Development Institute, Bonn.

Amaizo, Y. E. (2012). "An Alternative African Developmentalism: A Critique of Zero-sum Games and Palliative Economics". *Africa Development, 37*(4): 117–140.

Amin, A. A. (2002). "An Examination of the Sources of Economic Growth in Cameroon". African Economic Research Consortium Research Paper 116.

Amin, S. (1973). *Le développement inégal: Essai sur les formations sociales du capitalisme périphérique*. Paris.

Amin, S. (1990). *Delinking: Towards a Polycentric World*. London: Zed Books.

Ammah-Tagoe, F. A. (1990). *On Woodfuel, Total Energy Consumption and GDP in Ghana: A Study of Trends and Causal Relations*. Boston. MA: Center for Energy and Environmental Studies, Boston University (mimeo).

Amoako-Tuffour, J. and Armah, B. (eds) (2007). *Poverty Reduction Strategies in Action: Perspectives and Lessons from Ghana*. Lanham, MD: Lexington Books.

Amsden, A. (1989). *Asia's Next Giant: South Korea and Late Industrialization*. New York: Oxford University Press.

Amsden, A. (2000). *The Rise of the Rest: Challenges to the West from Late-Industrialization Economies*. New York: Oxford University Press.

Anand, S. and Kanbur, R. (1985). "Poverty under the Kuznets Process". *The Economic Journal, 95*(380a): 42–50.

Anand, S. and Kanbur, R. (1993). "The Kuznets Process and the Inequality–Development Relationship". *Journal of Development Economics, 40*(1): 25–52.

Ansorg, A. and Haastrup, T. (2016). "Brexit Beyond the UK's Borders: What It Means for Africa". *GIGA Focus*, 3 September. Available at: www.giga-hamburg.de/en/publication/brexit-beyond-the-uks-borders-what-it-means-for-africa.

Ansoms, A. and Rostagno, D. (2012). "Rwanda's Vision 2020 Halfway Through: What the Eye Does Not See". *Review of African Political Economy, 39*(133): 427–450.

Araya, S. (2007). "Misrepresentation of Africa", *Pambazuka News*, February 14.

Arndt, C. McKay, A., and Tarp, F. (2016). *Growth and Poverty in Sub-Saharan Africa. UNU-WIDER*. Oxford: Oxford University Press.

Atta-Mensah, J. (2017). "Theoretical Foundations of Africa's Economic Transformation and Growth". *Theoretical Economics Letters, 7*(5): 1150–1178. Available at: www.scirp.org/journal/tel.

Asek, S. N. (2017). "Towards Greater Emergence of Cameroon's Informal Sector Labor Market". Policy Brief, International Governance Institute,

Cameroon. Available at: www.igi-cameroon.com/wp-content/uploads/2017/07/IGI-CAMEROON-POLICY-BRIEF-JULY-2017.pdf.

Ashiagbor, D., Satyamurthy, N., Casey, M., and Asare, J. (2014). *Pension Funds and Private Equity: Unlocking Africa's Potential*. London: Commonwealth Secretariat.

Athukorala, P. C. and Menon, J. (1999). "Outward Orientation and Economic Development in Malaysia". *World Economy*, *22*(1): 119–139.

Auty, R. M. (2004). "Natural Resources and Civil Strife: A Two-Stage Process", in P. le Billon (ed.). The *G*eopolitics of *Resource Wars: Resource Dependence, Governance* and *V*iolence. London: Frank Cass, pp. 29–49.

Awoyomi, B. (1989). "Structural Adjustment, Risk Aversion and Livestock Production in Nigeria". *Rural Development in Nigeria*, *3*: 82–87.

Barth, J. R., Caprio Jr. G., and Phumiwasana, T. (2009). "The Transformation of China from an Emerging Economy to a Global Powerhouse". *The Milken Institute Series on Financial Innovation and Economic Growth*, *8*: 73–110.

Barton, D. and Leke, A. (2016). "3 Reasons Things Are Looking Up for African Economies", MGI and WEF. Available at: www.weforum.org/agenda/2016/05/what-s-the-future-of-economic-growth-in-africa/.

Batalha, L. and Carling, J. (eds) (2008). *Transnational Archipelago: Perspectives of Cape Verdean Migration and Diaspora*. Amsterdam: Amsterdam University Press.

Bates, B., Kundzewicz, Z. W., Wu, S., and Palutikof, J. (2008). "Climate Change and Water", Technical paper, Intergovernmental Panel on Climate Change, Geneva.

Bates, R. H. (1981). *Markets and States in Tropical Africa: The Political Basis of Agricultural Policy*. Berkeley, CA: University of California Press.

Battersby, J. (2016). "MDGs to SDGs – New Goals, Same Gaps: The Continued Absence of Urban Food Security in the Post-2015 Global Development Agenda". *African Geographical Review*, *36*(1): 1–15.

Bauer, G. (2013). "Gender Quotas and Women's Representation in African Parliaments. Democracy in Africa". Available at: http://democracyinafrica.org/gender-quotaswomens-representation-african-parliaments/.

Bauer, P. T. (1971). *Dissent on Development: Studies and Debates in Development Economics*. London: Weidenfeld & Nicolson.

Bayart, J. F. (1989). *L'État en Afrique. La politique du ventre*. Paris: Fayard.

BCG (Boston Consulting Group). (2016). *African Consumer Sentiment 2016: The Promise of New Markets*. Boston, MA: BCG.

Beck, T., de Jonghe, O., and Schepens, G. (2011). "Bank Competition and Stability: Cross-Country Heterogeneity", European Banking Center Discussion Paper, no. 019.

Behar, A. and Freund, C. (2011). "The Trade Performance of the Middle East and North Africa". Middle East and North Africa Working Paper Series (53).

Behuria, P. and Goodfellow, T. (2017). "The Disorder of 'Miracle Growth' in Rwanda", in L. Pritchett, K. Sen, and E. Werker (eds). *Deals and Development: The Political Dynamics of Growth Episodes*. Oxford: Oxford University Press.

Beresford, A. (2015). "Power, Patronage, and Gatekeeper Politics in South Africa". *African Affairs*, *114*(455): 226–248.

Beresford, A. (2016). "Africa Rising?" *Review of African Political Economy*, *43*(147): 1–7.

Berndt, E., Glennerster, R., Kremer, M., Lee, J., Levine, R., Weizsacker, G., and Williams, H. (2007). "Advance Market Commitments for Vaccines against Neglected Diseases: Estimating Costs and Effectiveness". *Health Economics*, *16*: 491–511.

Besada, H., Denton, F., and O'Bright, B. (2013). "Development and Sustainability in a Warming World: Measuring the Impacts of Climate Change". Background Research Paper, submitted to the High Level Panel on the Post-2015 Development Agenda, United Nations.

Besada, H., Denton, F., and O'Bright, B. (2015a). "Development and Sustainability in a Warming World: Measuring the Impacts of Climate Change in Africa", in G. Kararach, H. Besada, and T. Shaw (eds). *Development in Africa: Refocusing the Lens after the Millennium Development Goals*. Bristol: Policy Press.

Besada, H., Lisk, F., and Martin, P. (2015b). "Regulating Extraction in Africa: Towards a Framework for Accountability in the Global South". *Governance in Africa*, *2*(1): 1–12.

Bhagwati, J., Greenaway, D., and Panagariya, A. (1998). "Trading Preferentially: Theory and Policy". *The Economic Journal*, *108*(449): 1128–1148.

Bhengu, L. and Wallis, M. (2018). "Good Governance and Poverty Reduction: Exploring the 'Dark Hole'", in C. Landsberg (ed.). *Africa Rise Up: Perspectives on African Renewal*. Johannesburg: Real Africa Publishers.

Biedermann, Z. (2016). "The Case of Rwanda as a Developmental State", in L. Achtenhagen and E. Brundin (eds). *Entrepreneurship and SME Management across Africa*. Singapore: Springer, pp. 139–157.

Blades, D. (1980). "What Do We Know about Levels and Growth of Output in Developing Countries? A Critical Analysis with Special Reference to Africa". *Economic Growth and Resources: Proceedings of the Fifth World Congress, International Economic Association, Tokyo*, *2*: 68–75.

Bleasdale, S. and Tapsell, S. (1999). "Social and Cultural Impacts of Tourism Policy in Tunisia", in M. Robinson and P. Boniface (eds). *Tourism and Cultural Conflicts*. Oxford: CABI Publishing.

Bloomfield, A. I. (1992). "On the Centenary of Jacob Viner's Birth: A Retrospective View of the Man and His Work". *Journal of Economic Literature*, *30*(4): 2052–2085.

Blyden, E. W. (1872). "Africa for the Africans", *African Repository and Colonial Journal*, Washington, DC: January.

Blyden, E. W. (1887). *Christianity, Islam and the Negro Race*. London: W. B. Whittingham & Co.

Booth, A. (2007). "Night Watchmen, Extractive, or Developmental States? Some Evidence from Late Colonial South-East Asia". *Economic History Review*, *60*(2): 241–266.

Booth, D. and Golooba-Mutebi, F. (2012). "Developmental Patrimonialism? The Case of Rwanda". *African Affairs*, *111*(444): 379–403.

Booth, D. and Golooba-Mutebi, F. (2014). "How the International System Hinders the Consolidation of Developmental Regimes in Africa". Developmental Regimes in Africa Working Paper 4. London: Overseas Development Institute.

Bond, P. (2000). *Elite Transition: From Apartheid to Neo-liberalism in South Africa*. London: Pluto Press.

Bond, P. (2006). *Looting Africa: The Economics of Exploitation*. London: Zed Books and Pietermaritzburg: University of KwaZulu-Natal Press.

Bourdet, Y. and Falck, H. (2006). "Emigrants' Remittances and Dutch Disease in Cape Verde". *International Economic Journal*, *20*(3): 267–284.

Brand, U. (2012). "Green Economy – the Next Oxymoron?", *GAIA*, *21*(1): 28–32.

Brautigam, D. (2009) *The Dragon's Gift: The Real Story of China in Africa*. Oxford and New York: Oxford University Press.

Breznitz, D. (2007). *Innovation and the State: Political Choice and Strategies for Growth in Israel, Taiwan and Ireland.* New Haven, CT: Yale University Press.

Briguglio, L. (1995). "Small Island Developing States and Their Vulnerabilities". *World Development, 23*(9): 1615–1632.

Brunnschweiler, C. N. (2008). "Cursing the Blessings? Natural Resource Abundance, Institutions and Economic Growth". *World Development, 36*(3): 399–419.

Bryceson, D. F. (1999). "African Rural Labour, Income Diversification and Livelihood Approaches: A Long-Term Perspective". *Review of African Political Economy, 80*: 171–189.

Bryceson, D. F. 2000. "'African Peasants' Centrality and Marginality: Rural Labour Trans-formations", in D. F. Bryceson, C. Kay, and J. Mooij (eds). *Disappearing Peasantries? Rural Labour in Africa, Asia and Latin America.* London: Intermediate Technology Publications

Bush, R. (2013). "Making the Twenty First Century its Own: Janus Faced African (Under) Development". *Afrika Focus, 26*(1): 51–65.

Callaghan, C. (2013). "Mineral Resource Based Growth Pole Industrialisation Growth Poles and Value Chains". Research prepared for the Regional Integration Research Network Open Dialogues for Regional Innovation. Available at: www.trademarksa.org/sites/default/files/publications/6.%20TMSA%20Growth%20Poles%20-%20Growth%20Poles%20and%20Value%20Chains%20131006%20FINAL.pdf.

Camara, B. (2005). "Hegel and Africa". *Journal of Black Studies, 36*: 82–96.

Campbell, H., Stein, H., and Samoff, J. (1992). *Tanzania and the IMF: The Dynamics of Liberalisation.* Boulder, CO: Westview Press.

Campbell, L. M., Gray, N. J., Fairbanks, L. W., Silver, J. J., and Gruby, R. L. (2013). "Oceans at Rio+20". *Conservation Letters, 6*(6), 439–447.

Campbell, L. M., Gray, N. J., Fairbanks, L., Silver, J. J., Gruby, R. L., Dubik, B. A., and Basurto, X. (2016). "Global Oceans Governance: New and Emerging Issues". *Annual Review of Environment and Resources, 41*(1): 517–543.

Cardoso, K. A. L. R. (2004). "Diáspora: A (Décima) Primeira Ilha de Cabo Verde, A Relação Entre a Emigração e a Política Externa de Cabo Verde". Masters Thesis. Instituto Superior da Ciência do Trabalho e da Empresa.

Carling, J. and Akensson, L. (2009). "Mobility at the Heart of a Nation: Patterns and Meanings of Cape Verdean Migration". *International Migration, 47*(3): 123–155.

Carmody, P. (2011). *The New Scramble for Africa.* Cambridge: Polity Press.

Ceratti, M. (2014). *How to Reduce Poverty: A New Lesson from Brazil for the World?* Washington, DC: World Bank. Available at: www.worldbank.org/en/news/feature/2014/03/22/mundo-sin-pobreza-leccion-brasil-mundo-bolsa-familia.

Chabal, P. and Daloz, J-.P. (1999). *Africa Works: Disorder as Political Instrument.* Oxford: James Currey; Bloomington, IN: Indiana University Press.

Challinor, E. P. (2008). "Home and Overseas: The Janus Faces of Cape Verdean Identity". *Diaspora: A Journal of Transnational Studies, 17*(1): 84–104.

Chang, H.-J. (1996). *The Political Economy of Industrial Policy.* New York: St. Martin's Press.

Chang, H.-J. (2002). *Kicking Away the Ladder: Development Strategy in Historical Perspective.* London: Anthem Press.

Chang, H.-J. (2003). "Foreign Investment Regulation in Historical Perspective Lessons for the Proposed WTO Investment Agreement". *Global Policy*, March.

Chang, H.-J. (2007). *Bad Samaritans: Rich Nations, Poor Policies, and the Threat to the Developing World*. London: Random House.

Chang, H.-J. (2013). "Industrial Policy: Can Africa Do It?", in J. Stiglitz, J. Lin, and E. Patel (eds), *The Industrial Policy Revolution 2: Africa in the 21st Century*. Basingstoke, UK: Palgrave Macmillan, pp. 114–132.

Chang, H.-J. and Andreoni, A. (2016). "Industrial Policy in a Changing World: Basic Principles, Neglected Issues and New Challenges". *Cambridge Journal of Economics*, 40 Years Conference, Cambridge, July 13.

Chavula, H. K., Tefera, M. G., Kedir, A. and Awe, Y. M (2017). "Monetary and Other Financial Policies for Africa's Structural Transformation", in Lopes et al. (eds). *Macroeconomic Policy Frameworks for Structural Transformation*. Basingstoke, UK: Palgrave Macmillan.

Chatelard, O. G. (2012). "Africa Must Do More to Profit from China". BBC, 22 May. Available at: www.bbc.co.uk.

Chenery, H. B. (1960). "Patterns of Industrial Growth". *American Economic Review*, *50*(2): 624–654.

Chenery, H. B. (1979). *Structural Change and Development Policy*. New York: Oxford University Press.

Chenery, H. B. and Taylor, L. (1968). "Development Patterns Among Countries and Over Time". *Review of Economics and Statistics*, *50*(3): 391–416.

Chenery, H. B. and Syrquin, M. (1975). *Patterns of Development, 1950–1970*. London: Oxford University Press.

Chenery, H., Robinson S., and Syrquin, M. (eds) (1986). *Industrialisation and Growth: A Comparative Study*. World Bank: Oxford University Press.

Cheru, F. (2002). *African Renaissance: Roadmaps to the Challenge of Globalization*. London: Zed Books.

Cheru, F. (2017). "Africa's Development Trajectory: Past, Present, and Future Directions", in C. Lopes, A. Hamdok, and A. Elhiraika (eds). *Macroeconomic Policy Frameworks for Structural Transformation*. Basingstoke, UK: Palgrave Macmillan.

Cheru, F., Cramer, C., and Oqubay, A. (eds) (2019). *The Oxford Handbook of the Ethiopian Economy*. Oxford: Oxford University Press.

Chikozho, C. (2012). "Towards Best-Practice in Transboundary Water Governance in Africa: Exploring the Policy and Institutional Dimensions of Conflict and Cooperation over Water", in K. T. Hanson, G. Kararach, and T. Shaw (eds). *Rethinking Development Challenges for Public Policy*. London: Palgrave Macmillan, pp. 155–200.

Clapham, C. (2018). "The Ethiopian Developmental State". *Third World Quarterly*, *39(6)*: 1151–1165.

Clark, C. (1940). *The Conditions of Economic Progress*. London: Macmillan.

Collier, P. (2004). *Development Effectiveness in Fragile States: Spillovers and Turnarounds*. Oxford: Centre for the Study of African Economies.

Collier, P. (2015). "Africa: New Opportunities, Old Impediments". *Economic Affairs*, *35(2)*: 169–177.

Collier, P. and Hoeffler, A. (2004). "Greed and Grievance in Civil War". *Oxford Economic Papers*, *56*: 563–559.

Collier, P. and Venables, A. J. (2012). "Greening Africa? Technologies, Endowments and the Latecomer Effect". *Energy Economics*, *34*: S75–S84.

Cooper, A., Antkiewicz, A. and Shaw, T. (2007). "Lessons from/for BRICSAM about South–North Relations at the Start of the 21st Century: Economic Size Trumps All Else?" *International Studies Review*, *9*(3): 673–689.

Cooper, F. (2002). *Africa Since 1940: The Past of the Present*. Cambridge, UK: Cambridge University Press.

Cornelissen, S. (2009). "Awkward Embraces: Emerging and Established Powers and the Shifting Fortunes of Africa's International Relations in the Twenty-First Century". *Politikon*, *36*(1): 5–26.

Cornelissen, S., Cheru, F., and Shaw, T. (eds). (2012). *Africa and International Relations in the 21st Century*. London: Palgrave Macmillan.

Cornia, G. A., Stewart, F. and Jolly, R. (1987). *Adjustment with a Human Face*. Oxford: Oxford University Press.

Corson, C., MacDonald, K. I. and Neimark, B. (2013). "Grabbing 'Green': Markets, Environmental Governance and the Materialization of Natural Capital". *Human Geography*, *6*(1): 1–15.

Crisafulli, P. and Redmond, A. (2012). *Rwanda, Inc.: How a Devastated Nation Became an Economic Model for the Developing World*. Basingstoke, UK: Palgrave Macmillan.

Cross, C. and Omoluabi, E. (2006) "Introduction", in C. Cross, D. Gelderblom, N. Roux, and J. Mafukidze (eds). *Views on Migration in Sub-Saharan Africa*. South Africa: HSRC Press, pp. 1–23.

D'Alessandro, C. and Zulu, L. C. (2017). "From the Millennium Development Goals (MDGs) to the Sustainable Development Goals (SDGs): Africa in the Post-2015 Development Agenda. A Geographical Perspective". *African Geographical Review*, *36*(1): 1–18.

Dahlerup, D. (ed). (2006). *Women, Quotas and Politics*. London and New York: Routledge.

Daka, E. and Toivanen, H. (2014). "Innovation, the Informal Economy and Development: The Case of Zambia". *African Journal of Science, Technology, Innovation and Development*, *6*(4): 243–251.

Dasgupta, P. (2001). *Human Wellbeing and the Natural Environment*. Oxford: Oxford University Press.

Dasgupta, P. and Heal, G. M. (1979). *Economic Theory and Exhaustible Resources*. Cambridge, UK: Cambridge University Press.

De Haas, H. (2008). "Migration and Development: A Theoretical Perspective", IMI Working Paper No. 9, Oxford University.

De Haas, H. (2012). "The Migration and Development Pendulum: A Critical Review on Research and Policy". *International Migration*, *50*(3): 8–25.

Dempsey, J. and Robertson, M. M. (2012). "Ecosystem Services: Tensions, Impurities, and Points of Engagement within Neoliberalism". *Progress in Human Geography*, *36*(6): 758–779.

Devarajan, S. (1999). "Cameroon", in P. Collier and J. W. Gunning (eds). *Trade Shocks in Developing Countries, Volume 1: Africa*. New York: Oxford University Press.

de Vries, G. J., de Vries, K., and Timmer, M. P. (2013). "Structural Transformation in Africa: Static Gains, Dynamic Losses". *GGDC Research Memorandum*, 136.

de Vries, G., Timmer, M. and De Vries, K. (2015). "Structural Transformation in Africa: Static Gains, Dynamic Losses". *Journal of Development Studies*, *51*(6): 674–688.

Diamond, J. (1997). *Guns, Germs and Steel: The Fates of Human Societies*. New York: W. W. Norton.

Diawara, M. (2000). "Globalization, Development Politics and Local Knowledge". *International Sociology, 15*(2): 361–371.

Díaz-Bonilla, E. (2009). "Global Macroeconomic Developments: Implications for Poverty", in J. von Braun, R. E. Hill, and R. Pandya-Lorch (eds). *The Poorest And Hungry: Assessments, Analyses, and Actions*. An IFPRI 2020 book. Washington, DC: IFPRI.

Diop, C. A. (1955/1974). *The African Origin of Civilization: Myth or Reality*. Westport, CT: Lawrence Hill.

Diop, C. A. (1974). *The African Origins of Civilisation: Myth or Reality*. New York: Lawrence Hill.

Diop, C. A. (1987). *Precolonial Black Africa: A Comparative Study of the Political and Social System of Europe and Black Africa, from Antiquity to the Formation of Modern States*. Westport, CT: Lawrence Hill.

Dixit, A. K. and Newbery, D. M. (1985). "Setting the Price of Oil in a Distorted Economy". *Economic Journal, Supplement*: 71–82.

Donna, D. R., Widodo, T., and Adiningsih, S. (2017). "Pattern of Comparative Advantage in Middle East and North Africa (MENA)", MPRA Paper No. 78109. Available at: https://mpra.ub.uni-muenchen.de/78109/1/MPRA_paper_78109.pdf.

Donnenfeld, Z., Porter, A., Cilliers, J., Moyer, J. D., Scott, A. C., Maweni, J., and Aucoin, C. (2017). "Ethiopia Development Trends Assessment". Institute of Security Studies and Frederick S. Pardee Center.

Douya, E. (2001). "Accès aux Marchés des Produits Pérennes Camerounais: Cas de la Filière Cacao". *Colloque International, 4*(9): 1–21.

Durand, J., Parrado, E., and Massey, D. (1996). "Migradollars and Development: A Reconsideration of the Mexican Case", *International Migration Review, 30*(2): 423–444.

Dutt, A. and Wilber, C. (2010). *Economics and Ethics: An Introduction*. Basingstoke, UK: Palgrave Macmillan.

ECA (United Nations Economic Commission for Africa) (1990). *African Alternative Framework to Structural Adjustment Programmes for Socio-economic Recovery and Transformation*. Addis Ababa: ECA.

ECA (2004). *Assessing Regional Integration in Africa: From the Early Years to the African Union*. Addis Ababa: ECA.

ECA (2009). *African Governance Report II*. Oxford: Oxford University Press.

ECA (2010a). *Assessing Regional Integration in Africa (ARIA): Enhancing Intra-African Trade*. Addis Ababa: ECA.

ECA (2011). *Economic Report on Africa 2011: Governing Development in Africa – the Role of theSstate in Economic Transformation*. Addis Ababa: ECA.

ECA (2013). *Millennium Development Goals Report 2013: Assessing Progress in Africa Towards the Millennium Development Goals Food Security in Africa: Issues, Challenges and Lessons*. Addis Ababa: ECA.

ECA (2014a). *Economic Report for Africa: Dynamic Industrial Policy in Africa*. Addis Ababa: ECA.

ECA (2014b). *Tunisia: Economic Situation and Outlook in the Current Transition Phase*. Addis Ababa: ECA.

ECA (2014c). *Twenty-Year Review of the Implementation of the Beijing Declaration and Platform for Action (Bpfa) + 20 Africa Regional Review Summary Report 1995–2014*. Addis Ababa: ECA.

ECA (2015a). *Economic Report for Africa 2015: Industrialization Through Trade*. Addis Ababa: ECA.

ECA (2015b). *Millennium Development Goals Report 2015: Assessing Progress in Africa towards the Millennium Development Goals Lessons from the Millennium Development Goals Experience*. Addis Ababa: ECA.

ECA (2015c). *Poverty Reduction, Inequality and the Financing Gap for Sustainable Development Goals (SDGs) in Africa*. Addis Ababa: ECA.

ECA (2015d). *Illicit Financial Flow. Report of the High Level Panel on Illicit Financial Flows from Africa*. Addis Ababa: ECA.

ECA (2015e). *Innovative Financing for Africa's Economic Transformation, African Development Forum Book*. Addis Ababa: ECA.

ECA (2015f). *Africa Investment Report*. Addis Ababa: ECA.

ECA (2016a). *Economic Report for Africa 2016: Greening Africa's Industrialization*. Addis Ababa: ECA.

ECA (2016b). *Macroeconomic Policy and Structural Transformation of African Economies*. Addis Ababa: ECA.

ECA (2016c). *Transformative Industrial Policy for Africa*. Available at: www.uneca.org/sites/default/files/PublicationFiles/tipa-chap4_en.pdf.

ECA (2016d). *African Governance Report: Measuring Corruption in Africa: The International Dimension Matters*. Addis Ababa: ECA.

ECA (2016e). *The Handbook on the Blue Economy*. Addis Ababa: ECA.

ECA (2017). *Economic Report on Africa*. Addis Ababa: ECA.

ECA (2018). *African Governance Report V: Natural Resources and Domestic Resources Mobilisation For Africa's Development*. Addis Ababa: ECA.

ECA and AUC (African Union Commission) (2013). *Economic Report on Africa 2013: Making the Most of Africa's Commodities: Industrializing for Growth, Jobs and Economic Transformation*. Addis Ababa: ECA.

ECA and AUC (2014). *Economic Report on Africa 2014: Dynamic Industrial Policy in Africa: Innovative Institutions, Effective Processes and Flexible Mechanisms*. Addis Ababa: Economic Commission for Africa.

ECA and AUC (2015). *Joint African Union Commission: Economic Commission for Africa Elements Paper for the Regional Consultation on Financing for Development*. Addis Ababa: ECA.

ECA and UN-HABITAT (2016). *Towards an African Urban Agenda*. Addis Ababa: ECA.

ECA, AU, and AfDB (2012). *Assessing Regional Integration in Africa V: Towards an African Continental Free Trade Area*. Addis Ababa: ECA.

Economist (2010). "Cartography: The True Size of Africa". Available at: www.economist.com/blogs/dailychart/2010/11/cartography.

Economist (2013). "A Hopeful Continent: Africa Rising – A Special Report", *Economist* Online Edition, 2nd March. Available at: www.economist.com/special-report/2013/03/02/a-hopeful-continent.

Economist (2017). "The History of Growth Should Be All about Recessions", *Economist* Online, 8 April. Available at: www.economist.com/finance-and-economics/2017/04/08/the-history-of-growth-should-be-all-about-recessions.

Economist (2018). "After a Good Run of Growth, China's Economy Braces for Bumps". *Economist* Online, 17 April.

Ekeh, P. P. (1975). "Colonialism and the Two Publics in Africa: A Theoretical Statement". *Comparative Studies in Society and History*, *17*(1): 91–112.

Ekpo, A. H. (2012). "Public Debt and Growth in Selected West African Countries: Implications for Economic Integration". *African Journal of Economic Policy, 19*(2): 1–25.

Elhiraika, A. B. and Bodart, C. (2012). "Development Planning and Public Expenditure Effectiveness: Lessons from Botswana and Malaysia", paper presented at the 50th Anniversary of IDEP, ECA, Dakar, Senegal, 5–7 November.

Elhiraika, A. and Mbate, M. (2014). "Assessing the Determinants of Export Diversification in Africa". *Applied Econometrics and International Development, 14*(1): 147–160.

Elhiraika, A. and Sloan, J. (2014). "Can Africa Move from Resource Dependence to Structural Transformation?", in E. Zedillo, O. Cattaneo and H. Wheeler (eds). *Africa at a Fork in the Road: Taking Off or Disappointment Once Again?* New Haven, CT: Yale Center for the Study of Globalization, Yale University, pp. 373–393.

Elhiraika, A., Aboubakar, O. and Muhammad, K. (2014, Spring). "Promoting Manufacturing to Accelerate Economic Growth and Reduce Growth Volatility in Africa". *Journal of Developing Area, 48*(2): 1–20.

Ellis, R. E. (2013). "The Strategic Dimension of Chinese Engagement with Latin America", Perry Paper 1. Washington, DC: William J. Perry Centre for Hemispheric Defence Studies.

Ernst & Young and AVCA (African Private Equity and Venture Capital Association) (2016). *How Private Equity Investors Create Value*. London: Ernst & Young.

Erol, U. and Yu, E. S. H. (1987). "On the Causal Relationship between Energy and Income for Industrialized Countries". *Journal of Energy and Development, 13*: 113–122.

Euromonitor (2015). *Apparel and Footwear in 2015: Trends, Developments and Prospects, Euromonitor International*. Available at: www.euromonitor.com/apparel-and-footwear-in-2015-trends-developments-and-prospects/report.

European Investment Bank (EIB) (2015). *Recent Trends in Banking in Sub-Saharan Africa: From Financing to Investment*. Luxembourg: EIB.

European Union (EU) (2009). Submission to UNFCCC. Available at: http://unfccc.int/files/kyoto_protocol/application/pdf/ecredd191108.pdf.

Evans, A. and Steven, D. (2012). "*Beyond the Millennium Development Goals: Agreeing to a Post-2015 Development Framework*". An MGO Working Paper. Washington, DC and New York: Brookings and CIC NYU.

Ezeala-Harrison, F. (1996). *Economic Development: Theory and Applications*. Westport, CT: Praeger.

Faist, T. (2009). "Transnationalization and Development: Toward an Alternative Agenda". *Social Analysis, 53*(3): 38–59.

Fama, E. F. and Jensen, M. C. (1983). "Separation of Ownership and Control". *Journal of Law and Economics, 26*(2): 301–325.

Fanon, F. (1952). *Black Skin, White Masks*. France: Editions de Seuil.

Fanon, F. (1963). *The Wretched of the Earth*. New York: Grove Weidenfeld.

Field, C. B. et al. (eds) (2014). "Climate Change 2014: Impacts, Adaptation, and Vulnerability. Part A: Global and Sectoral Aspects". Contribution of Working Group II to the Fifth Assessment Report of the Intergovernmental Panel on Climate Change, Cambridge, UK: Cambridge University Press.

Financial Times (FT) (2018). "Tap creative industries to boost Africa's economic growth". *Financial Times*, 22 March. Available at: www.ft.com/content/9807a468-2ddc-11e8-9b4b-bc4b9f08f381.

Findley, S., Traore, S., Ouedraogo, D., and Diarra, S. (1995). "Emigration from the Sahel". *International Migration* (Special Issue: *Emigration Dynamics in Developing Countries*), *33*(3–4): 469–520.

Fioramonti, L. (2016). "Horizontal Economy: How Africa Can Build a Thriving Economy in the 21st Century", in V. Gumede (ed.). *The Great Recession and its Implications for Human Values: Lessons for Africa*. Johannesburg: MISTRA.

Fisher, A. G. B. (1935). *The Clash of Progress and Security*. London: MacMillan.

Fisher, A. G. B. (1939). "Production: Primary, Secondary and Tertiary". *Economic Record*, *75*: 112–125.

Food and Agriculture Organization (FAO) (with UN Statistics Commission) (2010). *Global Strategy to Improve Agricultural and Rural Statistics*. Report of the Friends of the Chair on Agricultural Statistics United Nations Economic and Social Council Statistical Commission 41st Session, 23–26 February. Available at: https://unstats.un.org/unsd/statcom/doc10/BG-AgriStats.pdf.

Food and Agriculture Organization (FAO) (2015). *Regional Overview of Food Insecurity: Africa 2015*. Accra: Author.

Fukuda-Parr, S. (2008). "Are the MDGs Priority in Development Strategies and Aid Programmes? Only Few Are!" (No. 48). Working Paper, International Poverty Centre.

Fukuyama, F. (1992). *The End of History and the Last Man*. New York: The Free Press.

Gaillard, J. C. (2010). "Vulnerability, Capacity and Resilience: Perspective for Climate and Development Policy". *Journal of International Development*, *22*(2): 218–232.

Gardner, B. L. (2002). *American Agriculture in the Twentieth Century: How it Flourished and What it Cost*. Cambridge, MA: Harvard University Press.

Gerschenkron, A. (1962). *Economic Backwardness in Historical Perspective: A Book of Essays*. Cambridge, MA: Belknap Press of Harvard University Press

Glaeser, E. (2011). *Triumph of the City: How Our Greatest Invention Makes Us Richer, Smarter, Greener, Healthier, and Happier*. New York: The Penguin Press.

Global Fund (The Global Fund to Fight AIDS, Tuberculosis and Malaria) (2012). *The Global Fund Annual Report 2012*. Geneva. Available at: www.theglobalfund.org/en/publications/2013-07-24_Annual_Report_2012/.

Global Witness (2017). *Uganda: Undermined*. London. Available at: www.globalwitness.org/sv/campaigns/oil-gas-and-mining/uganda-undermined/.

Gören, E. (2013). "How Ethnic Diversity Affects Economic Development". ZenTra Working Papers in Transnational Studies 14. Oldenberg and Bremen, Germany: ZenTra Center for Transnational Studies.

Grant, R. (2015). *Africa: Geographies of Change*. Oxford: Oxford University Press.

Greenwald, B. and Stiglitz, J. (2003). *Towards a New Paradigm in Monetary Economics*. Cambridge, UK: Cambridge University Press.

Griffin, K. B. and Enos, J. L. (1970). *Planning Development*. London: Addison-Wesley.

Grosen, M. and Coflkun, B. (2010). "A Decade of Saps, Market Liberalization and Environment in Tanzania (1987–1998)". *European Journal of Economic Policy Studies*, *2*: 53–71.

GSMA Intelligence (2016). *The Mobile Economy in Africa 2016*. London: GSMA Intelligence.

Gumede, W. (2014). "Comparative Country Long-Term Development Planning: Lessons for South Africa", OR Tambo Debate Series, Wits School of Governance, University of the Witwatersrand, Johannesburg, South Africa.

Gumede, V. (2017). "Presidencies and Policy in Post-Apartheid South Africa". *Politeia*, *36*(1): 1–17.

Haas, P. M. (2012). "The Political Economy of Ecology: Prospects for Transforming the World Economy at Rio Plus 20". *Global Policy*, *3*(1): 94–101.

Haastrup, T. (2013). *Charting Transformation Through Security: Contemporary EU–Africa Relations*. Basingstoke, UK and New York: Palgrave Macmillan.

Halter, M. (1993). *Between Race and Ethnicity: Cape Verdean American Immigrants 1860–1965*. Urbana, IL: University of Illinois Press.

Handley, A. (2008). *Business and the State in Africa: Economic Policy-Making in the Neo-Liberal Era*. Cambridge, UK: Cambridge University Press.

Hanson, K. (2016). "Capacity Development for Natural Resource Management: Findings from the 2013 Africa Capacity Indicators Report", in H. Besada (ed.). *Governing Natural Resources for Africa's Development*. London and New York: Routledge, pp. 39–63.

Hanson, K. and Leautier, F. (2013). "Jobless Economic Growth in Africa: Is There a Role for Agriculture?" *Journal of African Development*, *15*(2): 1–17. Available at: www.jadafea.com/wp-content/uploads/2014/09/JAD_vol15_fall_ch1.pdf.

Hanson, K., Kararach, G., and Shaw, T. (2012). *Rethinking Development Challenges for Public Policy: Insights from Contemporary Africa*. Basingstoke, UK: Palgrave Macmillan.

Hanson, K., Puplampu, K. P., and Shaw, T. M. (2017). "Crystalising the Africa Rising Narrative with Sustainable Development", in K. Hanson, K. P. Puplampu, and T. M. Shaw (eds). *From Millennium Development Goals to Sustainable Development Goals: Rethinking African Development*. London: Routledge.

Harrington, J. and Walton, T. L. (2008). *Climate Change in Coastal Areas in Florida: Sea Level Rise Estimation and Economic Analysis to Year 2080*. Tallahassee, FL: Florida State University.

Harris, J. and Todaro, M. (1970). "Migration, Unemployment and Eevelopment: A Two Sector Analysis". *American Economic Review*, *60*: 126–142.

Harrison, G. (2016). "Rwanda: An Agrarian Developmental State?" *Third World Quarterly*, *37*(2): 354–370.

Hart, G. (2001). "Development Critiques in the 1990s: Culs de Sac and Promising Paths". *Progress in Human Geography*, 25(4): 649–658.

Haskins, J. (2012). "Building Resilience in Small Island Economies: From Vulnerabilities to Opportunities", C1A Policy Brief No. 8, November. Available at: www.cpahq.org/cpahq/cpadocs/Building%20Resilience%20in%20Small%20Island%20Economies.pdf.

Hatton, T. and Williamson, J. (2003). "Demographic and Economic Pressure on Emigration out of Africa". *Scandinavian Journal of Economics*, *105*: 465–486.

Hausman, D. and McPherson, M. (2006). *Economic Analysis, Moral Philosophy, and Public Policy*. Cambridge, UK: Cambridge University Press.

Hausmann, R. (2012). "A Comment on: The New Structural Economics: A Rethinking of Development Economics and Policy". Washington, DC: The World Bank, 6 March. Available at: http://siteresources.worldbank.org/DEC/Resources/84797-1104785060319/598886-1104852366603/599473-1223731755312/Hausmann_comment_on_Justin_Lin.pdf

Hausmann, R. and Rodrik, D. (2005). "Self-Discovery in a Development Strategy for El Salvador". *Journal of Lacea Economia*, *6*(1): 1–29.

Hausmann, R. and Klinger, R. (2006). "*Structural Transformation and Patterns of Comparative Advantage in the Product Space*". Working Paper 128. Center for International Development. Cambridge, MA: Harvard University.

Hausmann, R., Pritchett, L., and Rodrik, D. (2005). "Growth Accelerations". *Journal of Economic Growth, 10*: 303–329.

Henderson, G. and Waterstone, M. (eds). (2009). *Geographic Thought: A Praxis Perspective*. New York: Routledge.

Henderson, J. V., Storeygard, A., and Weil, D. N. (2012). "Measuring Economic Growth from Outer Space". *American Economic Review, 102*(2): 994–1028.

Herbel, D., Bamou, E., and Mkouonga, H. F. (2002). *Elaboration et Evaluation des Politiques Agricoles*. Yaoundé: Ministère de l'Agriculture, Division des Etudes et Projets.

Herbst, J. (2000). *States and Power in Africa*. Princeton, NJ: Princeton University Press.

Hickel, J. (2015). "Five Reasons to Think Twice about the UN's Sustainable Development Goals". *Africa at LSE* (23 September 2015).

Hidalgo, C. A., Klinger, B., Barabasi, A.-L., and Hausmann, R. (2007). "The Product Space Conditions the Development of Nations", Papers 0708.2090, arXiv.org.

Hisali, E., Birungi, P. and Buyinza, F. (2011). "Adaptation to Climate Change in Uganda: Evidence from Micro Level Data". *Global Environmental Change, 21*(4): 1245–1261.

Hoste, J. C. (2011) "Where Was United Africa in the Climate Change Negotiations?" Africa Policy Brief, Egmont Institute, Belgium. Paper presented to the seminar, Emerging Agents of Change? Africa in International Negotiations, Chatham House, London, 3 February 2011.

Hotelling, H. (1931). "The Economics of Exhaustible Resources". *Journal of Political Economy, 39*(2): 137–175.

Hruby, A. (2018). "Tap Creative Industries to Boost Africa's Economic Growth". *Financial Times*. Available at: www.ft.com/content/9807a468-2ddc-11e8-9b4b-bc4b9f08f381.

Human Rights Watch (2017). *Human Rights Watch: World Report*. Available at: www.hrw.org/sites/default/files/world_report_download/wr2017-web.pdf

IEA (International Energy Agency) (2010). *World Energy Outlook Report For 2010*. Paris: IEA.

Igbedioh, S. O. and Aderiye, J. B. I. (1994). "Increase in Food Prices and Food Consumption Pattern in Some University Students in Makurdi, Nigeria". *Ecology of Food and Nutrition, 31*: 219–226.

Independent Expert Advisory Group Secretariat (2014). "A World that Counts: Mobilising the Data Revolution for Sustainable Development". Technical report; New York: UN.

Institute of Water Modelling (IWM) and Center for Environmental and Geographical Information Services (CEGIS) (2007). *Investigating the Impact of Relative Sea-Level Rise on Coastal Communities and Their Livelihoods in Bangladesh*, IWM, CEGIS, Dhaka.

InterAcademy Council (2004). *Realizing the Promise and Potential of Africa Agriculture: Science and Technology to Improve Food Security and Agricultural Productivity in Africa*. Amsterdam: InterAcademy Council.

Inter-American development Bank (IADB) (2014). *Rethinking Productive Development: Sound Policies and Institutions for Economic Transformation*. Basingstoke, UK: Palgrave Macmillan.

Intergovernmental Panel on Climate Change (IPCC) (2007). *Summary for Policy Makers. Climate Change 2007: Synthesis Report.* Fourth Assessment Report of the Intergovernmental Panel for Climate Change. Available at: www.ipcc.ch/pdf/assessment-report/ar4/ syr/ar4_syr_spm.pdf.

International Monetary Fund (IMF) (2009). *Regional Economic Outlook: Sub-Saharan Africa – Weathering the Storm.* Washington, DC: IMF.

International Peace Information Service (IPIS) (2008). *Democratic Republic of The Congo, Mining Contracts: State of Affairs.* Antwerp, Belgium: IPIS.

Jackson, T., Suyuki, D., Marchant, J., Daly, H., Speth, G., Else, L., Simms, A., George, S., and Soper, K. (2008). "Special Report: Why our Economy is Killing the Planet". *New Scientist*, 15 October.

Jeffrey, H. L. and Bleasdale, S. (2017). "Tunisia: Mass Tourism in Crisis?", in D. Harrison and R. Sharpley (eds). *Mass Tourism in a Small World.* Wallingford, UK: CABI.

Jerven, M. (2013). *Poor Numbers: How We Are Misled by African Development Statistics and What to Do About It.* Ithaca, NY: Cornell University Press.

Johnson, S. (2016). "Africa's Life Expectancy Jumps Dramatically". *Financial Times.* Available at: https://next.ft.com/content/38c2ad3e-0874-11e6-b6d3-746f8e9cdd33.

Johnson, T. (2013). "Rwanda's Great Turnaround", *UC Observer*, 15 September, www.ucobserver.org.

Jolly, R., Emmerij, L. and Weiss, T. (2009). *UN Ideas that Changed the World.* Bloomington and Indianapolis, IN: Indiana University Press.

Kanbur, R. (2012). "Does Kuznets Still Matter?", in S. Kochhar (ed.). *Policy-Making for Indian Planning: Essays on Contemporary Issues in Honor of Montek S. Ahluwalia.* London: Academic Foundation Press, pp. 115–128.

Kanbur, R. (2017). "Structural Transformation and Income Distribution: Kuznets and Beyond". Working Paper Series No. 2 66. Abidjan, Côte d'Ivoire: African Development Bank.

Kanbur, R. and Zhuang, J. (2013). "Urbanization and Inequality in Asia". *Asian Development Review, 30*(1): 131–147.

Kaplinsky, R. (2000). "Globalisation and Unequalisation: What Can Be Learned from Value Chain Analysis?" *Journal of Development Studies, 37*(2): 117–146.

Kararach, G. (1997). "Ideology of Development and Sector-Led Growth in Tanzania: An Essay in the Reconstruction of Economic Theory". PhD Thesis. Leeds, UK: University of Leeds.

Kararach, G. (2011). *Macroeconomic Policy and the Political Limits of Reform Programmes in Developing Countries.* Nairobi: African Research and Resource Forum.

Kararach, G. (2014). *Development Policy in Africa: Mastering the Future?* Basingstoke, UK: Palgrave Macmillan.

Kararach, G. (2017). "Translating the Extractive Resources to Economic Growth and Transformation". *Journal of Sustainable Development, Law and Policy, 8*(1): 90–120.

Kararach, G. and Hanson, K. (2011). "The Challenges of Knowledge Harvesting and the Promotion of Sustainable Development for the Achievement of the MDGs in Africa", *ACBF Occasional Paper 12.*

Kararach, G. and Odhiambo, W. (2016). "Natural Resources, Global Economic Volatility, and Africa's Growth Prospects", in H. Besada (ed.). *Governing Natural Resources for Africa's Development.* Oxford: Routledge.

Kararach, G. and Yepes, T. (2017). "Water and Sanitation in Africa: Current Status, Trends, Challenges and Opportunities", in M. Ncube and C. Leyeka Lufumpa (eds). *Infrastructure in Africa: Lessons for Future Development*. Bristol: Policy Press.

Kararach, G. and Kedir, A. (2019). "Nutrition, Health and Productivity in Africa: Evidence from Ethiopia", in R. Jha (ed.). *Hunger and Malnutrition as Major Challenges of the 21st Century*. Singapore: World Scientific Publishing.

Kararach, G., Hanson, K. T., and Léautier, F. A. (2011). "Regional Integration Policies to Support Job Creation for Africa's Burgeoning Youth Population". *World Journal of Entrepreneurship, Management and Sustainable Development*, 7(2/3/4).

Kararach, G., Hanson, K., and Shaw, T. (2012). "Introduction: Africa's Second Half-Century: Enhancing Capacity for Sustainable Human Development and Human Security", in K. Hanson, G. Kararach, and T. Shaw (eds). *Rethinking Development Challenges for Public Policy: Issues from Contemporary Africa*. Basingstoke, UK: Palgrave Macmillan.

Kararach, G., Léautier, F. A., and Luhanga, T. (2013): "South–South Cooperation: How Does Gender Equality Factor in the Emerging Multilateralism?", in H. Besada and S. Kindornay (eds). *Multilateral Development Cooperation in a Changing Global Order*. Basingstoke, UK: Palgrave Macmillan.

Kararach, G., Besada, H., and Shaw, T. (2015). *Development in Africa: Refocusing the Lens after the MDGS*. Bristol, UK: Policy Press.

Kararach, G., Kedir, A., Suominen, H., and Ajambo, E. (2017). "Fiscal Policy, Long Term Growth and Structural Transformation in Africa", in C. Lopes, A. Hamdok, and A. Elhiraika, (eds). *Macroeconomic Policy Frameworks for Structural Transformation*. Basingstoke, UK: Palgrave Macmillan.

Karinganire, E. (2012). "Rwanda: Vision 2020 National Targets Revised", *The Rwanda Focus*, 12 March. Available at: http://focus.rw.

Karl, T. L. (1997). *The Paradox of Plenty: Oil Booms and Petro-States*. Berkeley, CA: University of California Press.

Karp, L. and Newbery, D. M. (1991). "Optimal Tariffs on Exhaustible Resources". *Journal of International Economics*, *30*: 285–299.

Kates, R. W. and Dasgupta, P. (2007). "African Poverty: A Grand Challenge for Sustainability Science". *Proceedings of the National Academy of Sciences*, *104*(43): 6747–6750.

Kates, R. W., Clark, W. C., Corell, R., Hall, J. M., Jaeger, C. C., Lowe, I., McCarthy, J. J., Schellnhuber, H. J., Bolin, B., Dickson, N. M., Faucheux, S., Gallopin, G. C., Grubler, A., Huntley, B., Jager, J., Jodha, N. S., Kasperson, R. E., Mabogunje, A., Matson, P., Mooney, H., Moore III, B., O'Riordan, T., and Svedlin, U. (2001). "Sustainability Science". *Science*, *292*(5517): 641–642.

Kaufmann, D. (2006). *Governance Matters V: Aggregate and Individual Governance Indicators for 1996–2005*. Available at: http://siteresources.worldbank.org/INTWBIGOVANTCOR/Resources/1740479-1150402582357/2661829-1158008871017/gov_matters_5_no_annex.pdf.

Kedir, A., Kararach, G., Alessandro, C., and Gauci, A. (2016). *Tax Compliance and Service Delivery in Africa*. Sheffield, UK: Management School, University of Sheffield.

Kelsall, T. (2013). *Business, Politics and the State in Africa: Challenging the Orthodoxies on Growth and Transformation*. London: Zed Books.

Khan, M. (2010). "Political Settlements and the Governance of Growth-Enhancing Institutions". Research Paper Series on Governance for Growth. School of Oriental and African Studies, University of London. Available at: http://mercury.soas.ac.uk/users/mk17.

Killick, T. (1976). "The Possibilities of Development Planning". *Oxford Economic Papers*, *28*: 161–184.

Kobou, G. (1993). "Dysfonctionnement du Marché du Travail au Cameroun: Quelles Alternatives pour une Politique de l'Emploi?". Paper presented to the colloquium on the methodology of creating employment policies, Ministère du Travail et de la Prévoyance Sociale, 22–26 September: 1–27.

Kobou, G., Fouda S. M., and Njinkeu, D. (2003). "Explaining African Economic Growth: 1960–2000 the Cameroon Case Study". Report submitted to AERC.

Kok, P., Gelderblom, D., Oucho, J. O., and Van Zyl, J. (eds) (2003). *Post-Apartheid Patterns of Internal Migration in South Africa*. Cape Town: HSRC Press.

Konde, P. C. B. (2018). "Industrialisation and Economic Growth through Diversification of Products and the Promotion of Trade Integration in Africa", in C. Landsberg (ed.). *Africa Rise Up: Perspectives on African Renewal*. Johannesburg: Real Africa Publishers.

Kraft, J. and Kraft, A. (1978) "On the Relationship between Energy and GNP". *Journal of Energy and Development*, *3*: 401–403.

Kuznets, S. (1955). "Economic Growth and Income Inequality". *American Economic Review*, *49*: 1–28.

Kuznets, S. (1966). *Modern Economic Growth*. New Haven, CT: Yale University Press.

Lagarde, C. (2015). "Rwanda: Taking on the Future, Staying Ahead of the Curve". Speech made in the Parliament of Rwanda. Kigali, Rwanda.

Lakdawalla, D. N. (2018). "Economics of the Pharmaceutical Industry". *Journal of Economic Literature*, *56*(2): 397–449.

Lall, S. (1995). "Malaysia: Industrial Success and the Role of the Government". *Journal of International Development*, *7*(5): 759–773.

Lall, S. (2002). "Selective Policies for Export Promotion: Lessons from the Asian Tigers", in G. K. Helleiner (ed.). *Non-Traditional Export Promotion in Africa: Experience and Issues*. New York: Palgrave Macmillan.

Landsberg, C. (2018). "Introduction: Bolstering a Pan-African Agency – from Africa Rising to Africa Rise Up", in C. Landsberg (ed.). *Africa Rise Up: Perspectives on African Renewal*. Johannesburg: Real Africa Publishers.

Lawrence, P. and Graham, Y. (2015). "Structural Transformation and Economic Development in Africa", Blog, *ROAPE*. Available at: http://roape.net/2015/12/18/structural-transformation-and-economic-development-in-africa/.

Léautier, F. (2009). "Leadership in a Globalized World: Complexity, Dynamics and Risk", Lecture PPT Notes. The Fezembat Group, February 26, 2009.

Léautier, F. (2014). *Leadership in a Globalised World: Complexity, Dynamics and Risks*. London: Palgrave Macmillan.

Léautier, F., Schaeffer, M., and Shen, W. (2015). "A Port City in the New Maritime Silk Road: The Case of Bagamoyo". *Businesstimes*. Available at: www.businesstimes.co.tz/index.php?option=com_content&view=article&id=5617:part-ii-a-port-city-in-the-new-maritime-silk-roadthe-case-of-bagamoyo&catid=1:latest-news&Itemid=57.

Lee, D. (2011). "African Activism in the WTO: How Effective Diplomatic Agency Can (Sometimes) Overcome Structural Power Constraints in the Global Trade Regime". Paper presented to the seminar, Emerging Agents of Change? Africa in International Negotiations, Chatham House, London, 3 February 2011.

Leipziger, D. M. and Thomas, V. (1993). *Lessons of East Asia*. Washington, DC: World Bank.

Lema, R., Quadros, R., and Schmitz, H. (2012). "Shifts in Innovation Power to Brazil and India: Insights from the Auto and Software Industries". IDS Research Report 73. Institute of Development Studies, Brighton, Sussex.

Le Pere, G. (2018). "African Economic Forum", mimeo. African Capacity Building Foundation.

Lewis, W. A. (1951). *Principles of Economic Planning*. Washington, DC: Public Affairs Press.

Lewis, W. A. (1954). "Economic Development with Unlimited Supplies of Labor". *Manchester School of Economic and Social Studies, 22*(2): 139–191.

Lewis, W. A. (1976). "Development and Distribution", in A. Caircross and P. Mohinder (eds). *Employment, Income Distribution and Development Strategy: Problems of the Developing Countries* (Essays in honour of H. W. Singer). New York: Holmes & Meier, pp. 26–42.

Leys, C. (1975). *Underdevelopment in Kenya: The Political Economy of Neo-Colonialism*. London: James Currey.

Lin, J. Y. (2010). "New Structural Economics: A Framework for Rethinking Development". Policy Research Working Paper No 5197, The World Bank, Washington, DC.

Lin, J. Y. (2011). "From Flying Geese to Leading Dragons: New Opportunities and Strategies for Structural Transformation in Developing Countries", WIDER Lecture. Maputo, Mozambique.

Lin, J. (2012). *New Structural Economics, A Framework for Rethinking Development and Policy*. Washington, DC: World Bank.

Lin, J. and Chang, H. (2009). "Should Industrial Policy in Developing Countries Conform to Comparative Advantage or Defy It? A Debate between Justin Lin and ha-Joon Chang". *Development Policy Review, 27*(5) (2009): 483–502.

Lin, J. Y. and Monga, C. (2010). "The Growth Report and New Structural Economics". Policy Research Working Paper 5336, The World Bank, Washington, DC.

Lin, J. and Monga, C. (2011). "Growth Identification and Facilitation: The Role of the State in the Dynamics of Structural Change", Policy Research Working Paper Series 5313, World Bank.

Lin, J. Y. and Monga, C. (2012). "Growth Identification and Facilitation: The Role of the State in the Dynamics of Structural Change", in J. Y. Lin (ed.). *New Structural Economics: A Framework for Rethinking Development and Policy*. Washington, DC: World Bank.

Lin, J. Y. and Wang, Y. (2014). "China–Africa Co-operation in Structural Transformation: Ideas, Opportunities and Finances". Working Paper 2014/046, United Nations University World Institute for Development Economics Research, Helsinki.

Lin, J. Y. and Wang, Y. (2017). *Going beyond Aid: Development Cooperation for Structural Transformation*. Cambridge, UK: Cambridge University Press.

Lindert, P. H. (1991). "Historical Patterns of Agricultural Policy", in C. P. Timmer (ed.). *Agriculture and the State: Growth, Employment and Poverty in Developing Countries*. Ithaca, NY: Cornell University Press.

Links, A. L. M., Hart, T. and Jacobs, P. (2014). "The Dynamics of Local Innovations Among Formal and Informal Enterprises: Stories from Rural South Africa". *African Journal of Science, Technology, Innovation and Development*, *6*(3): 175–184.

Lipton, M. (1995). "Rural Financial Services, Demography and Migration: International Experience". Report to South African Commission of Enquiry into Rural Financial Services.

Lopes, C. (2013a). "Moving from Early Pan-Africanism Towards an African Renaissance". *Executive Secretary's Blog*. Available at: www.uneca.org/es-blog/moving-early-pan-africanism-towards-african-renaissance.

Lopes, C. (2013b). "Pan Africanism and African Renaissance". Remarks by Dr Carlos Lopes at the Intergenerational Youth Forum on 24 May 2013 in Addis Ababa, Ethiopia.

Lopes, C. (2013c). "Global Value Chains: Africa, the factory floor of the world?" Africa Cheetah Run, Executive Secretary, ECA Blog.

Lopes, C. (2014a): "Africa: A New Era for Partnerships with the South". Africa Cheetah Run – Executive Secretary Blog. Available at: www.uneca.org/es-blog/africa-new-era-partnerships-south.

Lopes, C. (2014b). "The Paradox of Africa's Small Island Developing Nations". Executive Secretary Africa Cheetah Run Blog. Available at: www.uneca.org/es-blog/paradox-africa%E2%80%99s-small-island-developing-nations.

Lopes, C. (2014c). "Governance and Large Scale Agricultural Investments in Africa". Executive Secretary Africa Cheetah Run Blog. Available at: www.uneca.org/es-blog/governance-and-large-scale-agricultural-investments-africa.

Lopes, C. (2015a). "Emerging Africa, its Middle Class and New Development Challenges". Lecture delivered at International Institute of Social Studies in The Hague, Part of Erasmus University Rotterdam. Available at: www.iss.nl/fileadmin/ASSETS/iss/Documents/Conference_presentations/lecture_carlos_lopes.pdf.

Lopes, C. (2015b). "2015: African Economic Prospects". Speech at the 26th Ordinary Session of the African Union Executive Council held in Addis Ababa on 26 January 2015.

Lopes, C. (2015c). "How Can Africa Profit from Its Creative Industries?" *Blog WEF*. Available at: www.weforum.org/agenda/2015/09/how-can-africa-profit-from-its-creative-industries/.

Lopes, C. (2015d). "Harnessing FDI", in ECA (2015). Africa Investment Report, Addis Ababa: ECA.

Lopes, C. (2015e). "Industrialization: The Good Road Ahead", in E. Zedillo, O. Cattaneo and H. Wheeler (eds). *Africa at a Fork in the Road: Taking Off or Disappointment Once Again?* New Haven, CT: Yale University, Yale Center for the Study of Globalization eBook, pp. 45–51.

Lopes, C. (2019a). *Africa in Transformation: Economic Development in the Age of Doubt*, Basingstoke, UK: Palgrave Macmillan.

Lopes, C. (2019b). "Three sectoral policies in Ethiopia's structural transformation", in F. Cheru, C. Cramer, and A. Oqubay (eds). *The Oxford Handbook of the Ethiopian Economy*. Oxford: Oxford University Press.

Lopes, C. and Theisohn, T. (2003). *Ownership, Leadership and Transformation: Can We Do Better for Capacity Development?* New York/London: UNDP/Earthscan.

Lopes, C., Hamdok, A., and Elhiraika, A. (eds) (2017). *Macroeconomic Policy Frameworks for Structural Transformation*. Basingstoke, UK: Palgrave Macmillan.

Low, P. (2013). "The Role of Services in Global Value Chains". Fung Global Institute Working Paper FGI-2013-1.

Luengo-Cabrera, J. (2016). "Africa: Weakened Economies, Tamed Democracies". *Africa Policy Journal*, August 21.

Maathai, W. (2011). "Challenge for Africa". *Sustainability Science*, *6*(1): 1–2.

McAfee, K. (1999). "Selling Nature to Save It? Biodiversity and Green Developmentalism". *Environment and Planning D: Society and Space*, *17*: 133–154.

McAfee, K. (2012). "The contradictory logic of global ecosystem services markets". *Development and Change*, *43*(1): 105–131.

MacDonald, K. I. and Corson, C. (2012). "'TEEB Begins Now': A Virtual Moment in the Production of Natural Capital". *Development and Change*, *43*(1): 159–184.

McLeman, R. and Smit, B. (2006) "Migration as an Adaptation to Climate Change". *Climatic Change*, *76*(1–2): 31–53.

McMillan, M. S. and Headey, D. (2014): "Introduction: Understanding Structural Transformation in Africa". *World Development*, *63*: 1–10.

McMillan, M. S. and Rodrik, D. (2011). "*Globalization, Structural Change and Productivity Growth*". Working Paper 17143. Cambridge, MA: National Bureau of Economic Research.

McMillan, M., Rodrik, D., and Verduzco-Gallo, I. (2014). "Globalization, Structural Change, and Productivity Growth, with an Update on Africa". *World Development*, *63*: 11–32.

Mafukidze, J. (2006). "A Discussion of Migration and Migration Patterns and Flows in Africa", in C. Cross, D. Gelderblom, N. Roux, and J. Mafukidze (eds). *Views on Migration in Sub-Saharan Africa*. South Africa: HSRC Press.

Makinda, S. M. (2012). "Africa's Leadership Malaise and the Crisis of Governance", in K. Hanson, G. Kararach, and T. Shaw (eds). *Rethinking Development Challenges for Public Policy: Insights from Contemporary Africa*. New York: Palgrave Macmillan.

Malyamkono, T. L. and Bagachwa, M. S. D. (1990). *The Second Economy in Tanzania*. London: Villiers Publications.

Mamdani, M. (1996). *Citizen and Subject: Contemporary Africa and the Legacy of Late Colonialism*. Princeton, NJ: Princeton University Press.

Mandy, T. (2007). "The Scramble for Africa". *The Guardian*, Wednesday, 2 May.

Mann, L. (2018). "Corporations Left to Other Peoples' Devices: A Political Economy Perspective on the Big Data Revolution in Development". *Development and Change*, *49*(1): 3–36.

Mann, L. and Berry, M. (2016). "Understanding the Political Motivations that Shape Rwanda's Emergent Developmental State". *New Political Economy*, *21*(1): 119–144.

Mansfield, B. (2001). "Property Regime or Development Policy? Explaining Growth in the U.S. Pacific Groundfish Fishery". *Professional Geographer*, *51*(3): 384–397.

Manzambi, O. (2017). "Creative Industries and Informal Sector". *Africa Investment Review Q3, Quantum Global Research Laboratory*. Available at: https://quantumglobalgroup.com/wp-content/uploads/2017/09/Africa_Investment_Review_Q3_2017_web2.pdf.

Markwell, D. (2008). *John Maynard Keynes and International Relations: Economic Paths to War and Peace*. Oxford: Oxford University Press.

Marques, M., Santos, R. and Araújo, F. (2001). "Ariadne's Thread: Cape Verdean Women in Transnational Webs". *Global Networks*, *1*(3): 283–306.

Martins, P. M. G. (2015) "Sub-Regional Perspectives on Structural Change". Credit Research Paper. No. 15/03.

Mazrui, A. A. (1972). "The Political Economy of World Order: Modernization and Reform in Africa", in J. N. Bhagwati (ed.). *Economics and World Order: From the 1970s to the 1990s*. New York: Macmillan.

Mazrui, A. A. (1973). "African Diplomatic Thought and Supranationality", in A. A. Mazrui and H. H. Patel (eds). *Africa in World Affairs: The Next Thirty Years*. New York: Third Press.

Mbate, M. (2016). "Structural Change and Industrial Policy: A Case Study of Ethiopia's Leather Sector". *Journal of African Trade*, *3*(1–2): 85–100.

Mbeki, M. (2009). *Architects of Poverty: Why African Capitalism Needs Changing*. Johannesburg: Picador Africa.

Meffe, D. (2013). "The Distorted Size of Africa". Available at: www.africareview.com/Special-Reports/The-distorted-size-of-Africa/-/979182/2071294/-/4x8ptsz/-/index.html.

Meier, G. (2001). "The Old Generation of Development Economists and the New", in G. M. Meier and J. E. Stiglitz (eds). *Frontiers of Development Economics: The Future in Perspective*. Oxford: Oxford University Press.

Meillassoux, C. (1977). *Women, Barns and Capital*. Mexico, XXI Century.

Midelfart-Knarvik, K. H., Overman, H. G., and Venables, A. (2003). "Monetary Union and the Economic Geography of Europe". *Journal of Common Market Studies*, *41*(5): 847–868.

Milanovic, B. (2016). *Global Inequality: A New Approach for the Age of Globalization*. Cambridge, MA: Harvard University Press.

Minten, B. and Barrett, C. B. (2008). "Agricultural Technology, Productivity, and Poverty in Madagascar". *World Development*, *36*: 797–822.

Mkandawire, T. (1997). "Globalization and Africa's Unfinished Agenda". *Macalester International*, *7*: 71–107.

Mkandawire, T. (2001). "Thinking about Developmental States in Africa". *Cambridge Journal of Economics*, *25*(3): 289–314.

Mkandawire, T. (2014). "Can Africa Turn from Recovery to Development?" *Current History*, *113*(793): 171–177.

Mkandawire, T. (2015). "Neopatrimonialism and the Political Economy of Economic Performance in Africa: Critical Reflections". *World Politics*, *67*(3): 563–612.

Mkandawire, T. (2017). "State Capacity, History, Structure, and Political Contestation in Africa", in M. A. Centeno, A. Kohli, D. J. Yashar, and D. Mistree (eds). *States in the Developing World*. Cambridge, UK: Cambridge University, pp. 184–216.

Moghalu, K. C. (2014). *Emerging Africa: How the Global Economy's "Last Frontier" Can Prosper and Matter*. London: Penguin Books. Mohammed, I., Mirghani, M., Salih, A., and Gumaa, Y. (2011). "Impacts of Sudan Macroeconomic Policy on Agriculture". *International Trade Journal*, *3*(134): 22–32.

Momoh, S. (1995). "Food Production Policies and Nutritional Status in Nigeria". *Agricultura Tropica et Subtropica*, *28*: 15–22.

Monga, P. (2010). "Powering Industrial Growth: The Challenge of Energy Security for Africa", The OPEC Fund for International Development (OFID) Pamphlet Series 39.

Morgan, K. (2001). "The Exaggerated Death of Geography: Localised Learning, Innovation and Uneven Development". Paper presented at the Future of Innovation Studies Conference, The Eindhoven Centre for Innovation Studies, Eindhoven University of Technology, 20–23 September 2001. Available at: http://citeseerx.ist.psu.edu/viewdoc/download?doi=10.1.1.564.1384&rep=rep1&type=pdf.

Morris, M. and Fessehaie, J. (2014). "The Industrialisation Challenge for Africa: Towards a Commodities Based Industrialisation Path". *Journal of African Trade*, *1*(1): 25–36.

Moseley, W., Schnurr, M., and Bezner Kerr, R. (2015). "Interrogating the Technocratic (Neoliberal) Agenda for Agricultural Development and Hunger Alleviation in Africa". *African Geographical Review*, *34*(1): 1–7.

Moss, T. (2010) Available at: http://blogs.cgdev.org/globaldevelopment/2010/11/ghana-says-hey-guess-what-we%E2%80%99re-not-poor-anymore.php.

Motoki, T. (2001). "The Creation of Developmental States: Arguments and the Reality in Africa", in E. Kurimoto (ed.). *Rewriting Africa: Towards Renaissance or Collap*se. Japan Centre for Area Studies Symposium Series. No. 14.

Moussa, H. (1998). "Economic Policy and Economic Development in Tunisia", in J. Y. Lin (ed.). *Contemporary Economic Issues: Regional Experience and System Reform*. Basingstoke, UK: Palgrave Macmillan.

Mudenda, D. (2009). "Trade and Industrialisation Policies Experienced from Zambia". *Industrial Policy Thematic Working Group, 1–29*. Available at: www.saipar.org:8080/eprc/handle/123456789/204.

Mugobo, V. V., Mutize, M., and Aspeling, J. (2016). "The Ownership Structure Effect on Firm Performance in South Africa". *Corporate Ownership and Control*, *13*(2): 462–465.

Murphy, J. T., Carmody, P., and Surborg, B. (2014). "Industrial Transformation or Business as Usual? Information and Communication Technologies and Africa's Place in the Global Information Economy". *Review of African Political Economy*, *41*(140): 264–283.

Murphy, K. M., Shleifer, A., and Vishny, R. W. (1989). "Industrialization and the Big Push". *Journal of Political Economy*, *97*(5): 1003–1026.

Naidu, S., Corkin, L., and Herman, H. (2009) "China's (re) Emerging Relations with Africa: Forging a New Consensus?" *Politikon*, *36*(1): 87–115.

Nakhooda, S. and Norman, M. (2014). "Climate Finance: Is It Making a Difference?", Special Report, London: ODI. Available at: www.odi.org/sites/odi.org.uk/files/odi-assets/publications-opinion-files/9358.pdf.

Ncube, M. and Shimeles, A. (2012). "The Making of the Middle Class in Africa", mimeo. African Development Bank. Available at: www.uneca.org/sites/default/files/uploaded-documents/AEC/2012/aec2012-399.pdf.

Ndahiro, I. (2015). "Explaining Imihigo Performance in Gicumbi District, Rwanda: The Role of Citizen Participation and Accountability (2009–2014)". Research Paper, Institute of Social Sciences, The Hague, 28–29. Available at: http://hdl.handle.net/2105/32926.

Ndikumana, L. and Boyce, J. K. (2012). "Rich Presidents of Poor Nations: Capital Flight from Resource-Rich Countries in Africa". *ACAS Bulletin*, *87*: 2–7.

Ndikumana, L. and Boyce, J. (2018). "Capital Flight from Africa: Updated Methodology and Estimates." PERI Working Paper, June. Available at: www.peri.umass.

edu/publication/item/1083-capital-flight-from-africa-updated-methodology-and-new-estimates.

Ngugi, W. T. (1986). *Decolonising the Mind*. London: James Currey.

Nhamo, G. (2013). "Green Economy Readiness in South Africa: A Focus on the National Sphere of Government". *International Journal of African Renaissance*, *8*(1): 115–142.

Niëns, L. M., Cameron, A., Van de Poel, E., Ewen, M., Brouwer, W. B. and Laing, R. (2010). "Quantifying the Impoverishing Effects of Purchasing Medicines: A Cross-Country Comparison of the Affordability of Medicines in the Developing World". *PLoS Med*, *31*(7– 8): e1000333.

Nkrumah, K. (1965). *Neo-Colonialism, The Last Stage of Imperialism*. London: Thomas Nelson & Sons.

North, D. (1990). *Institutions, Institutional Change and Economic Performance*. Cambridge, UK: Cambridge University Press.

North–South Institute (2010). "Domestic Resource Mobilisation in Africa: An Overview", Ottawa: North–South Institute. Available at: http://www.nsi-ins.ca/wp-content/uploads/2012/10/2010-Domestic-Resource-Mobilization-in-Africa-An-Overview.pdf

Ocampo, J. A. (2006). "Latin America and the World Economy in the Long Twentieth Century", in K. S. Kumo (ed.). *The Long Twentieth Century, the Great Divergence: Hegemony, Uneven Development and Global Inequality*. New Delhi: Oxford University Press.

Ocran, R. K. (2014). "Women's Political Participation: A Comparative Study on Ghana and Tanzania". Thesis for International Master's Degree Program in Border Crossings: Global & Local Societies in Transition (Sociology). Faculty of Social Sciences University of Eastern Finland.

OECD/DAC (2018). "Development Finance Data". Available at: www.oecd.org/dac/financing-sustainable-development/development-finance-data/

Office for National Statistics (2016). "The UK's Trade and Investment Relationship with Africa: 2016. Recent Changes in The UK's Trade and Investment Relationship with Africa". Available at: www.ons.gov.uk/economy/nationalaccounts/balanceofpayments/articles/theukstradeandinvestmentrelationshipwithafrica/2016.

Oguh, C. (2015): "The Representation of Africa in Western Media: Still a 21st Century Problem", MA Thesis; Department of Journalism and Publishing, Edinburgh Napier University, UK.

Okafor, H. O. (2018). "Multilateralism, Regionalism, and the Effectiveness of Trade Policy in sub-Saharan Africa", in C. Landsberg (ed.). *Africa Rise Up: Perspectives on African Renewal*. Johannesburg: Real Africa Publishers.

Okimoto, D. I. (1989). *Between MITI and the Market: Japanese Industrial Policy for High Technology*. Stanford, CA: Stanford University Press.

Oloruntoba, S. (2018). "The State, Regional Integration, and Economic Development in Africa: Rethinking the Neoliberal Paradigm", in C. Landsberg (ed.). *Africa Rise Up: Perspectives on African Renewal*. Johannesburg: Real Africa Publishers.

Onesti, M. (2012). "Latin America and the Winding Road to Rio+20: From Sustainable Development to Green Economy Discourse". *Journal of Environment and Development*, *21*(1): 32–35.

Onuoha, G. (2016). "A 'Rising Africa' in a Resource Rich Context: Change, Continuity and Implications for Development". *Current Sociology*, *64*(2): 277–292.

Oqubay, A. (2015). *Made in Africa: Industrial Policy in Ethiopia*. Oxford: Oxford University Press.

Osei, B. and Mubiru, A. M. (2010). "Chinese Trade and Investment Activities in Africa", *African Development Bank Policy Brief*, Volume 1, Issue 4, July.

Ovadia, J. S. and Wolf, C. (2018). "Studying the Developmental State: Theory and Method in Research on Industrial Policy and State-Led Development in Africa". *Third World Quarterly*, *39*(6): 1056–1076.

Owusu, F. (2012). "Organizational Culture and Public Sector Reforms in a Post-Washington Consensus Era: Lessons from Ghana's Good Reformers". *Progress in Development Studies*, *12*(2–3): 135–151.

Oxfam (2015). *Entering Uncharted Waters: El Niño and the Threat to Food Security*. Oxfam Media Briefing. Oxford: OXFAM.

Oyama, N., Nair, J., and Levitan, J. (2012). "Africa's Water Crisis: The Miracle and the Mirage: What Policy Mix, Strategies and Institutional Steps Are Vital?", in K. Hanson, G. Kararach, and T. Shaw (eds). *Rethinking Development Challenges for Public Policy: Insights from Contemporary Africa*. Basingstoke, UK: Palgrave Macmillan.

Pack, H. and Saggi, K. (2006). "Is There a Case for Industrial Policy? A Critical Survey". *World Bank Research Observer*, *21*(2): 267–297.

Paes de Barros, R., Ferreira, F. H. G., Vega, J. R. M., Saavedra, J. C., De Carvalho, M., Franco, S., FreijeRodriguez, S., and Gignoux, J. (2009). *Measuring Inequality of Opportunities in Latin America and the Caribbean*. Washington, DC: World Bank.

Parry, M. L., Canziani, O.F., Palutikof, J.P., van der Linden, P.J., and Hanson, C.E. (eds) (2007). "Climate Change 2007: Impacts, Adaptation and Vulnerability". Contribution of Working Group II to the Fourth Assessment Report of the Intergovernmental Panel on Climate Change. Cambridge, UK: Cambridge University Press.

Peters, A. (1980). *The New Cartography*. New York: Friendship.

Phillips, J., Hailwood, E., and Brooks, A. (2016). "Sovereignty, the 'resource curse' and the limits of good governance: a political economy of oil in Ghana", Review of African Political Economy, *43*(147): 26–42.

Piketty, T. (2006). "The Kuznets' Curve, Yesterday and Tomorrow", in A. Banerjee, R. Benabou, and D. Mookherjee (eds). *Understanding Poverty*. Oxford: Oxford University Press.

Piketty, T. (2014). *Capital in the 21st Century*. Cambridge, MA: Harvard University Press.

Pillay, D. (2016). "The Africa Rising Narrative in the Context of the Global Economic and Ecological Crisis", in V. Gumede (ed.). *The Great Recession and Its Implications for Human Values: Lessons for Africa*. Johannesburg: MISTRA.

Poirier, R. A. (1995). "Tourism and Development in Tunisia". *Annals of Tourism Research*, *22*(1): 157–171.

Polanyi, K. (1944). *The Great Transformation*. Boston, MA: Beacon Press.

Posel, D. (2004). "Have Migration Patterns in Post-Apartheid South Africa Changed?" Paper presented to Stellenbosch Mini-Conference on Migration and Poverty, Stellenbosch, March.

Prah, K. K. (2011). "Culture: The Missing Link in Development Planning in Africa", in L. Keita, (ed.). *Philosophy and African Development: Theory and Practice*. Dakar: CODESRIA.

Prebisch, R. (1950). "The Economic Development of Latin America and Its Principal Problems". New York, United Nations. Reprinted in *Economic Bulletin for Latin America*, *7*(1): 1–22.

Prichard, W. (2009). "The Mining Boom in Sub-Saharan Africa: Continuity, Change and Policy Implications", in R. Southall and H. Melber (eds). *A New Scramble for Africa? Imperialism, Investment and Development*. KwaZulu-Natal: University of KwaZulu-Natal.

PricewaterhouseCoopers (PwC) (2015). "Asset Management 2020 and Beyond: Transforming Your Business for a New Global Tax World". Available at: www.pwc.com/gx/en/asset-management/publications/pdfs/am-tax-2020.pdf.

Pritchett, L. (2010). "The Problem with Paper Tigers: Development Lessons from the Financial Crisis of 2008", in N. Birdsall and F. Fukuyama (eds). *New Ideas in Development after the Financial Crisis*. Baltimore, MD: Johns Hopkins University Press.

Ratha, D. (2003). "Workers' Remittances: An Important and Stable Source of Development Finance", in *Global Development Finance*. Washington, DC: World Bank Group, pp. 157–175.

Ratha, D. and Shaw, W. (2007). "South–South Migration and Remittances". World Bank Working Paper No. 102. Washington, DC: World Bank.

Ratha, D., Mohapratha, S. and Scheja, E. (2011). "Impact of Migration on Economic and Social Development: A Review of Evidence and Emerging Issues", Policy Research Working Paper 5558. Washington DC: World Bank Group

Rawls, J. (1971). *A Theory of Justice*. Boston, MA: Belknap Press.

Read, R. (2010). "Trade, Economic Vulnerability, Resilience and the Implications of Climate Change in Small Island and Littoral Developing Economies", ICTSD Issue Paper No. 12.

Resende-Santos, J. (2015). "Cape Verde and Its Diaspora: Economic Transnationalism and Homeland Development". *Journal of Cape Verdean Studies*, *2*(1): 69–107.

Reyntjens, F. (2011). "Constructing the Truth, Dealing with Dissent, Domesticating the World: Governance in Post-Genocide Rwanda". *African Affairs*, *110*(438): 1–34.

Robinson, S. (1976). "A Note on the U-Hypothesis Relating Income Inequality and Economic Development", *American Economic Review*, *66*(3): 437–440.

Rocha, C. M., Tolentino, A. C. and Tolentino, N. C. (2008). *A Importância e o Impacto das Remessas dos Emigrantes em Portugal no Desenvolvimento de Cabo Verde*. Lisbon: ACIDI.

Rodney, W. (1972). *How Europe Underdeveloped Africa*. London: Bogle-L'Ouverture Publications.

Rodrik, D. (2003): "Growth Strategies", Working Paper, No. 0317, Johannes Kepler University of Linz, Department of Economics, Linz.

Rodrik, D. (2008). "The Real Exchange Rate and Economic Growth", Brookings Papers on Economic Activity, 2.

Rodrik, D. (2009). "Industrial Policy: Don't Ask Why, Ask How". *Middle East Development Journal*, *1*: 1–29.

Rodrik, D. (2013). "Structural Change, Fundamentals, and Growth: An Overview", Institute of Advance Study, Princeton University, Princeton, NJ. September. Available at: www.sss.ias.edu/files/pdfs/Rodrik/Research/Structural-Change-Fundamentals-and-Growth-An-Overview_revised.pdf.

Rodrik, D., Subramanian, A., and Trebbi, F. (2004). "Institutions Rule: The Primacy of Institutions over Geography and Integration in Economic Development". *Journal of Economic Growth*, *9*: 131–165.

Roemer, J. (1998). *Equality of Opportunity*. Cambridge, MA: Harvard University Press.

Romer, P. (1990). "Endogenous Technological Change". *Journal of Political Economy*, *98*: 245–275.

Rosegrant, M. W., Ewing, M., Yohe, G., Burton, I., Huq, S., and Valmonte-Santos, R. (2008). "Climate Change and Agriculture: Threats and Opportunities". Paper prepared for GTZ Climate Protection Programme for Developing Countries. Available at: www.preventionweb.net/files/11890_gtzclimatechangeagriculture1.pdf.

Rostow, W. W. (1960). *The Stages of Economic Growth: A Non-Communist Manifesto*. Cambridge, UK: Cambridge University Press.

Rouis, M. and Tabor, S. R. (2013). *Regional Economic Integration in the Middle East and North Africa beyond Trade Reform*. Washington, DC: The World Bank.

Rowden, R. (2013). "The Myth of Africa's Rise: Why the Rumors of Africa's Explosive Growth Have Been Greatly Exaggerated". *Foreign Policy*. Available at: http://foreignpolicy.com/2013/01/04/the-myth-of-africas-rise/.

Rucipero, R. (2001). "Rebuilding Confidence in the Multilateral Trading System: Closing the Legitimacy Gap", in G. P. Sampson (ed.). *The Role of the World Trade Organization in Global Governance*. New York: United Nations University Press.

Rutten, M. M. E. M., Leliveld, A. H. M., and Foeken, D. W. J. (eds) (2008). *Inside Poverty and Development in Africa: Critical Reflections on Pro-poor Policies*. Leiden/Boston, MA: Brill.

Sachs, J. D. and Warner, A. M. (1997). "Sources of Slow Growth in African Economies". *Journal of African Economies*, *6*(3): 335–376.

Sahn, D. E. and Stifel, D. C. (2003). "Progress toward the Millennium Development Goals in Africa". *World Development*, *31*(1): 23–52.

Sampath P. G. (2016). "Sustainable Industrialization in Africa: Toward a New Development Agenda", in P. G. Sampath and B. Oyelaran-Oyeyinka (eds). *Sustainable Industrialization in Africa*. London: Palgrave Macmillan.

Saul, J. (1974). "The State in Post-Colonial Societies: Tanzania". Paper was originally presented in the "Views from the Left" Lecture Series, Toronto, Canada. Available at: file:///C:/Users/KAU105623/Downloads/5321–7196–1-PB.pdf.

Sawyer, M. (2016). "Financialization, Financial Structures, Economic performance and Employment", FESSUD Working Paper, No. 93.

Schiller, N. G. (2012). "Unravelling the Migration and Development Web: Research and Policy Implications". *International Migration*, *50*(3): 92–97.

Schmidhuber, J. and Tubiello, F. N. (2007). "Global Food Security under Climate Change". *PNAS*, *104*(5): 19703–19788.

Schumacher, E. F. (1973). *Small Is Beautiful: A Study of Ecomonics as if People Mattered*. London: Vintage Books.

Schumpeter, J. A. (1954). *History of Economic Analysis*. London: Allen & Unwin.

Scitovsky, T. (1954). "Two Concepts of External Economies". *Journal of Political Economy*, *62*(2) (April): 143–151.

Seguino, S. (2014). "How Economies Grow: Alice Amsden and the Real World Economics of Late Industrialization", Presented at the Alice H. Amsden Memorial Lecture, University of Witwatersrand, Johannesburg, South Africa, September 4. Available at: http://tips.org.za/files/paper_stephanie_seguino_amsden_memorial_lecture.pdf.

Seme, Pixley ka Isaka (1905–6). "The Regeneration of Africa". *Royal African Society, 4*: 75–81.
Sen, A. (1987). *On Ethics and Economics*. Oxford: Blackwell.
Sen, A. (1999). *Development as Freedom*. New York: Oxford University Press.
Senghor, L. S. (1971). *Nation et voie africaine du socialisme*. Paris: Seuil.
Shaw, T. M. (2012). "Africa's Quest for Developmental States: 'Renaissance' for Whom?" *Third World Quarterly, 33*(5): 837–851.
Shaw, T. M. (2015). "From Post-BRICS Decade to Post-2015: Insights from Global Governance and Comparative Regionalisms". *Palgrave Communications, 1*(1): January.
Shaw, T. (2018). "Conclusion: The Future Nexus of African Foreign Policies, International Institutions, and Developmental Regionalism", in J. Warner and T. M. Shaw (eds). *African Foreign Policies in International Institutions*. Basingstoke, UK: Palgrave Macmillan.
Shaw, T. M. and Newbury, M. C. (179). "Dependence or Interdependence: Africa in the Global Political Economy", in Mark W. DeLancey (ed.). *Aspects of International Relations in Africa*. Bloomington, IN: African Studies Program, Indiana University.
Shaw, T. and Polonenko, L. (2015). "Public Diplomacy for Developmental States: Implementing the African Mining Vision", in G. Kararach, H. Besada, and T. Shaw (eds). *Development in Africa: Refocusing the Lens After the Millennium Development Goals*. Bristol, UK: Policy Press.
Shelton, G., Funeka, Y. A., and Li, A. (eds) (2015). *FOCAC 2015: A New Beginning of China–Africa Relations*. Pretoria: Africa Institute of South Africa.
Shleifer, A. and Vishny, R. W. (1986). "Large Shareholders and Corporate Control". *Journal of Political Economy, 94*(3): 461–488.
Shumuye, M. Y. (2015). "The Role of Developmental State in Development: The Case of Ethiopia". *International Journal of African and Asian Studies, 14*: 96–110.
Silver, J. J., Gray, N. J., Campbell, L. M., Fairbanks, L. M., and Gruby, R. L. (2015). "Blue Economy and Competing Discourses in International Oceans Governance". *Journal of Environment and Development, 24*(2): 135–160.
Simon, H. A. (1957). "Rationality and Administrative Decision Making". *Models of Man, 196*: 196–198.
Singer, H. (1950). "Comments to the Terms of Trade and Economic Development". *Review of Economics and Statistics, 40*: 84–89.
Skeldon, R. (2008). "International Migration as a Tool in Development Policy: A Passing Phase?" *Population and Development Review, 34(1)*: 1–18.
Skidelsky, R. (2012). "Inequality Is Killing Capitalism", Project Syndicate, November 21. Available at: www.project-syndicate.org/commentary/the-need-for-redistribution-of-wealth-and-income-in-order-to-save-capitalism-from-its-current-crisis-by-robert-skidelsky?barrier=accesspaylog.
Smaoui, A. (1979). "Tourism and Employment in Tunisia", in E. de Kadt (ed.). *Tourism: Passport to Development?* Oxford: Oxford University Press, pp. 101–110.
Smith, J. B., Schneider, S. H., Oppenheimer, M., Yohe, G. W., Hare, W., Mastrandrea,M. D., Patwardhan, A., Burton, I., CorfeeMorlot, J., Magadza, C. H. D., Fussel, H., Pittock, A. B., Rahman, A., Suarez, A., and Van Ypersele, J. (2009). "Assessing Dangerous Climate Change through an Update of the Intergovernmental Panel on Climate Change 'Reasons for Concern'". *Proceedings of the National Academy of Sciences, 106*(11). Washington, DC.

Solow, R. M. (1956). "A Contribution to the Theory of Economic Growth". *Quarterly Journal of Economics*, *70*: 65–94.

Southall, R. (2009). "Scrambling for Africa? Continuities and Discontinuities with Formal Imperialism", in R. Southall and H. Melber (eds). *A New Scramble for Africa? Imperialism, Investment and Development*. KwaZulu-Natal: University of KwaZulu-Natal.

Southall, R. and Melber, H. (eds). (2009). *A New Scramble for Africa? Imperialism, Investment and Development*. KwaZulu-Natal: University of KwaZulu-Natal.

Sriskandarajah, D. (2005) *Reassessing the Impacts of Brain Drain on Developing Countries*. Washington, DC: Migration Policy Institute.

Standard Chartered Bank (SCB) (2012). "Standard Chartered's Africa Social and Economic Impact". Available at: www.sc.com/en/resources/global-en/pdf/sustainabilty/Africa_impact_report.pdf.

Steinberg, P. E. (2008). "'It's So Easy Being Green: Overuse, Underexposure, and the Marine Environmentalist Consensus". *Geography Compass*, *2*(6): 2080–2096.

Stiglitz, J. (2006). "Scrooge and Intellectual Property Rights". *British Medical Journal*, *333*: 1279–1280. Available at: https://pdfs.semanticscholar.org/694c/512ba40a001cde96609030359df0ba82e370.pdf.

Stiglitz, J. E. (2017). "Structural Transformation, Deep Downturns, and Government Policy". Working Paper Series No. 301. African Development Bank.

Stiglitz, J. and Weiss, A. (1981). "Credit Rationing in Markets with Imperfect Information". *American Economic Review*, *71*: 393–410.

Stiglitz, J., Lin, J., Monga, C., and Patel, E. (2013). "Industrial Policy in the Context of Africa", Policy Research Working Paper 6633. World Bank: Available at: https://openknowledge.worldbank.org/bitstream/handle/10986/16850/WPS6633.pdf.

Suarez, D. and Corson, C. (2013). "Seizing Center Stage: Ecosystem Services, Live, at the Convention on Biological Diversity". *Human Geography*, *6*(1): 64–79.

Suárez de Vivero, J. L. (2013). "The Extended Continental Shelf: A Geographical Perspective of the Implementation of Article 76 of UNCLOS". *Ocean and Coastal Management*, *73*:13–126.

Syrquin, M. (1988). "Patterns of Structural Change", in H. B. Chenery and T. N. Srinivasan (eds). *Handbook of Development Economics, vol 2*. Amsterdam: North-Holland, pp. 197–273.

Tafirenyika, M. (2011). "Information Technology Super-Charging Rwanda's Economy", United Nations (UN), April. Available at: http://www.un.org.

Takizawa, H., Gardner, E. H., and Ueda, K. (2004). "Are Developing Countries Better Off Spending Their Oil Wealth Upfront?" IMF Working Paper WP/04/141. Washington, DC: IMF.

Taylor, I. (2016). "Dependency Redux: Why Africa Is Not Rising". *Review of African Political Economy*, *43*(147): 8–25.

Teixeira, R., Bertella, M., and Mendes, A. (2014). "Industrialization in Sub-Saharan Africa and Import Substitution Policy". *Brazilian Journal of Political Economy*, *34*(1): 120–138.

Tekere, M. (2001). "Trade Liberalization Under Structural Economic Adjustment: Impact on Social Welfare in Zimbabwe". *Structural Adjustment Program Review Initiative*: 1–43. Available at: www.saprin.org/zimbabwe/research/zim_trade_lib.pdf.

Theroux, P. (2013). *The Last Train to Zona Verde: Overland from Cape Town to Angola*. London: Penguin Books.

Thomas, C. (1974). *Dependence and Transformation: The Economics of the Transition to Socialism*. New York and London: Monthly Review Press.

Thompson, C. (2009). "The Scramble for Genetic Resources", in R. Southall and H. Melber (eds). *A New Scramble for Africa? Imperialism, Investment and Development*. KwaZulu-Natal: University of KwaZulu-Natal Press.

Timmer, C. P. (2007). *The Structural Transformation and the Changing Role of Agriculture in Economic Development: Empirics and Implications*. Available at: http://iis-db.stanford.edu/pubs/22133/Timmer_wendt_lecture.pdf.

Timmer, P. and Akkus, S. (2008). "*The Structural Transformation as a Pathway Out of Poverty: Analytics, Empirics and Politics*". Working Paper 150. Washington, DC: Center for Global Development.

Tinbergen, J. (1967). *Development Planning*. London: Weidenfeld & Nicolson.

Tirole, J. (2017). *Economics for the Common Good*. Princeton, NJ: Princeton University Press.

Tisdell, C. (2009). "Economic Challenges Faced by Small Island Economies: An Overview", School of Economics, University of Queensland, Working Paper No. 58.

Todaro, M. (1976). *Internal Migration and Economic Development: A Review of Theory, Evidence, Methodology and Research Priorities*. Geneva: International Labour Organization.

Trachtman, J. P. (1998). "Cyberspace, Sovereignty, Jurisdiction and Modernism." *Indiana Journal of Global Legal Studies*, *5*: 561–582.

Tumwebaze, P. (2014). "World Bank Hails Rwanda's Growth"". *New Times*. 10 April.

Uberti, S. D., De Lombaerde, P., Nita, S. and Legovini, E. (2015). "Analyzing Intra-regional Migration in sub-Saharan Africa: Statistical Data Constraints and the Role for Regional Organizations". *Regions and Cohesion*, *5*(2): 77–133.

UN (2010). *Re-thinking Poverty: Report on the World Social Situations*. New York: United Nations.UNAIDS (Joint United Nations Programme on HIV/AIDS) (2012). *UNAIDS Report on the Global Aids Epidemic*. Geneva: UNAIDS.

UNCTAD (2016). *World Investment Report, 2016*. Available at: http://unctad.org/en/pages/PublicationWebflyer.aspx?publicationid=1555.

UNCTAD (2017). *World Investment Report 2017: Investment and the Digital Economy*. Geneva: UNCTAD.

UNCTAD (2018). *World Investment Report 2018: Investment and New Industrial Policies*. Geneva: UNCTAD. Available at: https://unctad.org/en/PublicationsLibrary/wir2018_en.pdf.

UNCTAD (United Nations Conference on Trade and Development) and UNIDO (United Nations Industrial Development Organization), 2011. *Economic Development in Africa Report: Fostering Industrial Development in Africa in the New Global Environment*. Special Issue, United Nations.

UNDP (United Nations Development Programme) (2013a). *Human Development Report: The Rise of the South: Human Progress in a Diverse World*. New York: UNDP.

UNDP (United Nations Development Programme) (2013b). *Impact Investment in Africa: Trends, Constraints and Opportunities*. New York: UNDP.

UN-ENERGY (2007). *Energy for Sustainable Development: Policy Options for Africa*. UNENERGY/Africa publication to CSD15.

UNESCO (United Nations Educational, Scientific and Cultural Organization) (2010). *UNESCO Science Report 2010: The Current Status of Science Around the World*. Paris: UNESCO.

UNESCO-UIS (UNESCO Institute for Statistics) (2011). *Global Education Digest 2011: Comparing Education Statistics Across the World*. Montreal: UNESCO Institute for Statistics.

UN-Habitat (2013). *State of the World's Cities 2012/2013: Prosperity of Cities*. Nairobi.

UN-Habitat (2014). *Structural Transformation in Ethiopia: The Urban Dimension*. Nairobi: Author.UNU-IHDP (United Nations University International Human Dimensions Programme on Global Environmental Change) and UNEP (United Nations Environment Programme) (2012). *Inclusive Wealth Report 2012: Measuring Progress Toward Sustainability*. Cambridge, UK: Cambridge University Press.

UN World Commission on Environment and Development (1987). *Our Common Future*. Oxford: Oxford University Press.

van der Meer, C. L. J. and Yamada, S. (1990). *Japanese Agriculture: A Comparative Economic Analysis*. London: Routledge.

van der Ploeg, F. (2010). "Aggressive Oil Extraction and Precautionary Saving: Coping with Volatility". *Journal of Public Economics*, *94*: 431–433.

Varshney, K. R., Chen, G. H., Abelson, B., Nowocin, K., Vivek Sakhrani, V., Xu, L. and Spatocco, B. L. (2015). "Targeting Villages for Rural Development Using Satellite Image Analysis". *Big Data*, *3*(1): 41–53.

Versi, A. (2014). "Angola's Urban Transformation". *African Business*. Available at: http://africanbusinessmagazine.com/sectors/infrastructure/angolas-urban-transformation/.

Viner, J. (1950). "The Customs Union Issue". New York: Carnegie Endowment for International Peace.

von Braun, J. and Mengistu, T. (2009). "Poverty and the Globalization of the Food and Agriculture System", in J. von Braun, R. E. Hill, and R. Pandya-Lorch, R. (eds). *The Poorest and Hungry: Assessments, Analyses, and Actions*. An IFPRI 2020 book. Washington, DC: IFPRI.

Vu, T. (2010). "Studying the State through State Formation", *World Politics*, *62*(1): 148–175.

Wachira, G. M. (2017). "Strengthening the Peace and Governance Nexus within the African Union", Norwegian Institute of International Affairs Research Report, 7. Available at: https://trainingforpeace.org/wp-content/uploads/2017/11/Strengthening-Peace-Governance-Nexus-AU.pdf.

Wade, R. (1990). *Governing the Markets: Economic Theory and the Role of Government in East Asian Industrialization*. Princeton, NJ: Princeton University Press.

Wakiaga, J. (2015). "The Post-2015 Development Agenda: Building a Global Convergence on Policy Options", in G. Kararach, H. Besada, and T. M. Shaw (eds). *Development in Africa: Refocusing the Lens after the Millennium Development Goals*. Bristol: Policy Press, pp. 25–46.

Wallerstein, I. (1974). *The Modern World-System, vol. I: Capitalist Agriculture and the Origins of the European World-Economy in the Sixteenth Century*. New York/London: Academic Press.

Weiss, T. G. and Daws, S. (2007). *The Oxford Handbook on the United Nations*. Oxford: Oxford University Press.

Welter, F., Smallbone, D., and Pobol, A. (2015) "Entrepreneurial Activity in the Informal Economy: A Missing Piece of the Entrepreneurship Jigsaw Puzzle". *Entrepreneurship and Regional Development*, *27*(5–6): 292–306.

Werner, K. (2015). "African Development through Peace and Security to Austainability", in G. Kararach, H. Besada, and T. M. Shaw (eds). *Development in Africa: Refocusing the Lens after the MDGs*. Bristol: Policy Press, University of Bristol.

Whitfield, L., Buur, L., Therkildsen, O., and Kjaer, M. (2015). *The Politics of African Industrial Policy: A Comparative Perspective*. Cambridge, UK: Cambridge University Press.

Wilkinson, R. and Pickett, K. (2010). *The Spirit Level: Why Equality is Better for Everyone*. London: Penguin.

Wolf, A. (1998). "Conflict and Cooperation along International Waterways". *Water Policy, 1*: 251–265.

Woods, N. (2006). *The Globalizers: The IMF, the World Bank and Their Borrowers*. Ithaca, NY: Cornell University Press.

Woods, N. (2010). "Global Governance after the Financial Crisis: A New Multilateralism or the Last Gasp of the Great Powers?" *Global Policy, 1*(1): 51–63.

World Bank (2007). *Export Diversification in Egypt, Lebanon, Jordan, Morocco and Tunisia: Research Report, Social and Economic Development Sector Unit Middle East and North Africa Region*. Washington, DC: World Bank. Available at: http://siteresources.worldbank.org/INTEXPCOMNET/Resources/Export_Diversification_in_Egypt,_Lebanon,_Jordan,_Morocco,_and_Tunisia.pdf.

World Bank (2013a). *Doing Business 2013: Smarter Regulations for Small and Medium-Size Enterprises*. Washington, DC: World Bank.

World Bank (2013b). *Capital for the Future: Saving and Investment In an Interdependent World. Global Development Horizons Report*. Washington, DC: World Bank.

World Bank (2014). *Revisiting the Sources of Growth: The Quality of Basic Education. Cameroon Economic Update*. Washington, DC: World Bank.

World Bank (2015). *World Development Indicators*. Washington, DC: World Bank.

World Bank (2016a). *MENA Economic Monitor*. Washington, DC: World Bank. Available at: http://pubdocs.worldbank.org/en/234021460138331314/MEM-Tunisia.pdf.

World Bank (2016b). *Africa's Pulse: An Analysis of Issues Shaping Africa's Economic Future*. Washington, DC: World Bank.

World Bank (2018a). *World Bank Group Enterprise Surveys*. Washington, DC: World Bank

World Bank (2018b). *World Bank in Uruguay*. Available at: www.worldbank.org/en/country/uruguay/overview.

World Economic Forum (WEF) (2017). *Global Gender Gap Report*. Geneva: WEF. Available at: www3.weforum.org/docs/WEF_GGGR_2017.pdf.

World Economics (2016). *Measuring GDP in Africa*. Available at: www.worldeconomics.com/Papers/Measuring%20GDP%20in%20Africa_2c4addf3-b795-44f2-8d30-23b9e22f284e.paper.

World Travel and Tourism Council (2018). *Travel & Tourism Economic Impact 2018 Tunisia*. Available at: https://hi-tek.io/assets/tourism-statistics/Tunisia2018.pdf.

World Wide Fund for Nature (WWF) (2011). *The Energy Report:100% Renewable Energy By 2050*. Gland, Switzerland: WWF International.

Wunder, S. (2005). "Payments for Environmental Services: Some Nuts and Bolts". CIFOR Occasional Paper, vol. 42. Center for International Forestry Research, Bogor, Indonesia.

Wunder, S. and Sunderlin, W. D. (2004). "Oil, Macroeconomics, and Forests: Assessing the Linkages". *World Bank Research Observer, 19*: 231–257.

Xie, D., Li, F., Yao, B., Li, G., Chen, Z., Zhou, L. and Guo, M. (2016). "Simba: Spatial In-Memory Big Data Analysis". Paper presented at the 24th ACM SIGSPATIAL International Conference on Advances in Geographic Information Systems, San Francisco, CA, USA, October 31–November 3.

Xu, H. (2011). "Growth Accelerations Revisited", *Economic Journal Watch*, *8*(1): 39–56.

Yates, D. A. (1996). *The Rentier State in Africa: Oil Rent Dependency and Neocolonialism in the Republic of Gabon*. Trenton, NJ: Africa World Press.

Yeats, A., Amjadi, A., Reincke, U., and Ng, F. (1996). "What caused Sub-Saharan Africa's Marginalization in World Trade". *Finance & Development*. December: 38–41. Available at: www.imf.org/external/pubs/ft/fandd/1996/12/pdf/yeats.pdf.

Yilmaz, G. (2015). "Decomposition of Labor Productivity Growth: Middle Income Trap and Graduated Countries." Working Paper No. 15/27. Central Bank of the Republic of Turkey, Istanbul, Turkey.

Young, A. (2012). "The African Growth Miracle". *Journal of Political Economy*, *120*(4): 696–739.

Yu, E. S. H. and Hwang, B. (1984). "The Relationship between Energy and GNP: Further Results". *Energy Economics*, 6: 186–190.

Yu, E. S. H. and Choi, J-Y. (1985). "The Causal Relationship between Energy and GNP: An International Comparison". *Journal of Energy and Development*, *10*: 249–272.

Yusuf, S. (2012). "Garment Suppliers Beware: The Global Garments Value Chain is Changing". International Growth Centre, Pakistan and LSE, London.

Zack-Williams, A. (2013). "Neo-Imperialism and African Development". *Review of African Political Economy*, *40*(136): 179–184.

Zartman, W. (1976). "Europe and Africa: Decolonization or Dependency?" *Foreign Affairs*, *54*: 325–343.

Zeleza, P. (2018). "Africa's Renewal: The Challenges and Opportunities of Sustainability and Leadership", in C. Landsberg (ed.). *Africa Rise Up: Perspectives on African Renewal*. Johannesburg: Real Africa Publishers.

Zhou, X. (2001). "Understanding the Determinants of Managerial Ownership and the Link between Ownership and Performance". *Journal of Financial Economics*, *62*(3): 559–571.

Zondi, S. (2011). "Africa in Multilateral Negotiations: A Critique of African Common Positions". Paper presented to the seminar, Emerging Agents of Change? Africa in International Negotiations, Chatham House, London, 3 February 2011.

Index

Note: Bold page numbers refer to figures; *italic* page numbers refer to tables and page numbers followed by "n" denote endnotes.

2030 Agenda for Sustainable Development 70

Abramowitz, M. 17
Abuja Declaration and Charter for African Cultural Renaissance 119
Abuja Treaty 50
Accelerated Industrial Development of Africa 103
accountability 88, 149–50, 164
action levers 200–3, **201**
Adams, R. 67
Adaptation Fund 147, 172
Adebajo, A. 68
Afghanistan 87
Africa: context 16–17, 19–21; portrayal of 1–3, 71–2, 202
Africa Continental Free Trade Area (ACFTA) 40, 59, 102
Africa First 29
African agency 17, 31–2
African, Caribbean and Pacific–European Union (ACP–EU) 50
African common position 57
African Development Bank 9, 64, 168; Land Policy Initiative 164
African Development Forum 156
African Economic Research Consortium 84
African Governance Architecture 151
African Mining Vision 136–7, 139, 153
African Moment, the 26
African Peace and Security Architecture 151, 197–8
African Peace Facility 198
African renaissance 98–9
African Union 57, 71–3, 75, 85, 149, 157
African Union Commission 164
African Union Summit, 2013 99
Africapitalism 107
Africa Regional Review Report 129–30
Africa rising narrative 3, 4, 10–12, 26, 30, 31, 41
agency 3, 11, 34, 125; African 17, 31–2, 125–7; local 10; national 16; and ownership 73
Agenda 2063 40, 42, 50–1, 74, 155, 157, 165, 172
Agenda for Transformation, Cape Verde 182
Aghion, P. 200
Agreement on Trade-related Aspects of Intellectual Property Rights 85
agriculture 4; and AI 199; climate change adaptation 78–9; climate-smart revolution 82; exports 77; GDP share 14–16, 77; labour force 20; labour productivity 15; Large Scale Land Based Investments 163–5; productivity 8, 20, 99, 139, 170; public expenditure 164; smallholder producers 163
aid 169, 189
Aid for Trade 83–4, 181
AIDS 120, 121, 165, 196
air transport 177
Akamatsu, K. 18
Akkus, S. 15
Alavi, H. 33–4
Algeria 129, 176
alliance formation 126
allocative inefficiencies 59
Al Qaeda in the Maghreb 151
Amin, S. 33

Amsden, A. 22
Angola 129, 139, 151, 195
apps 132
AppsTech 178
Arab League 176
Arab spring 174
Argentina 107
artificial intelligence 198–9
Asian experience 27
Asian Tigers, the 86
assets under management 138
asset values 46–7
asylum seekers 68
Atlantic Music Expo 118
AU/Economic Commission for Africa (ECA) system 73
AU-NEPAD 131
Australia 107
authoritarianism 187
autonomy 41, 72, 124

Baker, S. 2
Bali agreement 176
Bandung Conference 84
Barrett, C. B. 139
BASEL III 156
Bates, B. 34–5
Bayart, J.F. 35
Beijing Declaration and Platform for Action 128, 154n2
Benin 97
big data 98
big push approach 91–2
biodiversity 195; loss of 61–2, 145
biomass 111
black people, demeaning portrayal of 2
Blades, D. 95
blood diamonds syndrome 152
blue economy, the 112–13, **112,** 153; exclusive economic zones 143; exploitation 142–7; governance 142
Boko Haram 12, 38, 71, 151
Bolsa Familia Programme, Brazil 84, 104
Bond, P. 52
Botswana 94, 104, 124n1, 166–7
branding challenge 11
Brazil 22–3, 39, 53, 65, 83, 109, 134, 181; *Bolsa Familia* Programme 84, 104; foreign direct investment 4
Bretton Woods institutions 52, 92
Brexit 147, 197–8, 203
BRICS 65, 76, 83, 125
Brundtland Report 52–3
Bryceson, D. F. 66–7
bureaucracy. 184
Burkina Faso 32, 192
Burundi 97, 121, 129
Bush, R. 32

Cambodia 27
Cameroon, transformation experiences 173, 177–80, *177*, 190
capacity building 66
capacity deficits 136
capacity-related constraints 170
Cape Verde 94, 113, 117–18, 129, 144, 146; transformation experiences 173, 180–3, *183*, 190
capital accumulation 17
capital expenditures 47
capitalism 5, 21–2
carbon-intensive development, benefits of 78
cartography 1, 3
catching-up process 17
central banks 160
Chad 139
challenges 193–5; tackling 200–3, **201**
Chang, H.-J. 203
Chenery, H. B. 15, 17, 19
China 39, 65, 74, 83, 102, 103, 188; Africa policy 85; development success 107; economic growth 83; economic recalibration 37; economic slow-down 46; engagement with 76, 192, 195; and Ethiopia 189, 190; foreign direct investment 4, 76, 162; GDP 4; GDP growth 31, 109, 138; global competitiveness 18; growth and environmental preservation 53; high-tech sector 131; industrialisation 23; investment in South Africa 86; investment stock holdings 38; labour force 12n5; multilateralism 64; rise of 18; Special Economic Zones 115, 131; trade relations 84
China Development Bank 64
China Eximbank 64
China National Offshore Oil Corporation 195
China National Petroleum Corporation 195
cinema industry 118
circumstances, realignment of 46–8, 61
citizenship rights 63
civil society 93
Clapham, C. 187, 187–8
Clark, C. 13, 15

climate change 49, 55, 57, 61–2, 68, 77–82, 87, 101, 108, 110, 126, 153, 170, 171, 182, *183*, 193; adaptation 78–9, 82; burden sharing 81; concerns 79–80; and development 80–2; financing 81; health effects 79; impacts 78, 82; and migration 80; mitigation 79, 82; as opportunity 80; policy ownership 81; sea level rise 80, 144–5; vulnerability 79
climate finance 170
climate science 146
climate services 146
CO_2 emissions 110
coastal erosion 145
coffee 107, 108
collective action 85
colonial attitudes 1
colonial exploitation 35
colonialism 10–11, 30–1, 35, 75, 92
colonisation 2
commodities, value addition 101
commodity-based industrialisation 25–6, 28
commodity dependency 31, 46
commodity price index 138
commodity prices 4, 7, 25, 38, 89, 138
commodity volatility 88
commodity windfalls 26
Common Market for Eastern and Southern Africa (COMESA) 50, 149
Communauté Économique des États de l'Afrique Centrale (CEEAC) 50
Comoros 113
company revenues 13
Compaore, Blaise 32
comparative advantage 43n1, 60, 90, 175
competition 43n1
conceptual issues 14–19
conflict 27, 38, 127; causes 151; emergence of new types 62
conflict prevention 62–3, 87
conflict resolution strategies 151
Conrad, J. 2
consumerism, growth of 62
consumer preferences 47
consumer spending 7
consumption: domestic 101–2; growth 175
Continental Free Trade Agreement 176
Continental Free Trade Area 114
Convention on the Protection and Promotion of the Diversity of Cultural Expressions 119
COP 21 62
Copenhagen Accord 126
copyright 119
Cornelissen, S. 74
corporate governance 43
corruption 31, 44, 49, 61, 88; combating 127–8
Côte d'Ivoire 105
Cotonou Agreement 77
creative economy 117–19
Creative Economy Reports 119
creativity 135, 153
credit, domestic 159–60
criminal activities 62
crisis response 193
cross-border money transfer 37
Cross, C. 67
Culture Bank 118
currencies, undervaluation 60
Curse of Berlin, the 10–11

data, challenge of 57
data divide, the 98
data revolution 98
debt 58
debt cancellation 58
debt control 38
decolonisation 44, 202
decolonisation perspective 71–2
De Haas, H. 67
deindustrialisation 31
democracy 44; participatory 184
Democratic Republic of Congo 147, 195
democratic transitions 150
democratisation 188–9
demographic changes 49, 63, 66, 69
demographic dividend 19, 71
demographic profile 39–40
demographics 3, 5–7, 43, 54
demographic transition 15, 17
Deng Xiaoping 103, 131
dependency 19, 30–1, 42, 70–2, 146
dependency theories 32
developing countries, economic integration 60
development 14; growth without 14
development agenda 203–4; ownership 85
development aid 169
developmentalism 9
developmental regionalism 9, 12
developmental state, the 9–10, 24–5, 33, 36, 41, 91, 94, 99, 103, 152, 174, 180, 184, 186–8, 193

developmental vision 180–1, 184
Development Assistance Committee 168
Development Bank of Southern Africa 64
development cooperation 86
development economists 90–1
development enablers 180
development financing 47, 155–72, 179; domestic resource mobilization 157, 159–60; domestic sources 166–7, **166**; Ethiopia 188–9; foreign direct investment 160–5, **161**; harnessing 165–6; innovative sources 166–72, **166**, **167**, 202; outcomes 155; policy initiatives 156–7; potential 155–60, **156**; tax-based 157–8; tool selection 203
development-led mining 136–8
development narrative, taking control of 192
development objectives 137
development planning 90–4, 123
development policies 40–1
development strategy 20, 85–6, 180
development trajectory: ownership 73–4; planning 203–4
de Vries, G. J. 20–1
Diaspora communities 181
Diawara, M. 10
digital revolution 118–19
Diop, C. A. 202
disaster recovery programmes 145
disease: burden 120; climate-sensitive 79–80; economic costs 122
disequilibrium 46
disruptive technologies 198–200
diversification 8, 14, 20, 42, 115–17
diversity management 150
diversity recognition 128
Doha Declaration on Financing for Development 159
domestic credit 159–60
domestic resource mobilization 157, 159–60, 166–7, **166**, 170
domestic sector, the 35–6
donor-driven private sector promotion 7
drought 4, 81
drug and drug trafficking 12, 151
dual economy models 59

earnings, lag 16
Ease of Doing Business Report, World Bank 190–1
East African Community (EAC) 50, 149
East Asia 60
Economic Commission for Africa 164
Economic Community of West African States (ECOWAS) 50
economic development 6–8, 19, 51; debates 13–14
economic diversification 42, 115–17
economic environment 169
economic growth 3–4, 6, 7, 11, 20, 29–33, 165; China 83; fragility 31; and job creation 104–5; origins of 32–3; and productivity 33; and the resource-curse 135–6; resurgence in 13
economic institutions 135–6
economic integration 60, 147–8, 181
economic liberalisation 61
Economic Partnership Agreements 77, 85
economic performance 7, 9, 19, 192
economic policy 101
economic prospects 36–41, 192
Economic Report on Africa, 2013 105
economic shocks *183*
economic transformation 103; development strategy for 85–6
economies of scale 29
ecotourism 146
education 92; decline in 46
Egypt 2, 107, 122
elections 150
electoral models 129
electrification rates 111, 179
Elhiraika, A. B. 25
emerging economies, partnerships 76
empirical dimensions 15
employment 20; in industry 5
employment creation 149
enablers 180
energy challenges 111
energy demands 111
energy poverty 139
energy resources 139–41
energy sector 139–41
energy security 139–41
Enhanced Integrated Framework 181
Enonchong, R. 178
enterprise performance 186
entrepreneurs 116, 132, 178, 179, 184
environmental degradation 57, 61–2, 68, 78, 101, 108, 109
environmental devastation 108
environmental impacts 18
environmental management 51
environmental policy 143

environmental preservation, and growth 53
environmental standards, compliance certification 51
environment-versus-development debate 22
equity 52
Ethiopia 8, 75, 81, 94, 107, 117, 126, 130, 166, 192; authoritarianism 187; challenges facing 189; and China 189, 190; development financing 188–9; diplomatic repositioning 189; experience of statehood 187–8; food security 188; foreign direct investment 189; GDP 186–7; governance 189; growth 186; human capital development 188; human rights 189–90; infrastructure 188; investments in renewable energy 188; service sector 187; transformation experiences 174, 186–90, *187*; value addition 186–7, *187*
ethnic divisions 34
EU–Africa partnership 76–7
EU–Africa Summit 36
Euromonitor 118
Europe 175; economic stagnation 37; industrialisation 21–2; migration crisis 65–7; partnerships 76–7; pull factors 68
European Central Bank 143
European Investment Bank 133
European Monetary Union 147
European Renaissance 2
European Union 76–7, 85, 147, 176, 197–8; Economic Partnership Agreements 114
Eurozone 147; sovereign debt crisis 77
excess labour 60
exclusive economic zones 143
exports 113; agriculture 77; commodities 142; primary product 4, 40; primary resource 31, 75; Tunisia 176
Extractive Industries Transparency Initiative 137, 139
Extractive Industries Transparency International guidelines 152
Ezulwini Consensus 126, 154n1

factionalism 179
Fanon, F. 202
fashion industry 118
finance 29
financial crises 56
financial deregulation 61
financial flows, illicit 49, 150–2, 158, 201
financialisation 61
financial potential 155–60, **156**
financial resources 156
financial services, mobile 133
financial systems 101
financing gap 156–7, 159
financing, innovative 166–71, **166**, **167**
Finland 107, 185, 186
Fintech 199
fiscal policy 25, 38, 157–8
Fisher, A. G. B. 13, 15
five-year planning phases 92
flood incidents 142
flying geese model 18
Food and Agriculture Organization 6, 64, 97
food security 6–7, 78, 79, 82, 139, 170, 188
foreign direct investment 4, 13, 38, 60, 171; British 197; development financing 160–5, **161**, *162*; diversification 76; Ethiopia 189; over-dependence risk 163; trends 160–3, **161**
fossil fuel consumption 140
freedom of speech 184
Frontex 67
frugal innovation 118, 132
Fukuda-Parr, S. 52
Fukuyama, F. 2
future, the, readiness for 70–4

G20 83, 126
gas 138, 178
gatekeeper states 31
GDP 4; agriculture 14–16, 77; base years 95; as benchmark 57; calculation 95–7, **95**, **96**; and China 31; Ethiopia 186–7; growth 109, 138; growth drivers 13; growth rates 140; industry share 5; manufacturing share 89; mobile ecosystem 132; rebasing 11, **95**, 96; sectoral composition 28; and trade 39; underestimation **96**
gender: budgeting 130; equality 128; inequality 130
geographical advantage 181
geography 1–3
geopolitical changes 74–7
geopolitics 38
geothermal energy 7
Germany 4

Gerschenkron, A. 17
Ghana 11, 94, 96, 105, 107, 133, 158, 163
Gini coefficient 17, 196
global compacts 64
global environment 29, 61
Global Environment Facility 170
globalisation 36, 45, 50, 87, 125; challenge to multilateralism 59–65; potential 192–3; resistance to 203; shaping 51
Global North 74, 76, 203
Global South, the 49, 52; partnerships with 82–7; rise of 87; trade 84
global value chains 28–9, 56, 100–1, 114–17, 175
global warming 109
Global Witness 136
Google Maps 1
governance 41, 44–6, 125, 159; Agenda 2063 and 51; blue economy 142; corporate 43; corruption 128; Ethiopia 189; failures of 58; global 82, 83; target challenges 201; undermining 151
Great Britain 197
Green Climate Fund 170
green economy 108–13, **112**, 142–3
greenhouse gas emissions 110, 140
greenhouse gases 77–9
green industrialisation 8
growth 3–5, 26–7; boom-and-bust cycle 180; challenges 168; consumption 175; data 94–8; drivers 4, 89; and environmental preservation 53; Ethiopia 186; GDP 109, 138; global forecast 37; greening 108–13, **112**; inclusive 13; patterns 14, 15; prospects 36–41; quality 196; Rwanda 183–5; sustaining 195–7; and technical change 139; without development 14
Growth Miracle, the 25
GSMA Intelligence 133
Guiding Principles on Large-Scale Land Based Investments 164
Guinea 97
Guinea-Bissau 129, 144
Gumede, W. 90

Haas, P. M. 142
Handley, A. 34–5
Hart, G. 10
Hatton, T. 68
Hausmann, R. 41
healthcare 120, 146, 98
Henderson, J. V. 97
Herfindahl-Hirschmann Index 4
higher education system 134
high-growth countries 59
High-Level Panel on Alternative Sources of Financing 156–7
High-Level Panel on Illicit Financial Flows 157, 158
High-Level Panel Report 57
historical experience 29
HIV/AIDS 120, 121, 165, 196
Hong Kong 18, 184
household consumption 96–7
Hubs 133
human capital 46, 49, 188, 198
human development 51
human resource training 134
human rights 43, 44, 51, 68, 164, 184, 189–90
human trafficking 12, 38, 151
hunger 6, 7
hydroelectricity 81, 101, 111

IMF 64, 65, 82, 157; global growth forecast 37
impact investing 169, 171
implementation 41
import competition 60
imports: food 4; processed food 101
import substitution 20, 28, 101
incentives 202
Inclusive Wealth Index 109
income, and productivity 22
India 27, 39, 53, 65, 74; engagement with 76, 192; foreign direct investment 4, 76, 162; investment stock holdings 38; labour force 12n5; rise of 83
Indonesia 27, 105
industrialisation 6, 8, 11, 20, 28, 47, 74–6, 88–117, 123–4, 153, 163, 196–7, 203; attitude towards 102; Brazil 22–3; Cameroon 179; Cape Verde 182; causes of failure 89; challenges 93, 107; China 23; commodities-based 25–6, 28, 70, 75, 104–8; development planning 90–4, 123; and diversification 115–17; drivers 105–8, **106**; Europe 21–2; global context 104; greening 108–13, **112**; importance of 88; import-substituting 28; and job creation 104–5; learning from others 99–101, 105; Malaysia 23; myths about 103–5; need for credible data 94–8; pillars 103; policy 88–90, 101, 124; and pollution 104; South

Korea 22; stakeholders 93; state role 89–90; strategic vision 90; strategies 101–2; and trade policies 113–15; United Arab Emirates 23
industrial potential 75
inequality 31, 42–3, 43n1, 48, 55, 61, 72, 74, 89, 100, 130, 196; and disruptive technologies 200; of opportunity 48; rural 17; urban 17
infant mortality 140
informal sector 132; contribution 126–7
information and computer technology 17, 63, 132
infrastructural development 74
infrastructure 20, 169, 181, 188, 192, 202
innovation 36, 37; exploiting 130–5
innovative financing 166–71, **166**, **167**
Instant Cash 37
institutional inertia 81
institutions, role of 24
insurance sector 167
intellectual property rights 119–21
inter-African trade 4, 126
Inter-America Development Bank 64
interest rates 49
intergenerational equity 52, 53
internal consumption 38
internal migration 68–9
international community, challenge facing 45
international development cooperation 49–50
international order, qualitative change 44
international trade 99–100
Internet connectivity 7
internet of things 7
internet traffic 98
Inter Parliamentary Union 128
intra-Africa investments 161
intra-African trade 175–6
investment: booms 9; coordination 25; opportunities 41; planning 91; public 23; scaling up 23; streams 99
Iraq 87

Japan 18, 188; economic stagnation 37
Jerven, M. 10, 30, 31, 95, 96
Jihadist movements 27
job creation 6; and economic growth 104–5
jobless growth 117
Joint Africa–EU Strategy 76–7

Kaldor-Verdoorn's law 60
Kanbur formalisation, the 205–7
Kashmir 27
Kenya 11, 38, 80, 108, 113, 118, 131, 133, 198, 199; election, 2017 11
Killick, T. 94
Kimberly Process 137, 152
kinship 145
knowledge, investment in 29
knowledge transfer 16
Korea 18
Kruse, K. 2
Kuznets-Lewis framework 17, 39, 44–5, 48; Kanbur formalisation 205–7
Kuznets, S. 15, 48
Kyoto Protocol 57

labour: costs 18; global division of 4; market flexibility 61; productivity growth 19; reallocation 15, 19
labour force 5, 12n5, 20, 116, 142; sectoral shifts 15
labour productivity, agriculture 15
Lakdawalla, D. N. 120
land governance 164
Landlocked Developing Countries 55
Land Policy Initiative, African Development Bank 164
land status **106**
land tenure system 164
Large Scale Land Based Investments 163–5
late capitalism 32
Latin America 60, 101, 110
leadership 184–6, 201; transformational 105
Least Developed Countries 55
Lee Kuan Yew 184
Leopold of Belgium 30
Lesotho 95
Lewis, A. 32–3
liberalisation 22; economic 61; trade 4–5, 58, 114
Liberia 151
Libya 68
life expectancy 140, 165
Limitless 178
Lin, J. Y. 13–14, 18, 64
linkage development 108
Lipton, M. 66
List, F. 15
literature 14, 19
local agency 10
London School of Economics 96–7
Lopes, C. 16, 25

McKinsey Global Institute 13
McMillan, M. S. 20–1, 59
macroeconomic frameworks 74, 148–9
macroeconomic stability 58
macro stability 23
macro-tendencies 194
Madagascar 113
Maghreb African Union (MAU) 50
malaria 122, 145
Malawi 131
Malaysia 23, 27, 38, 105, 106, 107
Mali 121
Mandela, Nelson 102
manufacturing 5, 19–20; GDP share 89
maps 1
Maputo Declaration 164
maritime zones 1–2
market-led development models 28
market liberalisation 22
markets: failure of 46–7; need for 40
Martins, P. M. G. 19
Marx, K. 35
Mauritius 34, 113, 144, 146
medicines 121
megatrends 195–6
Meier, G. 91
Meillassoux, C. 35
Mercator projection 1, 2
mergers and acquisitions 161–2, *162*
micro-credit 118
Middle-Income Countries 55
migrants, remittances 170–1
migration 20, 56, 63, 193; and climate change 80; debate 65–70; driving forces 65–8; Harris-Todaro model 66; internal 68–9; international 67; outward 69; and poverty 67; pull factors 68; rural-to-urban 17; and socio-economic improvements 66–7
migration crisis 65–7
Millennium Development Goals (MDGs) 6, 52, 57, 58, 61, 97, 165, 195, 196
Mindanao conflict, the 27
mining companies, net profits 135, 136
mining, development-led 136–8
Minten, B. 139
misperceptions 2–3, 71–2; changing 202
mistakes, avoiding 99–101
Mkandawire, T. 9
mobile banking 133
mobile financial services 37, 133
mobile penetration 132
mobile technology 7, 49
mobility 56
modernisation theory 32, 33
Moghalu, K. C. 59
monetary policy 160
monetary unions 147–8
Monga, C. 13–14
monopolies 120
Monterrey Consensus 157
Morocco 116, 122, 131, 192
Moss, T. 96
Motoki, T. 92
Mozambique 113, 129, 142
Mugabe, Robert 32
multilateralism 45; challenges to 64–5; disappointment of 82; globalisations challenge to 59–65; importance of 64; redefinition of 49; renewal 63–4
murky protectionism 56
Murphy, J. T. 25
music economy 118

Naidu, S. 74
Nairobi Plan of Action on Cultural Industries 119
Namibia 95, 128, 164
national agency, role of 16
national development plans 92
National Development Strategies 93
national income 14
nationalism 72, 148
National Strategy for the Development of Statistics 97
natural language processing 199
negative portrayals 1–3
neoliberalism 32, 51, 203
New Green Revolution 7
Newly Industrialised Economies, East Asia 23
New Partnership for Africa's Development 50, 93; Planning and Coordination Agency 156
New Scientist 194
New York Times, The 130
Niger 97
Nigeria 11, 37, 75, 94, 96, 107, 131, 133, 166–7, 199
Nollywood 118
non-market networking activities 5
non-state actors 72–3
Norway 107

Obama, B. 36
Ocampo, J. A. 22–3
oceans governance 142

OECD 158
oil 8, 40, 75, 138, 160, 177, 178, 195; prices 138
Okafor, H. O. 50
Omoluabi, E. 67
opportunity, inequality of 48
organised crime 12, 38
Organization of African Unity 75
out-migration 65
over-indebtedness 58
ownership 73–4, 93; and agency 73; development agenda 85

Page, J. 67
Pakistan 27
Pan-African Economic community 50
Pan-Africanism 8, 72, 73, 75, 125, 126
Panama Papers 158
PARIS21 97, 124n2
Paris Agreement on Climate Change 61–2, 77, 156
participatory democracy 184
partnerships 64, 73, 181; emerging economies 76; Europe 76–7; with Global South 82–7; strategic 87; strategy 77
patron–client relationships 31
peace and security 149–54, 180
peace dividend 151
peacekeeping 62–3
pension funds 167
pensions 158
performance, tracking 97
pessimism 2
Peters, A. 1
Petty, W. 15
pharmaceutical sector 120–3
Philippines, the 27
Piketty, T. 48
piracy attacks 27
planning institutions 41
Pliny the Elder 30
Polanyi, K. 21–2
policy correction 17
policy environment 29
policy implementation 24
policy objectives 94
political agenda 168
political economy 32, 94
political environment 169
political leadership 29
political processes, failure of 46–7
pollution 104
population growth 54, 101–2
populism 11–12, 197
portrayal, of Africa 1–3
Posel, D. 67
post-colonial state, the 33–4, 36
post-structuralist perspective 10, 34
potential 11; recognising 202
poverty 42, 55, 70, 97, 100, 182, 192–3, 196, 204n1; and debt 58; drivers 58; and migration 67
poverty reduction 12, 93, 94, 99
power generation 111
power relationships 46–7
power structures, preserving 47–8
Praia Declaration 119
Preferential Trade Area (PTA) 50
Preqin 168
PricewaterhouseCoopers 138
primary production, shift from 102
priorities 165
private equity 168–9
private sector development 6
private sector leaders 106–7
productivity 14, 20–1, 35, 140; agriculture 20, 99, 139, 170; gains 19; gaps 59; and growth 33; and income 22
Programme for Infrastructure Development in Africa 141, 159
property rights 127, 164
pro-poor policies 8
protectionism 56, 113, 114, 124
Protocol of the African Charter on the Rights of Women in Africa 128
public and private collaboration 108
public–private partnerships 7, 142, 159
public sector reform 6
public transportation, and AI 199

quality of life 140, 142

R&D expenditure 131
Rawls, J. 52
rebranding 202
regional cooperation bodies 50
Regional Economic Communities 85, 148, 149
regional integration 29, 102, 116, 141, 147, 153, 168, 185–6; economic 147–8; institutional environment 147; macroeconomic policy framework 148–9; political dimensions 148; and trade 147–9
regionalism 50
regional value chains 149, 175, 176

religious extremism 68
remittances 166, 170–1
renewable energy 105, 111, 141, 146, 170, 180, 188
renewable resources 7
rent-seeking 88, 106, 113, 152, 188
resilience 184, 185, 193
resource-curse, the 32, 135
resource dependency 31–2
resources 3, 4, 8, 25–6; abundance 41, 49, 75, 105, 108; capacity deficits 136; comparative advantage 60; control of 75, 151–2; energy 139–41; finite 14; mobilisation 25, 29, 99; new finds 135–42; potentials **26**; pricing 136; renewable 7; revenue bases 137; scramble for 195; sectoral transfer 27–8; soft 130–5; stocktaking 137; taxing mechanisms 136
responsibilities, reappraising 56–7
Rio +20 142
Rio Declaration 56
risks 59, 74, 168
Rodney, W. 30–1, 202
Rodrik, D. 20–1, 41, 59
Roemer 48
Rostow, W. W. 33
Rousseau, J.-J. 55–6
Rowden, R. 95
rule of law 41, 61
rural inequality 17
rural-to-urban migration 17
Russia 37, 53, 65; engagement with 76; foreign direct investment 4
Rwanda 80, 128, 130, 131, 158, 163, 166; growth 183–5; National Dialogue 184–6; regional integration agenda 185–6; trade imbalance 185; transformation experiences 174, 183–6, 190–1

Saarinen, T.F. 2
Sachs, J. D. 29–30
Saul, J. 33–4
savings 159
scepticism 2
Schumacher, E.F. 143–4, 153
Schumpeter, J. 97
science, technology, and innovation (STI) 130–5
Scitovsky, T. 91
Scotland 107
Scramble for Africa 30; new 193, 195
sea level rise 80, 144–5
security 127, 149–52
self-confidence 135
self-employment 5
self-reflection 32
self-reliance 50–1, 185
Seme, P.I. 99
Senegal 128
Senghor, L. 98
services sector 162, 187
Seychelles, the 113, 128, 144
Al-Shabab 38, 151
Silver, J. J. 143
Singapore 18, 184–6
Sinopec 195
skills development 66, 106
slavery 69
Sloan, J. 25
slums 42, 110
smallholder producers 163
Small Island Developing States 55, 112, 153, 169; climate change adaptation measures 146–7; economic and structural transformation 145–6; renewable energy 146; resource endowments 146; tourism 146; vulnerabilities 143–7, 182
smartphones 132–3
smart protectionism 114, 124
Smith, T. 178
social capital 145
social change 17
social compacts 185
social contract, the 54–6
social equity 127
social inclusion 42–3
social justice 52
socio-economic improvements 66–7
soft resources 130–5
solar energy 7
Solow, R. 139
Somalia 27, 38, 68
South Africa 34, 65, 67, 81, 107, 109, 113, 118, 122, 126, 128–31, 133, 164, 176, 192, 198, 199
South Africa–China Comprehensive Strategic Partnership 86
Southern African Development Community (SADC) 50, 149
South Korea 22, 27, 103, 188
South–South cooperation 126, 171
sovereign debt 38
sovereign wealth funds 166–7
Special Economic Zones 115–17, 131, 153
stability, maintaining 23

stakeholders 41, 93
state intervention 9, 91, 108
State of Food Insecurity in the World (SOFI) 6
state, the: accountability 88; burden 34–6; centrality of 34; colonial 33; ethnic ownership 34; industrialisation role 89–90; post-colonial 33–4, 36; role of 9–10, 24, 40–1, 70, 119; stigmatisation of 35
statistical capacity 94–8
statistical horizon 194
Stiglitz, J. 46, 47, 120
stock market capitalisation 160
Strait of Malacca 27
strategic capacities 16
strategic choices 41
strategic management 186
strategic partnerships 49
strategic planning 200
structural adjustment 28
Structural Adjustment Programmes 9, 12, 28, 75, 92–3
structural change 17
structural constraints 33
structural deficit 182
structuralist tradition 33
structural transformation: African context 16–17; conceptual issues 14–19; definition 14–15; dimensions 15; phases 21
structural variables 46
Sub-Saharan Africa, economic development 6
subsistence economy 35
Sudan 126, 139, 195
Sunderlin, W. D. 178
sustainability 53, 180, 194
sustainable development 13, 52–3, 55, 58, 143, 180; challenges 56; financing requirements 165–6; pillars of 56
Sustainable Development Goals 49–59, 61, 87, 140, 155; considerations 55–9
sustainable livelihoods 79–80
sustainable production 51
Sweden 107
Syria 87

Taiwan 18, 184
Tanzania 8, 37, 80, 113, 129, 130
target challenges 201–2
tariffs 5, 40, 60, 113, 114
tax-based financing 157–8
tax compliance 158
Taylor, I. 15
Taylor, L. 31
technical change, and growth 139
technological divides, bridging 132
technological revolution 134
technology 47
technology diffusion 7
technology preferences 101
Teixeira, R. 203
TerraPa 37
terrorism 11, 27, 38, 68, 151, 174
textile industry 178
Thailand 27, 105, 107
Theisohn, T. 16
Theroux, P. 2
Thionng'o, N. W. 202
Thomas, C. 22
Thompson, C. 195
Timmer, C. P. 14–15
tourism 113, 146, 176–7, 182, 190
trade: and GDP 39; Global South 84; increasing role of 39; and industrialisation 113–15; institutional environment 147; inter-African 4, 126; international 99–100; intra-Africa 164; intra-regional 149; liberalisation 4–5, 58, 114; negotiation space 137; policies 40, 84–5; and regional integration 147–9; South–South 42, 83; tariff bias 5; *see also* exports; imports
trade agreements, asymmetric 40
Trade Related Aspects of Intellectual Property Rights 122
traditional values 36
transformation agenda 86
transformational leadership 105
transformation ambitions 20
transformation challenges, handling 23–24
transformation experiences 173–91; Cameroon 173, 177–80, *177*, 190; Cape Verde 173, 180–3, *183*, 190; Ethiopia 174, 186–90, *187*; Rwanda 174, 183–6, 190–1; Tunisia 173–7, *174*, 190
transparency 88, 164
transportation revolution 61
Tropical Storm Dineo 142
Trump, Donald 11–12, 62, 197
Tunisia 122, 129; competitiveness 175; economic outlook 174–5, *174*; European market 175; exports 176; intra-African trade 175–6; tourism 176–7, 190; transformation experiences 173–7, *174*, 190
Turkey 76

Uganda 37, 94, 111, 130, 131, 136, 139, 158, 164, 166
UN Convention on the Law of the Sea 143
UNCTAD 119
underdevelopment 72
unemployment 42, 61, 117, 179; youth 54, 70–1, 178
UNESCO 131, 134
UN-Habitat projects 110–11
United Arab Emirates 23
United Nations 51–2, 59, 72, 126; conferences 194; democracy fund 44; Food and Agriculture Organization 6, 64, 97; peacekeeping 62–3
United Nations Children Fund (UNICEF) 51
United Nations Committee of Experts on International Cooperation in Tax Matters 159
United Nations Development Programme (UNDP) 51, 52
United Nations Economic Commission for Africa 9
United Nations Framework Convention on Climate Change 144
United Nations Security Council 65
United States of America 107; agricultural subsidies 12n4; Consumer Protection Act 137; Dodd-Frank Wall Street Reform 137; GDP 4; GDP growth 109; growth 37; pharmaceutical sector 120; Trump presidency 11–12, 197
urban inequality 17
urbanisation 7, 8, 15, 17, 39, 42, 110–11, 118
urban population 12n6
urban renewal 110–11
urban transformation 6
urgency, sense of 71
Uruguay 185, 186
US-Africa Leaders' Summit 36

value addition 101, 104–9, 114, 123–4, 142, 186–7, *187*
value chains 178; global 28–9, 56, 100–1, 114–17, 175; regional 149, 175, 176
van der Meer, C. L. J. 15
Venezuela 105, 107
Viner, J. 148
Vision 2030 124n1, 182
vision, clarity of 29

Wang, Y. 64
Warner, A. M. 29–30
water management 82, 141–2, 145
water stress 79
wealth creation 61
wealth, richest individuals 40
welfare challenges 6
Western civilisation, dominance of 2
Williamson, J. 68
wind energy 7
windfall earnings 135
women 125; economic empowerment 129–30; economic role 67; educational achievements 129; empowerment 128–30; ministers 129; in parliaments 128–9; pay equality 129; representation of 128, 196
Woods, N. 82
worker's rights 102
World Bank 10, 64, 65, 82, 96, 157; Ease of Doing Business Report 190–1
World Bank Catastrophe Risk Insurance Facility 147, 172
World Bank Global Partnership for Oceans 142
World Economic Forum 170
World Economics 11
world financial crises, 2008/2009 61, 83, 88, 168
World Health Organization 51, 121
world outlook 202
World Summit on Sustainable Development 53
World Trade Organization 57, 58, 64, 121, 171; Ninth Ministerial Conference 84–5
world-views 35–6
Wunder, S. 178

Yamada, S. 15
young talents: exploitation 178; exploiting 130–5
youth bulge 19, 40, 71
youth unemployment 54, 70–1, 178

Zambia 107, 137, 195
Zeleza, P. 34–6
Zimbabwe 32, 164

For Product Safety Concerns and Information please contact our EU representative GPSR@taylorandfrancis.com
Taylor & Francis Verlag GmbH, Kaufingerstraße 24, 80331 München, Germany

www.ingramcontent.com/pod-product-compliance
Ingram Content Group UK Ltd.
Pitfield, Milton Keynes, MK11 3LW, UK
UKHW010959180926
475701UK00004B/467

* 9 7 8 1 0 3 2 0 9 1 6 3 1 *